GODDESS OF THE MARKET

GODDESS OF THE MARKET

Ayn Rand and the American Right

Jennifer Burns

OXFORD

UNIVERSITY PRESS

2009

OXFORD
UNIVERSITY PRESS

Oxford University Press

Oxford University Press, Inc., publishes works that further
Oxford University's objective of excellence
in research, scholarship, and education.

Oxford   New York
Auckland   Cape Town   Dar es Salaam   Hong Kong   Karachi
Kuala Lumpur   Madrid   Melbourne   Mexico City   Nairobi
New Delhi   Shanghai   Taipei   Toronto

With offices in
Argentina   Austria   Brazil   Chile   Czech Republic   France   Greece
Guatemala   Hungary   Italy   Japan   Poland   Portugal   Singapore
South Korea   Switzerland   Thailand   Turkey   Ukraine   Vietnam

Copyright © 2009 by Oxford University Press, Inc.

Published by Oxford University Press, Inc.
198 Madison Avenue, New York, New York 10016

www.oup.com

Oxford is a registered trademark of Oxford University Press.

Library of Congress Cataloging-in-Publication Data
Burns, Jennifer, 1975–
Goddess of the market : Ayn Rand and the American Right / Jennifer Burns.
p.   cm.
Includes bibliographical references and index.
ISBN 978-0-19-532487-7
1. Rand, Ayn.   2. Rand, Ayn—Political and social views.
3. Rand, Ayn—Criticism and interpretation.   4. Novelists, American—20th
century—Biography.   5. Women novelists, American—Biography.
6. Philosophers—United States—Biography.
7. Political culture—United States—History—20th century.
8. Right and left (Political science)—History—20th century.
9. United States—Politics and government—1945–1989.   I. Title.
PS 3535.A547Z587 2009
813'.52—dc22   2009010763

3 5 7 9 8 6 4 2

Printed in the United States of America
on acid-free paper

TO MY FATHER

CONTENTS

GODDESS OF THE MARKET

Introduction

SHER EYES WERE what everyone noticed first. Dark and widely set, they dominated her plain, square face. Her "glare would wilt a cactus," declared *Newsweek* magazine, but to Ayn Rand's admirers, her eyes projected clairvoyance, insight, profundity. "When she looked into my eyes, she looked into my soul, and I felt she saw me," remembered one acquaintance. Readers of her books had the same feeling. Rand's words could penetrate to the core, stirring secret selves and masked dreams. A graduate student in psychology told her, "Your novels have had a profound influence on my life. It was like being reborn....What was really amazing is that I don't remember ever having read a book from cover to cover. Now, I'm just the opposite. I'm always reading. I can't seem to get enough knowledge." Sometimes Rand provoked an adverse reaction. The libertarian theorist Roy Childs was so disturbed by *The Fountainhead*'s atheism that he burned the book after finishing it. Childs soon reconsidered and became a serious student and vigorous critic of Rand. Her works launched him, as they did so many others, on an intellectual journey that lasted a lifetime.[1]

Although Rand celebrated the life of the mind, her harshest critics were intellectuals, members of the social class into which she placed herself. Rand was a favorite target of prominent writers and critics on both the left and the right, drawing fire from Sidney Hook, Whittaker Chambers, Susan Brownmiller, and William F. Buckley Jr. She gave as good as she got, calling her fellow intellectuals "frightened zombies" and "witch doctors."[2] Ideas were the only thing that truly mattered, she believed, both in a person's life and in the course of history. "What are your premises?" was her favorite opening question when she met someone new.

Today, more than twenty years after her death, Rand remains shrouded in both controversy and myth. The sales of her books are

1

extraordinary. In 2008 alone combined sales of her novels *Atlas Shrugged*, *The Fountainhead*, *We the Living*, and *Anthem* topped eight hundred thousand, an astonishing figure for books published more than fifty years ago.[3] A host of advocacy organizations promote her work, and rumors swirl about a major motion picture based on *Atlas Shrugged*. The blogosphere hums with acrimonious debate about her novels and philosophy. In many ways, Rand is a more active presence in American culture now than she was during her lifetime.

Because of this very longevity, Rand has become detached from her historical context. Along with her most avid fans, she saw herself as a genius who transcended time. Like her creation Howard Roark, Rand believed, "I inherit nothing. I stand at the end of no tradition. I may, perhaps, stand at the beginning of one." She made grandiose claims for Objectivism, her fully integrated philosophical system, telling the journalist Mike Wallace, "If anyone can pick a rational flaw in my philosophy, I will be delighted to acknowledge him and I will learn something from him." Until then, Rand asserted, she was "the most creative thinker alive."[4] The only philosopher she acknowledged as an influence was Aristotle. Beyond his works, Rand insisted that she was unaffected by external influences or ideas. According to Rand and her latter-day followers, Objectivism sprang, Athena-like, fully formed from the brow of its creator.

Commentary on Rand has done little to dispel this impression. Because of her extreme political views and the nearly universal consensus among literary critics that she is a bad writer, few who are not committed Objectivists have taken Rand seriously. Unlike other novelists of her stature, until now Rand has not been the subject of a full-length biography. Her life and work have been described instead by her former friends, enemies, and students. Despite her emphasis on integration, most of the books published about Rand have been essay collections rather than large-scale works that develop a sustained interpretation of her importance.

This book firmly locates Rand within the tumultuous American century that her life spanned. Rand's defense of individualism, celebration of capitalism, and controversial morality of selfishness can be understood only against the backdrop of her historical moment. All sprang from her early life experiences in Communist Russia and became the most powerful and deeply enduring of her messages. What Rand confronted in her work was a basic human dilemma: the failure of good intentions. Her indictment of altruism, social welfare, and service to others sprang from her belief that these ideals underlay Communism, Nazism, and the wars that wracked the century. Rand's solution, characteristically, was extreme: to eliminate all virtues that could possibly be used in the service of totalitarianism. It was also simplistic. If Rand's great strength as a thinker was to grasp interrelated underlying principles and weave them into an impenetrable logical edifice, it was also her great weakness. In her effort to find a unifying cause for all the trauma and bloodshed of the twentieth century, Rand was attempting the impossible. But it was this deadly serious quest that animated all of her writing. Rand was among the first to identify the problem of the modern state's often terrifying power and make it an issue of popular concern.

She was also one of the first American writers to celebrate the creative possibilities of modern capitalism and to emphasize the economic value of independent thought. In a time when leading intellectuals assumed that large corporations would continue to dominate economic life, shaping their employees into soulless organization men, Rand clung to the vision of the independent entrepreneur. Though it seemed anachronistic at first, her vision has resonated with the knowledge workers of the new economy, who see themselves as strategic operators in a constantly changing economic landscape. Rand has earned the unending devotion of capitalists large and small by treating business as an honorable calling that can engage the deepest capacities of the human spirit.

At the same time, Rand advanced a deeply negative portrait of government action. In her work, the state is always a destroyer, acting to frustrate and inhibit the natural ingenuity and drive of individuals. It is this chiaroscuro of light and dark—virtuous individuals battling a villainous state—that makes her compelling to some readers and odious to others. Though Americans turned to their government for aid, succor, and redress of grievances ever more frequently during the twentieth century, they did so with doubts, fears, and misgivings, all of which Rand cast into stark relief in her fiction. Her work sounded anew the traditional American suspicion of centralized authority, and helped inspire a broad intellectual movement that challenged the liberal welfare state and proclaimed the desirability of free markets.

Goddess of the Market focuses on Rand's contributions as a political philosopher, for it is here that she has exerted her greatest influence. Rand's Romantic Realism has not changed American literature, nor has Objectivism penetrated far into the philosophy profession. She does, however, remain a veritable institution within the American right. *Atlas Shrugged* is still devoured by eager young conservatives, cited by political candidates, and promoted by corporate tycoons. Critics who dismiss Rand as a shallow thinker appealing only to adolescents miss her significance altogether. For over half a century Rand has been the ultimate gateway drug to life on the right.

The story of Ayn Rand is also the story of libertarianism, conservatism, and Objectivism, the three schools of thought that intersected most prominently with her life. These terms are neither firmly defined nor mutually exclusive, and their meaning shifted considerably during the period of time covered in this book. Whether I identify Rand or her admirers as libertarian, conservative, or Objectivist varies by the context, and my interchangeable use of these words is not intended to collapse the distinctions between each. Rand jealously guarded the word Objectivist when she was alive, but I use the term loosely to encompass a range of persons who identified Rand as an important influence on their thought.

I was fortunate to begin this project with two happy coincidences: the opening of Rand's personal papers held at the Ayn Rand Archives and the beginning of a wave of scholarship on the American right. Work in Rand's personal papers has enabled me to sift through the many biased and contradictory accounts of her life and create a more balanced picture of Rand as a thinker and a human being. Using newly available documentary material I revisit key episodes in Rand's dramatic life, including her early years in Russia and the secret affair with a young acolyte that shaped her mature career. I am less concerned with judgment than with analysis, a choice Rand would certainly condemn. Though I was granted full access to her papers by the Ayn Rand Institute, I am not an Objectivist and have never been affiliated with any group dedicated to Rand's work. I approach her instead as a student and a critic of American thought.

New historical scholarship has helped me situate Rand within the broader intellectual and political movements that have transformed America since the days of the New Deal. At once a novelist and a philosopher, a moralist and a political theorist, a critic and an ideologue, Rand is difficult to categorize. She produced novels, plays, screenplays, cultural criticism, philosophic essays, political tracts, and commentary on current events. Almost everything she wrote was unfashionable. When artists embraced realism and modernism, she championed Romanticism. Implacably opposed to pragmatism, existentialism, and Freudian psychology, she offered instead Objectivism, an absolutist philosophical system that insisted on the primacy of reason and the existence of a knowable, objective reality. Though she was out of fashion, Rand was not without a tradition or a community. Rather than a lonely genius, she was a deeply engaged thinker, embedded in multiple networks of friends and foes, always driven relentlessly to comment upon and condemn the tide of events that flowed around her.

This book seeks to excavate a hidden Rand, one far more complex and contradictory than her public persona suggests. Although she preached unfettered individualism, the story I tell is one of Rand in relationship, both with the significant figures of her life and with the wider world, which appeared to her alternately as implacably hostile and full of limitless possibility. This approach helps reconcile the tensions that plagued Rand's life and work. The most obvious contradiction lies on the surface: Rand was a rationalist philosopher who wrote romantic fiction. For all her fealty to reason, Rand was a woman subject to powerful, even overwhelming emotions. Her novels indulged Rand's desire for adventure, beauty, and excitement, while Objectivism helped her frame, master, and explain her experiences in the world. Her dual career as a novelist and a philosopher let Rand express both her deep seated need for control and her genuine belief in individualism and independence.

Despite Rand's lifelong interest in current events, the escapist pleasures of fiction tugged always at the edges of her mind. When she stopped writing novels she continued to live in the imaginary worlds she had created, finding her characters as real and meaningful as the people she spent time with every day. Over time she retreated ever further into a universe of her own creation, joined there by a tight band of intimates who acknowledged her as their chosen leader. At first this closed world offered Rand the refuge she sought when her work was blasted by critics, who were often unfairly harsh and personal in their attacks. But Objectivism as a philosophy left no room for elaboration, extension, or interpretation, and as a social world it excluded growth, change, or development. As a younger Rand might have predicted, a system so oppressive to individual variety had not long to prosper. A woman who tried to nurture herself exclusively on ideas, Rand would live and die subject to the dynamics of her own philosophy. The clash between her romantic and rational sides makes this not a tale of triumph, but a tragedy of sorts.

PART I

The Education of Ayn Rand, 1905–1943

Alisa Rosenbaum, Leningrad, Russia, 1925.

CHAPTER ONE

From Russia to Roosevelt

$IT WAS A wintry day in 1918 when the Red Guard pounded on the door of Zinovy Rosenbaum's chemistry shop. The guards bore a seal of the State of Russia, which they nailed upon the door, signaling that it had been seized in the name of the people. Zinovy could at least be thankful the mad whirl of revolution had taken only his property, not his life. But his oldest daughter, Alisa, twelve at the time, burned with indignation. The shop was her father's; he had worked for it, studied long hours at university, dispensed valued advice and medicines to his customers. Now in an instant it was gone, taken to benefit nameless, faceless peasants, strangers who could offer her father nothing in return. The soldiers had come in boots, carrying guns, making clear that resistance would mean death. Yet they had spoken the language of fairness and equality, their goal to build a better society for all. Watching, listening, absorbing, Alisa knew one thing for certain: those who invoked such lofty ideals were not to be trusted. Talk about helping others was only a thin cover for force and power. It was a lesson she would never forget.

Ayn Rand's father, Zinovy Rosenbaum, was a self-made man. His bootstrap was a coveted space at Warsaw University, a privilege granted to only a few Jewish students. After earning a degree in chemistry, he established his own business in St. Petersburg. By the time of the Revolution he had ensconced his family in a large apartment on Nevsky Prospekt, a prominent address at the heart of the city. His educated and cultured wife, Anna, came from a wealthy and well-connected background. Her father was an expert tailor favored by the Russian Army, a position that helped shield their extended family against anti-Semitic violence.

Anna and Zinovy elevated Enlightenment European culture over their religious background. They observed the major Jewish holidays, holding a seder each year, but otherwise led largely secular lives. They spoke Russian at home and their three daughters took private lessons in French, German, gymnastics, and piano. They taught their eldest daughter, Alisa, born in 1905, that "culture, civilization, anything which is interesting…is abroad," and refused to let her read Russian literature.[1]

In their urbane sophistication and secularism, the Rosenbaums were vastly different from the majority of Russian Jews, who inhabited shtetls in the Pale of Settlement. Regulated and restricted by the czar in their choice of occupation and residence, Russia's Jews had found an unsteady berth in the empire until the 1880s, when a series of pogroms and newly restrictive laws touched off a wave of migration. Between 1897 and 1915 over a million Jews left Russia, most heading for the United States. Others emigrated to urban areas, where they had to officially register for residence. St. Petersburg's Jewish community grew from 6,700 in 1869 to 35,000 in 1910, the year Alisa turned five.[2]

By any standard, Russian or Jewish, the Rosenbaums were an elite and privileged family. Alisa's maternal grandparents were so wealthy, the children noted with awe, that when their grandmother needed a tissue she summoned a servant with a button on the wall.[3] Alisa and her three sisters grew up with a cook, a governess, a nurse, and tutors. Their mother loved to entertain, and their handsome apartment was filled with relatives and friends drawn to her evening salons. The family spent each summer on the Crimean peninsula, a popular vacation spot for the affluent. When Alisa was nine they journeyed to Austria and Switzerland for six weeks.

Alisa's childhood was dominated by her volatile mother. At a young age Alisa found herself ensnared in an intense family rivalry between Anna and her sister's husband. Both families had three daughters and lived in the same apartment building. Her mother was delighted each time Alisa bested her cousins in reading, writing, or arithmetic, and showed her off before gatherings of friends and relatives. Privately she berated her eldest daughter for failing to make friends. Alisa was a lonely, alienated child. In new situations she was quiet and still, staring out remotely through her large dark eyes. Anna grew increasingly frustrated with Alisa's withdrawn nature. "Why didn't I like to play with others? Why didn't I have any girlfriends? That was kind of the nagging refrain," Alisa remembered.[4] At times Anna's criticisms erupted into full-blown rage. In a "fit of temperament" she would lash out at her children, on one occasion breaking the legs of Alisa's favorite doll and on another ripping up a prized photo of Alexander Kerensky. She declared openly that she had never wanted children, hated caring for them, and did so only because it was her duty.

Zinovy, a taciturn and passive man, did little to balance his mercurial wife. He worked diligently to support his family and retreated in his spare time to games of whist, a popular card game. Despite the clashes with her mother, Alisa knew she was unquestionably the family favorite. Her grandmother doted on her, showering her with trinkets and treats during each visit. Her younger sisters idolized her, and although her father remained in the background, as was customary for fathers in his time, Alisa sensed that he approved of her many accomplishments.

After extensive tutoring at home, Alisa enrolled in a progressive and academically rigorous gymnasium. During religion classes at her school, the Jewish girls were excused to the back of the room and left to entertain themselves.[5] What really set Alisa apart was not her religion, but the same aloof temperament her mother found so troubling. Occasionally she would attract the interest of another girl, but she was never able to maintain a steady friendship. Her basic orientation to the world was simply too different. Alisa was serious and stern, uncomfortable with gossip, games, or the intrigues of popularity. "I would be bashful because I literally didn't know what to talk to people about," she recalled. Her classmates were a mystery to Alisa, who "didn't give the right cues apparently." Her only recourse was her intelligence. Her high marks at school enabled her to gain the respect, if not the affection, of her peers.[6] Alisa's perspective on her childhood was summarized in a composition she wrote as a young teen: "childhood is the worst period of one's life."

She survived these lonely years by recourse to fantasy, imagining herself akin to Catherine the Great, an outsider in the Russian court who had maneuvered her way to prominence. Like Catherine, Alisa saw herself as "a child of destiny." "They don't know it," she thought, "but it's up to me to demonstrate it."[7] She escaped into the French children's magazines her mother proffered to help with her language studies. In their pages Alisa discovered stories rife with beautiful princesses, brave adventurers, and daring warriors. Drawn into an imaginary universe of her own creation she began composing her own dramatic stories, often sitting in the back of her classroom writing instead of attending to the lessons.

Alisa's most enthusiastic audience for these early stories were her two sisters. Nora, the youngest, shared her introversion and artistic inclinations. Her specialty was witty caricatures of her family that blended man and beast. Alisa and Nora were inseparable, calling themselves Dact I and Dact II, after the winged dinosaurs of Arthur Conan Doyle's fantastic adventure story *The Lost World*.[8] The middle sister, Natasha, a skilled pianist, was outgoing and social. Both Nora and Natasha shared a keen appreciation for their elder sister's creativity, and at bedtime Alisa regaled them with her latest tales.

As the turmoil of Russia's revolutionary years closed in around the Rosenbaums, the family was forced to forgo the luxuries that had marked Alisa's childhood. Trips abroad and summer vacations receded into the distant past. Watching the disintegration of St. Petersburg, now renamed Petrograd, Anna convinced Zinovy they must relocate to Crimea. There, in czarist territory, he was able to open another shop, and the family's situation stabilized briefly. Alisa, entering her teenage years, enrolled at the local school, where her superior city education made her an immediate star.

But Crimea was a short-lived refuge. Red and White Russians battled for control of the region, and the chaos spilled into Yevpatoria, where the Rosenbaums lived. Communist soldiers rampaged through the town, once again robbing Zinovy. Piece by piece the family sold Anna's jewelry. Like a good peasant daughter, Alisa was put to work. She took a job teaching soldiers how to read.

In the middle of these bleak years Alisa unexpectedly broke through to her distant father. The connection was politics. Although forbidden to read the newspapers or talk about politics, she had followed the news of the Revolution with great interest. When Zinovy announced his departure for a political meeting one evening, Alisa boldly asked to accompany him. Surprised yet pleased, Zinovy agreed to take her, and afterward the two had their first real conversation. He listened to Alisa respectfully and offered his own opinions.

Zinovy was an anti-Communist and, as the mature Rand phrased it, "pro-individualist." So was she. In her adventure stories heroic resisters struggling against the Soviet regime now replaced knights and princesses. She filled her diary with invective against the Communists, further bolstered by her father's position. Their new connection was a source of great joy for Alisa, who remembered it was "only after we began to be political allies that I really felt a real love for him...." She also discovered that her father had an "enormous approval of my intelligence," which further confirmed her emerging sense of self.[9]

As in Petrograd, she remained unpopular with her classmates. They were eager to ask for her help on school assignments, but Alisa was not included in parties or invited on dates. Underneath their rejection Alisa sensed a certain resentment. Did her classmates dislike her because she was smarter? Were they penalizing her for her virtues? It was the first glimmer of an idea that would surface later, in her fiction. "I *think* that is what is the matter with my relationships," she began to believe, but worried this was "too easy" an explanation.[10]

Most likely, her classmates simply found Alisa abrasive and argumentative. She had an admitted tendency to force conversations, a violent intensity to her beliefs, an unfortunate inability to stop herself from arguing. But from her perspective, their jealousy had forced her into a lonely exile. Alisa was starting to understand herself as a heroine unfairly punished for what was best in her. Later she would come to see envy and resentment as fundamental social and political problems.

Turning to her interior world, Alisa became concerned not only with *what* she thought but *how* she thought. In her preteen years she had taken her family's casual attitude toward religion a step farther, deciding that she was an atheist. Now she discovered the two corollaries of her unbelief: logic and reason. When a teacher introduced the class to Aristotle and syllogisms it was "as if a light bulb went off." Consistency was the principle that grabbed her attention, not surprising given her unpredictable and frightening life. Consistency as Alisa understood it was the road to truth, the means to prevail in the heated arguments she loved, the one method to determine the validity of her thoughts.[11]

Three years after leaving Petrograd, in 1921, the Rosenbaums returned. There was nowhere left to go, for Crimea and the rest of the country had fallen to the Communists. Anna had begged Zinovy to leave Russia, to flee with his family across the Black Sea, but for once he stood firm against her. The decision to return was not wise. Their apartment and adjoining property had been given to other families, although the Rosenbaums were able to secure a few rooms in the building Zinovy had once owned outright.

Years later Alisa described in her fiction the grim disappointment of her family's return to Petrograd: "Their new home had no front entrance. It had no electrical connections; the plumbing was out of order; they had to carry water in pails from the floor below. Yellow stains spread over the ceilings, bearing witness to past rains." All trappings of luxury and higher culture had vanished. Instead of monogrammed silver, spoons were of heavy tin. There was no crystal or silver, and "rusty nails on the walls showed the places where old paintings had hung."[12] At parties hostesses could offer their guests only dubious delicacies, such as potato skin cookies and tea with saccharine tablets instead of sugar.

Under the Soviet New Economic Plan Zinovy was able to briefly reopen his shop with several partners, but it was again confiscated. After this latest insult Zinovy made one last, futile stand: he refused to work. Alisa silently admired her father's principles. To her his abdication was not self-destruction but self-preservation. His refusal to work for an exploitive system would structure the basic premise of her last novel, *Atlas Shrugged*. But with survival at stake it was no time for principles, or for bourgeois propriety. Anna found work teaching languages in a school, becoming her family's main source of support. But her teacher's salary was not enough for a family of five, and starvation stalked the Rosenbaums.

Even with money it would have been difficult to find enough to eat, for 1921–22 was the year of the Russian famine, during which five million Russians starved to death. In the city limited food supplies were parceled out to a subdued population through ration cards. Millet, acorns, and mush became mainstays of the family diet. Anna struggled to cook palatable meals on the Primus, a rudimentary Soviet stove that belched smoke throughout their living area. In later years Alisa remembered these bleak times vividly. She told friends she wrapped newspapers around her feet in lieu of shoes and recalled how she had begged her mother for a last dried pea to stave off her hunger.

Living under such dire circumstances, the Rosenbaums continued to prize education and culture. Alisa, now a full-time university student, was not asked to work. When her parents scraped together enough money to pay her streetcar fare she pocketed the money and used it to buy tickets to the theater. Musicals and operettas replaced fiction as her favorite narcotic.

At Petrograd State University Alisa was immune to the passions of revolutionary politics, inured against any radicalism by the travails her family was enduring. When she matriculated at age sixteen the entire Soviet higher education system was in flux. The Bolsheviks had liberalized admission policies and made tuition free, creating a flood of new students, including women and Jews, whose entrance had previously been restricted. Alisa was among the first class of women admitted to the university. Alongside these freedoms the Bolsheviks dismissed counterrevolutionary professors, harassed those who remained, and instituted Marxist courses on political economy and historical materialism. Students and professors alike protested the new conformity. In her first year Alisa was particularly outspoken. Then the purges began. Anticommunist professors and students disappeared, never to be heard from again. Alisa herself was briefly expelled when all students of bourgeois background were dismissed from the university. (The policy was later reversed and she returned.) Acutely aware of the dangers she faced, Alisa became quiet and careful with her words.

Alisa's education was heavily colored by Marxism. In her later writing she satirized the pabulum students were fed in books like *The ABC of Communism* and *The Spirit of the Collective*. By the time she graduated the school had been renamed Leningrad State University (and Petrograd had become Leningrad). Like the city itself, the university had fallen into disrepair. There were few textbooks or school supplies, and lecture halls and professors' offices were cold enough to freeze ink. Ongoing reorganization and reform meant that departments and graduation requirements were constantly changing. During her three years at the university Alisa gravitated to smaller seminar-style classes, skipping the large lectures that were heavy on Communist ideology. Most of her coursework was in history, but she also enrolled in classes in French, biology, history of worldviews, psychology, and logic. Her degree was granted by the interdisciplinary Department of Social Pedagogy.[13]

Alisa was skeptical of the education she received at the university, and it appears to have influenced her primarily in its form rather than its content. Her time at the University of Leningrad taught her that all ideas had an ultimate political valence. Communist authorities scrutinized every professor and course for counterrevolutionary ideas. The most innocuous statement could be traced back to its roots and identified as being either for or against the Soviet system. Even history, a subject Alisa chose because it was relatively free of Marxism, could be twisted and framed to reflect the glories of Bolshevism. Years later she considered herself an authority on propaganda, based on her university experience. "I was trained in it by experts," she explained to a friend.[14]

The university also shaped Alisa's understanding of intellectual life, primarily by exposing her to formal philosophy. Russian philosophy was synoptic and systemic, an approach that may have stimulated her later interest in creating an integrated philosophical system.[15] In her classes she heard about Plato and Herbert Spencer and studied the works of Aristotle for the first time. There was also a strong Russian tradition of pursuing philosophical inquiry outside university settings, and that was how she encountered Friedrich Nietzsche, the philosopher who quickly became her favorite. A cousin taunted her with a book by Nietzsche, "who beat you to all your ideas."[16] Reading outside of her classes she devoured his works.

Alisa's first love when she left university was not philosophy, however, but the silver screen. The Russian movie industry, long dormant during the chaos of war and revolution, began to revive in the early 1920s. Under the New Economic Plan Soviet authorities allowed the import of foreign films and the Commissariat of Education began supporting Russian film production. Hoping to become a screenwriter, Alisa enrolled in the new State Institute for Cinematography after receiving her undergraduate degree. Movies became her obsession. In 1924 she viewed forty-seven movies; the next year she watched 117. In a movie diary she ranked each film she saw on a scale of one to five, noted its major stars, and started a list of her favorite artists. The movies even inspired her first published works, a pamphlet about the actress Pola Negri and a booklet titled *Hollywood: American Movie City*. In these early works she wrote knowledgably about major directors, artists, and films and explained the studio system, the way directors worked, even the use of specially trained animals.[17]

In the movies Alisa glimpsed America: an ideal world, a place as different from Russia as she could imagine. America had glamour, excitement, romance, a lush banquet of material goods. She described Hollywood in reverent tones: "People, for whom 24 hours is not enough time in a day, stream in a constant wave over its boulevards, smooth as marble. It is difficult for them to talk with one another, because the noise of automobiles drowns out their voices. Shining, elegant Fords and Rolls-Royce's fly, flickering, as the frames of one continuous movie reel. And the sun strikes the blazing windows of enormous, snow white studios. Every night an electric glow rises over the city."[18]

Her interest in America surged when the family received an unexpected letter from Chicago. Almost thirty years earlier Harry Portnoy, one of Anna's relatives, had emigrated to America, and her family had helped pay the passage. Now one of Harry's children, Sara Lipski, wrote inquiring about the Rosenbaums, for they had heard nothing during the wartime years. Alisa saw her chance. Using her connections to the Portnoys she could obtain a visa to visit the United States, once there she could find a way to stay forever. She begged her mother to ask their relatives for help. Her parents agreed to the idea, perhaps worried that their outspoken daughter would never survive in the shifting political climate.

Or perhaps they agreed because Alisa's unhappiness was palpable. Amid the privations of Petrograd she had made a life for herself, even attracting an attentive suitor, a neighbor her family referred to as Seriozha. But daily life continually disappointed. Film school seemed a road to nowhere, for Alisa knew that as a Russian screenwriter she would be expected to write Soviet propaganda, to support a system she loathed. Seriozha was little comfort. The two had met when their families rented adjacent cabins one summer for a brief vacation. Back in Leningrad Alisa continued to accept his overtures, but her heart lay with the memory of another man. Her first adolescent crush had been on the darkly attractive Lev, whom she met through a cousin. Years later his memory lingered as the character Leo in We the Living: "He was tall; his collar was raised; a cap was pulled over his eyes. His mouth, calm, severe, contemptuous, was that of an ancient chieftain who could order men to die, and his eyes were such as could watch it."[19] Fascinated by the intense young Alisa, Lev for a time became a regular visitor to the Rosenbaum household. But he had no genuine interest in a romance, soon abandoning her for other pursuits. Alisa was crushed. Lev symbolized all the lost possibility of her life in Russia.

As she listened to her beloved eldest daughter shouting with despair behind her bedroom door, Anna knew she must get Alisa out of Russia.[20] It took months to lay the groundwork. The first step was English lessons. Next Anna, Natasha, and Nora began a new round of fervent Communist activity intended to prove the family's loyalty to the Revolution, even as Anna began securing the permits for Alisa's escape. The Rosenbaums claimed that Alisa intended to study American movies and return to help launch the Russian film industry, a lie made plausible by her enrollment at the film institute and the fact that her relatives owned a theater. All of Anna's Chicago relatives, the Portnoy, Lipski, Satrin, and Goldberg families, pledged their support.

Alisa's impending departure made the entire family tense. At each bureaucratic hurdle Alisa was struck with panic attacks at the prospect that she might not escape. Even as they urged her to use any means necessary to stay in the United States, the Rosenbaums were devastated by her departure. Alisa appeared more sanguine. Going to America was like "going to Mars," and she knew she might never see her family again. Yet she was supremely confident about her own prospects, and also shared her father's sense that the Communist government could not last. "I'll be famous by the time I return," she shouted to her stricken family as the train pulled out of the Leningrad station in January 1926. Aside from the lovelorn Seriozha, who would accompany her as far as Moscow, Alisa was on her own. She carried with her seventeen film scenarios and a precious stone sewn into her clothes by Anna. Nora, Natasha, and her cousins chased after the train as it faded into the distance. Zinovy returned home and wept.[21]

Leaving Russia was only the first step, for Alisa still had to receive immigration papers from the American consulate in neighboring Latvia. Just a year earlier, responding to rising nativist sentiment, the U.S. Congress had moved to severely restrict immigration from Russia and other Eastern European countries. As she waited for her appointment, staying with family friends, Alisa soothed her nerves at the cinema, seeing four films during her brief stay. A quick fib about a fiancé secured her the necessary American papers, and then she was off, taking a train through Berlin and Paris, where more family connections smoothed her way. At the Hague she sent a last cable to Leningrad and then took passage on an ocean liner bound for New York. Once there, she would be met by yet more family friends, who would shepherd her to Chicago.

Onboard the *de Grasse* Alisa was flattened by seasickness. But as she lay pinned to her berth by the motion of the sea she began refashioning herself. In Russia she had experimented with using a different surname, Rand, an abbreviation of Rosenbaum. Now she jettisoned Alisa for a given name inspired by a Finnish writer.[22] Like a Hollywood star she wanted a new, streamlined name that would be memorable on the marquee. The one she ultimately chose, Ayn Rand, freed her from her gender, her religion, her past. It was the perfect name for a child of destiny.

The rat-tat-tat of Ayn's typewriter drove her Chicago relatives crazy. She wrote every night, sometimes all night. In America nothing was going to stand in her way. Whenever possible she went to the Lipskis' cinema, watching films repeatedly, soaking in the details of the filming, the acting, the story, the plot. In the six months she spent in Chicago she saw 135 movies. Her English was still poor, and matching the subtitles to the action helped her learn.

Completely focused on her own concerns, Rand had little time for chit-chat with her relatives. Asked about family affairs in Russia she gave curt answers or launched into long tirades about the murderous Bolsheviks. The many generations of Portnoys were baffled by their strange new relative. They began trading her back and forth, for no household could long stand her eccentricities. By the end of the summer their patience was exhausted.

Rand was eager to leave Chicago anyway. She was particularly discomfited by the exclusively Jewish social world in which her relatives lived. Since her arrival in New York, nearly everyone she had met was Jewish. This was not, she thought, the real America. She longed to break out of the stifling ethnic enclave of her extended family and experience the country she had imagined so vividly in Russia. The Portnoys bought her train ticket to Hollywood and gave her a hundred dollars to start out. Rand promised them a Rolls Royce in return.[23]

In Russia Rand had imagined Hollywood as a microcosm of the globe: "You will meet representatives of every nationality, people from every social class. Elegant Europeans, energetic, businesslike Americans, benevolent Negroes, quiet Chinese, savages from colonies. Professors from the best schools, farmers, and aristocrats of all types and ages descend on the Hollywood studios in a greedy crowd."[24] Despite its international image, Hollywood itself was little more than a glorified cow town that could not compare to the glitz of its productions. When Rand arrived in 1926 the major studios were just setting up shop, drawn by the social freedoms of California and the warm climate, which meant films could be shot year-round. Roads were haphazard and might dead-end suddenly into a thicket of brush; chaparral covered the rolling hills to the east, where rattlesnakes and mountain lions sheltered. Besides movies, the main exports were the oranges and lemons that grew in groves at the edge of town. Near the studios a surreal mix of costumed extras wandered the streets. "A mining town in lotus land" is the way the novelist F. Scott Fitzgerald described early Hollywood. More negative was the verdict of his contemporary Nathanael West, who called the city "a dream dump."[25] But Rand had little exposure to the movie industry's dark side.

Instead, arriving in Hollywood was like stepping into one of the fantasy tales she wrote as a child. Her timing was fortuitous. The industry was still young and relatively fluid; moreover, the mid-1920s were the last years of the silent pictures, so even though Rand had barely mastered English she could still hope to author screenplays. Movie dialogue, which appeared in subtitles at the bottom of the screen, was necessarily brief and basic. The action in movies was driven instead by popular piano music, which Rand loved. In Chicago she had written several more screenplays in her broken English.

Her first stop was the De Mille Studio, home of her favorite director. None of De Mille's religious films had been released in Russia, where he was famous for "society glamour, sex, and adventure," as Rand recalled.[26] She had a formulaic letter of introduction from the Portnoys and a sheaf of her work in hand. A secretary listened politely to her tale before shunting her out the door. And then she saw him, Cecil B. De Mille himself. By the gates of the studio De Mille was idling his automobile, engrossed in conversation. She stared and stared. De Mille, used to adulation, was struck by the intensity of her gaze and called out to her from his open roadster. Rand stammered back in her guttural accent, telling him she had just arrived from Russia. De Mille knew a good story when he heard it and impulsively invited Rand into his car. He drove her through the streets of Hollywood, dropped famous names, pointed out noteworthy places, and invited her to the set of *King of Kings* the next day. When it was all over Rand had a nickname, "Caviar," and steady work as an extra.

She quickly parlayed her personal connection with De Mille into a job as a junior writer in his studio. Her own screenwriting efforts were unpolished, but Rand could tell a good movie from a bad one. By the time she arrived in Hollywood she had watched and ranked more than three hundred movies. As a junior writer she summarized properties De Mille owned and wrote suggestions for improvement. It was almost too good to be true. Less than a year after leaving Russia, Rand had realized some of her wildest dreams. She took lodgings at the new Studio Club, a charitable home for eighty aspiring actresses located in a beautiful, Mediterranean-style building designed by Julia Morgan. Founded by concerned Hollywood matrons, the Studio Club aimed to keep the starstruck "extra girl" out of trouble by providing safe, affordable, and supervised refuge. Men were not allowed into the rooms, and the residents were provided with a variety of wholesome social activities, such as weekly teas.

These aspects of the Studio Club held little attraction for Rand, who struck her fellow boarders as an oddball. In contrast to the would-be starlets who surrounded her, Rand rarely wore makeup and cut her own hair, favoring a short pageboy style. She stayed up all night to write and loved combative arguments about abstract topics. "My first impression is that this woman is a freak!" remembered a Hollywood acquaintance. Rand herself knew she was different. "Try to be calm, balanced, indifferent, normal, and not enthusiastic, passionate, excited, ecstatic, flaming, tense," she counseled herself in her journal. "Learn to be calm, for goodness sake!"[27]

Even in a town of outsize ambitions Rand was extraordinarily driven. She lashed at herself in a writing diary, "Stop admiring yourself—you are nothing yet." Her steady intellectual companion in these years was Friedrich Nietzsche, and the first book she bought in English was *Thus Spoke Zarathustra*. Nietzsche was an individualist who celebrated self-creation, which was after all what Rand was doing in America. She seemed to have been deeply affected by his emphasis on the will to power, or self-overcoming. She commanded herself, "The secret of life: you must be nothing but will. Know what you want and do it. Know what you are doing and why you are doing it, every minute of the day. All will and all control. Send everything else to hell!"[28] Set on perfecting her English, she checked out British and American literature from the library. She experimented with a range of genres in her writing, creating short stories, screenplays, and scenarios. She brought her best efforts into the De Mille studio, but none were accepted.

Rand was also absorbed by the conundrums of love, sex, and men. Shortly after arriving in Chicago she had written Seriozha to end their relationship. Her mother applauded the move, telling her daughter it was "only the fact that you had been surrounded by people from the caveman days that made you devote so much time to him." She was less understanding when Rand began to let ties to her family lapse. "You left, and it is though you divorced us," Anna wrote accusingly when Rand did not respond to letters for several months.[29] Rand was becoming increasingly wary of dependence of any kind. The prospect of romance in particular roused the pain of Lev's rejection years earlier. To desire was to need, and Rand wanted to need nobody.

Instead she created a fictional world where beautiful, glamorous, and rich heroines dominated their suitors. Several short stories she wrote in Hollywood, but never published, dwelled on the same theme. *The Husband I Bought* stars an heiress who rescues her boyfriend from bankruptcy by marrying him. Another heiress in *Good Copy* saves the career of her newspaper boyfriend, again by marrying him, while in *Escort* a woman inadvertently purchases the services of her husband for an evening on the town. In several stories the woman not only has financial power over the man, but acts to sexually humiliate and emasculate him by having a public extramarital affair. In Rand's imagination women were passionate yet remained firmly in control.[30]

Real life was not so simple. On a streetcar heading to work during her first days in Hollywood she noticed a tall and striking stranger. Frank O'Connor was exactly the type of man Rand found most attractive. To her joy, she realized they were both heading to the same destination, De Mille's *King of Kings* set. After changing into her costume she spotted him again, attired as a Roman soldier, complete with toga and head-dress. Rand followed his every move for days. On the fourth day she deliberately tripped him as he did a scene and apologized profusely after he fell. Her words made it clear she was not American, and like De Mille before him, Frank was struck by this odd foreign woman. They chatted briefly. Nerves thickened Rand's accent, and Frank could barely under-stand a word she said. Then he was distracted by someone else, and the next minute he was gone.

Never one to doubt herself, Rand was sure it was love. Finding Frank and then losing him shattered her. Homesickness, loneliness, anxiety over her future—all her pent-up emotions poured forth as she fixated on the handsome stranger. For months she sobbed audibly in her bed-room at the Studio Club, alarming the other girls. Then she found him again, this time in a library off Hollywood Boulevard. They spoke for several hours, and he invited her to dinner. From then on their court ship was slow but steady.

Raised in a small town in Ohio, Frank was the third of seven children born to devout Catholic parents. His father was a steelworker, his mother a housewife who aspired to greater things. Overbearing and ambitious, she dominated her large brood and her passive, alcoholic husband. After his mother's untimely death, Frank left home at age fifteen with three of his brothers. They worked their way to New York, where Frank began acting in the fledgling movie industry. A few years later he followed the studios west, arriving in Hollywood around the same time as Rand. Like her, he was entranced by the flash and sophistication of the movies.

The similarities ended there. Where Ayn was outspoken and bold, Frank was taciturn and retiring. She was mercurial, stubborn, and driven; he was even-keeled, irenic, and accommodating. Most important, Frank was used to strong women. He was intrigued by Ayn's strong opinions and intellectual bent and was willing to let her steer the relationship. Rand was captivated, both by Frank's gentle manner and by his good looks. She worshipped the beauties of Hollywood, but with her square jaw and thick features she knew she could never be counted among them. Frank, however, was movie-star handsome, with a slender build, an easy grace, and a striking visage. Her neighbors at the Studio Club began to notice a new Ayn, one more relaxed, friendly, and social than before. An incident the other girls found hilarious sheds some light on her priorities. "She apparently had terrible financial problems and owed money to the club," recounted a fellow boarder. "Anyhow, a woman was going to donate $50 to the neediest girl in the club, and Miss Williams picked out Ayn. Ayn thanked them for the money and then went right out and bought a set of black lingerie."[31]

Rand's financial problems were triggered by the advent of the talkies, which shook the movie industry to the core. In 1927 De Mille closed his studio, and with talking pictures now ascendant Rand could not find another job in the industry. Unskilled and anonymous, she had to settle for a series of odd jobs and temporary positions. She fell behind on her rent and started skipping meals. This was not the fate she had expected when she disembarked in New York years earlier. Though she accepted small loans from her family, she was unwilling to ask Frank for help, or even to reveal the extent of her problems to him. On their dates she kept up appearances, never letting him see the despair that was beginning to suffuse her life.

Under the surface Rand's unfulfilled ambitions ate away at her. When the tabloids filled with the sensational case of William Hickman, a teen murderer who mutilated his victim and boasted maniacally of his deed when caught, Rand was sympathetic rather than horrified. To her, Hickman embodied the strong individual breaking free from the ordinary run of humanity. She imagined Hickman to be like herself, a sensitive individual ruined by misunderstanding and neglect, writing in her diary, "If he had any desires and ambitions—what was the way before him? A long, slow, soul-eating, heart-wrecking toil and struggle; the degrading, ignoble road of silent pain and loud compromises."[32] Glossing over his crime, Rand focused on his defiant refusal to express remorse or contrition.

She began to plan "The Little Street," a story with a protagonist, Danny Renahan, modeled after Hickman. It was the first of her stories to contain an explicit abstract theme. She wanted to document and decry how society crushed exceptional individuals. In a writing notebook she explained her attraction to the scandal: "It is more exact to say that the model is not

Hickman, but what Hickman suggested to me." Still, Rand had trouble interpreting the case as anything other than an exercise in mob psychology. She wrote, "This case is not moral indignation at a terrible crime. It is the mob's murderous desire to revenge its hurt vanity against the man who dared to be alone." What the tabloids saw as psychopathic, Rand admired: "It is the amazing picture of a man with no regard whatever for all that society holds sacred, and with a consciousness all his own. A man who really stands alone, in action and in soul."[33]

Rand appeared to be drawing from both her own psychology and her recent readings of Nietzsche as she mused about the case and planned her story. She modeled Renahan along explicitly Nietzschean lines, noting that "he has the true, innate psychology of a Superman." To Rand a Superman was one who cared nothing for the thoughts, feelings, or opinions of others. Her description of Renahan as Superman echoed her own self-description as a child: "He is born with a wonderful, free, light consciousness—resulting from the absolute lack of social instinct or herd feeling. He does not understand, *because he has no organ for understanding,* the necessity, meaning or importance of other people."[34]

Rand's understanding of the Superman as a strong individual who places himself above society was a popular, if crude, interpretation of Nietzsche's *Übermensch.*[35] What stands out is her emphasis on Renahan's icy emotional alienation. Rand clearly admired her imaginary hero's solipsism, yet she had chosen a profession that measured success by popularity. The tension between her values and her goals produced an ugly frustration. "Show that humanity is petty. That it's small. That it's dumb, with the heavy, hopeless stupidity of a man born feeble-minded," she wrote.[36] This anger and frustration, born from her professional struggles, was itself the greatest obstacle to Rand's writing career.

Rand's bitterness was undoubtedly nurtured by her interest in Nietzsche. Judging from her journals, unemployment precipitated a new round of reading his work. Her notes filled with the phrases "Nietzsche and I think" and "as Nietzsche said." Her style also edged in his direction as she experimented with pithy aphorisms and observations. More significantly, Nietzsche's elitism fortified her own. Like many of his readers, Rand seems never to have doubted that she was one of the creators, the artists, the potential Overmen of whom Nietzsche spoke.[37]

On some level Rand realized that her infatuation with Nietzsche, however inspirational, was damaging to her creativity. The idea of the Superman had lodged in her mind with problematic force. She struggled to resist: "Try to forget yourself—to forget all high ideas, ambitions, superman and so on. Try to put yourself into the psychology of ordinary people, when you think of stories."[38] Convinced of her own worth yet stymied by her low position, Rand alternated between despair and mania.

When she began writing to her family again after a long lapse, Anna was shocked at the dark tone that had crept into her letters. She sensed that Rand's expectations were part of the problem, reminding her daughter that success would not come without a struggle: "Your talent is very clearly and firmly established. Your gift manifested itself very early in life and long ago. Your talent is so clear that eventually it will break through and spurt like a fountain."[39] As her mother intuited, Rand's silence was due in part to her fear of disappointing her family. They had pinned their hopes on her, and after such a promising start Rand had little to report.

She did, however, have one success to share: a new husband. After a year of regular dates Rand moved out of the Studio Club into a furnished room that afforded her and Frank more privacy. Soon she began pushing for marriage, reminding Frank that after several extensions her visa was soon to expire. They were married in 1929, the year of the Great Crash. A few months later Rand applied for citizenship as Mrs. Frank O'Connor.

As it turned out, Rand's stories about dashing heiresses and feckless suitors proved a useful meditation for her marriage to Frank. A struggling actor, he had always worked episodically and the economic depression made jobs even more difficult to find. Rand was the breadwinner from the start. Soon after their marriage she was hired as a filing clerk in the wardrobe department at RKO Radio Pictures after another Russian employed there had given her a lead on the job. Focused, organized, and desperate for work, Rand was an ideal employee. Within a year she had risen to head of the department and was earning a comfortable salary, which allowed the newlyweds to establish a stable life together. They owned a collie and an automobile and lived in an apartment large enough to accommodate long-term guests. When close friends of the

O'Connor family went through a wrenching divorce, Ayn and Frank sheltered Frank's ten-year-old goddaughter for a summer.

Through the mundane negotiations of married life a current of exoticism kept their attraction strong. In a letter home Rand described Frank as an "Irishman with blue eyes," and he took to wearing Russian Cossack-style shirts.[40] Still, Rand found the rhythms of domesticity exhausting. She rose early in the morning to write and then left for RKO, where her days could stretch to sixteen hours. Each night she rushed home to cook Frank dinner, a responsibility she prized as a sign of wifely virtue. Over Frank's protestations she insisted on boiling water to scald the dishes after every meal, having inherited her mother's phobia about germs. After dinner and cleanup she returned to her writing.

In her off-hours she completed a film scenario called *Red Pawn*, a melodramatic love story set in Soviet Russia. A well-connected neighbor passed the scenario along to an agent, and Rand used her RKO position to access unofficial channels. She sent her work to a Universal screenwriter, Gouverneur Morris, a writer of pulpy novels and magazine stories (and great-grandson of the colonial statesman). The two had never met, but Morris's tightly plotted work had impressed Rand. Morris groaned at the request from an unknown wardrobe girl, but to his surprise he enjoyed the story. Meeting Rand he pronounced her a genius. When Universal purchased *Red Pawn* in 1932 Morris claimed full credit, and he pressed the studio to hire her on as a writer. Universal paid Rand seven hundred dollars for her story and an additional eight hundred dollars for an eight-week contract to write a screenplay and treatment.[41]

Rand's luck was beginning to turn. *Red Pawn* was never produced, but a few prominent stars showed interest in the property, sparking a brief flurry of news coverage. "Russian Girl Finds End of Rainbow in Hollywood" was the *Chicago Daily News* headline to a short article that mentioned Rand's Chicago connections, her meeting with De Mille, and plans for the movie.[42] The screenwriting job was far more lucrative than working in the wardrobe department, and by the end of the year Rand was flush enough to quit work and begin writing full time. The next two years were her most productive yet. In 1933 she completed a play, *Night of January 16th,* and the next year finished her first novel, *We the Living.*

As she began writing seriously, Rand was not shy about drawing from the work of other authors. Copying was one of the few honored traditions in Hollywood; no sooner had one studio released a popular movie than the others would rush a similar story into production. Similarly, Rand was inspired to write a play set in a courtroom after seeing *The Trial of Mary Dugan*. When her play *Night of January 16th* was first produced the *Los Angeles Times* noted uneasily, "It so closely resembles 'The Trial of Mary Dugan' in its broader aspects as to incorporate veritably the same plot."[43]

It is safe to say, however, that the author of *Mary Dugan* was not trying to advance individualism through theater. That goal was Rand's alone. *Night of January 16th* was Rand's first successful marriage of entertainment and propaganda. She hoped to both entertain her audience and spread her ideas about individualism. Like "The Little Street," the play was heavily tinctured with her interpretation of Nietzsche. She drew on yet another highly publicized criminal case to shape one of her characters, Bjorn Faulkner, who was loosely modeled on the infamous "Swedish Match King" Ivar Kreuger. In 1932 Kreuger shot himself when his financial empire, in reality a giant Ponzi scheme, collapsed in scandal.

Rand still found criminality an irresistible metaphor for individualism, with dubious results. Translated by Rand into fiction, Nietzsche's transvaluation of values changed criminals into heroes and rape into love. Rand intended Bjorn Faulkner to embody heroic individualism, but in the play he comes off as little more than an unscrupulous businessman with a taste for rough sex. He rapes his secretary, Karen Andre, on her first day of work. Andre immediately falls in love with him and remains willingly as his mistress, secretary, and eventual business partner. When Faulkner dies under mysterious circumstances, Andre becomes the prime suspect. She goes on trial for Faulkner's murder, and the entire play is set in a courtroom. What really made *Night of January 16th* was a crowd-pleasing gimmick: each night a different jury is selected from the audience. Rand constructed the play so that there was approximately equal evidence indicting two characters and wrote two endings to the play, to be performed according to the verdict of the audience jury.

This unusual staging attracted the attention of Al Woods, a seasoned producer who wanted to take the play to Broadway. It was the big break she had been waiting for, but Rand was wary of Woods. As much as she wanted fame, she wanted it on her own terms. *Night of January 16th* was encoded with subtle messages about individualism and morality. The ambitious and unconventional Karen Andre was a softer version of Danny Renahan from "The Little Street." If the audience shared Rand's individualistic inclinations they would vote to acquit Andre of the crime. Rand feared that Woods, intent on a hit, would gut the play of its larger meaning. She turned down his offer.

Even as literary fame lay within reach, Rand's ambitions were racing onward. In early 1934 she began a philosophical journal. She would write in it only episodically in the next few years, accumulating about ten pages before she shifted her focus back to fiction. It was only "the vague beginnings of an amateur philosopher," she announced modestly, but by the end of her first entry she had decided, "I want to be known as the greatest champion of reason and the greatest enemy of religion."[44] She recorded two objections to religion: it established unrealizable, abstract ethical ideas that made men cynical when they fell short, and its emphasis on faith denied reason.

From these first deliberations Rand segued to a series of musings about the relationship between feelings and thoughts. She wondered, "Are instincts and emotions necessarily beyond the control of plain thinking? Or were they trained to be? Why is a complete harmony between mind and emotions impossible?" During her first spell of unemployment Rand had chastised herself for being too emotional. Now she seemed to be convincing herself that emotions could be controlled, if only she could think the right thoughts. Couldn't contradictory emotions, she ventured, be considered "a form of undeveloped reason, a form of stupidity?"[45]

Over the next few months Rand's commitment to reason deepened. Where before she had seen herself as moody and excitable, she now imagined, "my instincts and reason are so inseparably one, with the reason ruling the instincts." Her tone alternated between grandiosity and self-doubt. "Am I trying to impose my own peculiarities as a philosophical system?" she wondered. Still she had no doubt that her musings would eventually culminate in "a logical system, proceeding from a few axioms in a succession of logical theorems." "The end result," she declared, "will be my 'mathematics of philosophy.'"[46]

She also began responding to Nietzsche's call for a new, naturalistic morality that would transcend Christianity. The key to originality, she thought, would be to focus exclusively on the individual. "Is ethics necessarily and basically a social conception?" she asked in her journal. "Have there been systems of ethics written primarily on the basis of an individual? Can that be done?" She ended with a Nietzschean peroration: "If men are the highest of animals, isn't *man* the next step?" Tentatively, slowly, Rand was sketching out the foundations of her later thought.[47]

In the meantime her playwriting career was beginning to take off. Rejecting Woods was an audacious move that only heightened his interest in *Night of January 16th*. After the play was successfully produced by a local Hollywood theater Woods tried again. This time he agreed to small changes in the contract that gave Rand more influence. He also requested that Rand relocate to New York immediately to assist with production of the play. Setting aside her misgivings, Rand accepted Wood's new offer. She was more than happy to move to New York. Hollywood had never been to her liking, but the few brief days she spent in New York had left a lasting impression. There was little keeping the O'Connors in California, for Frank's acting career had sputtered to an effective end. In November 1934 they packed up their few possessions and set out on the long drive to New York.

By the time they arrived the young couple was nearly destitute. Rand had drained her savings to write and spent the last of her money on the move. Woods was unable to find funding for the play, so for the foreseeable future Rand would receive only minimal monthly payments. A small furnished room was all they could afford. They borrowed money from a few friends, and Frank's brother Nick, a bachelor, became a frequent dinner guest and helped contribute to their expenses.

As in Hollywood, they socialized infrequently. Rand detested small talk, often sitting mute at social gatherings. At parties Frank would surreptitiously hand her notes suggesting conversational topics and partners.[48] She became animated only when the talk moved on to territory where she could hang an argument. At any mention of religion, morality, or ethics she would transform from a silent wallflower into a raging tigress, eager to take all comers. Neither persona made for pleasant company. But Nick O'Connor, who had a taste for intellectual discussion, enjoyed spending time with Rand. A few other friends gravitated into the O'Connor orbit, including Albert Mannheimer, a young socialist with whom Rand loved to argue, and a few Russians Rand had met through family connections. Frank's niece Mimi Sutton was also a frequent visitor to their home. By and large, though, Rand contented herself with the attentions of a few close friends. She and Frank, or "Cubbyhole" and "Fluff" as they now called one another, drew closer. Though he never pretended to be an intellectual, Frank cultivated a dry wit that she found hilarious. Serious and focused in her professional life, Rand could be silly and girlish with Frank. A long-haired Persian cat, Tartallia, rounded out the family.

As she waited for the play to go up, Rand turned her attention to selling her novel, completed a year before. *We the Living* is the most autobiographical of Rand's works. It is set in a milieu she knew well, the world of the Russian cultured classes who had lost nearly everything in the Revolution. The novel follows the fate of two bourgeois families, the Argounovs and the Ivanovitches, who, like the Rosenbaums, tumble from an exalted position in society to a life of poverty. The main characters are Kira, Leo, and Andrei, three young people who struggle against the injustices and violence of the Soviet regime. Petrograd itself is a palpable presence in the novel. Her tone elegiac and wistful, Rand describes its streets and monuments with evocative detail.

Rand's anti-Communism is woven into every scene in the novel and its overall structure. Kira, the heroine, is an independent and determined career woman who boldly flouts social convention, sharing an apartment with her lover, Leo, the son of a famous general executed for counterrevolutionary activity. Due to their class background, Leo and Kira are expelled from university and are unable to find work because they do not belong to the Communist Party. When Leo falls ill with tuberculosis he is denied medical care for the same reason. "Why—in the face of the Union of Socialist Soviet Republics—can't one aristocrat die?" an official asks Kira.[49] In desperation Kira begins a clandestine affair with Andrei, a sexy Communist with connections to the secret police. Andrei passes his salary on to Kira, who uses it to fund Leo's stay in a sanatorium.

Rand's sympathetic portrait of Andrei is striking, particularly when contrasted to her later villains. For all Rand's hatred of Communism, Andrei is one of her most fully realized and compelling characters. Ruthless in pursuit of his ideals, he has the strength and wisdom to recognize the corruption inherent in the Communist system. In one of the book's most gripping scenes, Andrei raids Leo's apartment and discovers his connection to Kira. When Kira confesses that money was a primary motivation for her affair with him, Andrei is devastated. She is unapologetic: "If you taught us that our life is nothing before that of the State—well then, are you really suffering?" Stung by her words, Andrei begins to understand the consequences of his ideals in action. He is further disillusioned when his superiors prosecute Leo for speculation yet hush up the involvement of several Communist Party members in the scheme. At his next Party Club meeting Andrei denounces the Party and defends individualism. Soon afterward he commits suicide, an act Rand frames as the final, noble decision of a man who recognizes the evil of the system he has served yet refuses to let it poison his soul.[50]

The novel ends on an even bleaker note. Kira has saved Leo's life but not his spirit. Denied gainful employment, he turns to crime and then abandons Kira for a wealthy older woman. Kira concludes, "It was I against a hundred and fifty million people. I lost." At the end of the story Kira is shot while attempting to cross the Siberian border to freedom. Rand paints her death in dramatic detail: "She lay on the edge of a hill and looked down at the sky. One hand, white and still, hung over the edge, and little red drops rolled slowly in the snow, down the slope." Through all the romantic intrigue Rand's didactic message is clear: Communism is a cruel system that crushes the virtuous and rewards the corrupt.[51]

We the Living was Rand's first attempt to link her idée fixe of individualism to larger social and political problems. It exhibits much of her previous contempt for the masses, but its overall theme has a gravity and relevance missing from her earlier work. In her notes for the novel she used the word "collectivism" for the first time; her book would demonstrate "its spirit, influence, ramifications," she jotted in a brief aside. Rand's use of the concept demonstrated her new familiarity with contemporary American language. As the country sank deeper into depression during the mid-1930s there was much discussion of collective solutions and collective action.[52] Like many others, Rand saw Russia as emblematic of collectivism. This identification lay at the heart of her attack.

According to Rand, collectivism was inherently problematic, for it prioritized the common good over the lives of individuals. Russia, with its purges, secret police, and stolen property, provided the clearest example of this truth. But she wanted her novel to show that the problem went beyond Russia, for it was the very principles of Communism, not just the practice, that were flawed. Rand was unwilling to grant collectivism any moral high ground. As Kira informs Andrei, "I loathe your ideals."[53] This was the first germ of Rand's critique of altruism. It also marked an important expansion and maturation of her thought. Her first works had focused on the clash between exceptional individuals and their immediate society. Now she began to examine how these forces played out on a larger canvas.

This move to a social framework transformed Rand's writing. In Soviet Russia she found a setting that could give full and plausible expression to her own embedded emotional patterns. When set within an oppressive society, the lonely, embattled individual became not an antisocial loner but an admirable freedom fighter. Drawing from her past also helped Rand check her wilder flights of imagination. The novel's plot is fanciful, but most of the book's characters ring true. Rand based many of them on people she knew in Russia and drew liberally from her own experiences to describe the frustration and angst of living under Soviet Communism.[54]

Rand expected the novel to sell quickly. She knew it was not the best work she could produce, but it was far better than anything she had written before. She also had some powerful connections on her side. Her Hollywood booster, Gouverneur Morris, called her latest work "the *Uncle Tom's Cabin* of Soviet Russia" and sent the manuscript to his friend H. L. Mencken, the famed book critic. Like Rand, Mencken had a strong appreciation for Nietzsche. An unabashed elitist, he delighted in mocking the stupidity and pretensions of the American "boo-boisie." With time Mencken was growing increasingly conservative politically, and he proved receptive to Rand's individualist message. He reported back to Morris that *We the Living* was "a really excellent piece of work," and the two of them lent their names to Rand's manuscript. Even so, Rand's agent reported one failure after another.[55]

It began to dawn on Rand that there were Communist sympathizers, or "pinks," in America. At first she had assumed, "[T]hey did not matter in the least...this was *the* capitalist country of the world, and by everything I could observe, Leftism or socialism was not an issue."[56] But now she began to hear that although publishers liked the book, they found its politics objectionable. Reviewers and editorial board members explained to Rand's agent that she was simply wrong about Soviet Russia and misunderstood the noble experiment being conducted there. Some added that though conditions might have been poor in the revolutionary period that Rand described, everything was different now.[57]

It is true that *We the Living* flew in the face of everything most educated Americans thought they knew about Russia. As the Great Depression ground on and unemployment soared, intellectuals began unfavorably comparing their faltering capitalist economy to Russian Communism. Karl Marx had predicted that capitalism would fall under the weight of its own contradictions, and now with the economic crisis gripping the West, his predictions seem to be coming true. By contrast Russia seemed an emblematic modern nation, making the staggering leap from a feudal past to an industrial future with ease.[58]

High-profile visitors to Russia reinforced this perception. Important Americans who visited the USSR were given the red carpet treatment and credulously reported back the fantasy they had been fed. More than ten years after the Revolution, Communism was finally reaching full flower, according to the *New York Times* reporter Walter Duranty, a Stalin fan who vigorously debunked accounts of the Ukraine famine, a man-made disaster that would leave millions dead. The Soviet economy was booming; Russia had even eliminated juvenile delinquency, prostitution, and mental illness, according to the psychiatrist Frankwood Williams, author of the optimistic *Russia, Youth, and the Present-Day World*.[59]

There was a sense of inevitability about it all. In educated, reform-minded circles it became conventional wisdom that the United States would simply have to move toward Communism or, at the very least, socialism. Whittaker Chambers, a Communist since the 1920s, remembered the Party's sudden surge in popularity: "These were the first quotas of the great drift from Columbia, Harvard, and elsewhere...from 1930 on, a small intellectual army passed over to the Communist Party with scarcely any effort on its part." Many who did not join remained sympathetic fellow travelers. During the Popular Front period of 1935–39, when the Communist Party encouraged an alliance with the American left, well-meaning liberals flocked to myriad antifascist, pro-labor front organizations. Far more than just a political party, Communism was a whole climate of opinion.[60]

Nowhere was the mood more pronounced than in New York's artistic and literary circles. One of the Party's most powerful front groups was the American Writers' Congress, which called for a "new literature" to support a new society, and even convinced President Roosevelt to accept an honorary membership. "The Stalinists and their friends, under multiform disguises, have managed to penetrate into the offices of publishing houses, the editorial staffs of magazines, and the book-review sections of conservative newspapers," wrote Phillip Rahv, founder of *Partisan Review*, in 1938. The result was de facto censorship, he asserted.[61] Not that Rahv was opposed to Marxism; indeed, he led the charge of the Trotskyites, a rival Communist faction. The debate was not about the merits of Communism; it was about *what form* of Communism was best.

Rand had fled Soviet Russia only to find herself still surrounded by Communists. None of the talk about a new economic order impressed her. Her struggles in Hollywood only reinforced her belief in individualistic values, and she remained committed to the competitive market system her father had thrived under during her youth. Even now, in the depth of the depression, Rand scoffed at any collective solution to the country's economic agony.

She was particularly outraged by the glowing reports about life in Russia. The Rosenbaums' letters made clear that conditions had only deteriorated in the years since she had left. Even her highly educated and extremely resourceful family was just scraping by. Her artistic sisters were working as tour guides and dutifully attending political meetings to keep their employment. In his new role as house husband Rand's father scoured the streets for days in search of a lightbulb. The household rejoiced when Anna Rosenbaum was once able to purchase an entire bag of apples.[62] Rand had a manuscript that exposed the horrors of life under Communism, but wealthy New Yorkers who had never been to Russia only sniffed at her testimony.

Adding to her cynicism was a battle with Al Woods over *Night of January 16th* that consumed most of 1935. The clash was in some ways inevitable. Rand was a jealous author, unwilling to consider any changes to her plot or dialogue, especially those monologues about the importance of individualism. Woods was a moneymaker, primarily interested in the play for its unusual jury setup. He had little interest in arguing with Rand, instead steamrolling her by talking about all the other hits he had produced. By the time of the first performance she had essentially disowned the play. Later the two would enter arbitration over her royalties.[63] It was the start of a pattern that would mark Rand's career. Her name was finally in lights above Broadway, but fame, when it came, was almost as difficult for her as anonymity.

Just as Rand reached her lowest point with Woods, she learned that her new literary agent had managed to sell *We the Living* to Macmillan. Like other publishers, the editorial board at Macmillan had balked at the novel's ideological messages but eventually decided to take a gamble on the work.

The reviews that *We the Living* garnered when it was published in 1936 only reinforced Rand's suspicions that something was terribly wrong in America. The newspapers were filled with propaganda about Russia, but it was Rand's true-to-life novel that was dismissed as a sham. "The tale is good reading, and bad pleading. It is not a valuable document concerning the Russian experiment," wrote the *Cincinnati Times-Star*. *The Nation* doubted that "petty officials in Soviet Russia ride to the opera in foreign limousines while the worker goes wheatless and meatless." Trying to strike a conciliatory note, a Toronto newspaper noted that the 1920s were "a transition period in the life of the nation." That Rand's testimony was inconsistent with "the descriptions of competent observers like Anna Louis Strong and Walter Duranty does not necessarily discredit it entirely."[64] Even reviewers who praised Rand's writing seemed to assume that her rendition of life in Russia was as imaginative as the improbable love triangle that structured the plot.

There were a few exceptions, mostly among journalists suspicious of the new vogue for all things Soviet. Elsie Robinson, a spirited Hearst columnist, praised Rand effusively: "If I could, I would put this book into the hands of every young person in America....While such conditions threaten any country, as they most certainly threaten America, no

one has a right to be carefree."[65] John Temple Graves, a popular southern writer, was also taken with the book and began touting Rand in
his genteel Birmingham dispatch "This Morning." Another subset of
readers was deeply touched by the novel's emotional power. Rand was
unsurpassed at singing the proud, forlorn song of the individual soul.
One reader told Rand, "I write in difficulties. The book made such an
impression on me that I am still confused. I think it's the truth of all you
say that is blinding me. It has such depth of feeling."[66] It was the first of
the adoring fan letters Rand would receive throughout her career.

In some important ways *We the Living* was an unquestioned success.
The novel was widely reviewed, and almost all reviewers marveled at her
command of English and made note of her unusual biography. Rand's
picture appeared in the newspapers, along with several short profiles.
When she spoke at the Town Hall Club about the evils of collectivism
the column "New York Day by Day" pronounced her an "intellectual
sensation." Yet sales of the book were disappointing. Macmillan printed
only three thousand copies and destroyed the type afterward. When
their stock sold out the book effectively died. Rand's chance at literary
success had been nipped in the bud.[67]

Disillusioned by the slow demise of *We the Living*, Rand began to
ruminate on the state of the nation. She came to political consciousness during one of the most powerful and rare phenomena in American
democracy: a party realignment. The old Republican coalition of midwestern moralists and eastern urbanites lay crushed under the weight of
the Great Depression. Bank failures, crop failures, and soaring unemployment had scorched across the familiar political landscape, destroying old assumptions, methods, and alliances. Out of the ashes President
Franklin Delano Roosevelt was assembling a new coalition among
reformers, urban workers, and African Americans that would last for
most of the century.

At the base of this coalition was the "New Deal" Roosevelt had offered
to American voters in the campaign of 1932. The current depression was
no ordinary event, he told his audiences. Rather, the crisis signaled that the
era of economic individualism was over. In the past liberalism had meant
republican government and laissez-faire economics. Now, Roosevelt
redefined liberalism as "plain English for a changed concept of the duty
and responsibility of government toward economic life." His federal

government would assume an active role in moderating and managing the nation's economy. Of course he wasn't sure exactly just how. "Bold, persistent experimentation" was all that Roosevelt could promise.[68]

Rand voted for Roosevelt in 1932, drawn primarily by his promise to end Prohibition, but as she struggled to sell *We the Living* her opinion changed. "My feeling for the New Deal is growing colder and colder. In fact, it's growing so cold that it's coming to the boiling point of hatred," she wrote Gouverneur Morris's wife, Ruth, in July 1936. Her distaste for Roosevelt was cemented by her sense that he was somehow "pink." She told Ruth, "You have no idea how radical and pro-Soviet New York is—particularly, as everyone admits, in the last three years. Perhaps Mr. Roosevelt had nothing to do with it, but it's a funny coincidence, isn't it?"[69] In a letter to John Temple Graves she moved closer to a conservative position. She agreed with Graves that "big business is crushing individualism and that some form of protection against it is necessary." But she added, "The term 'umpired individualism' frightens me a little."[70] Rand wondered just who the umpire would be.

The 1936 election did little to reassure. Threatened by populist demagogues like Huey Long and Father Coughlin, Roosevelt tacked hard to the left. During the campaign he pounded away at "economic royalists," framing himself as the only responsible champion of the common man. Roosevelt's presidency set the terms of modern politics, establishing such institutions as Social Security, the Federal Deposit Insurance Corporation, the Securities and Exchange Commission, the National Labor Board, the Federal Aviation Administration, and the Federal Communications Commission. He was creating the basic outlines of the administrative state, securing both the livelihood of impoverished Americans and his own political fortunes.[71]

Rand watched all this with growing suspicion. The idea that government had a "duty" to manage economic life reminded her of those soldiers who had taken over her father's business. She was further unnerved by the radicals that seemed to swarm around Roosevelt and had wormed their way into the highest citadels of American intellectual and political life. Rand could see little difference between armed Communist revolution and Roosevelt's rapid expansion of the federal government. She railed against both. It was an opposition that quickened her pulse and fired her pen. A lifelong obsession with American politics had begun.

CHAPTER TWO

Individualists of the World, Unite!

$ ONCE SHE SPOTTED the first pink, Rand began to see them everywhere. They had even infiltrated the movie studios, she soon discovered. Despite her success as a novelist and playwright, Rand could find no work in the lucrative film industry, a failure she blamed on her outspoken opposition to Soviet Russia. She turned instead to the novel that would become *The Fountainhead*. Politics soon emerged as a welcome distraction. As Roosevelt launched his historic program of government reforms Rand watched closely. She read the New York newspapers regularly and began dipping into the work of authors critical of the president. By 1940 her interest in politics had become all-consuming. Fired to action by the presidential campaign of Wendell Willkie she stopped work on her novel and began volunteering full time for the New York City Willkie Club.

The Willkie campaign helped Rand crystallize the political nature of her work and resolve unarticulated tensions about American democracy and capitalism that surfaced during her early work on *The Fountainhead*. At first Rand was hesitant to ascribe political meaning to the novel. She wanted her new book to be philosophical and abstract, not rooted in historic circumstance, as was *We the Living*. Nor was she certain of what her political ideas were, beyond principled anti-Communism. Rand was suspicious of both democracy and capitalism, unsure if either system could be trusted to safeguard individual rights against the dangers of the mob.

A few months' immersion in the hurly-burly of American politics washed away this cynicism. The campaign was an unexpected window into her adopted country, spurring new understandings of American history and culture. Afterward Rand began to praise America in terms that would have been utterly alien to her only months before. Like any small-town booster she touted the glories of American capitalism and individualism, voicing a newfound nationalism that celebrated the United States as a moral exemplar for the world. Her volunteerism completed a transformation that shaped her passage through the second half of the 1930s. Rand entered that politically charged decade an ingénue, focused relentlessly on her own personal ambitions. Ten years later she had located herself firmly on the broad spectrum of domestic public opinion.

The essence of Rand's new novel had come to her shortly after her marriage to Frank. While working at RKO she became friendly with a neighboring woman who was also a Jewish Russian immigrant. Rand was fascinated by her neighbor's daughter, the executive secretary to an important Hollywood producer. Like Rand the daughter was fiercely ambitious and dedicated to her career. At her mother's urging she introduced Rand to an agent who eventually succeeded in selling *Red Pawn*, giving Rand her first important success. Even so, Rand disliked the secretary, feeling that somehow, despite their surface similarities, the two were quite different. One day she probed this difference, asking the other woman what her "goal in life" was. Rand's abstract query, so typical of her approach to other people, brought a swift and ready response. "Here's what I want out of life," her neighbor lectured Rand. "If nobody had an automobile, I would not want one. If automobiles exist and some people don't have them, I want an automobile. If some people have two automobiles, I want two automobiles."[1]

Rand was aghast. This piece of petty Hollywood braggadocio opened an entire social universe to her. Here, she thought furiously, was someone who appeared selfish but was actually self-less. Under her neighbor's feverish scheming and desperate career maneuverings was simply a hollow desire to appear important in other people's eyes. It was a motivation Rand, the eternal outsider, could never understand. But once identified the concept seemed the key to understanding nearly everything around her.

Swiftly Rand expanded her neighbor's response into a whole theory of human psychology. The neighbor's daughter was a "second-hander," someone who followed the ideas and values of others. Her opposite would be an individualist like Rand, someone who wanted to create certain ideas, books, or movies rather than attain a generic level of success. Within days Rand had identified the differences between her and the neighbor as "the basic distinction between two types of people in the world." She visualized the dim outlines of two clashing characters, the second-hander and the individualist, who would drive the plot and theme of her next novel.[2]

Rand put these ideas on hold for the next few years, her energies absorbed with the move to New York. Once she got started again she was methodical in her approach. For once, money was no object. Much as she hated Woods, the producer's populist touch gave Rand what she wanted the most: enough money to let her write full time. Some weeks royalties from *Night of January 16th* could reach $1,200 (in today's dollars, about $16,000), income that freed both Ayn and Frank from paid work.[3] By then she had determined that the background of her book would be architecture, the perfect melding of art, science, and business. With the help of librarians at the New York Public Library she developed an extensive reading list on architecture, filling several notebooks with details that would color her novel. As with her earlier work, she also wrote extensive notes on the theme, the goal, and the intention of the project she called "Second Hand Lives."

In its earliest incarnations the novel was Rand's answer to Nietzsche. The famous herald of God's death, Nietzsche himself was uninterested in creating a new morality to replace the desiccated husk of Christianity. His genealogy of morals, a devastating inquiry into the origins, usages, and value of traditional morality, was intended to clear a path for the "philosophers of the future."[4] Rand saw herself as one of those philosophers. In her first philosophical journal she had wondered if an individualistic morality was possible. A year later, starting work on her second novel, she knew it was.

"The first purpose of the book is a defense of egoism in its real meaning, egoism as a new faith," she wrote in her first notes, which were prefaced by an aphorism from Nietzsche's *Beyond Good and Evil*. Her novel was intended to dramatize, in didactic form, the advantages of egoism as morality. Howard Roark, the novel's hero, was "what men should be." At first he would appear "monstrously selfish." By the end of the book her readers would understand that a traditional vice—selfishness—was actually a virtue.[5]

To effect this transvaluation of values Rand had to carefully redefine selfishness itself. Egoism or selfishness typically described one who
"puts oneself above all and crushes everything in one's way to get the
best for oneself," she wrote. "Fine!" But this understanding was missing
something critical. The important element, ethically speaking, was "not
what one does or how one does it, but why one does it."[6] Selfishness
was a matter of motivation, not outcome. Therefore anyone who sought
power for power's sake was not truly selfish. Like Rand's neighbor, the
stereotypical egoist was seeking a goal defined by others, living as "they
want him to live and conquer to the extent of a home, a yacht and a full
stomach." By contrast, a true egoist, in Rand's sense of the term, would
put "his own 'I,' his standard of values, above all things, and [conquer]
to live as he pleases, as he chooses and as he believes." Nor would a truly
selfish person seek to dominate others, for that would mean living for
others, adjusting his values and standards to maintain his superiority.
Instead, "an egoist is a man who lives for himself."[7]

What sounded simple was in fact a subtle, complicated, and potentially confusing system. Rand's novel reversed traditional definitions of
selfishness and egoism, in itself an ambitious and difficult goal. It also
redefined the meaning and purpose of morality by excluding all social
concerns. "A man has a code of ethics primarily for his own sake, not
for anyone else's," Rand asserted.[8] Her ideas also reversed traditional
understandings of human behavior by exalting a psychological mind-
set utterly divorced from anything outside the self.

As Rand described Howard Roark, she reverted to her earlier celebration of the pathological Hickman from "The Little Street," again mixing
in strong scorn for emotions. "He was born without the ability to consider others," she wrote of Roark. "His emotions are entirely controlled
by his logic…he does not suffer, because he does not believe in suffering." She also relied liberally on Nietzsche to characterize Roark. As she
jotted down notes on Roark's personality she told herself, "See Nietzsche
about laughter."[9] The book's famous first line indicates the centrality of
this connection: "Howard Roark laughed."

Like Nietzsche, Rand intended to challenge Christianity. She shared
the philosopher's belief that Christian ethics were destructive to
selfhood, making life "flat, gray, empty, lacking all beauty, all fire, all
enthusiasm, all meaning, all creative urge." She also had a more specific

critique, writing that Christianity "is the best kindergarten of communism possible."[10] Christianity taught believers to put others before self, an ethical mandate that matched the collectivist emphasis on the group over the individual. Thus a new system of individualist, non-Christian ethics was needed to prevent the triumph of Communism.

Although her ethical theory was firm, Rand was less certain of the other messages her book would impart. In her first notes she thought she "may not include" Communism in the novel. By early 1938 she described it to an interested publisher as "not political, this time." "I do not want to be considered a 'one-theme' author," she added.[11] Not a single Russian or Communist would appear, she assured him. At the same time Rand had always sensed a connection between politics and her conception of the second-hander. Indeed, her neighbor's statement had rocked her precisely because it seemed to illuminate a puzzling question: What made some people collectivists and others individualists? Before, Rand had never understood the difference, but now she believed that the basic collectivist principle was "motivation by the value of others versus your own independence."[12] Even as she professed a purely philosophical intent, the book's very origins suggested its possibilities as political morality play. Still, Rand was ambivalent about writing that kind of book.

Part of the problem was that outside of the Russian setting, Rand wasn't sure where she stood politically. By the early 1930s she was expanding her range of nonfiction reading beyond Nietzsche, and she gravitated first to writers who were deeply skeptical of democracy, such as H. L. Mencken, Oswald Spengler, Albert Jay Nock, and José Ortega y Gasset.[13] These thinkers did little to shake Rand out of her Nietzschean fixation on the superior individual. Indeed, they may even have shaped her understanding of Nietzsche, for the writers she selected had themselves been deeply influenced by the German philosopher. Mencken was one of Nietzsche's foremost American interpreters, and Nietzsche's ideas strongly influenced Spengler's *Decline of the West* and Ortega y Gasset's *Revolt of the Masses,* which in turn exerted its powers on Nock's *Memoirs of a Superfluous Man.* Rand's reading was a Nietzschean hall of mirrors with a common theme: forthright elitism.

Accordingly, her reflections on American society were both tentative and deeply pessimistic. Rand doubted that America was hospitable to her values, an impression furthered by the popularity of Communism in New York. In a writing notebook she wondered "if there are things in capitalism and democracy worth saving" and speculated, in a Spenglerian aside, that perhaps the white race was degenerating.[14] She qualified every reference to America's individualistic economic system with sarcastic asides such as "so-called" or "maybe!"[15] According to Rand the primary "fault" of liberal democracies was "giving full rights to quantity." Instead, she wrote, there should be "democracy of superiors only."[16] As she began the book the connections between her vaunted individualism and American society were far from clear to Rand.

By contrast, her characters were starkly etched in her mind. Rand designed an elegant, almost geometric structure for the book. Howard Roark was her ideal man, an uncompromising individualist and creator. The other primary characters were variations on his theme. As she explained in a notebook, "Howard Roark: the man who can be and is. Gail Wynand: the man who could have been. Peter Keating: the man who never could be and doesn't know it. Ellsworth M. Toohey: the man who never could be—and knows it."[17] Rand also created two love interests for Roark, Vesta Dunning and Dominique Francon.

Rand's characterizations flowed directly from her architectural research, her knowledge of current events, and her developing opposition to American liberalism. To give Roark form and specificity she drew on the career of the modernist pioneer Frank Lloyd Wright, whose avant-garde style she admired. Numerous details of Wright's life as described in his autobiography would recur in the novel, and she gave Roark a cranky, embittered mentor in the vein of Wright's own teacher, Louis Sullivan. Second-hander Peter Keating was based on a contemporary mediocrity, the popular architect Thomas Hastings. As Rand noted excitedly after reading a book on Hastings, "If I take this book and Wright's autobiography, there is practically the entire story."[18]

Other titans appeared in the novel as well. Gail Wynand was modeled after William Randolph Hearst, whose career Rand had closely followed. She was struck in particular by his failed bids for mayor and governor of New York. Here was a man who claimed great influence but had little success in actually grasping the levers of power. Hearst had been thoroughly humbled, Rand thought, overlooking his two terms in Congress and the authority he continued to wield through his media empire. To her Hearst's strength was a chimera. His power was not his own, but could be granted or withheld by the masses whom he served. In her novel Wynand would illustrate this principle, with his failings contrasted starkly to Roark's independence and agency.

Her villain, Ellsworth Toohey, promised to transform Rand's supposedly nonpolitical novel into a sharp satire on the leftist literary culture of 1930s New York. One evening she and Frank reluctantly accompanied two friends to a talk by the British socialist Harold Laski at the leftist New School for Social Research. When Laski took the stage Rand was thrilled. Here was Ellsworth Toohey himself! She scribbled frantically in her notebook, sketching out a brief picture of Laski's face and noting his every tic and mannerism. She and Frank went back twice more in the following evenings.

Most of Rand's notes on Laski's lecture, and her resultant description of Toohey, showcased her distaste for all things feminine. Rand was repelled by the women in the New School audience, whom she characterized as sexless, unfashionable, and unfeminine. She and Frank scoffed at their dowdy lisle stockings, trading snide notes back and forth. Rand was infuriated most by the "intellectual vulgarity" of the audience, who seemed to her half-wits unable to comprehend the evil of Laski's socialism. What could be done about such a "horrible, horrible, horrible" spectacle, besides "perhaps restricting higher education, particularly for women?" she asked in her notes on the lecture. This misogyny rubbed off on Rand's portrait of Toohey, who was insipidly feminine, prone to gossip, and maliciously catty "in the manner of a woman or a nance." Through Toohey, Rand would code leftism as fey, effeminate, and unnatural, as opposed to the rough-hewn masculinity of Roark's individualism.[19]

Before she saw Laski, Toohey was an abstracted antithesis of Roark. But a socialist intellectual fit her purposes just as well, even as the characterization shifted the novel ever closer to a commentary on current events. Laski was not the sole inspiration, for Rand also used bits of the American critics Heywood Broun, Lewis Mumford, and Clifton Fadiman to round out Toohey's persona. Fitting Toohey so squarely into the leftist literary culture signaled Rand's emerging dual purposes for the book and ensured that when it was finally published, the novel would be understood as a political event as much as a literary achievement.

This painstaking research also enabled Rand to surpass the limitations of her first attempts at fiction. Characterization had always been a particular problem for Rand. In *Night of January 16th* her characters are powerful symbols but unconvincing human beings. *We the Living* circumvented this weakness because Rand made most of her characters composites of people she had known in Russia. Now she repeated this technique by drawing liberally on biography and observation.

The great exception to this method was Dominique. To capture the psychology of Dominique, a bitter and discontented heiress, Rand conjured up her own darkest moods. She tapped into all the frustration and resentment of her early years, her feeling that the world was rigged in favor of the mediocre and against the exceptional, and then imagined, "[W]hat if I really believed that this is all there is in life."[20] In the novel Howard would teach Dominique to let go of these poisonous attitudes, just as Rand herself had become more optimistic with her professional success and freedom to write.

She combined this introspection with a new analysis of Frank, her beloved but troubling husband. When they first met, Frank was brimming with hopes and plans for his Hollywood career. He had several near misses, including a screen test with D. W. Griffith for a part that helped establish Neil Hamilton (later famous on TV as *Batman*'s Police Commissioner Gordon). But as Rand's fortunes soared ever upward, Frank's collapsed. In New York, with Rand's income sufficient to support them both, Frank idled. He took charge of paying the household bills but made little effort to establish himself in a new line of work. It was an inexplicable turn of events for Rand, who valued career above all else.

Now, as she crafted Dominique, Rand hit on a satisfying explanation for Frank's passivity. Dominique, like Frank, would turn away from the world in anger, "a withdrawal not out of bad motives or cowardice, but out of an almost unbearable kind of idealism which does not know how to function in the journalistic reality as we see it around us."[21] Dominique loves Howard, yet tries to destroy him, believing he is doomed in an imperfect world. Confusing and conflicted, Dominique is among Rand's least convincing creations. More important, though, was the effect this character had on Rand's marriage. Seeing Frank as Dominique glossed over his professional failures and cast his defeated resignation in terms Rand could understand. Bits of Frank found their way into Rand's hero too. Roark's cat-like grace and easy physicality struck the couple's friends as a precise portrait of Frank.

Frank had become increasingly important to Rand as connections with her family in Russia snapped. In 1936, putting a long-held dream in motion, she began a torturous round of paperwork to bring her parents to the United States. She petitioned the U.S. government for an immigration visa, obtaining letters from Universal describing her screenwriting work. She and Frank wrote a notarized deposition testifying to her financial independence. She even prepaid her passage on the United States Lines. It was all to no avail. In late 1936 the Rosenbaums' visa application was denied, and an appeal proved fruitless. Rand got the final word in a brief telegram sent from Leningrad in May 1937: "Cannot get permission."[22]

It was one of their last communications. Rand stopped responding to family letters shortly afterward, believing that Russians who received mail from America could be in grave danger. It was a cruel kindness, for the Rosenbaums had no explanation for her sudden silence. They pleaded with her to write. And then, ominously, the letters stopped coming.[23] Rand was irrevocably cut off from her family.

Although she and Frank were now financially secure, it appears that they never seriously contemplated having children of their own.[24] Rand's books would be her children, to be carefully tended and agonizingly birthed.

As it turned out, "Second-Hand Lives" was a problem child. With the main characters sketched out, Rand turned to the much more difficult work of plotting the novel, beginning an "enormous progression of experimenting, thinking, starting from various premises." The framework would be Roark's career, but beyond this basic line Rand was unsure how events should proceed. She spent months trying out "a lot of pure superstructure calculations. What would be the key points of Roark's career, that is, how would he start, what would be the difficulties on the early stage, how would he become famous?"[25] She wrote a detailed outline of Hugo's *Les Miserables* to grasp its underlying structure and create a model for herself.

The most difficult part was the climax, "really a mind-breaker." Rand wanted a single dramatic event that would draw together the novel's disparate story lines, dramatize her theme, and thrill readers. Until the climax was set everything else in the novel had to remain tentative. Even worse, she felt like "a fake anytime I talk about my new novel, when I don't yet know the central part of it, when nothing is set."[26] She writhed in agony at her writing desk, caught in her first ever case of "the squirms," her phrase for writer's block.

As Rand planned and drafted *The Fountainhead* her dislike of Roosevelt continued to fester. To most Americans, Roosevelt was a hero, a paternal figure who had soothed their fears and beveled the sharp edges of economic crisis. He was unquestionably the most popular political figure of the decade, if not the century. But among a small subset of commentators dark mutterings about Roosevelt were becoming more common. Criticism came from many quarters. To adherents of traditional laissez-faire economic doctrine, Roosevelt was foolhardy in his clumsy attempts to right the economy with state power. To his opponents Roosevelt was a virtual dictator, wantonly trampling on the Constitution as he expanded the government's reach into business, law, and agriculture. Like few presidents before, his actions spawned a cottage industry dedicated to attacking him, known as the "Roosevelt haters."[27]

Rand avidly consumed this literature. Mencken remained a particular favorite. She had first been drawn to his work by their shared interest in Nietzsche. Now she began regularly reading *American Mercury*, the magazine he founded, and absorbed his growing suspicion of Roosevelt. She also followed the writing of Albert Jay Nock, a magazine editor, essayist, and the author of *Our Enemy, the State*. Nock and Mencken were the first to call themselves "libertarians," a new coinage meant to signify their allegiance to individualism and limited government, now that Roosevelt had co-opted the word "liberal." Libertarians were few and far between, although some had gained positions of prominence. At the *New York Herald Tribune* a columnist for the weekly book review, Isabel Paterson, was making waves with her vitriol against Roosevelt. Rand read Paterson regularly.[28]

In 1937 Rand added her voice to this growing chorus, dispatching a blistering letter to the *New York Herald Tribune* in response to Roosevelt's proposal that additional justices be added to the Supreme

Court. "No tyranny in history has ever been established overnight," Rand warned. She traced the recent history of Russia and Germany, asking, "If Mr. Roosevelt is empowered to pass his own laws and have his own men pass on these laws, what is to prevent him from passing any law he pleases?" Her solution, even at this early date, was activism. "There must be a committee, an organization, or headquarters created at once to lead and centralize the activity of all those who are eager to join their efforts in protest," she declared. Her letter urged readers to write immediately to Congress, lest they lose their lives and possessions. She closed with a reference to her favorite Sinclair Lewis novel: "'It can't happen here,' you think? Well, it's happened already!"[29] Rand's letter was never printed, but more prominent commentators shared its basic sentiments. Roosevelt's disastrous bill, widely condemned as a court-packing scheme, went down to stunning defeat in Congress and emboldened his opposition. The influential columnist Walter Lippmann emerged as a new Roosevelt critic, throwing darts at the president in his national columns. In 1938 Texas Congressman Martin Dies began investigating Communist infiltration of the federal government, eventually releasing a list of more than five hundred government employees who also belonged to known Communist fronts, a move intended to blur the line between Communist, socialist, and New Deal liberal.

But it seemed almost impossible to launch any effective opposition to the popular president. A rich man himself, Roosevelt was skilled at caricaturing his opposition as tools of the rich. Often it was not caricature at all. The one organized anti-Roosevelt group, the Liberty League, *was* a secretive cabal of wealthy businessmen hoping to wrest control of government from the masses. Although the Liberty League made several awkward attempts at populism, its main financial backers were the conservative Du Pont family. Tarred as fascists after several of the group's members praised Mussolini and called for an American dictator, the Liberty League disintegrated within a few years of its founding.[30]

Even as she dwelled on Roosevelt's perfidy, Rand pursued a number of side projects. Prompted by the interest of a theater producer, she began a stage adaptation of *We the Living,* entitled *The Unconquered.*[31] When Frank found work in a summer stock production of *Night of January 16th* the two spent an idyllic few weeks in Stonington, Connecticut. There, in a flash of inspiration, Rand completed a new manuscript, a novel of scarcely a hundred pages that she titled *Anthem*. Again Rand did not hesitate to borrow an idea that had worked well for another writer. She began the project after reading a short science fiction story, "The Place of the Gods," in the *Saturday Evening Post*. Many of *Anthem*'s basic elements mirror those of the story and another famous science fiction work, Evgeny Zamyatin's *We*, a novel that circulated *samizdat* in Russia when Rand lived there.[32] Unlike these other works, however, Rand's fable emphasized individual creativity and the destructive power of state control.

Although set in a generic dystopia, *Anthem* is Rand's extrapolation of Communist Russia far into the future, to a time when even the word "I" has been lost. The novel opens with the first line of Equality 7–2521's furtive diary, "We know it is a sin to write this," and continues in the first-person plural, giving the novel a sonorous, almost biblical quality. Over the course of the story Equality 7–2521 finds a hidden tunnel where he can escape his oppressive collectivist society, finds love with Liberty 5–3000, and invents electricity. Rather than welcoming Equality 7–2521's lightbulb, the despotic Council of Elders tries to kill him and destroy his invention. The two lovers flee into the forest, where Equality rediscovers the word "I."

Anthem was a significant departure from Rand's earlier work because the story's hero is a creative and productive individual rather than an alienated misanthrope. Rand was moving from a reactive depiction of individualism to a more dynamic and positive celebration of individual creativity and accomplishment. Much of this must have come from her research into Frank Lloyd Wright, whose architectural brilliance far outweighed the crimes of William Hickman and Ivar Kreuger, her previous literary inspirations. Integrating technology, discovery, and invention into her story broadened her reach and made the book a relevant commentary on the potentially destructive nature of state control.

Strange in style and provocative in substance, *Anthem* aroused little interest among American publishers but was recognized as a trenchant political parable in Britain. It was released there in 1938 by Cassells, the same firm that handled British distribution of *We the Living*. Despite the cool reception it initially received in the United States, Rand considered *Anthem* one of her favorite pieces of writing. The brief novel was her hymn to individualism, "the theme song, the goal, the only aim of all my writing."[33] It had been a welcome break from the planning of her novel-in-progress.

Anthem had not, however, cured her of the squirms. Returning to New York in the fall of 1937 Rand still found it impossible to complete the plot and outline of her larger novel. She couldn't begin writing until she had the whole narrative structure down, but the pieces of the story remained stubbornly fragmented and inchoate. She decided to escape her daily struggle by volunteering in the office of a noted New York architect, the modernist Ely Jacques Kahn. She worked for him without pay for six months in an arrangement that was kept secret from the rest of the office staff. Kahn was flattered and pleased to have attracted the interest of a budding novelist, and Rand earned his gratitude by expertly rearranging his files during her tenure. He took his new "employee" under his wing, offering her anecdotes from his own career and gossipy tidbits about other prominent architects. Rand cast him in the novel as Guy Francon, a once talented architect who is an incurable social climber.

One morning Kahn suggested a resolution to her creative impasse when he told her that the greatest problem architects face was housing. Rand remembered, "[T]he moment he said 'housing,' something clicked in my mind, because I thought, well now, there is a political issue and an architectural issue; that fits my purpose."[34] Thinking over his words at lunch, Rand quickly visualized the rest of the story. Peter Keating would seek a commission to build a public housing project. He would convince Roark, who is motivated by the intellectual challenge of the housing problem, to design it for him. Roark agrees to help on the condition that his building be built exactly as designed. When Roark's plans are nonetheless altered he would destroy the building, an action that would allow Rand to explain the supremacy of the individual creator over the needs of society. The rest of the characters would react accordingly. Toohey would attack Roark, Wynand would try to defend him, Peter would retreat in shame, and Dominique would return to him.

Rand's excitement over the central unifying idea of housing indicated how significantly her sense of the novel had shifted. It had begun as an abstract tale about the superior man struggling against the suffocating mob, a thematic remnant from her obsessive reading of Nietzsche and her earliest stabs at fiction. The writing of *Anthem*, which for the first time featured a triumphant hero, marked an important move away from this dark view of human possibility. Now her attraction to the symbolic issue of public housing, which both fit her topic and encapsulated her political views, indicated that Rand had come to see the novel as an overtly political work. The presentation of her hero remained primary, but Rand had ceased resisting the larger implications that could be drawn from the story.

With the plot finally set Rand began writing. The book would be divided into four parts, with each of the central characters the focus of one section. She began with her second-hander, Peter Keating. The first three chapters she wrote toggled between Keating and Roark, describing their very different paths through architecture school at the Stanton Institute for Technology. The writing was slow and painful, but it was progress nonetheless.

Rand showed her completed chapters to two outside readers, her literary agent and Frank Lloyd Wright. Rand idolized Wright, seeing him as a true creative genius and the embodiment of the Overman Nietzsche celebrated. She was sure he was a kindred spirit who would appreciate what she had written. But Wright, who had never heard of Rand before, sent the chapters back with a brusque note, rudely telling her the novel was implausible because no architect could have red hair like Roark. Rand was undeterred. Kahn helped her secure an invitation to a formal banquet where Wright was to speak. She spent three hundred dollars on a matching black velvet dress, shoes, and a cape, a splurge she could ill afford as her savings dwindled. After a formal introduction Wright again rebuffed her overtures. Rand was simply another unknown hoping to cash in on his fame.[35]

Rand's agent, Ann Watkins, was more appreciative. She began shopping the chapters around, and in 1938 brought Rand an offer from Knopf. Rand would receive five hundred dollars upon signing and another five hundred dollars upon completion of the manuscript. Knopf also committed to publishing Rand's book as a "leader," publicly identifying it as one of the most important books of the season. The catch was that Rand had one year to complete the book. It was an impossible task. She wrote as fast as she could, but even a year's extension of the original contract was not enough time. In October 1940 Knopf canceled the deal.[36] She had completed slightly more than a quarter of her projected book.

It was at this juncture that Rand became smitten with Wendell Willkie. The last of the dark horse presidential candidates in American politics, Willkie swept to the 1940 Republican presidential nomination on a feverish surge of support at the Party's National Convention.[37] He had first come into the public eye as the chairman of Commonwealth and Southern (C&S), a utility company fighting Roosevelt's proposed Tennessee Valley Authority. The TVA was intended to bring electricity to the blighted towns of Tennessee, northern Alabama, and Mississippi, a region bypassed by the forces of modernization. Roosevelt's solution was the creation of publicly owned utilities that would provide affordable electricity for the conveniences of modern life, such as refrigerators and radios, to customers otherwise overlooked by private industry. As part of the plan the utility companies would have to sell their holdings to TVA-backed public utilities. It was the kind of government assault on private industry that made Rand's blood boil.

As chairman and former general counsel for C&S, one of the major companies targeted by Roosevelt's reform, Willkie had fought the government's plan. His efforts were ultimately unsuccessful, and when the courts upheld Roosevelt's legislation TVA proceeded to purchase private holdings and lower electricity costs for homeowners. Willkie himself helped negotiate some of the agreements. In the meantime, though, he had made a name for himself as a Roosevelt foe. He had certainly caught Rand's attention, for she thought he had delivered an honest and effective defense of the utility company's rights. Willkie also claimed to be representing a constituency larger than his company. During congressional hearings on the TVA a flood of telegrams expressed support for the company's suit.[38]

Now, in the summer of 1940, Willkie claimed to be arousing similar support in his last-minute bid for the Republican presidential nomination. His claim to a groundswell of genuine popular enthusiasm was questionable; as Alice Roosevelt Longsworth quipped, Willkie's support came "from the grass roots of a thousand country clubs."[39] Allegations of fraud dogged both his nomination and his earlier work for the utility companies. The telegrams touted as spontaneous manifestations of his popularity turned out to be part of a carefully orchestrated corporate campaign.

In a season of lackluster candidates, however, Willkie was popular enough to briefly unite a powerful faction of Republicans behind his candidacy. He was championed by the cosmopolitan East Coast Republicans, who valued his business experience and progressive openness to involvement in world affairs. Rallying behind Willkie they chose to overlook the unfortunate reality that only a year before their standard bearer had been a registered Democrat. This fact outraged the Republican Old Guard, the Party's isolationist wing. They saw Willkie as a tool of eastern moneyed interests who would drag them into the European war. Willkie thus presided uneasily over a deeply divided party that was momentarily united by their hunger for victory over Roosevelt.

Characteristically, Rand's take on Willkie's campaign was idiosyncratic. Willkie is remembered for his optimistic internationalism, typified by his postwar best-seller *One World*, and his willingness to present a united front with Roosevelt on aid to Europe during the presidential campaign. Rand, however, focused almost entirely on Willkie's defense of capitalism. To be sure, this was a part of Willkie's persona. In 1940 he told a campaign audience, "I'm in business and proud of it. Nobody can make me soft-pedal any fact in my business career. After all, business is our way of life, our achievement, our glory." Rand appreciated how he framed his opposition to the New Deal as a "very forthright ideological, intellectual, moral issue."[40] She saw him as a fellow crusader for individualism. She also mistakenly believed he was a populist candidate who was beloved by the masses.

Genial, upbeat, and hopelessly green, Willkie was no match for the Roosevelt juggernaut. He lacked the killer instinct necessary to unseat an incumbent running for his third term. Genuinely concerned about the gathering hostilities in Europe, he acceded to Roosevelt's entreaty that he not take a public stance against Lend-Lease, a policy controversial with isolationists. Deprived of the one substantive issue that might have contrasted him sharply with Roosevelt, Willkie struggled to define himself. Instead, with a few broad strokes, Roosevelt painted him as a tool of big business and the rich.

Such stereotyping did little to discourage Rand; in fact it had the opposite result. Convinced for the first time that domestic politics truly mattered, she and Frank signed on with the New York City branch of the Willkie Club, a network of volunteer organizations that was vital to the campaign. It was a risky move. Neither she nor Frank had worked regularly for years, and their savings were nearly depleted. But it was characteristic of Rand that she never did anything halfway. Politics had been a growing fixation of hers for years. Here was the chance to live her principles, to act on behalf of a politician she supported. She would never have been able to do the same in Russia. Setting aside her unfinished novel, she eagerly joined the cause.

The New York Willkie Club was tailor-made for a young, Republican-leaning author. Willkie's mistress, Irita von Doren, the book editor of the *New York Herald Tribune,* had a strong influence on the New York campaign, which brimmed with writers, editors, and other literati. Here were people like Rand: passionate about ideas, articulate, willing to argue endlessly about politics. These were no bohemian radicals talking about revolution, but establishment figures who mingled easily with the city's business elite. She told a friend, "I have met a greater number of interesting men and women, within a few months, than I did in my whole life, during the Willkie campaign of 1940."[41]

Rand began her volunteer work as a humble typist and filing clerk. Her ascent through the ranks was swift, and within weeks she spearheaded the creation of a new "intellectual ammunition department." Rand taught other volunteers how to skim newspapers for damning statements by Roosevelt or his running mate, Henry Wallace. These quotations would then be compiled for use by campaign speakers or other Willkie clubs. Wallace, in particular, proved a fertile source of objectionable rhetoric, and Rand sent several volunteers to the local library to comb through material from his earlier career.

At times Rand butted heads with her superiors in the Willkie campaign. Her instinct was to highlight Roosevelt's negative qualities, his collectivist ideology, and his antagonism to business. The campaign managers, however, chose to advertise Willkie like a new kind of soap, stressing his positive qualities. Such mild tactics disgusted Rand. When she wasn't researching Roosevelt's misdeeds, she visited theaters where Willkie newsreels were shown, staying afterward to field questions from the audience. These sessions were among the most exciting parts of the campaign for Rand, who reveled in the chance to share her strong opinions and argue with strangers. "I was a marvelous propagandist," she remembered.[42]

Her coat emblazoned with Willkie campaign buttons, she joined the ranks of the city's soapbox preachers. On promising street corners she would begin an anti-Roosevelt, pro-Willkie diatribe, quickly drawing crowds attracted by the novelty of a woman campaigner with a Russian accent. When a listener jeered at her for being a foreigner, Rand jeered right back. "I chose to be an American," she reminded him. "What did you do?"[43]

These spontaneous sessions began to shake Rand loose from her pre-conceived notions about American voters. Before campaigning, Rand had been suspicious of American democracy. Instead of government of, for, and by the people, she thought the state should be "a means for the convenience of the higher type of man."[44] Her earliest fiction, heavy with contempt for the masses, reflected this sensibility. Now she found herself impressed by the questions her working-class audience asked and their responsiveness to her capitalist message. She said of her time in the theaters, "[It] supported my impression of the common man, that they really were much better to deal with than the office and the Madison Avenue Republicans."[45] It seemed that the faceless crowds she condemned, rather than their social and intellectual betters, understood the dangers of the Roosevelt administration.

Most questions she fielded were about the war in Europe, however. Every voter wanted to know whether the candidate would involve the United States in the conflict. Most dreaded the idea of sending their boys overseas, even though the situation in Europe was deteriorating rapidly. Germany, Italy, and Spain had gone fascist, and Britain remained the lone outpost of liberal democracy. Britain's prime minister, Winston Churchill, beseeched Roosevelt for money and material. Roosevelt's hands were tied by restrictive neutrality acts, but he was increasingly convinced that the United States must play a role in the European war. Still, there were powerful pressures against any involvement. Neither candidate wanted to risk alienating the isolationists or the equally powerful internationalists. Both charted a careful course between the two.[46]

On the front lines of the campaign Rand sought to gloss over Willkie's equivocation. She herself doubted Willkie was sincere when he spoke out against the war, but she did her best to convince voters otherwise, walking the thinnest line between truth and falsehood. "[I]t would have been much better if he had come out against any help to the allies," she reflected later.[47] Toward the end of the campaign Willkie did turn in a markedly isolationist direction, telling his audiences he would not become involved in a war and eliciting a similar pledge from Roosevelt.

By then Rand's enthusiasm for Willkie had nearly ebbed away. More than his duplicity about the war she was bothered by his stance on capitalism. He had begun as a stalwart defender of free enterprise, but then shied away from using the term in his speeches. Instead "he talked about his childhood in Indiana—to show that he's a small town American, in effect—instead of talking about the issues."[48] What she wanted, more than anything else, was someone who would stand up and argue for the traditional American way of life as she understood it: individualism. She wanted the Republicans to attack Roosevelt's expansion of the federal government and to explain why it set such a dangerous precedent. The ideas and principles that Roosevelt invoked, she believed, were the very ones that had destroyed Russia.

Few Americans shared her views. Indeed voters were satisfied enough with Roosevelt that they elected him to an unprecedented third term. But it was not quite the coronation it seemed. For all its activity, the New Deal had not defeated the scourge of depression, and unemployment remained near 15 percent. Roosevelt had alienated powerful figures in both parties and his reform efforts had been thwarted in the past few years. But the increasing instability in Europe made voters skittish. Hitler had plowed over France, and his U-boats sniped at American ships in international waters. As the old adage went, it was unwise to switch horses midstream.

In the wake of Willkie's defeat new avenues opened before Rand. The campaign had profoundly redirected her intellectual energies. Rather than resume work on her novel full time, in the months following her volunteer work she poured forth a number of nonfiction pieces and began to see herself as an activist, not just a writer. With some of her Willkie contacts she planned a political organization, a group of intellectuals and educators who would pick up where the Republican candidate had left off.

Rand forged her own path into politics, eschewing established groups such as America First, which had picked up the mantle of organized opposition to Roosevelt. Founded in Chicago in the fall of 1940, America First was the institutional embodiment of midwestern isolationism. The idea that America should avoid entangling foreign alliances stretched all the way back to George Washington's farewell address in the early days of the republic. It was given modern relevance by the outcry against war profiteering following World War I. Now, watching another gathering storm in Europe, America First leaders and its 850,000 card-carrying members were convinced that the United States should stay out of the fray.[49] The organization lobbied vigorously against Roosevelt's plans to aid Britain, arguing that the United States should concentrate on fortifying its own defenses. Because it so staunchly opposed Roosevelt's foreign policy initiatives, America First drew many of the president's most bitter critics into its fold. It also attracted a sizable number of anti-Semites to its banner.

Although she shared its basic isolationist sentiments, Rand was not attracted to America First. To her the European war was simply a localized expression of a deeper conflict that structured world history: the clash between Individualism and Collectivism. Her concern lay primarily with American domestic politics, not with America's role in the world, and her loyalties remained with the Willkie Clubs, which she saw as a powerful grassroots network devoted to capitalism and individualism. But the Willkie Clubs had not long to live. Willkie had little desire to establish himself as a permanent opposition leader, and shortly after the election he gave his blessing to a decision by the Confederated Willkie Clubs to dissolve.[50]

Rand was deeply disappointed by the disappearance of the Willkie Clubs but intrigued by the idea of the Independent Clubs, a proposed successor organization. These clubs would be nonpartisan local organizations that would encourage "good citizenship" and political participation. Rand began to imagine a new organization along these lines, but national in scope and primarily educational in nature. It would become a headquarters for anyone who wanted to continue fighting the New Deal. Eventually the group would grow large enough to support a national office and a periodical. This new organization would build on and preserve the spirit of the campaign, which, at least in New York, had drawn together a group of serious intellectuals committed to a meaningful defense of capitalism. It was the kind of community Rand had always hoped to find someday, and she was loath to let it disappear.

She was also motivated by a deep sense of crisis, as evidenced by a rousing essay she wrote to attract members to the group she hoped to organize. "To All Fifth Columnists" was an alarmist portrait of America honeycombed with collectivists and Soviet agents, teetering on the brink of dictatorship. Her opening lines asserted, "Totalitarianism has already won a complete victory in many American minds and conquered all of our intellectual life." Rand assumed that totalitarian dictatorship in America was only a matter of time, and she blamed apathetic and ignorant citizens, the so-called "fifth column." Hard-working Americans who ignored politics and simply tried to provide for their families were making a grave mistake: "The money, home or education you plan to leave [your children] will be worthless or taken away from them. Instead, your legacy will be a Totalitarian America, a world of slavery, of starvation, of concentration camps and firing squads."[51]

The only way to forestall such a tragedy was for the true voice of America to make itself heard. The American way of life, according to Rand, "has always been based on the Rights of Man, upon individual freedom and upon respect for each individual human personality." These ideals were being overshadowed by Communist propaganda. Her response: to be heard, "we must be organized." Here Rand grappled briefly with the paradox of organizing individualists. Her group would be "an *organization against organization*...to defend us all from the coming compulsory organization which will swallow all of society."[52] There was no other alternative, she declared, for in the world today there could be no personal neutrality.

Rand's urgency stemmed directly from her experiences in the New York literary world, which convinced her that Communists were also a powerful force within American political life. In truth, the Party had been hemorrhaging members for years, since rumors of the 1936 Stalinist purges reached New York. The Soviet fever broke in 1939, with the revelation of the Nazi-Soviet nonaggression pact. American Communists were caught flat-footed by the sudden reversal of policy. They had always loudly boasted of their antifascist credentials, a position that was particularly popular among American leftists. Now Communist leaders could offer no convincing reason for the new alliance. Never large to begin with, Party membership plummeted. Friendly intellectuals and liberal fellow travelers began distancing themselves from the

Communist program. Though the wartime alliance between the Soviet Union and the United States would bring a few prominent intellectuals back into the fold, by 1940 Party affiliation was transforming from a badge of honor into a slightly embarrassing relic of youth.[53]

Yet Rand was still spooked by just how popular Communism and socialism had been. She was right to understand that the Communist threat had not vanished entirely, even though intellectual fashions had changed. Soviet spies remained in Washington, D.C., and some would successfully filch valuable military secrets during World War II. But the Communists were not on the verge of taking over the American political system. At the height of their influence they had mustered fewer than one million members and barely 100,000 votes.[54] Still, Rand's broadside made for exciting reading.

One of the first people Rand shared "Fifth Columnists" with was Channing Pollock, whom she had met during the Willkie campaign. Pollock was a newspaper columnist and moderately successful playwright who had been on the advisory board of the Liberty League and was well connected to wealthy conservatives. Like Rand he was a committed individualist and an implacable foe of Roosevelt. But unlike many of the president's opponents, Pollock favored aid to Britain and shared Roosevelt's sense that America's involvement in the war might be necessary. He traveled the country regularly delivering folksy speeches that denounced Communism, the New Deal, and isolationism in equal measure. He had even floated the idea of a "vigorous organization of the Great Middle Class" that would "rout the rotten forces of Communism, Fascism, collectivism and general nuttiness, and put America back on its feet—a hardworking, united United States."[55] His idea anticipated the group Rand herself hoped to start.

Rand contacted Pollock in early 1941. Pollock was a "name," someone who could attract both donors and attention to her proposed organization. Without help from him or somebody similarly prominent, Rand's idea would go nowhere. Pollock was interested, but not ready to commit immediately. He decided to test the concept during an upcoming lecture tour, asking anyone interested in a political group to contact him. He netted four thousand names, enough to convince him that Rand's idea had wings. Returning to New York in April he gave Rand the go-ahead. He sent out a brief letter to prospective backers and asked Rand to draw up a statement of principles to attract interested parties.

The result was Rand's thirty-two-page "Manifesto of Individualism," the first full statement of her political and philosophical beliefs. Pollock wanted something much shorter, but once she got going Rand couldn't stop. She spent an entire weekend pounding out an essay that would "present the whole groundwork of our 'Party Line' and be a basic document, such as the *Communist Manifesto* was on the other side."[56] In contrast to her novel, the "Manifesto" had practically written itself.

Rand's version of the Communist Manifesto bore the hallmarks of her later work. It was an all-encompassing vision that included a statement of rights, a theory of history and of social classes, and keen attention to human psychology. It was a first pass through many of the ideas she would later flesh out in both her fiction and her nonfiction. There were some critical differences, both in content and in tone. Rand was more expository and more nuanced in this first statement than she would be in her published work. Most significantly, she did not include reason as an important part of individualism, and she used the word "altruism" only twice. But many other features of her mature thought were there.[57]

The base of Rand's individualism was a natural rights theory derived from the Declaration of Independence. Each man had the right to life, liberty, and the pursuit of happiness, and these rights were "the unconditional, personal, private, individual possession of each man, granted to him by the fact of his birth and requiring no other sanction." The role of society, and its only purpose, is to ensure these individual rights Rand explained. Next Rand set up a dyad of opposing concepts, contrasting Totalitarianism to Individualism. Totalitarianism was defined by one basic idea, "that the state is superior to the individual." Its only opposite and greatest enemy was Individualism, which was the basic principle of natural rights. Individualism was the only ground on which men could live together in decency. As such, the doctrine of an absolute "common good" was "utterly evil" and "must always be limited by the basic, inalienable rights of the Individual."[58]

From there she moved quickly to divide society into two realms, the Political Sphere and the Creative Sphere. The creative sphere is the realm of all productive activity, and it belongs to "single individuals." Rand stressed repeatedly that creation was an individual, not a collective process. Making an analogy to childbirth, she argued, "[A]ll birth is individual. So is all parenthood. So is every creative process."[59] The Political Sphere was the opposite of the Creative Sphere and must be extremely limited in scope lest it destroy individual creativity.

Closely related to the two spheres was Rand's next dyad, of Active Man and Passive Man. Even as she set them up as polar opposites, Rand recognized that "in every one of us there are two opposite principles fighting each other: the instinct of freedom and the instinct of security." But both man and societies could be defined as either active or passive, and there was "a strange law in their relationship."[60] If society was geared toward the needs of the Passive Man, the Active Man would be destroyed; yet if society responded to the needs of the Active Man, he would carry along both Passive Man and all of society as he rose. Therefore modern humanitarians were caught in a paradox: in restricting the Active to benefit the Passive, they undercut their basic goal.

This clash between Active and Passive even structured world history, according to Rand. When the Active Man was ascendant, civilization moved forward, only to succumb to the lure of the security needed by the Passive Man. It was a cycle of light and dark that had continued for centuries, and now Rand saw another round dawning in America: "[W]hen a society allows prominence to voices claiming that Individual Freedom is an evil—the Dark Ages are standing on its threshold. How many civilizations will have to perish before men realize this?"[61]

Active and Passive Man were, at base, variations on the concepts of creator and the second-hander that underlay Rand's developing novel. Now appearing in nonfiction form, the same ideas gave Rand a class theory of sorts. She was quick to emphasize that the passive type of man was not necessarily a member of the working classes or the "so-called downtrodden." In fact, working men understood quite well the nature of individual effort and initiative. The highest concentration of collectivists would be found in two other classes, Rand ventured: the second-generation millionaires and the Intellectuals. Most intellectuals were second-raters with a lust for power, she alleged. It was they who had helped Stalin, while the millionaires helped Hitler, aided by "the lowest elements" in both cases. She concluded, "Tyrannies come from above and below. The great middle is the class of Freedom."[62]

Here was the clearest influence of the Willkie campaign on her thinking. Before, Rand had spoken only of the superior man and his contributions to society, showing little interest in distinguishing members of the faceless mob below. Now, without losing contempt for "the lowest elements" (which remained undefined), she allotted a new role to the vast American middle classes. These were the people she had met in the theater and on the street, ordinary voters who seemed naturally suspicious of Roosevelt and his promises of prosperity.

The "Manifesto" as a whole throbbed with a newfound love and respect for America. In Russia Rand had idealized America, but the 1930s had disillusioned her. Watching the spread of collectivism in literature and art, in 1937 she complained about "our degeneration in cultural matters—which have always been collective in America."[63] The "Manifesto" bore no such traces of cynicism. Instead it defined individualism and Americanism as essentially the same thing. America's establishment of individual liberty, according to Rand, "was the secret of its success." She praised the American Revolution as a rare historic moment when men worked collectively to establish "the freedom of the Individual and the establishment of a society to ensure this freedom," and called "give me liberty or give me death," Patrick Henry's dramatic words in support of the American Revolution, "the statement of a profound truth."[64]

Rand's final section, an extended defense of capitalism, likewise bore the marks of her campaign experience. Before Willkie she had been pro-capitalist yet pessimistic, writing, "The capitalist world is low, unprincipled, and corrupt." Now she celebrated capitalism as "the noblest, cleanest and most idealistic system of all." Despite her opposition to Willkie's managers, Rand seemed to have picked up on some of their tactics, marketing capitalism as the solution to all ills.[65]

Rand's newfound embrace of capitalism also reflected reading she had done since the campaign ended, particularly Carl Synder's *Capitalism the Creator: The Economic Foundations of Modern Industrial Society*.[66] Snyder, a well-known economist and statistician at the Federal Reserve Bank, argued that capitalism was the "only one way, that any people, in all history, have ever risen from barbarism and poverty to affluence and culture." From this premise Snyder developed a historically grounded, statistically supported case in favor of capital accumulation and against economic regulation and planning. Snyder supported centralized credit control, and indeed touted wise control of the money supply as the key to preventing future depressions and panics. He also gave grudging support to some government activities, such as the building of dams and conservation projects. But any further intervention, such as redistributive taxation, centralized planning boards, or wage and price controls, would be tantamount to "putting industry under the dead hand of government regulation."[67] Published with a glossy picture of Adam Smith for a frontispiece, Snyder's book was a rebuttal of the Keynesian theories that dominated academic economics and influenced Roosevelt's administration.

Snyder helped Rand codify and historicize the ideas she had already expressed in *Anthem*. In allegorical form Rand had emphasized the power of the individual and the importance of breakthrough innovations. Now Snyder set these ideas in an economic and historical context, arguing that economic prosperity was due to "some few [who] are very successful, highly talented, endowed with capacities and abilities far beyond the mass of their fellows."[68] As she read Snyder, Rand transformed the psychological categories of second-hander and creator into the economic concepts of Active and Passive Man.

In the "Manifesto" Rand followed Snyder's celebration of classical economics rather than introduce her own explosive concepts of morality. Altruism, which would play a significant role in *The Fountainhead,* is noticeably subordinate in the "Manifesto." It may have been that Rand's attention was far from the philosophy of her novel when she wrote the "Manifesto," or it may have been that she was unwilling to debut her ideas without the illustrative support of fiction. Whatever the reason, Rand celebrated selfishness in entirely economic terms. "One of the greatest achievements of the capitalist system is the manner in which a man's natural, healthy egoism is made to profit both him and society," she wrote, and went no further.[69] Similarly all of her attacks were leveled at the "absolute" common good, implying that a limited conception of the common good was acceptable.

Unlike her later work, the "Manifesto" did not spell out Rand's differences with Adam Smith's bounded "self-interest." Though he lauded self-interest in the economic realm, Smith also celebrated the natural concern people felt for the welfare of others, which he called "sympathy." Smith drew a distinction between self-interest and what he called the "the soft, the gentle, the amiable virtues." These two sets of values existed in a delicate balance, he argued, and "to restrain our selfish, and indulge our benevolent affections, constitutes the perfection of human nature." In her mature work Rand would attack any distinction between economic and social virtues, insisting that the same code of morality must apply to both. But in her first extended discussion of philosophy she was content to talk about capitalism's efficiencies and the benefits of freedom without integrating both into a new moral system.[70]

Rand closed her discussion of capitalism with a twist of her own devising. She asserted that for all the glories of capitalism she had sung, "we have never had a pure capitalist system." Collectivist elements, such as Monopoly Capitalists and the State, had conspired against capitalism from the beginning. These problems were not the fault of capitalism, but rather the result of encouraging collectivism. We must stop blaming capitalism, she wrote: "[I]t is time to say that ours is the noblest, cleanest and most idealistic system of all. We, its defenders, are the true Liberals and Humanitarians." Her readers faced a choice, and they must draw together in common action. They would find and recognize each other by "a single, simple badge of distinction," their devotion to freedom and liberty. She blared, "INDIVIDUALISTS OF THE WORLD, UNITE!"[71] Rand dispatched the final product to Pollock with an enthusiastic note. She was open to changes and amendments but hoped the "Manifesto" would be eventually published or made public, along with the signatures of the committee they would gather. "Let us be the signers of the new Declaration of Independence," she wrote hopefully.[72]

Rand's individualist "Manifesto" was the culmination of a series of shifts that had transformed her thinking since the publication of *We the Living* in 1935. Most obvious was her overt and enthusiastic embrace of politics. In this she was returning to an early interest, reprising the fascination with revolution and her father's political ideas that had marked her years in Russia. But American politics both challenged and reinforced her strongly held beliefs about the world. Working on the Willkie campaign helped shake Rand out of her reflexive elitism. She saw now that democracy might be more hospitable to capitalism than she had ever assumed. And she had come to believe that individualism was a fundamentally American value, one that had merely been disguised by collectivist propaganda. It was simply a question of getting the right ideas out to a broad audience.

The campaign also suggested another career path to her. Politics was now just as captivating to her as fiction. As *The Fountainhead* lay stillborn, Rand had found it easy to write thirty pages of political philosophy. In the 1940s she went on to forge a hybrid career, devoting herself to the spread of political ideas as much as the creation of dramatic stories and characters. It was the first step toward an identity she would later claim with pride: novelist and philosopher.

CHAPTER THREE

A New Credo of Freedom

$ BY THE TIME she completed the "Manifesto of Individualism" Ayn Rand's interest in politics was all-consuming and her literary life was at a standstill. She left *The Fountainhead* manuscript largely unattended and plunged into another round of organizing efforts. Wielding Channing Pollock's name and her writing, Rand began meeting as many New York "reactionaries" as possible. She was in a city known as the reddest in America; indeed the very phrase "New York intellectual" came to connote a certain type of leftist-literary thinker with Communist sympathies. What Rand joined instead was an alternate universe of *other* New York intellectuals, committed to free markets and laissez-faire.

These contacts, particularly her new friend Isabel Paterson, further introduced Rand to the American individualist tradition she had encountered through her opposition to Roosevelt. Rand found libertarian ideas compelling but the libertarian attitude alarming. The Willkie campaign had energized Rand and convinced her that Americans were receptive to capitalist ideas, but it had the opposite effect on others. Alone among her fellows, it seemed, she believed in the possibility of political change. Through months of letter writing, meetings, and impassioned talks, Rand found few willing to join her crusade to develop a "new credo of freedom."[1] Her organizing failures increased Rand's sense of urgency. As she wrote to Pollock, "Who is preaching *philosophical* individualism? No one. And if it is not preached, economic individualism will not survive."[2] Rand had a new sense of mission that would eventually find its way into her uncompleted manuscript.

When she finally secured a publisher for *The Fountainhead* Rand returned to the book a different person, with different ways of thinking about the world. In its origins *The Fountainhead* reflected Rand's earlier intellectual orientation toward Nietzsche and her deep-seated elitism. But in execution the novel bore the marks of what had happened since. The remaining two-thirds of the book, written in a tremendous year-long spurt of creativity, layered the themes of the "Manifesto" over the structure Rand had devised years earlier. The result showed Rand the writer at the height of her powers, even as Rand the thinker continued to emerge.

Since the expiration of her first contract in late 1940, few other publishers exhibited interest in Rand's unfinished manuscript. Her agent, Anne Watkins, racked up eight rejections in about as many months. The best she could do was help Rand secure an hourly position as a reader for Paramount Pictures, a job she started in the spring of 1941, just as her efforts with Pollock got under way. The string of rejections strained relations between agent and author. Watkins's interest in the book wavered, and she began to criticize Rand's writing. Rand gave no quarter, and the two argued unproductively over why the manuscript wasn't selling. The breaking point came just after Rand finished her "Manifesto." After another discussion of her novel, Watkins told Rand, "You always ask for reasons. I can't always give reasons. I just go by feelings." The statement came as a "traumatic shock" to Rand. To her it was a shameful confession of personal and intellectual inadequacy. She could tolerate criticism of her book that was carefully and consciously justified, but to be attacked on the basis of unspecified feelings galled her. Watkins's confession also destroyed any possibility of an ongoing professional relationship. Rand told her as much in a long philosophical letter announcing that she no longer wanted Watkins to represent her work.[3]

Rand's new boss at Paramount Pictures, Richard Mealand, was dismayed by the turn of events. He loved the parts of the novel he had read, and Rand immediately became one of his favorite employees. She was also beloved by her supervisor, Frances Hazlitt, who was an outspoken conservative. Frances was married to Henry Hazlitt, a journalist who would later become known in libertarian circles for his *Economics in One Lesson*. Together Hazlitt and Mealand gave Rand the pick of incoming stories and championed her writing career. When Mealand learned that her manuscript was languishing in obscurity, he pressed his services on Rand. He had contacts in the publishing world and was eager to help her out. Reluctantly she agreed to let him submit her chapters to Little, Brown, a publisher she viewed as relatively free from Communist influence.

At first it looked as if she had struck gold. An editor at the house pronounced the chapters "almost genius" and arranged to have dinner with Rand. There he probed her political views, assuming she was an anarchist. Rand set him straight: "I was telling him all about what I think of the New Deal, why this book is anti–New Deal, why I am for free enterprise, and what passages and what proves it."[4] It was a significant shift. Only a few years earlier she had been assuring prospective editors that her novel would *not* be political; now she insisted that her latest literary suitor recognize its deeper meaning.

Rand's spirits during this period were low. She had completely stopped working on the manuscript, and her work at Paramount further dampened her ambitions. Each day as she picked through yet another potboiler that the studio had bought, she moaned to Frank about the trash that was published while her work remained unnoticed. He was at once sympathetic, supportive, and suitably outraged, but with a gentle touch that cracked Rand's despair. "I know how you feel," he told her. "Here you are throwing pearls and you're not getting even a porkchop in return."[5] Rand crowed in delight and gave the line to one of her characters. After Little, Brown passed on the manuscript, Frank rose to the occasion masterfully. Rand was ready to junk the book entirely. Frank stayed up with her one long, terrible night, urging her to continue, reaffirming her genius, helping her believe the world was not the cold and hostile place it seemed. That was the night he "saved" the book, earning his place on the dedication page.

Despite her renewed resolve to finish the book, Rand's primary interest remained the new political organization. She chafed at Pollock's slowness in lining up converts and cash cows. George Sokolsky, a conservative columnist, came onboard at once. By June Pollock and Rand had discovered another important ally, DeWitt Emery. Based in Ohio, Emery owned a small manufacturing company that produced letterhead. A foot soldier of the anti–New Deal forces, he doubled as head of the National Small Business Men's Association, a lobbying concern.

After an initial introduction by Pollock, Rand and Emery met three times during a visit he paid to New York. Emery was deeply impressed by Rand. Her passion, clarity, and literary talents overwhelmed him, and he immediately pledged his support for the new organization.

Small business owners like Emery would always be among Rand's most consistent fans. Her emphasis on economic individualism coupled with her newfound patriotism resonated powerfully with politically conservative business owners. When she showed Emery her "Manifesto," he wanted the NSBMA to publish it. He passed it on to his friend Monroe Shakespeare, the owner of a Michigan-based company that manufactured fine fishing tackle. Shakespeare was similarly enthusiastic. He wrote Emery, "What do we have to do to get this Individualist Manifesto available for publication? I had a speaking engagement before the luncheon club at Three Rivers this past week and I condensed that down to a half-hour presentation and they were wild about it. They would have been twice as wild, if possible, if they could have seen the whole thing."[6] Soon Shakespeare was corresponding with Rand too.

Although Rand spoke in the coded language of individualism, her business audience immediately sensed the political import of her ideas. Many correctly assumed that her defense of individualism was an implicit argument against expanded government and New Deal reforms. Rand was a powerful polemicist because she set these arguments in terms both abstract and moral. She flew above the grubby sphere of partisan politics, using the language of right and wrong, the scope and scale of history to justify her conclusions.

We the Living was another effective weapon in Rand's arsenal. It established her, at least among political conservatives, as an expert on Soviet Russia and a living example of American superiority. After reading the novel Emery wrote her an emotional letter describing his reaction: "I thought I was one of the few who was really awake. I thought I knew and appreciated what we have, but I know now that I was at least half asleep."[7] Midway through the novel Emery paused to inspect his full refrigerator, newly grateful for the bounty contained therein.

As the "names" came in, Rand began telephoning and visiting potential recruits in the New York area. She visited Ruth Alexander, a Hearst columnist known for her conservative views, and briefly summarized the main points of the "Manifesto." Alexander agreed to support the project, provided it remained uncompromising in ideology and did not evade or pussyfoot "on major issues, such as the issue of defending capitalism," Rand reported to Pollock. Next on her list was Gloria Swanson, a famous actress from the silent movie era who had been a Willkie supporter. Swanson was originally reluctant to participate, but after reading Rand's "Manifesto" she agreed to join the committee and make further introductions. "I can't repeat what she said about the 'Manifesto,' it would sound too much like boasting on my part," Rand bragged to Emery.[8] During this time Rand also met John Gall, an attorney for the National Association of Manufacturers, who pledged to drum up interest and possibly funding among his colleagues.

With enough interest aroused, in the late summer and fall Rand and Pollock scheduled a series of meetings to discuss their plans and talk with professional fund-raisers. At least one of these meetings was held at Rand's apartment. Frank was present as Rand's escort during all meetings held at their home, but he did not participate actively in any of the planning. He had rung bells and passed out literature for the Willkie campaign but was uninterested in the intellectual and strategic questions that animated Rand.

During these meetings Rand had her first misgivings about the project. She was flattered but surprised by the reaction of her fellows to her "Manifesto," which she considered a "bromide" full of self-evident truths. Many of her contacts instead greeted it as a revelation, which aroused her suspicions. Now, meeting her group in person, she realized they were not intellectuals. She had pictured the organization as primarily educational in nature, but now she saw that "education would have to begin not with the provinces and the clubs, but with the headquarters, that we would have nobody to run it."[9]

Rand's disillusionment was particularly acute when she met Albert Jay Nock, one of their most prominent recruits. Unlike the others, Nock was a true intellectual. In the 1920s he had edited an idiosyncratic literary magazine, *The Freeman,* and had lately emerged as a vigorous critic of Roosevelt. In 1935 he published an individualist tract, *Our Enemy, the State.* He had been a member of the Liberty League and edited a *Review of Books* for the conservative National Economic Council. Along with H. L. Mencken, Nock was one of the few established men of letters who publicly identified himself as an individualist and opponent of the New

Deal. Rand admired Nock's writing and had high hopes for his participation in her organization. When she finally met the great man, however, she found him to be fatalistic, mystical, and gloomy. Nock was in
his seventies and appeared worn down. Freedom was a rare, accidental
exception in history, he told the group. Although he wished them well,
they didn't stand a chance. He argued that individualism as a political concept should be replaced by subjective "self sufficiency." Rand was
unconvinced. "Why surrender the world?" she retorted.[10]

Rand also became uneasy about Pollock's role in the organization.
She began to question his sincerity and his commitment to the cause;
too many people had joked to her about Pollock's wanting to run for
president. When he brought in the gravy boys, professional fund-raisers,
they talked only about how to raise money, eclipsing discussion of all
other issues. She sensed that Pollock and his contacts clung to individualism out of inertia rather than true commitment: "They were going out
of fashion. And that that fight was much more to retain the status quo or
the personal status of being leaders of public opinion, rather than what
did they want to lead the public to, nor what were their opinions."[11]
What bothered her most of all was a sense of resignation she detected.
Almost Marxists at heart, some of the group seemed to feel they had
ended up on the wrong side of history.

Rand was right to notice a whiff of decay around the advocates of
capitalism. Through the campaign and her organizing efforts she had
encountered the last remnant of nineteenth-century laissez-faire, loos-
ing its final breath into Willkie's anti–New Deal campaign. The pessimism of her compatriots was in many ways an accurate assessment of
reality, for the intellectual climate had shifted decisively against limited
government. Once influential free market economists like Frank Knight
and Joseph Schumpeter had raised dire warnings against government
interference in the economy, only to see their ideas eclipsed by the rising star of John Maynard Keynes, a Brit who argued that government
stimulation should play a vital role in supporting industrial economies.

First published in 1936, Keynes's *General Theory of Unemployment,
Interest, and Money* launched a full frontal assault on the received wisdom
of classical economics and the hands-off doctrine of laissez-faire. Instead
Keynes offered what came to be known as the theory of "pump prim-
ing." When the economy became sluggish, governments should intervene

with ambitious spending programs that would stimulate the economy. Unlike older economists Keynes was unconcerned about deficit spending, which he saw as a temporary measure to prevent small recessions from spiraling into deeper depressions. His timing could not have been better. Professors and politicians alike were casting about for explanations of and solutions to the economic malaise that gripped the globe. By 1940 Keynes's ideas had triumphed in both academia and government, making supporters of laissez-faire seem like relics from a bygone era.[12]

Indeed, to counter Keynesian economics, many of Rand's Willkie group reached for arguments popular during America's Gilded Age in the late nineteenth century. The British economist Herbert Spencer and his great American disciple, William Graham Sumner, were particular favorites. Most contemporary social scientists considered both thinkers hopelessly out of date. "Spencer is dead," the Harvard sociologist Talcott Parsons declared in his seminal 1937 work, *The Structure of Social Action*.[13] But Spencer was very much alive for Nock, who identified as a "Spencerian Individualist" and modeled *Our Enemy, the State* on Spencer's 1884 book, *The Man versus the State*. In 1940 Nock helped republish Spencer's volume, claiming in the introduction, "This piece of British political history has great value for American readers." It was this copy of Spencer that Rand had in her personal library, the pages thoroughly marked up.[14]

That this older tradition should persist, to be encountered anew by Rand during her political awakening, is not surprising. As Richard Hofstadter and other historians have detailed, arguments for laissez-faire saturated American society in the late nineteenth century, permeating both the intellectual climate of small-town America and commanding respect at the nation's most prominent universities. Sumner was among Yale's most popular (if controversial) teachers, and Spencer "was to most of his educated American contemporaries a great man, a grand intellect, a giant figure of thought."[15] Educated or well-read Americans in the 1930s and 1940s would have had at least a passing familiarity with the ideas of Sumner, Spencer, and other laissez-faire theorists, for they constituted a significant part of the American intellectual tradition.

Moreover, there seemed to be an almost natural structure to pro-capitalist thought. The writings of Spencer and Sumner, launched as polemics in an earlier age of state expansion, fit easily with vehement distaste for the New Deal. Both sets of thinkers had similar ground to cover. To argue convincingly against government action it was necessary to prove that government was incompetent, unfair, or both. Lacking extensive evidence about the ultimate success or failure of New Deal reforms, writers in the 1940s turned eagerly to theoretical and historical arguments articulated at an earlier time. These older thinkers lent an air of timeless wisdom to their critique of the state.

If Rand's associates replicated the arguments of nineteenth-century laissez-faire in many ways, they were noticeably circumspect about evolutionary theory, which had played such a dominant role in the thought of Spencer and Sumner. The earlier generation of capitalist boosters had based their arguments largely on evolutionary science and the corresponding idea that natural laws were at work in human societies. From this basis they argued that government interference in the economy was doomed to failure. Some of these arguments came close to the infamous social Darwinist position, in that they suggested government support for the poor might retard the evolution of the species.[16]

Vestiges of this scientific background still remained in 1940. On his cross-country speaking tour Channing Pollock came close to attacking New Deal relief programs in the old terms, arguing, "We can't afford a social order of the unfit, by the unfit, for the unfit."[17] Ruth Alexander referred to herself half-jokingly in a letter to Rand as a "bad jungle sister, who believes in survival of the fittest." Nock's receptivity to pseudoscience, such as his interest in the architect Ralph Adams Cram's theory that most people were not "psychically" human, also hinted at this earlier legacy. Rand too shared Cram's elitist affectation, a residue of her readings in Nietzsche. In a 1932 note about *We the Living* she remarked, "I do give a good deal about human beings. No, not all of them. Only those worthy of the name." But now Rand was beginning to drift away from this perspective. The campaign had been a taste of how a broader audience could actually appreciate her ideas. And in Nock and his fellows she saw how libertarian superiority could shade off into a debilitating pessimism.

As it turned out the only person who did not disappoint Rand was one who didn't even join the group: Isabel Paterson, a well-known columnist for the *New York Herald Tribune*. Rand sent Paterson an invitation to their meeting and followed up with a brief visit to her office. They had a cordial conversation, but Paterson explained that it was her policy not to join any group. Rand was surprised when, a few weeks later, Paterson found her home phone number and asked if they might meet again. More than twenty years Rand's senior, the divorced and childless Paterson had a formidable reputation. She had published several successful novels but wielded true influence through her weekly column, "Turns with a Bookworm." Written in a chatty, conversational style, Paterson's column mixed literary gossip with book reviews and ran for twenty-five years, from 1924 to 1949.[18]

Paterson had oddities to rival Rand's. At parties she sat silently by herself, refusing to talk to anyone she deemed uninteresting. She was openly rude. A friend recounted a typical anecdote from a publisher's luncheon given for a French author. After Paterson spoke disparagingly of H. G. Wells,

> the Frenchwoman turned most charmingly to Isabel and said, "You see, my dear Miss Paterson, it has been my great honor, privilege and happiness to know Mr. Wells most closely, most intimately. We have lived together, Mr. Wells and I, for seven happy years on the Riviera as man and wife."...Isabel then raised her lorgnette (being nearsighted as you know) and carefully looked at the Frenchwoman, from the table level slowly up and slowly down, and laying down the lorgnette she said, "I still say, H. G. Wells is a fool."[19]

Abrasive behavior was part of Paterson's shell and her persona, and it made her legendary among New York writers. A mention in her column could send book sales skyrocketing, but to curry favor with Paterson authors had to risk incurring her wrath. Always a contrarian, by the time of the Willkie campaign Paterson had become implacably opposed to Roosevelt. She peppered her columns with political commentary, a move that cost her readers and, eventually, her column.

Rand and Paterson's political friendship quickly became personal. Paterson invited Rand to her country home in Connecticut, an "enormous jump in the relationship," Rand remembered. "I was being very polite and formal, since it's just a political acquaintance. And she made it personal in very quick order." Initially hesitant, Rand soon found

Paterson to be a boon companion. She left Frank behind in New York and spent the weekend in Connecticut. The two women stayed awake "the whole first night, 'til seven in the morning—we saw the sunlight—talking philosophy and politics. And of course I was delighted with her for that reason."[20] Words and thoughts flowed easiest for Rand in the midnight hours, which she usually spent alone, buried in thought. That she so happily spent this time with Paterson, or "Pat" as Rand was now calling her, testified to the fast bond that grew between the pair. It was the first of many long talks that came to define their friendship.

Especially in the beginning, these conversations were decidedly one-sided. Paterson spoke and Rand listened. Educated only through high school, Paterson was nonetheless widely read, and friends recall the younger Rand literally "sitting at the master's feet" as Paterson discussed American history.[21] Paterson was working on a lengthy nonfiction treatise that would express her political views and had developed a commanding grasp of world history and economics that she gladly shared with Rand. She was an encyclopedia of knowledge. Rand would propose a topic—the Supreme Court, for example—and Paterson would hold forth for hours.

Like the other libertarians Rand met during this time, Paterson drew from an older tradition to make her case for limited government and individualism. Spencer was one of her favorites, and her column brimmed with references to his ideas. She was also taken by the concept of the status society versus the contract society, an idea first set forth by the British jurist and historian Sir Henry Maine but given legs by Spencer and later Sumner.[22] According to this theory, Western societies had evolved from a feudal system, in which relationships between individuals were determined by their status, to societies in which relationships were determined by contract. Although Maine was a Burkean conservative who believed firmly in ties of tradition and society, in American hands his idea of contract quickly became shorthand for a fluid, individualistic society that encouraged personal autonomy. Thinkers like Paterson interpreted Maine's ideas to mean that the New Deal betokened a return to the status society, or "rebarbarization."

Although she profited from the work of older and more obscure thinkers, as a prominent columnist and reviewer Paterson was well versed in contemporary intellectual debates. Where Rand spoke of "organization,"

Paterson warned against "planning" and "technocracy," invoking the more commonly used collectivist buzzwords. She also advanced a different kind of argument against organization. Rand used moral rhetoric about individual rights to make her case, but Paterson tended toward the practical, emphasizing that such planning simply could not work. There were several reasons why. Planners could never hope to determine the true value of goods and services, for such values were always in flux, as economic actors made individual decisions about what they wanted and how much they were willing to pay. Moreover, planning would interfere with invention and innovation, the very engine of the economy; before long, there would be nothing left to plan. And finally, Paterson worried, who would do the planning?

Paterson's particular preoccupation was energy. When she and Rand first met Paterson was working on the book that would become her only work of nonfiction, *God of the Machine*. She had been inspired by the dolorous *Education of Henry Adams*, and like Adams, she used energy as a central organizing metaphor. In Paterson's scheme the dynamo was individual man, who alone could generate energy through thought and effort. Energy could never be created by governments, but it could be directed—or misdirected—by state institutions and structures. More often than not government gummed up the works and stanched the flow of energy by interfering with individual freedom. Paterson hailed American government as a triumph of engineering design, for the careful balance of power between the states, federal government, and a free citizenry maximized the long circuit of energy released by individuals. She encouraged Rand to think not only about what made capitalism fail, but what made it succeed.

Paterson also had a handy explanation for the Great Depression, one that Rand would repeat throughout her later career. She was impressed by the analysis of the financial journalist Garet Garrett, who argued that the economic crisis had been brought about by government action. In the boom years of the crisis, Garrett argued, the Federal Reserve had inflated the money supply, leading to a speculative bubble that triggered the Depression.[23] As Paterson watched the government's efforts to repair the damage she saw only more of the same. Government had mismanaged the economy in the first place and was now making the problem worse through bungling efforts to fix it. The myriad shifting policies directed at ending the Depression had created a climate of uncertainty that was further drying up the free flow of capital. Paterson's prescription was to leave well enough alone; the government should pull out and let the economy recover on its own. Although her solution was unusual, her sense of the problem was not. Writers like Snyder and even members of Roosevelt's administration such as Stuart Chase fingered Federal Reserve policy as a cause of the depression. Most were willing on grounds of expediency to excuse government action to avert the crisis. Paterson, who set great stock in principles and consistency, was not.

Rand's encounter with Paterson constituted a virtual graduate school in American history, politics, and economics. She soaked up Paterson's opinions, using them to buttress, expand, and shape her already established individualism. Paterson helped shift Rand onto new intellectual territory, where Nietzsche's voice was one among many. Now Rand could draw from and react against the British classical liberal tradition and its American variants. Conversations with Paterson made Rand well versed in the major and minor arguments against the New Deal state.

Rand's relationship with Paterson also reinforced her growing preoccupation with reason. Both women shared a belief that with the world in political free fall, reason was their only hope and guide. In an episode that eerily mirrored Rand's break with her agent, Paterson described an argument she had with Rose Wilder Lane, another conservative writer. When Lane told Paterson she sometimes formed a conclusion by a feeling or a hunch, "…Isabel Paterson screamed at her over the phone, practically called her a murderess, explaining to her: how dare she go by feelings and hunches when the lives of other people are involved, and freedom and dictatorship. How can she go by anything but reason in politics, and what disastrous irresponsibility it is." To Rand, Paterson's arguments in favor of reason were "marvelous and unanswerable" and her anger in the face of disagreement understandable, even honorable.[24]

As her friendship with Paterson developed, Rand continued to work closely with Pollock and Emery. In October she drew up an "organization plan" and traded ideas with Emery on a potential name. He proposed American Neighbors, a name Rand rejected as too vague and meaningless. At one point the trio considered merging their efforts with the Independent Clubs of America, the group that had grown out of the Willkie Clubs. Rand drafted a fund-raising letter, noting that their

Declaration of Principles had been submitted as a possible declara-tion for the national group under the aegis of the New York Division. In another draft letter there is no mention of the Independent Clubs; instead recipients are invited to join the Educational Committee of the "'Intellectual Aristocrats' of our country, who will formulate a new credo of freedom, a faith for living, as complete, definite and consistent as the ideologies of our totalitarian enemies."[25]

Although the name and structure of the group remained inchoate, Rand grew increasingly clear on its purposes. Her group would offer a positive counterpoint to the New Deal, on an intellectual and philo-sophical level. They would be "the new teachers of a new Individualism." She consciously modeled her ideas on the methods of the left: "The New Deal has not won by bread alone. Nor by hams and baby blankets. The New Deal won by eight years of beautifully organized, consistent, sys-temic collectivist propaganda."[26] Her organization would counter this tide of leftism with its own publications, speeches, intellectuals, and ideas, making the case for individual rights and limited government. All Rand needed to make it happen was money, which had yet to material-ize. After months of appeals the organizers had received faint interest but no committed financial backers.

The problem was that in the political climate of mid-1941 Rand, Pollock, and Emery's efforts were doubly marginal. As opponents of Roosevelt they fell clearly outside the liberal order. Yet because Pollock was adamant that the group steer clear of "any crowd opposed to our aiding Britain" they were also cut off from the sources that were pump-ing funds into isolationist organizations. What Rand wanted to do would have been difficult at any time: create a group that was ideological yet practical, principled yet political. Her task was all the harder because her group cut across established lines of party politics.[27]

Around this time Rand's employer, Richard Mealand, once again inquired about her book. Always hesitant to accept favors, Rand had not considered asking Mealand for further help after Little, Brown turned down the book. A firm believer in her talent, Mealand was insistent and pressed Rand for the name of another publisher to approach. This time Rand suggested Bobbs-Merrill, which had recently published Eugene Lyon's *The Red Decade*, an exposé of Stalinist penetration in America. She guessed the firm might be favorable to a novel about individualism.

After Mealand made a few phone calls Rand walked her enormous manuscript, already several hundred pages and slightly more than one-fourth finished, over to Bobbs-Merrill. At first she didn't like the editor who would appraise her work, Archie Ogden. He had been hired only a few weeks earlier and was young, overly friendly, and insincere, Rand thought. Although he seemed to be a glad-hander, Ogden immediately recognized the potential in Rand's unfinished manuscript. He recommended publication of the book. His immediate supervisor was less impressed and vetoed the proposal. Fresh from reading Rand's heady tribute to individualism, Ogden sent a simple wire in response: "If this is not the book for you, then I am not the editor for you."[28] It was a bold, foolhardy, and ultimately brilliant move. Faced with mutiny, Ogden's supervisor relented and the press drew up a contract for Rand. She signed it on December 10, 1941, three days after Japanese forces attacked Pearl Harbor.

The outbreak of war put an immediate end to Rand's organizing efforts. Emery sent Rand an excited letter sharing his intention to join the armed forces. The president's critics muzzled themselves as the dangers of the New Deal paled beside the combined onslaught of Japan and Germany, which declared war on the United States only days after Pearl Harbor. Even America First disbanded, signifying the bankruptcy of isolationism as a political issue. Domestic concerns took a backseat to foreign affairs, and as the wartime economy shifted into high gear unemployment plummeted. World War II thrust the United States into a new international role, forever altering the dynamics of American politics. By the time the war was over a new set of concerns would structure the political landscape.

The ink on her contract had barely dried when Rand began writing again. She had only completed the first of four projected parts of the novel, entitled "Peter Keating," and six additional chapters. These sections served to introduce the major characters and foreshadow important later plot developments. She had described the early years of Howard Roark and Peter Keating, laying out their very different approaches to the world. In the book's opening scene Roark is expelled from the architecture school where Keating is about to graduate with honors. The next chapters describe Keating's easy rise through a big-name architecture firm, contrasting his experience to Roark's low-paying job with a washed-up master whose buildings he admires. Rand carefully interwove the careers of Roark and Keating, showing that Keating must rely on Roark to help complete his major commissions. She also laid out the explosive sexual dynamics between Dominique and Roark. The bulk of the novel, however, remained unwritten.

In the next twelve months Rand raced through the rest of the story. Bobbs-Merrill gave her a year to complete the manuscript, and this time Rand wasn't taking any chances. She had exhausted the reputable New York publishers and knew that if this contract fell through the book would never be published. Adding additional pressure was the fact that Rand still bore the primary financial burden in her marriage. Like so many men during the Depression era, Frank had been unable to find steady employment. He took the occasional odd job, at one point working as a clerk in a cigar store, but his income was never enough to support a household. Nor was Rand's thousand-dollar advance enough for her and Frank to live on, so she arranged to continue working on weekends for Paramount. The stress was considerable. Between writing and reading for Paramount, she was working virtually nonstop.

Rand now lived in two universes. Within *The Fountainhead* Roark continued his uneven career and his refusal to compromise for clients, while Keating's dizzying rise was topped by his marriage to Dominique, the daughter of his firm's founder. Rand's archvillain, Ellsworth Toohey, the focus of the book's second section, slowly wrapped his collectivist tentacles around the Wynand papers. Gail Wynand himself became disillusioned with his media empire, stole Dominique away from Peter, and befriended Roark. Back in the real world Rand kept impossible hours to meet her imminent deadline. The record, she told Ogden, was a mad burst of inspiration that lasted from 4 P.M. to 1 P.M. the next day.[29] On Sunday nights she did permit herself a rare indulgence, regularly stopping by Isabel Paterson's office at the *New York Herald Tribune* to help her proofread "Turns with a Bookworm." Paterson too was trying to finish a book, *God of the Machine*. She and Rand spurred each other on in a friendly contest, each hoping to finish first. Their jokes about competition made light of how deeply intertwined their creative processes truly were. Writing in tandem the two women shared ideas and inspiration freely.

Burning with ideas as she composed her novel, Rand stepped out of her passive, listening role and began to share her ideas about ethics. Paterson jousted back, during one conversation challenging Rand's view that self-interest must always be the first principle of action. Family was a sticking point for Paterson. Wasn't it true, she asked Rand, that parents must take care of their children before themselves? Rand countered swiftly, "If the child has no one but the parent, and the situation is such that the parent has to sacrifice himself and die, how long would the child survive thereafter?" Rand remembered, "[Paterson] gasped, in a pleased way, like an electric bulb going off. And she told me, 'of course that's the answer.' Now that's the last brick falling into place and she is convinced."[30] Paterson asked if she could draw on this conversation in her book, permission Rand gladly granted.

As 1943 approached Rand closed in on the final scenes of her novel. Here she made the first major changes that reflected her recent intellectual development. The final section of the book, named after her hero, was intended to celebrate Roark. Fleshing out the solution she had hit upon so many years earlier, Rand described Roark's design of a housing project, Cortland Homes, for Keating. It is a straightforward trade. Roark is intrigued by the problem of low-cost housing but knows he would never be chosen to design the project. He agrees to let Keating use his design, asking only one thing in return: the building must be built exactly as designed. But Cortland Homes is a government project, and everyone has a say. When built it blends Roark's design with the additions and amendments of several other architects. Appalled at the resulting compromise Roark dynamites the building late one night. Dominique is by his side in the storm of controversy that erupts, finally ready to love him openly.

From there Rand fell back on her trusty device of a trial, with a critical twist. Originally, an esteemed trial lawyer, roused from retirement by the Cortland case, was slotted to deliver a climactic defense of Roark. Now, as she neared completion of the novel, she decided that Roark would represent himself and deliver his own plea to the jury. It was a Hollywood-style scenario that injected a rare note of implausibility into an otherwise largely realistic novel. Having Roark deliver the speech, however, proved critical to expressing Rand's newfound appreciation for the average American. Roark's hand-selected jury mixed brawn and intellect: "two executives of industrial concerns, two engineers, a mathematician, a truck driver, a brick layer, an electrician, a gardener and three factory workers." Although several of the jurors are recognizable as men of exceptional achievement, the majority are manual workers of little distinction. Rand makes clear that they are hard-working types who have seen much of life, writing that Roark chose those with "the hardest faces."[31] If the jury understood Roark's argument, they would demonstrate their ability to recognize and reward individual genius.

First, though, the jury had to hear Rand's philosophy of life. Roark begins with a history lesson, arguing that all important achievements have come from creators who stood opposed to their time. Just as Rand emphasized in her "Manifesto," Roark explains to the jury that creativity is inextricably linked to individualism: "This creative faculty cannot be given or received, shared or borrowed. It belongs to single, individual men" (679). He situates the government's alteration of his design within the global struggle of collectivism versus individualism and repeats Rand's idea that good stems from independence and evil from dependence. Within this framework Roark's individual decision trumps the rights of government, future tenants, or any other involved parties, because "the integrity of a man's creative work is of greater importance than any charitable endeavor" (684).

Though it closely followed the "Manifesto," Roark's speech introduced a new theme that was to become one of Rand's signature ideas: the evil of altruism. In her first notes for the novel Rand had attacked Christian ethics, but now she attacked altruism. In the speech Roark identifies second-handers as preachers of altruism, which he defines as "the doctrine which demands that man live for others and place others above self" (680). The origins of Rand's shift from Christianity to altruism are unclear, but her conversations with the philosophically literate Paterson most likely played a role. Regardless of where she picked up the term, Rand's use of altruism reflected her refinement and abstraction of the concepts that had underlain the novel from the very start. At first she had understood the second-hander as a kind of glorified social climber. The frame of altruism significantly broadened this idea, allowing Rand to situate her characters within a larger philosophical and ethical universe. Identifying altruism as evil mirrored Rand's celebration of selfishness and completed the ethical revolution at the heart of *The Fountainhead*.

Along with creativity Roark's speech also celebrates reason, another theme of dawning importance to Rand. Here again was the influence of Paterson, who constantly ranted and raved about the importance of reason and the dangers of irrationality. The "Manifesto" did not mention rationality or the concept of reason, but Roark's speech lauds "the reasoning mind" and "the process of reason." At some points Roark distinguishes between thinking and creativity, at other times he collapses the terms, telling his audience, "The code of the creator is built upon the needs of the reasoning mind which allows man to survive" (681). He returns always to the basic point that individual rights must be valued above collective needs.

Swayed by Roark's argument, the jury promptly votes unanimously to acquit. The jury proved critical, helping Rand democratize her vision and reaffirm the basic wisdom of the free-thinking, independent American. Although none of the jurors are the history-making creator that Roark represents, Rand makes clear that they can share in his glory simply by understanding and affirming the principle of individualism.

After the trial scene Rand moved quickly to wrap up the loose ends of her story. In the pages preceding the trial she had dwelled at some length on the ordeal of Gail Wynand. Once a cocky and feared mogul, Wynand is humbled to discover that he cannot effectively defend Roark with his tabloids. Roark's destruction of Cortland has aroused public fury against him, and readers begin abandoning Wynand's publications when he takes Roark's side. Wynand has long believed he alone creates public opinion, but now he sees it is the public who owns him. Selling out his deepest values, he salvages his flagship newspaper, *The Banner*, by reversing course and attacking Roark. His fate is the most poignant in the book, for unlike Toohey and Keating, Wynand is "the man who could have been." In the novel's closing scenes Wynand shamefully rebuffs overtures from Roark, even as he commissions him to design and build a landmark building. Alone and desolate as the story ends, Wynand learns that his quest for power has brought him nothing in return.

Rand capped off her giant manuscript with a cinematic happy ending. Dominique, by now Mrs. Howard Roark, arrives at the construction site of the Wynand building. She takes an elevator up the side of the building, looking above to see "the sun and the sky and the figure of Howard Roark" (694). Her closing words were typed just before the firm deadline of January 1, 1943.

Now came the hard part. Both Rand and Ogden knew the manuscript was too long. Rand wanted to write everything down and then edit from there. She had only a few months to do it, for Bobbs-Merrill planned to release *The Fountainhead* in the spring. After nearly a year of nonstop writing Rand was now sleepy and unfocused when she sat at her desk. When she visited a doctor to consult about her chronic fatigue, he offered Benzedrine as a solution. At midcentury Benzedrine was a widely prescribed amphetamine and had a cult following among writers and artists. Jack Kerouac produced his masterwork *On the Road* in a three-week, Benzedrine-induced frenzy. Similarly Rand used it to power her last months of work on the novel, including several twenty-four-hour sessions correcting page proofs.[32]

Desperate to publish, Rand set aside her usual dislike of editorial advice and embraced many of the changes Ogden suggested. Most significant among these was the book's name. Rand's working title was "Second Hand Lives." When Ogden pointed out that this title highlighted her villains rather than her heroes, Rand agreed it must go. Her next choice, "The Mainspring," had been recently used. A thesaurus led her to "fountainhead," a word that never appears in the novel. Another important editorial force was Paterson. She advised Rand to prune all unnecessary adjectives, a change that would have gutted the novel. Rand did, however, find some of her suggestions useful. Following Paterson's advice, she weeded out proper names like Lenin, Hitler, Stalin, and Robespierre from Roark's courtroom speech to avoid tying the book to one historical moment.[33] The principles of her book were transcendent, Paterson reminded her.

In these last frantic months Rand also transformed Howard Roark. She decided to eliminate the character of Vesta Dunning, Roark's love interest before Dominique. The scenes between Vesta and Roark were among the first Rand wrote in 1938. Close in spirit to Rand's first heroes, the early Roark was cold and cruel, treating Vesta with dramatic indifference. By deleting these scenes in 1943 Rand softened Roark's character, making him less misanthropic and more heroic. Eliminating Vesta also

slimmed the manuscript and pruned complexity from Roark's character, allowing him to stand out more sharply as an idealized figure.

Even so, Roark's relations with women remained one of the most
troubling parts of the book. Often, as Rand struggled to make concrete
what she intended by the heroic, she described characters with icy emotional lives and distant, destructive relationships. Although their passions for each other are all-consuming, in another sense the novel's
characters never truly relate to one another. Friends find their greatest
moments of connection in silence, because it seems that in silence they
truly understand one another. Lovers don't hold hands, they hold wrists.
And then there is the infamous rape scene.

As in *Night of January 16th* the grand passion of *The Fountainhead*
begins in violence. The first encounters between Dominique and Roark
are charged with sexual tension. The two meet when Roark is working in
her father's quarry. Dominique requests that he be sent to repair a marble
fireplace she has deliberately scratched. Seeing through her ruse, Roark
smashes the marble, to Dominique's shocked delight, and then sends
another man to set the replacement. Encountering him again while on
horseback, Dominique slashes Roark across the face with a riding crop. He
returns a few nights later to finish what both have started, slipping through
her bedroom window. Rand wrote the scene to emphasize that even as she
resisted, Dominique welcomed Roark's advances. Yet it remained a brutal
portrayal of conquest, an episode that left Dominique bruised, battered,
and wanting more. Rand herself offered conflicting explanations for the
sadomasochistic scene. It wasn't real rape, she insisted to a fan, then called
it "rape by engraved invitation."[34] Certainly Rand perceived the encounter as an erotic climax for both characters. Risqué for its time, the rape
became one of the most popular and controversial parts of the book.[35]

The rape scene was a remnant of Rand's first intellectual preoccupa-
tions. In its basic structure *The Fountainhead* resembles many of Rand's
early works. Its hero is a principled criminal with a complicated love life,
and the plot culminates in a trial that affords the airing of philosophical views. Rand did what she could to improve the characterization of
Roark, sharpening and defining his sense of individualism as the novel
progressed.[36] But with a deadline looming, structural changes were
impossible. *The Fountainhead* is ultimately a hybrid work that caught
Rand in transition from one set of intellectual interests to another.

Along with deleting Vesta, Rand worked to purge the manuscript of her previous fixation on Nietzsche. In the first version of the manuscript she prefaced each of the four sections with an aphorism from *Beyond Good and Evil*. Now she removed these headings, and also removed several direct allusions to Nietzsche in the text of the novel. Still, she could not eliminate from *The Fountainhead* all of the vengeful scorn that had powered her earlier work. Particularly in the sections of the novel that treat Gail Wynand, her old horror at the mob returns. Rand demonstrated Wynand's lost possibilities by focusing on the masses to which he has sold his soul. One desperate night Wynand walks the streets of New York, his sense of degradation sharp as he smells the subway, "the residue of many people put together, of human bodies pressed into a mass," and passes drunks, tenement housewives, taxi drivers, and saloons. "I surrendered to the grocery man—to the deck hands on the ferryboat—to the owner of the poolroom," he thinks (661, 662). His discovery of his own value is twinned with disgust for these others, who "can produce nothing" (663). Pages later Rand tried to counterbalance these descriptions with her positive rendering of the jury, but her contemptuous attitudes still color the novel.

When contrasted with other contemporary celebrations of individualism, however, it becomes clear just how innovative *The Fountainhead* was. Elitism and populism were two impulses that had always coexisted uneasily in the defense of unregulated capitalism. Nock's *Memoirs of a Superfluous Man,* for example, is a credo shot through with educated disdain for the common man. At the same time opponents of the New Deal insisted that men, if left alone, could properly work out their own destiny. Like Sumner they glorified "the forgotten man," the ordinary workers who maintained what Paterson called "the set-up" without interference from government.[37] Defenders of laissez-faire invoked both elite privilege and the wonders of the ordinary, self-sufficient citizen, often in the same breath.

The Fountainhead finessed this contradiction and escaped libertarianism's fatal elitism through Rand's theory of ethics. For all her bluster, Rand's ethics were rather anodyne. Roark tells the jury, "Degrees of ability vary, but the basic principle remains the same; the degree of man's independence, initiative, and personal love for his work determine his talent as a worker and his worth as a man" (681). The book's hierarchy of values is not exclusive, for anyone could join Rand's elite simply by loving their work. Instead of talking about the wealthy, she talked about the independent, thereby sidestepping social class. Inequalities or differences between characters are discussed in specific, individual terms, without reference to larger social structures.[38] Denizens of Hell's Kitchen and the city's toniest drawing rooms are evaluated by the same standard of independence.

Even as it uncoupled libertarianism from its traditional elitism, *The Fountainhead* made a familiar argument that humanitarianism is simply a guise for those who seek power. The idea was not novel for a time that had seen the birth of two new totalitarianisms. Alfred Hitchcock's film *Foreign Correspondent,* released in 1940, depicted the head of Britain's peace party as a German agent, hiding his diabolical designs under the cover of pacifism. Paterson would make the point in her vividly titled chapter, "The Humanitarian and the Guillotine." In later years Rand claimed credit for the ideas in this chapter, a contention Paterson vigorously disputed. It is likely that Paterson did believe in an ethics of self-interest prior to meeting Rand, for such beliefs were not uncommon among supporters of laissez-faire. Paterson could have been paraphrasing William Graham Sumner, who was famously skeptical of humanitarianism, when she wrote, "Most of the harm in the world is done by good people, and not by accident, lapse, or omission. It is the result of their deliberate actions, long persevered in, which they hold to be motivated by high ideals toward virtuous ends." Rand was not the first thinker to criticize altruism or to suggest that noble sentiments often cloak base motives. Indeed in the early libertarians Rand had stumbled across a rare community where her attack on altruism was not taboo.[39]

What Rand offered was an unforgettable and highly stylized version of this argument set in a modern context. Her primary vehicle was *The Fountainhead*'s villain Ellsworth Toohey, who angles for power through the promotion of collectivist ideas. Subtly he influences the Wynand papers: "If a statement involved someone's personal motive, it was always 'goaded by selfishness' or 'egged by greed.' A crossword puzzle gave the definition of 'obsolescent individuals' and the word came out as 'capitalists'" (588). In a speech he parodies Roosevelt's Four Freedoms: "If you were assigned to a job and prohibited from leaving it, it would restrain the freedom of your career. But it would give you freedom from the fear of unemployment" (553). Toohey's most successful method, however, is to create a Union of Wynand Employees, which he uses as power base to take over the newspaper. Despite its high-minded rhetoric, the union is intended to benefit just one man.

Rand also pushed past traditional libertarian skepticism of charity to assault the very concept of altruism itself. Writers like Paterson and Sumner stressed that benevolence should not be compelled by the state, but supported private charity undertaken voluntarily. By contrast, Roark told his audience, "The only good which men can do to one another and the only statement of their proper relationship is—Hands off!" (683). Revising her earlier binary of Active Man and Passive Man, Rand now drew a primal distinction between independence and dependence and presented morality as a stark choice of either self-sacrifice or egoism. Unlike other libertarians Rand would let no hint of "social conception" taint her individualism.

As she neared the end of the project Rand was working at fever pitch, thanks to her new medication. She was thrilled by the long hours the drug made possible, freely telling friends about this latest discovery. In a few short months she had sliced the novel's length, reshaped its philosophical implications, and given a final polish to characters that had lived in her mind for nearly a decade. And she had done all this while holding down a part-time job. But Benzedrine had a boomerang effect. By the time the book was complete Rand's doctor diagnosed her as close to a nervous breakdown and ordered her to take two weeks of complete rest.[40]

Exhausted but happy, Rand decamped to Isabel Paterson's country house in Connecticut with Frank in tow. There she shocked Paterson by announcing she expected sales of at least 100,000. Otherwise she would consider herself a failure, Rand tactlessly informed Paterson, author of eight novels, none of which had sold more than several thousand copies. Although Paterson had been unfailingly supportive of Rand's writing, she was far from confident that Rand's novel would sell. *The Fountainhead* was not to her taste—too many adjectives, too much drama. She even declined to review the book for the *Herald Tribune,* a decision she carefully kept from Rand.

Rand had better luck with the *New York Times,* which gave *The Fountainhead* the best review of her career, in May, just a month after the book was released. Lorine Pruette called Rand "a writer of great power": "She has a subtle and ingenious mind and the capacity of writing brilliantly, beautifully, bitterly." Pruette went beyond the novel's style and also praised its content, writing that readers would be inspired to think "through some of the basic concepts of our times" and noting, "This is the only novel of ideas written by an American woman that I can recall." A host of lesser newspapers echoed her words. A reviewer in Pittsburgh said *The Fountainhead* "could conceivably change the life of anyone who read it," and the Providence *Journal* wrote, "With one book [Rand] at once takes a position of importance among contemporary American novelists." The exceptions came primarily from more highbrow literary outlets like the *Times Literary Supplement,* which found, "Miss Rand can only create gargoyles, not characters," and *The Nation,* where Diana Trilling sniffed about the book's caricatures.[41]

By the summer *The Fountainhead* began to appear on best-seller lists, driven both by review attention and positive word-of-mouth recommendations. Paterson undoubtedly played a role in the book's early success, for although she had declined to review *The Fountainhead* she plumped Rand from the safe distance of her column, mentioning her eight times in 1943.[42] In these years Paterson was at the height of her fame as a book reviewer, and "Turns with a Bookworm" was valuable publicity for Rand. Sales continued to grow into the fall, a development that confirmed Rand's expectations but confounded most others, including the business office of her publisher. Against the advice of Rand's editor, the press had printed only a small first run, expecting sales of ten thousand books at maximum. Soon they were scrambling to keep up with demand. By year's end they had sold nearly fifty thousand copies and gone through six printings. That Bobbs-Merrill failed to anticipate the book's success is understandable. *The Fountainhead* is a strange book, long, moody, feverish. Even after Rand's furious last-minute editing it took up nearly seven hundred pages.

What was it that readers found in *The Fountainhead*'s pages? At the most basic level the book told an exciting story, and told it well. When freighted with Rand's symbolic connotations, architecture became exciting and lively. In one striking scene Rand portrays a rebellious action by

Roark that wins him his first major client, Austen Heller. While Heller is looking at a watercolor drawing of his proposed house, which has drawn on Roark's ideas but blended them with those of other architects, Roark suddenly intervenes, destroying the watercolor by demonstrating how he had originally designed the house.

> Roark turned. He was at the other side of the table. He seized the sketch, his hand flashed forward and a pencil ripped across the drawing, slashing raw black lines over the untouchable watercolor. The lines blasted off the Ionic columns, the pediment, the entrance, the spire, the blinds, the bricks; they flung up two wings of stone; they rent the windows wide; they splintered the balcony and hurled a terrace over the sea. It was being done before the others had grasped the moment when it began....Roark threw his head up once, for a flash of a second, to look at Heller across the table. It was all the introduction needed; it was like a handshake. (126)

On the spot, Heller offers Roark his first major commission. Rand's tense, dramatic description brings the moment alive in all its emotional significance. As even the snooty *Times Literary Supplement* admitted, "She contrives from somewhere a surprising amount of readability."[43] With several plays, movie scenarios, and a novel behind her, Rand had developed a fast-paced, sweeping style that easily sustained her readers' interest.

Yet for many readers *The Fountainhead* was far more than a story. The book inspired a range of passionate reactions, as can be seen in the large volume of fan mail Rand began to receive.[44] In breathless, urgent letters, readers recounted the impact the book had on their lives. For many *The Fountainhead* had the power of revelation. As one reader told Rand after finishing the book, echoing DeWitt Emery's sentiments, "It is like being awake for the first time." This metaphor of awakening was among the most common devices readers used to describe the impact of Rand's writing. Adolescents responded with particular fervor to her insistence that dreams, aspirations, and the voice of self be heeded, whatever the consequences. An eighteen-year-old aspiring writer clung to the book as to a lifeline: "But now, when I reach the point—and I reach it often these days—where the pain can go down no further; I read part, any part, of *The Fountainhead*." Rand had anticipated responses like these, and indeed hoped to stir her reader's deepest feelings. Writing to Emery shortly after the book's release she told him, "It's time we realize—as the Reds do—that spreading our ideas in the form of fiction is a great weapon, because it arouses the public to an *emotional,* as well as intellectual response to our cause." Sales of *The Fountainhead* confirmed Rand's understanding. Rather than tapering off after reviews and commentary had faded from public memory, the book's sales increased steadily year after year. Readers were discovering the book, experiencing its powers, and pressing copies on all their friends.[45]

Among the most dedicated fans were many who used Rand's characters as templates for self-assessment and self-improvement. Worried by Rand's condemnation of "second-handers," they wondered if they fell into this category. An army lieutenant confessed to Rand, "However, admire him and agree with Roark as I do, I haven't the personal guts, if you call it that, to emulate him....Perhaps I am, after all, closer to Gail Wynand, because I have no reason to believe I could hold out longer than he did." Others credited *The Fountainhead* with rescuing them from conformity or surrender. After finishing the book one reader told Rand, "I was profoundly challenged and frightened. The challenge has outlived the fright....Thank you." A young woman compared herself to each of the book's characters in turn, finally concluding, "I am myself— believe in that, living by what I really want." By compelling readers to accept or reject parallels between themselves and her characters, Rand inspired many readers to reflect on their own choices and motivations in life.[46]

For others the book was a more intellectual experience. Rand's rejection of traditional morality and her counterintuitive theory of selfishness provoked many readers to thought, debate, and discussion. Her book was particularly popular among soldiers, who found in Rand's enormous tome both relief from boredom and a welcome meditation on the reasons for U.S. involvement in the war. As a serviceman stationed in Texas put it, "Though I do not entirely agree with hypotheses established in this book, I must admit that this material warrants much serious consideration. Indeed, superficially it appears to offer a logical recapitulation of the forces behind present-day global turmoil." Several letter writers told Rand that her novel was a hot commodity among their military units, eagerly passed from reader to reader. An army private wrote, "[*The Fountainhead* was] giving my brain some well needed exercise," and a book reviewer from Boston recounted, "My husband and I lived in [The Fountainhead] for several weeks, discussed it frontwards and backwards, in and out, the 'what' the 'why' the 'wherefore.'" Even those who disagreed with Rand enjoyed thinking through the questions she raised. This intellectual excitement was engendered by Rand's careful encoding of ideas in a fictional plot. Many who would never have read a treatise on ethics or politics found the novel drew them quickly into the world of ideas.[47]

From the start Rand hoped to twin the emotional and intellectual parts of the novel. Ideally readers would experience strong feelings of identification with both her characters and her political views. She told DeWitt Emery, "When you read it, you'll see what an indictment of the New Deal it is, what it does to the 'humanitarians' and what effect it could have on the next election—although I never mentioned the New Deal by name."[48] Rand's belief that fiction could have important political consequences sprang from her Russian background and her careful observations of the New York left. As anti-Communists were hustled out of Leningrad State University, Rand had realized that the most innocuous of literary works could have political meaning. She kept this in mind during her first years in the United States, when she sent her family American novels to translate into Russian. These books were an important source of income for the Rosenbaums, but they had to pass the Soviet censors. Rand became an expert in picking out which type of story would gain the approval of the Communists. These same works, she believed, were slowly poisoning the American system and had contributed to Willkie's defeat. "The people are so saturated with the collectivism of New Deal propaganda that they cannot even grasp what Mr. Willkie really stood for," she wrote in a fund-raising letter. "That propaganda has gone much deeper than mere politics. And it has to be fought in a sphere deeper than politics."[49] The Fountainhead would expose Americans to values and ideals that supported individualism rather than collectivism.

Plenty of readers understood and embraced The Fountainhead's deeper meaning. In a letter to Rand one woman attacked the Office of Price Administration, a federal government agency established to regulate commodity prices and rents after the war broke out: "I am assuming that you view with growing horror the government's paternal treatment of its poor and needy. I do, for when we begin trading our freedom for monetary security, we lose both." Another confessed, "My hatred of Roosevelt became in time almost a mania. He stood for almost everything I hated. It is quite clear that your own feeling equaled or exceeded mine." Rand's individualism ran against the mainstream intellectual currents of her day, but it echoed the common Victorian idea that dependence would create weakness or lead to moral degradation. As a Presbyterian minister from Indiana testified, "In Howard Roark I rediscovered the 'individual'—the individual I had been brought up to be and believe in, but who had been lost somewhere in the miasma of intellectual, moral, and spiritual confusions spawned in the unhealthy jungle of preachers, professors, and the poverty of the Depression." Rand was right to sense that there still existed a strong antigovernment tradition in America and an almost instinctual fear of bureaucratization, regulation, and centralization. Even as it promoted a new morality, politically the novel reaffirmed the wisdom of the old ways.[50]

To those who already leaned libertarian the novel offered a striking counterpoint to traditional ideas of laissez-faire. As she had intended, *The Fountainhead* made individualism a living, breathing faith. Rand's emphasis on creativity, productivity, and the power of individuals came as a bracing tonic to James Ingebretsen, who was just out of the army when he read *The Fountainhead* and Nock's *Memoirs of a Superfluous Man*. As he explained to a friend, "Howard Roark is the answer to Nock[,] meaning creation, not escape, is the answer to the messy world we are living in. Freedom, not enslavement to others, is the answer for all of us. And so my course is crystal clear to me now." Shortly after writing this letter Ingebretsen moved to Los Angeles, where he helped organize the Pamphleteers, one of the first libertarian groups founded in the postwar era. Similarly the journalist John Chamberlain found that the combination of old and new solidified his political opinions. Chamberlain read Rand's book in conjunction with Paterson's *God of the Machine* and yet a third libertarian book published in 1943, Rose Wilder Lane's *The Discovery of Freedom*. He remembered that the three writers "turned Nock's conception of social power into a detailed reality": "These books made it plain that if life was to be something more than a naked scramble for government favors, a new attitude towards the producer must be created." In the 1930s Chamberlain had been known for his mildly socialist leanings, but in the postwar era he would emerge as a high-profile voice of libertarianism, writing for the *Wall Street Journal, Life,* and *Time.*[51]

The Fountainhead offered renewed energy to libertarianism at a critical time. Somnolent for years, anti–New Deal groups such as the Committee for Constitutional Government and the American Economic Foundation began to reawaken in the early 1940s. These groups immediately recognized Rand as a kindred spirit. In the fall of 1943 she partook in a published debate sponsored by the American Economic Foundation. Her opponent was Oswald Garrison Villard, former editor of *The Nation,* and the question at hand, "Collectivism or Individualism—which promises postwar progress?" She sold a very condensed version of her "Manifesto" to the Committee for Constitutional Government, which placed it in *Reader's Digest* as "The Only Road to Tomorrow." Soon to become a font of popular anti-Communism, *Reader's Digest* helped Rand become identified as an overtly political author.[52]

Still, Rand feared she wasn't reaching her kind of readers. Most distressing were the ads for *The Fountainhead,* which presented the book as an epic romance rather than a serious treatment of ideas. She fired off an angry letter to Archie Ogden, detailing her dissatisfaction. Before long she took action herself, resurrecting her earlier political crusade, but now tying it directly to the fortunes of her novel. As she explained to Emery, she wanted to become the right-wing equivalent of John Steinbeck: "Let our side now build me into a 'name'—then let me address meetings, head drives, and endorse committees....I can be a real asset to our 'reactionaries.'" The key would be promoting *The Fountainhead* as an ideological and political novel, something Bobbs-Merrill would never do.[53]

Rand was careful to explain that her ambitions were not merely personal. The problem, she explained to Emery and several other correspondents, was that the intellectual field was dominated by a "Pink-New-Deal-Collectivist blockade" that prevented other views from being heard. This was why books like *The Fountainhead* were so important: If it went "over big, it will break the way for other writers of our side." Rand was convinced "the people are with us"; it was leftist intellectuals who stood in the way.[54] She set up meetings with executives at DuPont and the National Association of Manufacturers and pressed Monroe Shakespeare to pass her book along to Fulton Lewis Jr., a right-wing radio host.

In the end Hollywood gave *The Fountainhead* the boost it needed. The idea of a movie was particularly tantalizing to Rand. The novel was selling well, but she still worried it would suffer the same ignominy as *We the Living*. A movie would put her name before a wide audience and ensure the book's longevity. Rand turned down her first film offer only weeks after publication, sure her book would become more valuable with time. In the fall of 1943 her new agent reported a more promising proposal from Warner Brothers. Rand drove a hard bargain. After nearly two decades in the industry she had learned her lesson. "Red Pawn," the first scenario she sold, had doubled in price soon afterward, netting a tidy profit for the studio, which she had never seen. She would settle for nothing less than fifty thousand dollars, a princely sum. Scarcely two years earlier she had leapt at a paltry advance of a thousand dollars. Warner Brothers balked at the demand, but she wouldn't budge.

In November the offer came through. Almost better than the money was the studio's interest in having her write the script. It meant that she and Frank would return to Hollywood, a prospect Rand dreaded. But only by being there in person, Rand knew, could she hope to ensure the integrity of her story and preserve the essence of her ideas. Warner Brothers even dangled before her the prospect of consulting on the film's production. When the deal was finalized Frank and Isabel Paterson bundled her into a taxicab and set off for Saks Fifth Avenue. "You can get any kind of fur coat provided it's mink," Frank told his wife.[55] Rand's instinct was to hoard the money, to save every penny so she would always have time to write. Frank and Isabel knew better. After so many years of hard work, Rand had finally become a "name."

PART II

From Novelist to Philosopher, 1944–1957

Ayn Rand in her Chatsworth study where she began the writing of *Atlas Shrugged*.
J. Paul Getty Trust. Used with permission. Julius Shulman Photography Archive,
Research Library at The Getty Research Institute (2004. R. 10).

CHAPTER FOUR

The Real Root of Evil

$AYN AND FRANK arrived in Hollywood as celebrities. *The Fountainhead* was the hot property of the moment, and the town buzzed with speculation about who would be chosen for the choicest roles. Stars began to court Rand in the belief that she could influence the studio's choices. Joan Crawford threw a dinner for the O'Connors and came dressed as Dominique, in a long white gown and aquamarines. Warner Brothers set her up in an enormous office with a secretary out front and a $750 weekly salary. The contrast between Rand's arrival as a penniless immigrant in 1926 and her latest debut was sharp.

The Golden State's charms were lost on Rand, who complained about "the disgusting California sunshine."[1] Her heart was still in New York, and she hoped their time in California would be brief. She immediately set to work on *The Fountainhead* script, turning out a polished version in a few weeks. There would be no quick return east, however, for production of the film was suspended indefinitely due to wartime shortages. Rand resigned herself to a lengthy stay in California. When her work for Warner Brothers was done, she signed a five-year part-time screenwriting contract with the independent producer Hal Wallis, successfully negotiating six months off a year to pursue her own writing. She and Frank bought a house that perfectly suited them both, an architecturally distinguished modernist building that could easily have graced the pages of *The Fountainhead*. Designed by Richard Neutra and situated in rural Chatsworth, almost an hour's drive from Hollywood, the glass-and-steel house was surrounded by a moat and thirteen acres. In the end, they would live there for seven years.

Rand underwent two profound intellectual shifts during her time in California. The first was a reorientation of her thought toward a concept of reason she linked with Aristotle. When she arrived in California she was working on her first nonfiction book, a project she eventually abandoned in favor of her third novel. Much as *The Fountainhead* had showcased her ideas about individualism, this next book would reflect Rand's growing fealty to reason and rationality. After three years in California Rand had redefined the goal of her writing. Once individualism had been the motive power of her work; now she explained to a correspondent, "Do you know that my personal crusade in life (in the philosophical sense) is not merely to fight collectivism, nor to fight altruism? These are only consequences, effects, not causes. I am out after the real cause, the real root of evil on earth—the irrational."[2]

Soon after this development came Rand's dawning awareness of the differences that separated her from the libertarians or "reactionaries" she now considered her set. At issue was her opposition to altruism and, more significantly, her unwillingness to compromise with those who defended traditional values. In 1943 Rand had been one of the few voices to make a compelling case for capitalism and limited government. In the years that followed she would become part of a chorus, a role that did not suit her well.

Rand's move back to Hollywood immersed her in a cauldron of political activity that was dividing the film industry. The first stages of the Red Scare that would sweep the nation were already unfolding in California. Labor troubles paved the way. In 1945, shortly after her return, the Conference of Studio Unions launched an industry-wide strike, touching off a heated conflict that would last for nearly two years. At the gates of Warner Brothers rival unions engaged in a full scale riot that garnered national headlines and aroused the concern of Congress. Ensconced in far-away Chatsworth, Rand missed the excitement. She quickly signed on, however, with a group formed to oppose Communist infiltration of the entertainment unions and the industry more broadly, the Motion Picture Alliance for the Preservation of American Ideals. The group was founded by powerful Hollywood figures, including Walt Disney, John Wayne, and King Vidor, director of *The Fountainhead*. At the first meeting she attended Rand was surprised to be unanimously voted onto the Executive Committee.

Just as she had once dreamed, Rand was being tapped to head committees and lead drives, to lend her fame to a political cause. She also
joined the board of directors of the American Writers Association, an
alliance of writers formed to oppose the "Cain Plan," a proposed authors'
authority. Under the plan, which was supported by the Screenwriter's
Guild and a union of radio writers, the new authority would own copyright and marketing rights of authors' products. Rand and others immediately detected Communist agents at work. The American Writers
Association sent representatives to a meeting of the Authors League
in New York, held several meetings, and began publishing a newsletter. Rand was active in bringing several of her Hollywood connections
aboard, where they joined a prominent line-up of literary stars, including Dorothy Thompson, Hans Christian Andersen, Margaret Mitchell,
and Zora Neale Hurston. Through them Rand met another group
of right-wing activists, including Suzanne LaFollette, Clare Boothe
Luce, Isaac Don Levine, and John Chamberlain. When the Cain Plan
was soundly defeated, the American Writers Association attempted to
extend its ambit to a defense of writers who had suffered from political
discrimination, but it soon lapsed into inactivity.[3]

Rand was also taken up by business conservatives such as Leonard
Read, head of the Los Angeles Chamber of Commerce, who invited her
to dinner with several associates soon after she arrived in California.
The driving force behind the dinner was R. C. Hoiles, publisher of the
L.A.-area *Santa Ana Register.* Hoiles had given his family copies of *The
Fountainhead,* praised the book in his column, and swapped letters with
Rand while she was still in New York. The dinner created no lasting bond
between the two, perhaps because Hoiles liked to support his libertarianism with quotes from the Bible, but he continued to promote Rand in
his Freedom Newspapers, a chain that eventually grew to sixteen papers
in over seven western and southwestern states.[4]

Rand was more impressed by William C. Mullendore, an outspoken
executive at Con Edison. Mullendore admired *The Fountainhead* and
in turn she considered him a "moral crusader" and the only industrialist who understood "that businessmen need a philosophy and that
the issue is intellectual." It was Mullendore who had converted Read
to the "freedom philosophy," and under his tutelage Read transformed
his sleepy branch of the Chamber of Commerce into a mouthpiece for

libertarianism and a quasi–think tank, complete with a lecture series and educational programs. Stepping into an ideological vacuum, within a few years Read was able to "set the tone of the Southern Californian business community," as one historian observes.[5]

Read's activities built on larger trends shaping the region and the nation. With the war at its end and the economy recovering, business conservatives began to mount organized opposition to the New Deal order. Chief among their targets was organized labor. A wave of strikes and slow-downs that swept the country in 1945 was their opportunity. Business owners argued that labor had gained too much power and was becoming a dangerous, antidemocratic force. On the state level "right to work" laws, which outlawed the closed shop and other union-friendly measures, became political flashpoints, particularly in the fast grow-ing sunbelt region.[6] These initiatives were matched by developments on the national level. In 1947 the conservative Eightieth Congress over-rode President Truman's veto to pass the Taft-Hartley Act, a piece of legislation that rolled back many of the gains labor had made during Roosevelt's administration. Hoiles and Mullendore were emblematic of this new militancy, both taking a hard line when strikes hit the compa-nies they managed.

Read, Mullendore, and Hoiles rightly recognized Rand as a writer whose work supported their antiunion stance. It had not escaped their notice that *The Fountainhead*'s villain Ellsworth Toohey is a union orga-nizer, head of the Union of Wynand Employees. Read and Mullendore also suspected that Rand's more abstract formulations would resonate with businessmen. The two had a small side business, Pamphleteers, Inc., devoted to publishing material that supported individualism and free competitive enterprise. When Rand showed them a copy of *Anthem,* which had not been released in the United States, they decided to pub-lish it in their series. As Read and Mullendore anticipated, *Anthem* was eagerly picked up by a business readership. Rand received admiring letters from readers at the National Economic Council and Fight for Free Enterprise, and another Los Angeles conservative group, Spiritual Mobilization, presented a radio adaptation in its weekly broadcast.[7]

Anthem and *The Fountainhead* became particularly appealing to business readers in the wake of the 1947 Taft-Hartley Act, which permit-ted employers to educate their employees about economic and business matters, creating a vast new market for pro-capitalist writers.[8] Rand's principled defense of capitalism, which focused on individualism rather than specific political issues, was a perfect fit for these corporate efforts. The editor of the *Houghton Line,* published by a Philadelphia company that manufactured oils, leathers, and metal-working products, gave *The Fountainhead* a glowing review. In a weekly circular sent to customers the owner of Balzar's Foods, a Hollywood grocery store, referenced both *The Fountainhead* and *Anthem* and included a diatribe against the New Deal–created Office of Price Administration. A top executive at the Meeker Company, a leather goods company in Joplin, Missouri, distributed copies of Roark's courtroom speech to his friends and business acquaintances.[9] Much as Rand had always wished, capitalists were finally promoting her work of their own volition.

Business conservatives were also drawn to another best-selling book attacking state control of the economy, F. A. Hayek's *Road to Serfdom.* Written for a British audience, Hayek's book unexpectedly caught the attention of Americans, and he was mobbed by enthusiastic crowds when he toured the United States in 1944. Hayek made arguments very similar to those Rand had advanced during her post-Willkie activism. He tied his laissez-faire beliefs to the broader international situation, arguing that any movement toward state regulation of the economy would ultimately culminate in full-blown socialism and dictatorship. Like Rand, he warned, "The forces which have destroyed freedom in Germany are also at work here."[10] He shared her distrust of "the common good" and titled one of his chapters "Individualism and Collectivism." The reception of their work was also similar, for Hayek was snubbed by intellectuals yet embraced by businessmen and other Americans nervous about the implications of the New Deal. Both *The Fountainhead* and *Road to Serfdom* were even made into comic books, a testimony to their wide appeal.

The Road to Serfdom launched Hayek on a remarkable career as an intellectual and organizer that would culminate with his winning the 1974 Nobel Prize in Economics. The book's popularity caught the attention of the Kansas City–based Volker Fund, a newly active libertarian foundation, which eventually helped Hayek secure a position at the University of Chicago, a lone academic redoubt for libertarian ideas. During the war the economists Frank Knight, Henry Simons, and Alan

Director had assembled a critical mass of free market thinkers at the university. Hayek's arrival marked a high point in this campaign, even though he was rejected by the Economics Department and instead landed at the Committee for Social Thought, with a salary paid by the Volker Fund. Regardless of how he got there, once at Chicago Hayek quickly expanded on the earlier efforts of Knight and Director and helped transform the university into a powerhouse of market economics.[11] His most successful venture was the Mont Pelerin Society, an international society of economists he launched in 1947. Hayek drew on the same pool of conservative businessmen that Read and Mullendore first targeted with Pamphleteers, shaping an organization that bridged the worlds of commerce and academia.

Rand cast a gimlet eye on Hayek. In a letter to Rose Wilder Lane, a libertarian book reviewer, she called him "pure poison" and "an example of our most pernicious enemy." The problem was that Hayek was considered conservative, yet acknowledged there could be an important role for government-sponsored health care, unemployment insurance, and a minimum wage. "Here is where the whole case is given away," Rand noted in her copy of *The Road to Serfdom*. Addressing Lane, she compared him to Communist "middle of the roaders" who were most effective as propagandists because they were not seen as Communists.[12]

Rand's reaction to Hayek illuminates an important difference between her libertarianism and the classical liberal tradition that Hayek represented. Although the two terms are sometimes used interchangeably, classical liberals generally have a more capacious concept of the minimal state than do libertarians. Socialistic central planning and state ownership of economic enterprises overstep the line of permissible action, but up to that point classical liberals can be comfortable with a range of state action. Hayek himself remained a controversial figure on the right precisely because even his admirers thought he went too far in accepting an active government. In this respect Rand's critique of Hayek was not unique, but it fixed her on the far right of the libertarian spectrum.[13]

The rest of Rand's attack on Hayek was distinctive. "The man is an ass, with no conception of a free society at all," she scribbled in the margin of his best-seller. She assaulted Hayek on multiple fronts. She reacted angrily whenever he discussed how competition or societies might be guided or planned, or when he spoke favorably of any government action. She was unwilling to admit he had a point: "When and how did governments have 'powers for good?'" Some of her comments echoed the same disillusionment she felt with the fatalistic libertarians of the Willkie campaign, who underappreciated man's capacity for creation and growth. When Hayek spoke about the needs of different people competing for available resources Rand retorted, "They don't compete for the available resources—they create the resources. Here's the socialist thinking again." Hayek didn't truly understand either competition or capitalism, she concluded.[14]

Rand also objected to Hayek's definition of individualism, which she felt lacked moral grounding. Using wording Rand herself favored, Hayek defined individualism as "respect for the individual man *qua* man" and rooted it in Christianity, classical antiquity, and the Renaissance. However, he next referred to an individual's own sphere, "however narrowly that may be circumscribed." This qualification, like his willingness to tolerate limited government programs, outraged Rand. To her it was proof of why individualism had failed as a political ideology: "It had no real base, no moral base. This is why *my* book is needed." Hayek would have been surprised at Rand's contention that his individualism had no moral base. His work was motivated by a deep sense of spiritual crisis, and for an organization of economists the Mont Pelerin Society was unusually sensitive to questions of morality. Hayek originally wanted to name his group the Acton-Tocqueville Society, in reference to two great Catholic thinkers.[15]

But Rand and Hayek had very different understandings of what was moral. In *The Road to Serfdom* Hayek criticized people of goodwill and their cherished ideals, insisting that the West examine the ethical assumptions that underlay its descent into barbarism. As Rand detected, this was only a surface critique of altruism. Hayek also believed that a revival of traditional morals would save the West, and he was receptive to Christian values (although cagey about his personal religious beliefs). By contrast, she believed it was altruism itself that had brought Europe to the brink of destruction. At the end of Hayek's second chapter Rand summarized her thoughts: "Nineteenth Century Liberalism made the mistake of associating liberty, rights of man etc. with the ideas of 'fighting for the people,' 'for the downtrodden,' 'for the poor,' etc. They made it an altruistic movement. But altruism is collectivism. That is why collectivism took the liberals over."[16] The solution, then, was to shift the principles of nineteenth-century liberalism onto different ethical grounds that avoided altruism. Rand had a ready candidate at hand: her own system of selfishness that she had articulated in *The Fountainhead*.

Rand looked more favorably on Ludwig von Mises, Hayek's mentor, whose works she read during this time. As she explained to Leonard Read, Mises made mistakes when it came to morality, going "into thin air, into contradictions, into nonsense" whenever he discussed ethics. But at least he was "for the most part unimpeachable" on economics. Unlike Hayek, Mises was unwilling to consider political compromises that restricted the free market. Like Rand, he considered capitalism an absolute, and for that Rand was willing to forgive his failure to understand and reject altruism.[17]

Rand intended to make known her differences with Hayek and Mises in a short nonfiction work titled "The Moral Basis of Individualism." She proposed the project to Bobbs-Merrill as a booklet that would double as promotional material for *The Fountainhead*, but her ambitions for the project quickly grew. In her first notes she resurrected several concepts from her 1941 "Manifesto of Individualism," including Active Man and Passive Man. As her title indicated, however, there were significant differences between the two works. Where the "Manifesto" had skirted morality in favor of emphasizing the dangers of totalitarianism, now Rand wanted to make the case against altruism, which she called "spiritual cannibalism." She emphasized that her readers could choose from two alternatives: "Independence of man from men is the Life Principle. Dependence of man upon men is the Death Principle."[18] This was the dilemma she had brought to life through Howard Roark and Peter Keating. The challenge now was to explain it in simple terms linking her discussion to a defense of the capitalist system.

As it turned out, writing "The Moral Basis of Individualism" was much harder than Rand had anticipated. Nor did *The Fountainhead* need much help. Like most publishers, Bobbs-Merrill had a strict paper quota due to the war, and it was unable to keep up with demand for Rand's enormous novel until it subcontracted distribution of the book to Blakiston, a small press with a large paper quota. Blakiston released its own series of advertisements stressing the book's themes that finally satisfied Rand. In 1945 alone *The Fountainhead* sold 100,000 copies and finally cracked the New York best-seller lists, a milestone Rand had long anticipated. Both were notable feats for a book released two years earlier, and Rand capped off the year by approving a syndicated comic book version of the novel that appeared in newspapers nationwide. With each piece of good news her motivation to write a new book for publicity's sake dwindled.

Moreover, she was distracted by the idea for a new novel. As with *The Fountainhead,* inspiration had come all at once. In New York Rand and Isabel Paterson had been chatting about current events and the need for Rand to spread her ideas. Rand was indignant at the idea that she was obligated to write for anyone. Perhaps thinking of the new labor militancy that was sweeping the country, she asked Paterson, "What if I went on strike?" From there a story unfolded instantly in her mind. What if the all creators in the world went on strike, much like her father had in Russia? What would happen next? It was a refinement of the conflict she had dramatized through Dominique. Rand galloped ahead with this new idea, once alert to it seeing the concept of the strike everywhere.[19]

Her screenwriting job, however, permitted Rand little time to pursue either project. She was the first writer Hal Wallis had hired, and he was eager to make immediate use of her talents. Because Rand lived so far from Hollywood and gas rationing was still in effect, Wallis allowed her to work from home, coming in only when needed for story conferences. He put her to work rewriting properties he already owned, and her first two assignments, *Love Letters* and *You Came Along,* were both released as successful films in 1945. Next Wallis asked her to develop ideas for a movie based on the atomic bomb. Rand began a careful investigation of the Los Alamos project, even securing an extensive audience with the atomic scientist J. Robert Oppenheimer, head of the Manhattan Project. The film was never produced, but Rand's encounter with Oppenheimer provided fuel for a character in her developing novel, the scientist Robert Stadler.

While Rand busied herself with writing and networking, Frank thrived in California. The purchase of the Chatsworth property had been his decision, for Rand was unconcerned with where they lived. After carefully researching the local market, Frank determined that the outskirts of Los Angeles would boom in the postwar years once the price of gas declined. The distant ranch would appreciate sharply in value, he correctly gambled. Previously home to the director Joseph von Sternberg and the actress Marlene Dietrich, the house was extraordinary by any measure. Rand's office was on the ground floor, with glass doors that opened to a private patio. The master bedroom was set apart on the upstairs floor. Adjoining it was a mirrored bathroom and a roof pool that Frank filled with exotic fish. The open two-story living room was an arresting space, painted brilliant blue and dominated by a towering philodendron tree with leaves that Frank meticulously polished. Birds flew in and out of the house, and outside was a spacious patio that could hold two hundred people. The house was encircled by a goldfish-filled moat, lined by Japanese hyacinths. "Elemental in form, dynamic in color…designed for sun, steel and sky," enthused *House and Garden* in a four-page spread about the property that prominently featured Ayn and Frank.[20]

The house meant far more to Frank than an investment. Reinventing himself as a gentleman farmer, he grew lush gardens on their land and raised a flock of peacocks. In true individualist fashion the birds were not shut up in cages but flew shrieking about the property. Frank's agricultural dabbling soon revealed a true talent for horticulture. The fields filled with bamboo, chestnuts, pomegranate trees, and blackberry bushes. In a greenhouse he bred delphiniums and gladiolas and over the years developed two new hybrids, one called Lipstick and another called Halloween. He supervised a small staff of Japanese gardeners and in the high season opened a roadside vegetable stand to sell excess produce. After one of his employees taught him flower arranging he began selling gladiolas to Los Angeles hotels.[21] No longer living in Rand's shadow, Frank's talents drew admiration from his neighbors and customers.

Within the household, however, Frank continued to carefully defer to Ayn. Deep in concentration, she was often shocked to discover that he had silently glided into the house to tend the flowers or deliver the latest crop. At her request he agreed to wear a small bell on his shoe so she could hear him come and go. The rhythm of daily life revolved around her writing. She worked in the downstairs study with her door firmly shut and instructions to be left alone. A few days a week a secretary came in and took dictation. The house was large enough to accommodate live-in servants, typically a couple who divided household and outdoor tasks between them. Lunch was served on a regular schedule, but all understood they were not to speak to Ayn unless spoken to. If she was lost in thought the meal would be a silent affair. Dinner was more formal, with servants delivering a hot meal to the couple when summoned.[22]

Despite his new independence Frank remained an attentive and much needed consort for Rand. She did not drive, so he chauffeured her into Hollywood whenever business called. More important was his role as peacekeeper and social mediator. The O'Connors invited friends to their home on a regular basis. When the conversations stretched all night Frank retired midway through the evening, and when Rand hosted the Hollywood conservatives he remained on the sidelines, a gracious yet opinion-free host. But when social occasions became fraught or tense, Frank stepped in to manage the situation. One memorable afternoon Rosalie Wilson was visiting with her mother, Millie. As a child Rosalie had briefly lived with the O'Connors in Hollywood while her parents were divorcing. During a spirited political discussion Millie shocked the others by opining, "I don't think much of Hitler, but I'll have to agree with him he should have incinerated all those Jews." Rosalie remembered a silence that stretched to eternity. Then Rand said in a beautifully modulated tone, "Well, Millie, I guess you've never known, but I am Jewish." The silence continued as Frank walked the Wilsons to their car. Leaning through the window with tears on his face he squeezed Rosalie's shoulder one last time.[23]

Sometimes Frank was able to salvage relationships on the brink. Ruth Beebe Hill, a new acquaintance of the O'Connors, incurred Rand's wrath by mentioning that she had memorized Plato's *Republic* as part of a stage act. Hill did not know that Rand considered Plato the godfather of Communism (an opinion also held by Isabel Paterson). She could tell that she had said something wrong, though, for "the room became cold air, frigid, as if the room had frozen." Frank quickly came to Hill's rescue. He scooped her up off the floor where she had been sitting and resettled her in an armchair with a blanket tucked around her. "Ruth was just thinking back to college days, when she probably was required to memorize these different things," he told Ayn. "How about some coffee?" To Hill the incident was both a warning of Rand's capricious temperament and an important illumination of the O'Connor marriage. Although he seemed a passive adjunct to his more vibrant wife, Hill saw Frank as Ayn's rock, "the anchor to windward." Frank's cool collection was a vital counterbalance to Rand's uneven moods and fiery temperament.[24]

To others Rand seemed to be chafing at the bonds of marriage. Jack Bungay, an assistant to Hal Wallis, saw a sensuality in Rand that seemed barely contained. "There was a lot of sex in her face," he remembered, "beautiful eyes, black hair and very beautiful lips, very prominent lips, a lovely face, not especially big, but a beautiful smile." Although she was never fully comfortable with her looks, Rand had learned how to present herself to best advantage. The Benzedrine helped her shed excess weight, and she began wearing platform heels that boosted her height. She stepped out in dramatic clothing by Adrian, a designer favored by Hollywood stars. Rand enjoyed a close, flirtatious rapport with her boss Wallis, teasing and joking with him as they reviewed her scripts. Bungay, who spent a few months lodging with the O'Connors when he was between apartments, observed her fondness for a host of younger men who sought her counsel. Most prominent among these was Albert Mannheimer, an aspiring screenwriter whom Bungay believed to be Rand's heir after Frank.[25]

Troubled and intense, Mannheimer was a frequent visitor to the O'Connor household. He was reeling from the dramatic suicide of a former girlfriend, who killed herself in his apartment after a heated quarrel. Overcome by guilt at her death, Mannheimer clung to Rand's insistence that he bore no fault. The two grew noticeably close. She nicknamed him "Fuzzy" and he brought her extravagant gifts, including an enormous bottle of Chanel perfume. At times Mannheimer's feelings for her grew intense. "I love you Ayn, in a way I have never before loved anyone and never shall again," he told her in an impromptu letter written after one of their visits. He groped for images to describe their relationship, comparing her to the open country, the way a scientist feels "having discovered something new; or a writer loves the feeling of having created a beautiful phrase." It was impossible to feel depressed around her, he wrote, calling her "the ultimate in human beings I have known." Although she did not discourage such outpourings, Rand's letters to him were full of advice rather than suppressed passion. The two eventually drifted apart in the early 1950s.[26]

Other young men orbited around Rand during this time, including Thaddeus Ashby, a Harvard dropout and later an editor at the libertarian magazine *Faith and Freedom*. Like Mannheimer, Ashby enjoyed Rand's favor for several months. She offered him advice about his writing career, argued with him in long philosophical conversations, and offered him lodging at the ranch on several occasions. Eventually the O'Connors discovered that Ashby had fabricated details of his past and they cut him off. Although his friendship with Rand was platonic, he felt a distinct current of sexuality running beneath the surface of their interactions. Another young man who did editorial work for Rand, Evan Wright, reported a similar dynamic.[27]

Frank was both indispensable to Rand's happiness and unable to satisfy her completely. His unwillingness to engage her intellectually made their relationship possible, for she would never have tolerated dissent from her husband. Yet Frank's distaste for dispute and argument left a void that Rand sought to fill with others. Later she would confess to friends that during their years in California she had considered divorce. Frank, on the other hand, had found a comfortable accommodation with their differences. When Rand proclaimed to friends that Frank was the power behind the throne, he joked back, "Sometimes I think I am the throne, the way I get sat on."[28] Frank was well aware of the trade-offs he had made. Rand's wealth enabled him to work the land with little worry about finances. In return he did whatever was needed to keep her happy. On the surface he was dependent on her. But like Ruth Hill, Frank understood that Ayn needed him too.

As much as Rand despised California, these were intellectually rich years for her. When her first real break from screenwriting came in June 1945 she leapt at the opportunity to finally pursue her own intellectual interests. Early in the year she had mapped out her first notes for "The Strike," later to become *Atlas Shrugged*, but now her interest returned to nonfiction.[29] On the day of her last story conference with Wallis she lingered in Hollywood to buy five evening gowns and an enormous volume of Aristotle. The new purchase reflected her expanding plans for "The Moral Basis of Individualism." As she told Paterson, she had "realized the book must be much, much more than merely a restatement of my theme in *The Fountainhead*. It has to start further back—with the first axioms of existence." She confessed to Paterson that the effort was much harder than she had anticipated.[30]

Rand's turn to Aristotle reflected her sense that individualism as a political philosophy needed to be reconstituted from the ground up. The rise of Communism and fascism had convinced her that nineteenth-century liberalism, as she noted in the margins of *The Road to Serfdom,* "had failed." This sense that established ideologies were bankrupt was widely shared. Indeed the rise of totalitarianism had triggered a crisis in liberal political theory, for it called into question long held assumptions about human progress and rationality. As tensions between the United States and Russia grew, intellectuals across the political spectrum sought foundations that could bolster and support American democracy in its battle with Soviet Communism. The sudden popularity of the Protestant theologian Reinhold Niebuhr, who emphasized the innate sinfulness of mankind, reflected the urgent search for meaning that characterized the postwar era. Others looked to Aristotle, who appealed to many religious as well as secular thinkers. Catholics had long touted the wisdom of Thomist philosophy, proposing it as an alternative to relativism and naturalism, which they blamed for the collapse of the West. They had a high-profile convert in University of Chicago President Robert Hutchins, who a decade earlier had discovered in Aristotle a resource for the development of sound political ideas.[31] Rand too would embrace ancient philosophy as the antidote to modern political ills.

As she began to educate herself about philosophy Rand turned to Paterson for a durable frame of reference. In New York Paterson had ranted against Kant, Hegel, and Marx, quoting instead Aristotle and the dictum "A is A."[32] Now, as she read Aristotle and Plato, Rand told Paterson, "I think of you all the time—of what you used to say about them," and her first notes for the project were filled with allusions to Paterson's ideas and opinions. Both Paterson and Rand rejected the idea that man, like an animal, was controlled by instincts and subconscious drives. Instead they envisioned human nature as rational, voluntary, and defined by free will. "Man does not act to its kind by the pure instinct of species, as other animals generally do," Paterson wrote in one of her letters to Rand. She also asserted that any philosophical defense of liberty must be grounded in man's life. Speaking of others who had written on liberty she commented, "The issue is usually confused by a failure or refusal to recognize that one must begin with the simple fact of physical existence and the necessary conditions of physical existence on this earth."[33] As she returned to nonfiction Rand similarly criticized the idea of instincts and argued that morality must, above all, be practical.

Rand's writing now reflected a new emphasis on rationality, drawn from her reading of Aristotle. As a first step she critiqued her earlier notes and realized that they must be reorganized to give more thorough coverage to reason as the determining faculty of man. The idea that reason was the most important quality of humanity, indeed the very definition of human, had been a subtheme of her first drafts. Now she wanted to bring it front and center as the first major part of her discussion. She continued to sample from her earlier material, with an important change. Where the "Manifesto of Individualism" had celebrated the creative faculty as the province of individual men, something that could not be borrowed, stolen, or coerced, now Rand made the same points about the rational faculty. By mid-July she had brought her ideas about ethics, individualism, and rationality together: "The moral faculty is *not* something independent of the rational faculty, but directly connected with it *and proceeding from it.*" In turn the moral faculty must be exercised "according to the rules its nature demands, independently."[34] By August she had written a separate piece titled "The Rational Faculty."

Rand's newfound emphasis on reason stirred dormant tendencies in her thought. In July she identified "another hole in altruism." If goods were to be distributed equally in a collectivist society, it would have to be determined if everyone produced equally or if "men produce unequally." If the latter was true, then collectivism was based on exploitation of the more productive, "and this is one of the basic reasons why people advocate altruism and collectivism—the motive of the parasite."[35] Rand tried to resist the implications of this conclusion and return to the egalitarianism of *The Fountainhead*. "The moral man is not necessarily the most intelligent, but the one who independently exercises such intelligence as he has," she argued. To a hypothetical questioner who wondered what to make of his mediocre talents, Rand encouraged, "All men are free and equal, regardless of natural gifts." Still, the drift of her thought was tending back to the elitism of the early libertarians. At times old and new mingled together, as when she wondered, if perhaps, "the rational faculty is the dominant characteristic of the better species, the Superman."[36]

The way Rand integrated reason into her earlier ideas demonstrated her strong drive for consistency. She labored to define reason as inextricably linked to individuality, asserting, "The rational faculty is an attribute of the individual." Men could share the result of their thinking but not the process of thought itself, she argued. And since man's survival depended on his own thought, individuals must be left free. Rationality thus connected to laissez-faire capitalism, the only economic system that sought to maximize individual freedom.

Placing rationality at the heart of her philosophy also began to shift the grounding of Rand's ethics. In her early work independence had been the basic criterion of value. Now she wrote, "All the actions based on, proceeding from, in accordance with man's nature as a rational being are good. All the actions that contradict it are evil." Rand was feeling her way toward a connection she would make explicit in later years, the equation of the moral and the rational. "In other words," she wrote, "the intelligent man is the moral man if he acts as an intelligent man, i.e., in accordance with the nature of his rational faculty." Even selfishness, once her primary standard of morality, was beginning to recede behind rationality.[37]

After several months of intense work on "The Moral Basis of Individualism" Ayn and Frank made their first trip back to New York. She was eager to visit Paterson and immerse herself once more in the world of East Coast libertarianism. Rand's pilgrimage was part of a steady stream of traffic between conservative nodes on the East and West Coasts. Rand had finally met Henry Hazlitt, the husband of her former Paramount supervisor, Frances Hazlitt, when he paid a visit to California. Now that she was in New York Henry introduced her to Ludwig von Mises, who had recently arrived in the United States. Mises, a gentleman of the old school who did not expect women to be intellectuals, was particularly impressed by Rand's interest in economics. He considered *The Fountainhead* an important contribution to their cause, telling Henry Hazlitt she was the most courageous man in America."[38] Unfazed by Mises's sexism, Rand delighted in the compliment.

On their way back from New York Rand fulfilled a long held dream and paid a visit to Frank Lloyd Wright's compound Taliesin in

Wisconsin. Wright's changed attitude toward Rand had been among the sweetest fruits of *The Fountainhead*. It would have been impossible for him to ignore the novel, for many readers drew an immediate parallel between Roark and Wright. Privately Wright criticized the book, but in 1944 he sent Rand a complimentary letter, telling her, "Your thesis is *the* great one." Rand was thrilled and once again pushed for a meeting, telling Wright she wished to commission a house from him. She had not selected a site, but anticipating a move back to the East Coast told him it would be built in Connecticut. Once at Taliesin she was disappointed to observe the "feudal" atmosphere of the estate, where Wright's protégés shamelessly copied the master. The visit severely dimmed her admiration for Wright. From then on she would classify him as a Howard Roark professionally, but a Peter Keating personally. Her own Wright house remained unbuilt. Although she loved the design, Wright's exorbitant fee was far beyond even her substantial means.[39]

Back in California, as she resumed work for Wallis, Rand closely followed political developments on the right. Her hopes for political change rested almost entirely on Leonard Read, who moved to New York in 1946 and shortly thereafter started the Foundation for Economic Education (FEE). The most successful libertarian organization of the postwar years, FEE quickly replaced the scattershot efforts of myriad small anti–New Deal organizations. It was well funded, courtesy of corporate supporters including Chrysler, General Motors, Monsanto, Montgomery Ward, and U.S. Steel, and received its single largest donation from the Volker Fund. The Foundation got off to a quick start primarily through the charms of Read. Armed with a formidable Rolodex and an affable personality, Read inspired confidence in business donors and intellectuals alike. Even the dyspeptic Paterson pronounced him "good stuff."[40] He quickly ensconced the new organization in a rambling Westchester County mansion, a short trip from New York. From these headquarters FEE sponsored seminars with libertarian professors and commissioned writing on the free market ideal.

During FEE's founding year Read assiduously courted Rand. Her work for Pamphleteers had been a success, and Read had every expectation their collaboration could continue through FEE. In 1946 he described moving into FEE's new headquarters and deliberating on proper quotations to be hung on the wall: "Then, I got to thinking what

I should put up over the fireplace in my own office. So I came home, got into my slippers, provided myself with a good quantity of martini and was reading Roark's speech for the most suitable quotation." On another occasion he thanked Rand for praise she had given him, noting, "Your comments about my speech please me to no end. Getting that kind of approval from you is what I call 'passing muster.'" Read tapped Rand to serve as FEE's "ghost," asking her to read material he intended to publish to make sure it was ideologically coherent.[41] Rand was delighted with the chance to influence the new organization.

From the start she pushed Read to assume a stance that mirrored her own. She was particularly insistent that Read promote her moral views. He must explain that profit and individual gain were "the capitalist's real and proper motive" and ought to be defended as such. Otherwise, if the very motive of capitalism was "declared to be immoral, the whole system becomes immoral, and the motor of the system stops dead."[42] It was the same criticism she had made of Hayek: a partial case for the free market was worse than no argument at all. Read was naturally more cautious. Like Rand he believed that government functions such as rent control, public education, the Interstate Commerce Commission, military training, and the Post Office should all be done by "voluntary action." But he told her, "I had luncheon last week with the chief executive of the country's largest utility holding Corp. and a financial editor of the Journal American. They are regarded as reactionaries, yet each of these gents, while being [against] price controls generally, suffered rent control. This is typical." With an eye to public perception, Read had chosen the FEE's rather bland name rather than use the inflammatory word "individualism," as Rand had urged.[43] Although Rand was generally pleased with Read's efforts, she could see nothing but apostasy where others saw necessary compromises with political and economic realities. Despite their early productive collaboration, significant differences underlay Rand's and Read's approach to political activism.

Trouble came on the occasion of FEE's inaugural booklet, *Roofs or Ceilings?*, authored by Milton Friedman and George Stigler, then young economists at the University of Minnesota. Like her reaction to Hayek, Rand's reaction to Friedman is illuminating for the differences it highlights between her and another famous libertarian. *Roofs or Ceilings?* was written as Friedman, then a new faculty member at Minnesota, was moving away from a position he characterized as "thoroughly Keynesian" to his later libertarianism. Friedman had long opposed rent control for its inefficiencies. He and Stigler argued that by interfering with the free working of the market, rent control removed incentives to create more housing stock, improve existing units, or share housing. Therefore it created, rather than alleviated, the housing shortage. They did not question the underlying motivation for rent control, even identifying themselves as people "who would like even more equality than there is at present."[44] The problem with rent control was simply that it did not achieve its stated policy objectives.

This dispassionate tone infuriated Rand, who saw *Roofs or Ceilings?* through the lenses of her experience in Communist Russia. Friedman and Stigler's use of the word "rationing" particularly disturbed her. She did not know such usage was standard in economics, instead flashing back to her days of near starvation in Petrograd. "Do you really think that calling the free pricing system a 'rationing' system is merely confusing and innocuous?" she asked in an angry letter to Mullendore, a FEE trustee. She believed the authors were trying to make the word "respectable" and thus convince Americans to accept permanent and total rationing. Focusing entirely on the hidden implications of the pamphlet, Rand saw the authors' overt argument against rent control as "mere window dressing, weak, ineffectual, inconclusive and unconvincing."

Rand believed that Friedman and Stigler were insincere in their argument against rent control because they failed to invoke any moral principles to support their case. And when they did mention morality, it was to speak favorably of equality and humanitarianism. She fumed to Mullendore, "Not one word about the inalienable right of landlords and property owners…not one word about any kind of principles. Just *expediency*…and humanitarian…concern for those who can find no houses."[45] In addition to her eight-page letter to Mullendore, replete with exclamation points and capitalized sentences, Rand sent a short note to Read. She called the pamphlet "the most pernicious thing ever issued by an avowedly conservative organization" and told him she could have no further connection with FEE. To Rose Wilder Lane she described the incident as "a crushing disappointment," adding, "It is awfully hard to see a last hope go."[46]

The irony was that Read too disliked the pamphlet. Prior to publication he and the authors had tussled over several passages. The authors' implicit praise of equality as a social good was a particular sore spot. When Friedman and Stigler refused to alter their text, Read inserted a critical footnote, stating, "Even from the standpoint of those who put equality above justice and liberty, rent controls are the height of folly." His willingness to publish a pamphlet he disliked indicated the paucity of libertarian intellectual resources at the time. That two economists with legitimate academic positions would take a public stand against rent control was enough to ensure FEE's support. Still, the whole episode was problematic. In addition to incurring Rand's wrath the pamphlet alienated Friedman and Stigler, who were deeply offended by Read's unauthorized footnote. For many years they refused any collaboration with FEE or Read, until finally reconciling through their mutual connection to the Mont Pelerin Society. For her part, Rand felt betrayed by Read's failure to understand the principles at stake in their work and wounded by his disregard for their "ghost" agreement.[47]

Only weeks later Read added insult to injury when he sent Rand a sheaf of anonymous comments on her short article, "Textbook of Americanism." Rand had written the piece for *The Vigil*, the official publication of the Motion Picture Alliance for the Preservation of American Ideals, the Hollywood anti-Communist group that had recruited her to its board. "Textbook" was a very brief piece that included her first published discussion of rights. Written in the style of a catechism, the piece defined a right as "the sanction of independent action." Rand offered a secular defense of natural rights, which were "granted to man by the fact of his birth as a man—not by an act of society." Paramount in the "Textbook" was the noninitiation principle, the idea that "no man has the right to initiate the use of physical force against another man" (she capitalized the entire phrase for emphasis).[48] The noninitiation principle, sometimes called the nonaggression principle, can be traced to thinkers as varied as Thomas Aquinas, John Locke, and Herbert Spencer. Placing it at the center of her natural rights theory, Rand breathed new life into an old idea.

At Rand's urging, Read shared the "Textbook of Americanism" with the FEE staff and selected donors, all "men high in the country's business and academic life." The principle of noninitiation in particular appealed viscerally to Read. But most FEE friends were less enthusiastic. Rand had not spelled out or defended her basic premises, and much of what she wrote struck readers as pure assertion. "Her statement that these rights are granted to man by the fact of birth as a man not by an act of society, is illogical jargon," wrote one, advising, "If Miss Rand is to get anywhere she must free herself from theological implications." Another respondent was "favorably impressed by the goals which she seeks to attain, but the line of logic which she uses seems to me to be very weak." Such readers thought Rand left a critical question unanswered: *Why* did "no man have the right to initiate physical force"? Out of thirteen readers, only four recommended supporting the work in its present form.[49]

Rand, who saw herself as helping the unenlightened at FEE, was entirely unprepared for this criticism. She was livid, telling Read, his actions were "a most serious reflection on my personal integrity and a most serious damage to my professional reputation." She was particularly angered that the FEE readers evaluated her work as if she had requested financial backing. She informed Read, "I do not submit books for approval on whether I should write them—and my professional standing does not permit me to be thought of as an author who seeks a foundation's support for a writing project." Not only had Read disregarded her role as ghost, but now he had downgraded her from instructor to pupil and "smeared" her reputation. Rand demanded an apology and the names of the people who had written the comments on her work. Read refused both.[50] The breach would never heal.

Rand's break with Read drew her closer to Rose Wilder Lane, whom she had heard about through Isabel Paterson. The two established a correspondence shortly after Rand moved to California, but had never met. A magazine writer with a vaguely socialist background, Lane was the daughter of the famous children's author Laura Ingalls Wilder. Although she took no public credit, Lane was essentially a coauthor of the best-selling *Little House on the Prairie* series. She wove her libertarianism delicately through the nostalgic books, filling her fictional Fourth of July orations with musings on freedom and limited government and excising from her mother's past examples of state charity.[51] In 1943 she published *The Discovery of Freedom*, a historically grounded defense of individualism.

Like Paterson and Rand, Lane took a hard line on compromise of any type. As one friend remembered, "Rose used to go and talk about dead rats, that you'd bake a gorgeous, succulent cherry pie and cut into it and there in the middle of it would be a dead rat. She thought that Robert Taft supporting federal aid to education was such a dead rat."[52] Accordingly, Lane was sympathetic to Rand's anger. She told Rand that the problem with Read was simple: "He simply does not possess a mind that grasps abstract principle; he has no constant standard of measurement." Lane listed his many intellectual deficiencies but defended him against any challenge of malice. Read had also ignored advice that both she and Isabel Paterson had offered, she told Rand, although it was certainly "valid ground for the most extreme indignation" that he had reneged on their ghost agreement.[53] Grateful for her understanding, Rand sent Lane a copy of the censorious letter she had mailed to Mullendore.

In contrast to Paterson and Rand, who thrived on face-to-face contact, Lane was a homebody who exerted her influence through a network of well-placed correspondents. She was a guru figure to Jasper Crane, a wealthy DuPont executive who funded many libertarian causes, and exchanged dense philosophical letters with Frank Meyer, later an influential *National Review* editor. For many years Lane was employed by the Volker Fund to assess the ideological fitness of potential applicants. After the death of Albert Jay Nock she assumed the editorship of the National Economic Council's *Review of Books,* a slim publication sent mostly to corporate subscribers. Within the world of libertarianism Lane was a force to be reckoned with. In fact she played the kind of role Rand coveted: tablet keeper and advisor, sought after for her judgment and council.

Rand was keenly aware that Lane's book reviews could affect her reputation. In late 1945 she initiated their correspondence, writing to thank Lane for a favorable mention of *The Fountainhead* in the *NEC Review of Books.* Rand's first letter was polite and even flattering. She acknowledged Lane as an intellectual equal, telling her, "[I]t is such a rare treat to read intelligent book reviewing for a change." The next year Rand sent Lane her "Textbook of Americanism" and in a letter responded favorably to some of the corrections Lane suggested.[54]

As she had with Paterson, Rand tested out her developing theories on Lane, particularly her definition of rights. Lane was interested in Rand's theory of natural rights because she was "not certain, myself, of the basis of the definition of rights. Is a 'right' a thing, a fact, existing unalterably in the essential nature of the four dimensional world?" If rights were not a fact akin to an electron, then they must be moral or spiritual, she wrote. But then how could they survive in the physical world, given that "anyone can kill anyone else quite easily"? What she sought was a basis for rights "that doesn't have in it what seems to me the fallacy of dualism." Rand's theory of rights, or at least the brief exposition she had read in "Textbook" and Rand's earlier letters, did not seem to solve the problem. On the other hand, Lane was primarily enjoying the exploration of ideas rather than being set on finding a solution. As she admitted, "I'm only a fumbler, trying to think."[55] Rand's ideas were for her provocative, but not complete. There were enough areas of agreement between the two, however, to keep the correspondence productive. In the early stages it was enough that both women agreed individual rights must be clearly and explicitly defended.

Before long, more serious disagreements emerged as Rand's individualism clashed with Lane's holistic view of the world. Commenting on one of Lane's book reviews, Rand criticized Lane's invocation of "love thy neighbor as thyself," and her discussion of mutual effort. She warned Lane that both could be construed as supporting collectivism. This touched off a lengthy discussion about individualism, collectivism, and cooperation. Lane felt it would be "natural human action" to help others, citing the example of a neighbor's house catching fire. She asked Rand, "isn't there a vital distinction between cooperation and collectivism? It seems to me that the essential basis of cooperation is individualism....I think that it is literally impossible for one person on this planet to survive."[56] In her reply Rand emphasized that although human beings might choose to help one another, they should never be obligated to do so, and certainly they should never help another person to their own detriment. To argue that human beings should help others in need was "the base of the New Deal pattern of declaring one emergency after another." She tore apart Lane's logic, posing hypothetical situations in which it would be moral to not help a neighbor (if one's own house was on fire, for example). Aside from logic, Rand's response to Lane drew upon her own stark understanding of the world. She told Lane, "each man's fate is essentially his own."[57]

Lane was unconvinced. Calmly she told Rand, "you have perhaps shown me that I am a collectivist." But she simply couldn't believe that all human action should be or was motivated by self-interest. If that was the case, Lane asked, why did she herself oppose Social Security? Lane opposed Social Security because she thought it was bad for society as a whole, "which I can't deny is a do-good purpose." But opposing Social Security on "do-good" rather than self-interested grounds was not, Lane thought, inappropriate. Lane also rejected Rand's atomistic view of the world, recalling her frontier childhood to illustrate human interdependence. She described a typhoid epidemic in her small prairie town: "People 'helped each other out,' that was all....It was just what people did, of course. So far as there was any idea in it at all, it was that when you were sick, if you ever were, the others would take care of you. It was 'common neighborliness.'...The abnormal, that I would have thought about, would have been its not being there." She concluded, "There IS a sense of 'owing' in it, of mutuality, mutual obligation of persons to persons as persons."[58] Lane saw charity arising naturally from human societies. What bothered her was the coercion involved in government programs like Social Security, not the underlying moral principles they reflected. But it was just these underlying moral principles that Rand opposed.

As she wrote to Lane, Rand groped toward an explanation of how and why they differed. Both women agreed they were operating from different assumptions. Rand told her, "that is why I intend to write a book someday, stating my case from basic premises on."[59] Through their letters it became clear that Rand and Lane did not share the same understanding of human nature on either an individual or a social level. But these differences lay under the surface, for Rand had not yet explicitly formulated her moral and political philosophy. For instance, Rand told Lane, "now of course I don't believe that there is *any* 'natural' or instinctive human action. (I won't try to state my reasons here—that would have to be a treatise on the nature of man.)" This was a belief that Paterson shared but Lane did not. Presented without benefit of the treatise she hoped someday to write, Rand's ideas came across to Lane as assertions of dubious validity. Even Rand recognized this, acknowledging that her letters to Lane were a poor vehicle for communicating her complete philosophy. She asked Lane, "Do you know what I've written to you here? It's the theme of my next novel. This is only a brief, partial statement—the subject is extremely complex. If I haven't stated it clearly enough—you'll see me do better when I present it completely in the novel."[60]

As Rand's letter indicated, she had decided to forgo "The Moral Basis of Individualism" and turned instead to the book that would become *Atlas Shrugged*. The transition point came in the spring of 1946, when Rand clashed with Wallis over his decision to sell her atom bomb project to another studio. Frustrated that all her work had gone for naught, Rand convinced Wallis to give her an entire year off to get started on her novel. In long walks around the ranch property she began plotting the book's structure and imagining the major characters. By August she had a complete outline. In September she began writing.

Rand's creation of an imaginary world was interrupted by unhappy news from the country she had left behind. For eight years, since the Rosenbaums' American visa was denied, Rand had not communicated with her family. With the end of the war she hoped to reestablish contact, and asked a friend in New York to help her send two packages of food and supplies to her sisters in Leningrad. No sooner had Rand mailed off her request than she received a letter from Marie Strachnov, a close family friend and Rand's first English teacher. Trapped in a displaced persons camp in Austria, Strachnov had no news of Natasha or Nora, but reported that Rand's parents had died years before, of natural causes. Sorrowfully Rand told her, "you are now my only link to the past." She was adamant that Strachnov come to America, assuring her she would pay all costs and support her upon arrival. When Strachnov did finally make it to California, in large part due to Rand's indefatigable efforts on her behalf, she lodged with the O'Connors for nearly a year.[61]

The news from Russia fortified Rand's anti-Communism. She continued her work for the Motion Picture Alliance for the Preservation of American Ideals, authoring another article for *The Vigil*. This time she avoided political theory and instead concentrated on practical measures Hollywood studios could take to root out Communist influence. Her "Screen Guide for Americans," which would later be reprinted in the conservative magazine *Plain Talk,* nonetheless encapsulated much of her political thinking. In the guide Rand portrayed Hollywood Communists as veritable Ellsworth Tooheys, carefully smuggling "small casual bits of propaganda into innocent stories." Eventually these bits "will act like the drops of water that split a rock if continued long enough. The rock they are trying to split is Americanism."[62] To resist, movie producers and writers must understand that politics flowed from moral premises, Rand wrote. After this assertion, however, she backed away from sweeping statements, keeping most of her suggestions specific and practical. She opposed any formal movie code but listed thirteen ways to keep movies free of Communist undertones. Rand told moviemakers to avoid smearing the free enterprise system, industrialists, wealth, or the profit motive. They should celebrate success and avoid glorifying failure or the common man. Movies should also be careful about using current events or criticizing American political institutions.

Rand's "Screen Guide" caught the eye of a congressional committee, the House Un-American Activities Commission (HUAC), which was investigating Communist penetration of the movie industry. The committee had begun sniffing out Communists in 1938, and its activities picked up steam in the postwar years, eventually resulting in the celebrated confrontation between the former Communist Whittaker Chambers and the accused spy Alger Hiss that riveted the nation. In 1947, one year before the Hiss case broke, HUAC was just starting its first high-profile investigation, a probe into the political associations of famous actors, directors, and screenwriters.

Rand was eager to help. At HUAC's request she arranged her next trip east so that she could stop in Washington to appear as a friendly witness. Unlike most witnesses who were subpoenaed to testify about their past Communist associations, Rand took the stand willingly. After a few perfunctory remarks about her background, she launched into an attack on *Song of Russia*, a syrupy romance filmed at the height of America's wartime alliance with the Soviet Union. Her testimony gained notoriety when she told the committee that the movie was propaganda because it showed too many Russians smiling. "Doesn't anybody smile in Russia anymore?" a congressman queried. "Well, if you ask me literally, pretty much no," Rand responded, drawing laughter from the audience.[63]

What is most striking about the testimony, however, is how slow Rand was to understand that *Song of Russia* was not Communist propaganda, but American propaganda about a wartime ally. When Georgia Representative John Stevens Boyd questioned her about this, Rand seemed confused, asking, "What relation could a lie about Russia have with the war effort?" Later she asserted, "I don't believe the American people should ever be told any lies, publicly or privately....Why weren't the American people told the real reasons and told that Russia is a dictatorship but there are reasons why we should cooperate with them to destroy Hitler and other dictators?"[64] She had a real point to make about honesty in politics, but because she failed to appreciate the wartime context of *Song of Russia*, her testimony did little to support the inquiry into Communist subversion of American movies. Nor was the committee interested in hearing Rand's take on *The Best Years of Our Lives*, declining to ask her to testify a second day.

In retrospect Rand had mixed feelings about her appearance. She worried about the morality of government inquiries into Americans' political beliefs, assuring herself in private notes that the investigation was warranted because the committee was inquiring into the *fact* of Communist Party membership, not the belief in Communist ideals. That fellow travelers or Communist sympathizers would be swept up into the dragnet did not worry her. What bothered her was the ineffectiveness of the whole event, which seemed little more than a charade to get Congress off Hollywood's back. Later Rand became convinced that the hearings had triggered a reverse blacklist against the friendly witnesses. After HUAC's investigation many of her conservative friends, including Albert Mannheimer, had great difficulty finding work in the industry.[65]

Following her appearance in Washington Ayn and Frank continued on to New York, where she had scheduled a full gamut of literary activities. Chief among her goals was research for *Atlas Shrugged*. As the story developed Rand determined that railroads and steel, pillars of the modern industrial economy, would lie at the center of her story. As in *The Fountainhead*, she conducted painstaking research to make her story accurate. Her primary contact was with the New York Central Railroad. She grilled the vice president of operations, took a guided tour of Grand Central and its underground track systems, and visited a construction site in upstate New York. The highlight of her visit was a ride to Albany, where she was permitted to ride in the cab of the train's engine, an occasion that prompted the normally reticent Frank to declare, "You're marvelous!" In an effusive letter to Paterson, Rand described how the engineer even let her drive the train for a brief moment, to the surprise of observers along the track. When she disembarked, Frank continued to marvel, telling her, "You do such exciting things!"[66] In Chicago she had another series of appointments with executives at Kaiser Steel and toured one of the company's giant mills.

Rand's visit to New York also reinvigorated her connection to Paterson, which had seen its share of ups and downs. At first their rich friendship appeared to easily weather Rand's move to California. In New York their relationship was defined by long abstract conversations, often stretching into the early morning. When Rand relocated, they easily translated these conversations onto paper, sending each other lengthy letters and carrying on extended debates about intellectual matters. Paterson updated Rand on the comings and goings of New York libertarians, telling of her meetings with Herbert Hoover and DuPont executive Jasper Crane. The letters were also warm, with Paterson consoling Rand over publishing troubles, advising her on how to relate to the wives of her male friends, and praising her fashion choices. Paterson adopted a motherly role toward Rand. She was particularly concerned about Rand's continued use of Benzedrine to fuel her late-night conversations and lengthy writing days. "Stop taking that Benzedrine, you idiot," she told her. "I don't care what excuse you have—stop it."[67] Still enjoying the new creative capacity the stimulants engendered, Rand brushed off Paterson's hints that Benzedrine could become a dangerous habit.

Before long a chill crept into their letters. Busy with her writing, Rand was unable to maintain the relationship at a level that satisfied Paterson's emotional needs. After a three-month gap in correspondence Paterson felt neglected, telling Rand, "I assume that one speaks to a friend, or writes a letter, spontaneously. It is not a task."[68] Rand's silence hit a particularly sensitive spot for Paterson, who had noticed, "after authors have become successful I hear no more of them. They have many important affairs to attend to."[69] Paterson feared that Rand, like so many other aspiring writers, had simply cultivated her for professional advancement. Rand's affection for Paterson was genuine, but she had trouble soothing her friend's insecurities. It was another seven months, mid-1945, before Rand could reply, confessing, "I have been afraid to write you."[70] She explained in detail her anxiety about writing letters to friends, born of her correspondence with Russian family members, whose letters might be read by government censors; her fears she would be misunderstood; and her busy schedule. Paterson was not placated, telling Rand in response, "A person is not an object or lamp post, to be regarded as always 'there' for your convenience and having no other existence."[71] The rest of her letter was equally tart. Where before she had overflowed with effusive praise for Rand and her work, Paterson now challenged Rand's philosophical assumptions and her grasp of history.

Paterson was particularly harsh on Rand's new venture into philosophy. Responding to Rand's critical comments on the philosophers she had been reading, Paterson mused, "to be fair to them, one must envisage the whole problem of systematic thinking as from scratch." She then told Rand, "the 'frightening kind of rationality' you find in the philosophers is precisely your own kind."[72] Although she had once celebrated their joint achievement in working out "the necessary axioms and deductions of a free society," Paterson now doubted the whole goal of syllogistic reasoning.[73] The real problem was not creating a rational system, but making sure the assumptions that underlay it were correct. And she was not at all clear that Rand would do it right, observing, "in lesser matters, you talk a lot of 'reason,' but frequently don't use it, because you make assumptions that are not valid." She also had a few suggestions to make about Rand's behavior. It struck Paterson as rude that Rand constantly talked about sales of *The Fountainhead* when Paterson's book had failed commercially: "it appears to me that one could be a copper riveted individualist without being a solipsist."[74] Paterson's complaints about Rand and her ideas were a dramatic switch from earlier letters. No doubt her tone was partially inspired by her mood swings, but Rand's failure to carefully tend the relationship had also drawn forth this dyspeptic and angry response.

Rand was scandalized by the letter. She accused Paterson of putting words in her mouth and ignoring what she actually said. She rejected Paterson's comparison of her to other philosophers, insisting, "I have not *adopted* any philosophy. I have created my own. I do not care to be tagged with anyone else's labels." Though rigorously abstract, Rand's discourse was in many ways aggressively anti-intellectual. She was uninterested in placing herself within the broader community of thinkers and cared little about the intersections between different schools of thought. "I see no point in discussing what some fools said in the past and why they said it and what error they made and where they went off the rails," she told Paterson. Rand was also concerned that Paterson had brought up the issue of God, and was immediately suspicious that "you believe that unless I accept God, I will have betrayed the cause of individualism."[75] In response Paterson gave little quarter, sending a second critical missive to her friend. She did not think Rand knew what she was talking about when it came to reason or argumentation: "I suggest that you are confusing logical necessity with an assumed necessity of actually following a logical sequence from a given premise, whether in thought or in words or in action, and also with the fact that an act has its own consequences." And she rejected Rand's claim to originality, telling her, "if you should hold a theory which has already been thought out . . . I will use the word already existent for the thing."[76]

But as it turned out, Rand was right about Paterson and God. Paterson *did* think that belief in God was essential to individualism, arguing, "but if you do start with a statement of atheism, you won't have any basis for human rights." This was the same criticism that Lane and the FEE readers had made. Rand's theory of natural rights was based on fiat, on her stating it must be so. But in a world where rights were constantly challenged by despotic governments and violent crime, a more solid grounding was imperative. Paterson concluded her letter with another snide remark. Rand had written about Thaddeus Ashby, her new "adopted son," whom she characterized as a replica of herself. Paterson was sharp: "I don't know what would be interesting about a 'replica' of oneself. Would your replica write *The Fountainhead* again? It sounds kind of silly to me. However, it's your own business."[77] Intellectual differences, compounded by personal pride, began to snowball as the relationship between the two women deteriorated.

Before reaching the edge both Rand and Paterson pulled back. Rand had not yet responded to the latest blast when she received another letter from Paterson, this one friendly and happy and gossipy. Paterson had been invited to Maryland to meet several DuPont executives, and the meeting's success had buoyed her outlook. Rand wisely decided not to respond to the longer letter, for the two women would see each other soon in New York. It would be easier to iron out differences and resolve the communication problem in person. Both probably sensed the fragility of their connection, for in raising the issue of Rand's atheism Paterson had struck at a foundational difference between the two. Rand, not usually one to avoid an argument, did not press the point because Paterson was one of her most valued friends. In New York the two reached some sort of truce. As Rand described it to a fan, she had "an understanding…with all [her] friends" that she would not respond to letters when in an intense period of writing.[78] For two years she and Paterson stayed in touch over the telephone instead, until meeting again in person when Rand came east another time.

When their correspondence resumed in early 1948 it was marked by the same personal warmth and the same intellectual antagonism over religion. Rand still considered Paterson a valuable teacher, heeding her advice about deleting adjectives from her writing. She was writing steadily now and generously identified Paterson as part of the inspiration for her latest burst of creativity. Paterson responded with more New York gossip, including a tidbit about Don Levine's bizarre new concept of competing government agencies. It was the first glimmer of anarcho-capitalism, Rand's bête noire in the years ahead. But now Levine's strange views simply signaled to both Rand and Paterson that his newest venture was not worth supporting.

After more chitchat about current events Rand made a fatal slip, asking Paterson what she thought of the latest Fulton Sheen book. Sheen, soon to be ordained bishop of New York, was a prolific Catholic author. His latest book, the anti-Communist volume *Communism and the Conscience of the West,* had been sent to Rand from their shared publisher. Paterson brushed off Sheen as "not worth your time," but Rand pursued the point in a second letter, telling Paterson, "something awful seems to be happening to the Catholic thinkers." What concerned her was that Catholic thinkers like Sheen, long known for their anti-Communism, now appeared to be "turning quite deliberately toward Statism."[79] This drew forth a longer response from Paterson, in which she attempted to explain why Catholicism supported state action. Rand responded with outrage—not at Paterson, but at Catholic theology. And the battle was joined.

Although Paterson was not Catholic, she couldn't stand Rand's dismissive attitude toward religion. Sufficiently angered, she became cutting toward Rand's intellectual abilities. "You ought to get your creeds straight," she wrote, telling Rand she misunderstood the concepts of original sin and depravity. More problematic was Rand's willingness to reject Catholicism whole cloth. She accused Rand of misanthropy for her sweeping condemnation of Catholic philosophers: "Can you indict such a considerable number of the human race, including some of the greatest minds the human race has exhibited, without certain implications as to the human race itself?" Rand, for her part, was unapologetic. "Why yes, I certainly can," she told Paterson.[80]

This issue over Catholicism quickly led to more perilous territory, as the two women began to clash over how and whether Rand had influenced Paterson's thinking on morality. The question of influence was a particularly sensitive point for Rand, who now believed that Paterson had unfairly borrowed her ideas about altruism in *God of the Machine*. Prior to publication Paterson had asked Rand if she could draw on their discussions in her work without citing Rand specifically. Although Rand agreed to this arrangement, when the book was published she discovered sentences she described as "verbatim mine" from their conversations. Rand had never directly confronted Paterson about this, but her letter now hinted at this past history. In reply Paterson insisted that Rand had only helped clarify her thoughts on a specific application of "enlightened self interest."[81]

Points of contention began to multiply as the two women argued over specific conversations in the past, who had said what, and who had agreed with whom. Once more letters proved a poor medium for communication. Paterson thought the fault was Rand's: "I read your letters exactly, but sometimes you are not very exact." Again a scheduled visit helped smooth over the problems. Paterson was finally coming out to California, and Rand deferred further discussion until she arrived. She had high hopes for the visit and even agreed to pay Paterson's travel costs. Rand envisioned a return to the golden days of their friendship: "I am looking forward most eagerly to staying up with you all night, if you care to. Incidentally, the sun rises here are very beautiful, so I think we will have a good time." At the very least the California trip afforded a chance to resolve the many disagreements that were piling up.[82]

From the beginning Paterson's visit was a disaster. Rand discovered that her old friend "seemed to have lost interest in ideas. She talked much more about personal gossip of a literary nature: who is writing what, what authors are doing, what her old friends are doing." Paterson may have been trying to keep conversation on safe territory, but Rand had little interest in a nonintellectual relationship. Known for her irascible temperament, in California Paterson was particularly disagreeable. Rand had arranged several social evenings at her house, which Paterson systemically ruined. She called two of Rand's friends "fools" to their faces and told Rand after meeting Morrie Ryskind, "I don't like Jewish intellectuals." Rand was blunt in her response: "Pat, then I don't know why you like me."[83] Tension between the two old friends was building with each hour. Paterson even let it be known that she had passed up the chance to review *The Fountainhead* so many years before.

The final insult came when Paterson met William Mullendore, by now one of Rand's closest political allies. Paterson was seeking backing for a new political magazine, but when Mullendore began questioning her about the venture she lost her temper. Rand remembered, "She exploded, but literally. And she started yelling that none of them appreciated her, hadn't she worked hard enough, why should she have to write samples. Couldn't they take her word?" Mullendore, who had been forewarned about Paterson's character, was prepared for the outburst and kept his cool.[84] But Rand was mortified. When Paterson offered to leave the next day, Rand agreed. And when Paterson tried to change her mind in the morning, Rand held firm and sent Paterson on her way. It was the last time the two women would meet.

With the ending of their friendship, one of Rand's rare intellectual idols had crumbled. Rand had always been extravagant in her praise of Paterson, identifying her as one of the few people who had influenced her intellectual development. Even in the lead-up to their fight she was still assuring Paterson, "I learned *from you* the historical and economic aspects of Capitalism, which I knew before only in a general way." But afterward she would revise her estimate of Paterson, calling her "completely unoriginal....She was a good technical, competent, lady-novelist—and that was all." Paterson, famous in conservative circles for being "difficult," bears much of the responsibility for the ending of the friendship. As William F. Buckley Jr. later wrote in her obituary, Paterson was "intolerably impolite, impossibly arrogant, obstinately vindictive." But the friendship's end speaks to Rand's weaknesses as well. Unable to meet Paterson's demands for connection, she retreated into silence, a move that exacerbated any intellectual differences between the two. After their break she could no longer retain respect for Paterson, downgrading her to a second-rate novelist rather than an important thinker.[85]

Her changed estimate of Paterson changed Rand's own understanding of herself. If Paterson had not been so brilliant after all, then Rand had done most of her thinking alone. Erasing Paterson's contribution made Rand into the completely autonomous heroine of her own personal narrative. She would come to believe that her individual effort had solely shaped her ideas and driven her work, excluding her participation in the intellectual world that Paterson represented.

Personal relationships had always been troublesome for Rand. As she confessed to Paterson shortly after arriving in California, "I get furiously nervous every time I have to go out and meet somebody." Part of the problem was simply communicating her views to others. Rand found it difficult to be understood, no matter how long the letters she wrote. "I strongly suspect that we are not discussing the same theory or the same problem," she told Paterson as their relationship unraveled. The same gap in understanding had plagued her correspondence with Lane and shaped her reactions to Hayek, Friedman, and Read.[86]

The hope of building meaningful political alliances had compelled Rand to overcome her natural shyness and reach out to others. But after years of effort she began to wonder if it was all worth it. She had first been drawn to libertarianism because it broadened her perspective on the individualist themes that powered her writing. Her contact with Paterson and others had helped her move beyond the narrow Nietzscheanism that defined her early work. Now, more confident in her ideas, Rand was no longer looking for teachers, but for students.

CHAPTER FIVE

A Round Universe

$\mathbf{S}$ SPOTLIGHTS CRISSCROSSED THE sky as Ayn and Frank drove toward Hollywood for the long-awaited debut of the movie *The Fountainhead* in June 1949. While it was being shot Rand had been on the set almost daily, making sure the script she wrote was not altered. She paid special attention to Roark's courtroom speech. When King Vidor, the director, tried to shoot an abridged version of the six-minute speech, the longest in film history, she threatened to denounce the movie. Jack Warner joked later that he was afraid she would blow up his studio, and he told Vidor to shoot it as written. Rand also successfully battled film censors in the conservative Hays Office, who objected as much to her individualistic rhetoric as the movie's racy sexuality. But even Ayn Rand was no match for the Hollywood hit machine. At the movie's star-studded premiere she was devastated to discover the film had been cut, eliminating Howard Roark's climactic declaration, "I wish to come here and say that I am a man who does not exist for others."[1]

The movie's debut fueled a general disillusionment with her life in California. Now in her forties, Rand struggled with her weight, her moodiness, her habitual fatigue. The differences between her and Frank, once the source of fruitful balance in their relationship, had translated into a widening gap between them. Frank spent most of his days out in the garden while Rand worked in her study. At dinner they often had little to say to one another. Adding to her weariness was a contentious lawsuit against an anti-Communist colleague, Lela Rogers (mother of the dancer Ginger). Rand had coached Rogers before a political radio debate and was named party to a subsequent slander suit, then forced to answer court summons and consult with her lawyers.[2]

Salvation came from an unexpected quarter. Since the publication of *The Fountainhead* Rand had fielded thousands of fan letters. She had created a form response letter with brief biographical information to cope with the inundation. Occasionally, however, a letter impressed her enough that she would reach out to the writer. The first missives that Rand received from Nathaniel Blumenthal, a Canadian high school student, went unanswered. Blumenthal sounded like a confused socialist, and Rand had little time to tutor the ignorant. After entering UCLA as a college freshman, Blumenthal wrote again. His interest in Rand had not abated. This letter and his persistence impressed Rand, so she requested his phone number. After a brief phone conversation, in March 1950 she invited him to Chatsworth. It was the start of an eighteen-year relationship that would transform Rand's life and career.

When she first met Nathaniel Blumenthal, Rand had made a good start on her third novel. In contrast to *The Fountainhead,* she planned *Atlas Shrugged* rapidly, laying out the essentials of the plot and characters in six months during 1946, when she had a break from screenwriting. From there it was simply a matter of filling in the details of the scenes she had sketched out in a sentence or two. Regular cross-country trips helped her visualize the book's American setting. While driving back from New York, she and Frank visited Ouray, Colorado, a small town tucked in a seam of mountains. Right away Rand knew Ouray would be the model for her capitalist Shangri-la, the valley where her strikers would create their own utopian society.

Over time Rand had developed ingenious methods to combat the squirms. A visiting cousin was surprised to see Rand pricking her thumb with a pin, drawing dots of blood. "It keeps my thoughts sharp," she explained. At other times Rand would roam the Chatsworth grounds, picking up small stones along the way. Back in her study she sorted them according to color and size, filling the room with more than a hundred small boxes of them.[3] Perhaps her most effective method was writing to music. She tied specific melodies to different characters, using the music to set the proper mood as she wrote their starring scenes. Rand selected mostly dramatic classical pieces, so that as the plot thickened the music would reach a crescendo. Sometimes she found herself crying as she wrote.

At first Rand thought of the book as a "stunt novel" that would simply recapitulate the themes of *The Fountainhead,* but before long she widened its scope significantly. It remained an adventure story, with her heroes refusing to participate in an economy dominated by the welfare state. The main plotline drew from Rand's own biography, particularly her father's reaction to the Russian Revolution. Originally she thought "it would merely show that capitalism and the proper economics rest on the mind." Her reading of Aristotle and Plato, done for the forsaken nonfiction project, had sharpened her appreciation of rational philosophy. She decided her novel should demonstrate the connection between reason and reality. As she began making this theme concrete, a series of questions arose: "First of all, why is the mind important? In what particular way, what specifically does the mind do in relationship to human existence?" Pondering these questions, Rand realized her novel would be more than just an interesting political fable. By the time she began outlining the novel seriously, she saw it as a large-scale project that was primarily metaphysical in nature.[4] Still, she had trouble understanding the nature of the task she had shouldered.

Throughout the late 1940s Rand insisted the book was almost done. Certainly she was making progress. By July 1947 she had written 247 pages; a year later, with the book at 150,000 words, she still thought it would be shorter than *The Fountainhead*. When the manuscript topped three inches in width and five pounds in weight, Rand finally admitted it would be "bigger in scope and scale" than the earlier novel.[5] Even so, she had reason to believe the book was close to completion. The plotting and planning had gone faster than she could have imagined, and she had already finished much of her research. Her heroes and heroine were easy to imagine, and secondary characters developed quickly out of "the philosophical issues involved, and the generalized nature of the plot." In 1950 she convinced Hal Wallis to terminate her contract, freeing her to write full time. It now seemed entirely possible that she could finish in a matter of months. Rand did not yet understand that *Atlas Shrugged* had become, as she later put it, "the underestimation of my whole life."[6]

As Rand began writing seriously she continued to receive visitors. Ruth and Buzzy Hill visited nearly every weekend, and a small coterie from nearby Los Angeles State College were regulars. Rand had spoken to a political science class there at the invitation of the professor and invited students to visit her at home, provided they were not Communists. Their professor remembered, "She was welcoming and all that, but there was still a certain coldness about her. It was in her personality. She had her own mind and her own opinions—and that was that."[7] Rand sought, with some success, to convert students to her own point of view. One remembered, "I'd been confronted with 250 different philosophies, but it was all like a big wheel with its spokes all counterbalancing each other, and I didn't know what I thought anymore. She began removing spoke after spoke after spoke. Finally, the wheel began to turn. And I turned definitely in her direction."[8] In contrast to the mature conservatives she had met in New York and Hollywood, Rand found it easy to make converts out of the young seekers who flocked to her side.

In the group of students that crowded around Rand, Nathan Blumenthal stood out above all others. The connection between them was immediate. Rand liked him from the start, and Blumenthal had a simple feeling: "I'm home."[9] That first evening they dove into conversation, talking until the sun rose the next morning. It was shades of Isabel Paterson all over again, but this time Rand's counterpart was not her peer, but a handsome young man hanging on her every word. A few days later Blumenthal returned with Barbara Weidman, his future wife. Weidman too was entranced by Rand. She gazed into her luminous eyes, "which seemed to know everything, seemed to say that there were no secrets, and none necessary."[10] The couple soon became regulars at the ranch. Although Rand was always eager to talk philosophy and politics with her newfound friends, she also listened patiently to Barbara's personal troubles in long walks around the property. Chatsworth became a refuge for the two college students, who found their increasingly rightwing political views made them distinctly unpopular at UCLA. For her part, Rand had finally found a friendship in which she could feel comfortable. Blumenthal and Weidman didn't demand more than Rand could give, they never challenged her authority, and their appreciation for her work was a tonic.

An impressionable teenager in search of an idol when they met, Nathan slipped immediately into Rand's psychic world. He did not have far to go, for his basic mentality was strikingly similar to hers. Like Alisa Rosenbaum, Nathan was an alienated and angry child who felt divorced from the world around him. Where Alisa had movies, he sought refuge in drama, reading close to two thousand plays during his high school years.

By the time he met Rand he had memorized *The Fountainhead*. Told a sentence from the book, he could recite the one immediately before and immediately after. Now he began speaking to Rand on the phone several times a day and spent nearly every Saturday evening at her house. Rand was like an older, feminine version of himself—although at first, Nathan did not see her as a woman. Two months after their meeting Nathan gave her a letter to the editor he had published in the UCLA newspaper, inscribed "To My Father—Ayn Rand—the first step."[11]

The letter Nathan inscribed to Rand, which also listed Barbara as an author, was a virulent attack on F. O. Matthiessen, a literary critic and Harvard professor who had committed suicide while under investigation for past Communist associations. Matthiessen's widely publicized death was mourned by his colleagues on the left, who considered him the first scholarly martyr of the Cold War. Nathan and Barbara would have none of it. Instead they reinterpreted his death in Randian terms, attributing it to the irrationality of Communism. In his letter Blumenthal asked, "if a man places his hopes in an idea which contains an irreconcilable contradiction, and when he sees all exponents of this idea turned corrupt and fail in their aims—is there anything heroic about killing himself because an idea which can't work is not working?" Strident and tasteless, the letter averred that people like Matthiessen "deserve no pity whatsoever; rather do they deserve to be condemned to hell." The letter caused a bitter controversy at UCLA. It forever poisoned Barbara's relationship with a philosophy professor who had been close to Matthiessen. Before the letter was published the professor had been attentive and welcoming to Barbara, even joining the couple for a visit to Rand in Chatsworth, after which he pronounced himself deeply impressed. Now he counterattacked in the student newspaper and began criticizing Barbara openly in class. His hostility was so intense Barbara realized she would have to leave UCLA if she wanted to continue studying philosophy on the graduate level. Blumenthal was unfazed by the upheaval. He was a crusader who had found his cause.[12]

His allegiance now transferred to Rand, Nathan began to break free from his birth family. He picked a fight with his socialist older sister, berating her in angry letters for her immorality and inconsistency, his language taken straight from Rand. On a trip home he shouted so much he claimed, "my throat's getting hoarse." Rand, seeing her former self in his intemperance, counseled him on a better approach. It seemed to work, Nathan reported a year later. Instead of anger, he tried logic: "When they raise some objection—like taxation—I could refer them back to a premise they had already accepted, like immorality of initiated force, and they always had to cede the point."[13] Even if his family still persisted in their beliefs, Nathan was discovering the power of a defined and integrated philosophical system. By this time he was calling Rand "darling" in his letters. She reciprocated by elevating Nathan and Barbara above all others, letting them read early drafts of her work in progress.

Ultimately it was Rand who was unwilling to let their connection go. In early summer 1951 Nathan and Barbara moved to New York. Barbara intended to pursue a master's degree in philosophy at NYU, and Nathan transferred to be with her. After the couple left, Rand's restlessness grew intense. She had always wanted to move back to New York, and with *The Fountainhead* movie completed she saw no reason to remain. By the fall of 1951 she had convinced Frank they must leave. She knew he was "chronically and permanently happy" in California, but his preferences meant little compared to hers.[14] It had been more than twenty years since Frank supported himself. Increasingly Rand called the shots, and he was along for the ride. She phoned Nathan in high excitement to share the news. A few weeks later she and Frank were driving east. The Hills, who rented the Chatsworth property in their absence, found the house in disarray, as if the decision to leave had been made in great haste. Left behind was a box of old pictures, numerous pieces of furniture, and several stacks of railroad magazines. Frank asked the Hills to keep his gladiolas alive until he returned.

Back in New York Rand made no effort to rejuvenate her relationship with Isabel Paterson. Secure in her new triangle with Nathan and Barbara, she rejected overtures to conciliation by mutual friends and soon parted ways with Rose Wilder Lane, too. As Lane described it years later, Ayn and Frank visited her Connecticut home, where she and Ayn "had a hard struggle" over religion. Although Lane was not a churchgoer or an adherent to any traditional Christian doctrine, she firmly believed that the universe reflected a divine creator and thought Rand's atheism was "untenable." Writing to Jasper Crane, Lane described the scene after hours of conversation: "I was giving up, and murmured something about creativeness being obvious everywhere; and she struck me down by responding triumphantly, obviously feeling that she destroyed my whole position in one stroke, with the childish: 'then who created God?' I saw then that I had wholly misjudged her mental capacity. We parted amiably and I haven't seen her since." In Lane's recollection she was alienated both by Rand's statement and her manner; Rand spoke "with the utmost arrogant triumph," giving Lane a "'that squelches you' look" as she delivered her final question.[15] The incident confirmed Lane's doubts about Rand's ultra-individualistic position and laid bare the differences between them. Rand clearly felt that she had outgunned Lane. The following day Lane sent a lengthy letter further clarifying her position, which Rand covered with critical scribbles. She never responded to the letter and they had no further contact.

Rand's break with Lane foreshadowed the growing importance of religion on the political right. In the years since *The Fountainhead*, religion had moved to the forefront of American political discourse. Rand remembered the transition clearly. Until the mid- to late 1940s she "did not take the issue of religion in politics very seriously, because there was no such threat. The conservatives did not tie their side to God.... There was no serious attempt to proclaim that if you wanted to be conservative or to support capitalism, you had to base your case on faith." By 1950 all this was changing. As the Cold War closed in, Communism became always and everywhere Godless, and capitalism became linked to Christianity. William F. Buckley's best-selling debut, *God and Man at Yale*, famously recast Rand and Hayek's secular "individualism vs. collectivism" as an essentially religious struggle, arguing that it replicated on another level "the duel between Christianity and atheism." Two years later, in his iconic autobiography *Witness*, Whittaker Chambers defined Communism as "man without God," a substitute faith that flourished in the absence of traditional religion. Russell Kirk kicked off a vogue for "New Conservatism" with his 1953 book, *The Conservative Mind*, which asserted the importance of religious traditionalism. Even on the left, intellectuals gravitated toward the neo-Orthodox theology of the former socialist Reinhold Niebuhr.[16]

In turn Rand became an ever more devoted atheist. At a cocktail party she met the young Buckley, already a celebrated figure on the right. She was characteristically direct, telling him in her thick Russian accent, "You arrh too eentelligent to bihleef in Gott!!"[17] Buckley was both amused and offended. He sought the advice of other libertarians, including Isabel Paterson, as he pulled together *National Review,* the flagship magazine of American conservatism, but Rand became one of his favorite targets. Rand was not the only libertarian to reject the new supremacy of religion. The combination of conservatism, capitalism, and Christianity was a virtual hornet's nest on the right, sparking battles in the pages of FEE's *The Freeman* and among members of the Mont Pelerin Society.[18] By decade's end secular libertarianism would be overshadowed by the religious New Conservatism, but it never disappeared altogether. Rand and those she once sought as allies testified to its continued vitality.

Rand's opposition to religion grew stronger as she wrote *Atlas Shrugged.* The book originally included a priest, Father Amadeus, among the strikers. He would be her "most glamorized projection of a Thomist philosopher," a character who would "show theoretically the best that could be shown about a man who is attracted to religion by morality." Over the course of the story she intended Amadeus to realize the evil of forgiveness, and in an important scene he would go on strike by refusing to pardon one of her villains. Eventually Rand decided that the priest undermined her larger points about rationality. All of the other figures were taken from honorable professions that she wished to celebrate. Including a priest in this company would be tantamount to endorsing religion. She cut Father Amadeus from the novel.[19]

Despite the disappointments of Read, Lane, and Paterson, when she first returned to New York Rand was still interested in finding "reactionary" friends. Her California activism and years of letter writing kept her firmly embedded in multiple libertarian networks. Now she was again an active presence on the New York scene. Newly cautious in her approach, Rand eschewed formal organizations or partnerships. Never again would she find herself "committed to any idea that [she] didn't believe in." Instead she would be part of "a common intellectual front in an informal way."[20] Through her work for HUAC Rand had met J. B. Matthews, a dedicated anti-Communist who assisted Congressman Martin Dies and Senator Joseph McCarthy in their hunt for subversive Americans. Matthews included Rand in numerous conservative dinners and parties. At these events she met a group analogous to her Willkie associates. In the postwar era, however, conservatism was rapidly growing in size and strength, and Rand was no longer the sole intellectual of the crowd.

One of the first libertarians Rand reached out to was Ludwig von Mises, whom she had met briefly during one of her trips east. While other academics interested in the free market had found a welcoming home at the University of Chicago, Mises was so far outside the economics mainstream that no respected academic department would hire him. Ultimately the Volker Fund was able to secure him a visiting professorship at NYU, where they paid his salary (as they did for Hayek at Chicago). Mises's strongest connections were not to academia but to Leonard Read's Foundation for Economic Education, where he gave regular lectures and was considered an employee.[21] As his affiliation with FEE reminded her, Rand and Mises differed on important points, primarily concerning morality. Whereas outsiders saw Mises as a pro-capitalist hack, Mises firmly believed his economic theories were strict science, utterly divorced from his political preferences and beliefs. Misean economics pointedly did not concern itself with morality, to Rand a dangerous failing. Still, she remained hopeful that Mises and others could be converted to her point of view. She predicted, "it would only be a case of showing to them that I had the most consistent arguments."[22]

Rand's personal relationship with Mises was predictably rocky. Both were hot-tempered and principled, and tales about their conflicts were legendary in conservative circles. Russell Kirk liked to regale his audiences with a story about Mises taunting Rand as "a silly little Jew girl."[23] The truth as both Rand and Mises remembered it was more prosaic. At a dinner party with the Hazlitts, Rand began, as usual, trying to convert Mises to her moral position. Henry Hazlitt and Mises both assumed a utilitarian stance, arguing for capitalism on the basis of its benefit to society. Rand was testing out some of her ideas from *Atlas Shrugged,* talking about how man survived only due to his mind and defining the free use of rationality as a moral issue. According to Rand, Mises lost his patience and "literally screamed, because he was trying to prove that what I was saying was the same thing as Rousseau or natural rights, and I was proving to him that it wasn't." The dinner ended on a tense note, but Mises's wife later arranged a reconciliation. Rand was not unduly troubled by the incident, for Mises simply struck her as closed to persuasion: "I had the impression that von Mises had worked out his system, knew how he related his economics to the altruist morality, and that was that."[24] Mises's morality, however, did not ruin his entire approach. Unlike Hayek, Mises held capitalism as an "absolute," and thus she considered him worthy of study and respect.

Nathan and Barbara were puzzled by Rand's attitude toward Mises. They had seen the critical comments she left in the margins of his books, *Human Action* and *Bureaucracy*. "Good God!" she wrote angrily. "Why, the damned fool!" Why then did she continue to court Mises and recommend his books? Rare indeed was the person with whom Rand disagreed yet continued to see on a social basis. Her willingness to carve out an exception for Mises indicated the profound impact he had on her thought. As she told one of Mises's students, "I don't agree with him epistemologically but as far as my economics and political economy are concerned, Ludwig von Mises is the most important thing that's ever happened me." It was easy for Rand to appreciate Mises's intellectual orientation. He identified reason as "man's particular and characteristic feature" and based his work on methodological individualism, the idea that individuals should be the primary units of analysis. These premises underlay his approach to economics, a field about which Rand knew little but considered critically important.[25]

Mises had first made his name with an attack on socialism.[26] In his tome *Socialism* (first published in English in 1935) he argued that prices, which should be set by the free flow of market information, could never be accurately calculated under socialism; therefore fatal distortions were built into the very structure of a controlled economy, and collapse was inevitable. This analysis matched Rand's understanding of life under the Soviets. She also found the idea insightful for what it suggested about morality. In notes to herself she glossed Mises, writing, "Under altruism, no moral calculations are possible."[27] Mises's vision of an economy centered primarily on entrepreneurs rather than workers reinforced Rand's individualistic understanding of production and creativity.

Mises also provided economic support for Rand's contention that true capitalism had never been known, an idea she first advanced in the "Manifesto of Individualism" years earlier. Along with his exposition of the calculation problem under socialism, Mises was known for his argument against monopoly prices. According to Mises, in a truly free market a wily competitor would always undercut any attempt to establish artificially high prices. True monopoly prices could arise only if another party, such as the government, raised barriers to entry into the market, thereby preventing competition. Accordingly, antitrust laws were misguided and dangerous attempts to solve a problem that had been created in the first place by the state.[28] Rand now had two arguments to deploy against antitrust. The first was her moralistic argument that antitrust laws unfairly punished the successful. The second was Mises's contention that monopolies were not the fault of business, but of government regulation. Rand could therefore cite monopolies as evidence that the United States had never experienced true free-market capitalism. As Paterson had before, Mises helped Rand strengthen, define, and defend her ideas.

Cultural connections also bound the two. Mises was about twenty-five years older than Rand, but they both hailed from the same cosmopolitan European Jewish milieu. His Viennese family was similar to the Rosenbaums in many respects, secular yet conservative, cultured yet commercial. Mises had fled Austria in advance of the Nazis, an experience that profoundly shaped his views of the state. His style also suggested a model for Rand. He was famous for his Thursday evening *Privatseminar*, where curious NYU students mingled with libertarians of all ages, including the occasional famous visitor, such as the actor Adolph Menjou. Mises was formal and reserved toward his students, who in turn treated him reverently. Discussions were often so intense that the group typically reconvened at a nearby restaurant, with a number of students carrying on discussion without the professor until late in the night. Snubbed by the American intellectual establishment, Mises had nonetheless managed to establish himself as the leader of a small movement.

Soon Rand had her own salon to match Mises's. As she grew closer to Nathan and Barbara, Rand became ensconced within a new surrogate family, a tight kinship network consisting primarily of the couple's relatives and friends. The group included Barbara and Nathan's cousins, Leonard Peikoff and Allan Blumenthal, Nathan's sister and her husband, Elayne and Harry Kalberman, Barbara's childhood friend Joan Mitchell, and Joan's college roommate, Mary Ann Rukovina. Joan's boyfriend and briefly her husband, Alan Greenspan, was also a regular. Many were students at New York University, where Barbara and Nathan were now enrolled. These young people were fascinated by Rand, drawn by her strong personality, her bold presentation of ideas, and her literary fame. Rand's new group of fans dubbed themselves the "Class of '43" after *The Fountainhead,* or tongue-in-cheek, "The Collective." Rand granted her inner circle a rare privilege: the chance to read chapters of *Atlas Shrugged* as they poured off her typewriter. Objectivism as a philosophy had been long germinating in Rand's mind. Now Objectivism as a social world began to take shape around her.

Rand also remained a magnet for libertarians. She became friendly with Herbert and Richard Cornuelle, two brothers who worked for FEE and the Volker Fund. The Cornuelles were the same type of business-oriented libertarians she had met in California. After studying with Mises, Herbert pursued a corporate career with Dole Pineapple, and Richard served as the head of the National Association of Manufacturers and later as an advisor to Presidents Nixon and Reagan. Richard found Rand "electrifying." When he visited her apartment she seemed a dynamo of energy, perched high atop an ottoman "smoking cigarettes with a long holder with a very characteristic, rather severe hairdo and a kind of intensity in the way she looked at you when she was talking to you, which I found kind of fascinating and frightening almost." One evening the Cornuelles brought Murray Rothbard to Rand's home. A Brooklyn native, Rothbard had stumbled across organized libertarianism by way of the infamous *Roofs or Ceilings?* pamphlet that had caused so much grief for Leonard Read. Given a copy in 1946 while a graduate student, he contacted FEE and was then introduced to the work of Mises. By the time Rand returned to New York Rothbard was pursuing a Ph.D. in economics at Columbia University and was a regular at the Mises seminar.[29]

Meeting Rand, Rothbard quickly discovered that she was not his "cup of tea." It was a curious reaction, for the two had much in common. Both loved to argue, staked out extremist positions, and criticized any-one who strayed from pure ideology. Although he was an economist, Rothbard, like Rand, approached libertarianism from a moral point of view. But Rothbard found Rand exhausting. Her intensity, her "enor-mous hopped-up energy," overwhelmed him.[30] (He had no idea that Rand was a regular user of amphetamines, but he seems to have detected a strange edge to her personality.) A night owl who loved to stay up late arguing the fine points of economic theory, even Rothbard could not keep up with Rand. For days afterward he felt depressed.

Still, Rothbard's meeting with Rand had been eye-opening. Despite his allegiance to Mises, Rothbard was bothered by the Austrian's antipathy to natural rights. Like Rand, he was a natural moralist and wanted to ground his economics in something deeper than utilitarianism. Through Rand Rothbard learned about Aristotelian epistemology and "the whole field of natural rights and natural law philosophy, which [he] did not know existed."[31] He went on to explore these fields through his own reading. Eventually he combined Austrian economics and natural rights philosophy to create his own brand of anarchist libertarianism. Rothbard acknowledged that Rand had taught him something of value. Yet he disliked her intensely and kept his distance. Rand's growing charismatic powers could both attract and repel.

As Rand began training her own cadre of thinkers, she became less interested in the laborious task of converting others to her worldview. It was simply easier to start from scratch. Unlike Mises, Rothbard, and Hayek, the young people she met through Barbara and Nathan were not grounded in alternative approaches to politics or the free market. They were receptive to her comprehensive view of the world, her unified field theory of existence. Other libertarians wanted to argue with Rand, but the Collective merely listened.

Against this background Dwight Eisenhower's 1951 presidential nomination became a real turning point for Rand. In a tight convention Eisenhower, a decorated war hero, had narrowly ousted Senator Robert Taft, the presumptive Republican nominee. Taft, known in the Senate as "Mr. Republican," was the last major politician to vocalize views shared by Rand and her libertarian friends. He vigorously opposed the New Deal, fought against labor unions, and questioned the wisdom of American involvement overseas. By contrast, Eisenhower was a genial, noncontroversial figure who offered Americans a reassuring, steady hand at the tiller after the upheaval of the Depression and war. He was so popular, and his political views so moderate, that both parties courted him as a presidential prospect.

Rand was alert to the dangers of such a nominee. Eisenhower was akin to Hayek, a destroyer from within, a false friend who would dilute the principles she held dear. He did more damage than any Democrat possibly could, for his nomination "destroyed the possibility of an opposition" and meant "the end of any even semi-plausible or semi-consistent opposition to the welfare state." Rand was not alone in her reaction. Even the new religious conservatives she hated were tepid about the nonideological Eisenhower. In 1956 Buckley's *National Review* would offer a famously lukewarm endorsement: "We prefer Ike."[32] But now, to her dismay, most of Rand's New York friends swallowed their reservations and climbed aboard the Eisenhower bandwagon. Twenty years of Democratic rule had made them desperate for any Republican president. This struck Rand as foolish compromise and unforgiveable inconsistency. She realized, "[T]hey were not for free enterprise, that was not an absolute in their minds in the sense of real laissez faire capitalism. I knew then that there is nothing that I can do with it and no help that I can expect from any of them."[33] After a string of disappointments, she was ready to turn her back on conservatives altogether.

It was Nathan, stepping forward into a new role of advisor, who gently nudged Rand to this conclusion. The conservatives were not really "our side," he told Rand. "We have really nothing philosophically in common with them." Boldly he informed Rand that she was making "a great mistake" to ally herself with Republicans, conservatives, or libertarians. Rand was intrigued and relieved at Nathan's formulation, the last premise that she needed to clarify her thinking. Looking back a decade later, she remembered, "[F]rom that time on…I decided that the conservatives as such are not my side, that I might be interested in individuals or have something in common on particular occasions, but that I have no side at all, that I'm standing totally alone and have to create my own side."[34] Implicit in Nathan's words was the promise that he and the Collective could take the place of the allies Rand had forsaken.

The 1953 marriage of Nathan and Barbara accelerated Rand's move away from the broader libertarian community. She and Frank presided as matron of honor and best man at the wedding, a union Rand had done much to encourage. In California Barbara Wiedman had confessed to Rand her uncertainty about the relationship, but found the older woman unable to understand her hesitancy. Nathan was clearly an exceptional young man with a profound intelligence. Barbara admired Nathan and shared his values. According to Rand, they had all the necessary ingredients for a successful relationship. Against her instincts Barbara followed Rand's advice. Nathan and Barbara's subsequent decision to change their last name to Branden symbolized the new strength of Rand's growing circle. "Branden" had the crisp, Aryan ring of characters in Rand's fiction; it also incorporated Rand's chosen surname.[35] As in the case of young Alisa, the symbolism was clear enough. Barbara and Nathan were reborn not only as a married couple, but as a couple with an explicit allegiance to Rand.

After their marriage the Brandens and the Collective formed the nucleus of Rand's social life to the exclusion of all others. Rand sequestered herself during the day, laboring on *Atlas Shrugged*. At night she emerged for conversation, mostly about the book. Saturday nights were the highlight; no matter how intense her writing, Rand never canceled their salon. The Collective gathered at Rand's Thirty-sixth Street apartment, a small, dimly lit space "reeking with smoke" and filled with hair from the O'Connors' Persian cats.[36] The apartment could not compare with the magnificent estate at Chatsworth, but Rand loved that she could see the Empire State Building from a window in her office. Modernist furniture in her favorite color, blue-green, filled the apartment, and ashtrays were available at every turn. When Rand finished a chapter, it was a reading night, with the Collective silently devouring the pages she drafted. Other nights were dedicated to philosophical discussion.

During these evenings Rand taught the Collective the essentials of her philosophy. No longer content to celebrate individualism through her fiction, she now understood, "my most important job is the formulation of a rational morality of and for man, of and for his life, of and for this earth."[37] Objectivism, as she would soon be calling her ideas, was an ingenious synthesis of her ethical selfishness and the Aristotelian rationality that had captured her interest after she completed *The Fountainhead*. Stitching the two together, Rand argued that she had rationally proved the validity of her moral system. Unlike other systems, she claimed, Objectivist morality was not based on theological assumptions, but on a logically demonstrable understanding of what man's needs on earth were. In essence, Objectivism was Rand's rebuttal of the skeptical and relativistic orientation that had characterized American intellectual life since the rise of scientific naturalism.[38] What differentiated Objectivism was its ambition. Rather than simply reassert the idea of objective and transcendent truth, a project supported by a host of other neo-Aristotelian thinkers, Rand attempted at the same time to vindicate a controversial and inflammatory transvaluation of values that contradicted the basic teachings of Western religion and ethics.

The scope of her project awed her young followers, who considered her a thinker of world-historical significance. In her ideas they found a "round universe," a completely comprehensible, logical world. Rand's focus on reason led her to declare that paradoxes and contradictions were impossible. Thought, she explained, was a cycle of moving from abstract premises to concrete objects and events: "The cycle *is unbreakable;* no part of it can be of any use, until and unless the cycle is completed."[39] Therefore a premise and a conclusion could never clash, unless an irrational thought process had been employed. Nor could emotions and thoughts be at odds, Rand asserted. Emotions came from thought, and if they contradicted reality, then the thought underlying them was irrational and should be changed. Indeed even a person's artistic and sexual preferences sprang from his or her basic philosophical premises, Rand taught the Collective.

It was all adding up to one integrated system. Man was a rational creature who used his mind to survive. The rational faculty required independence and individuality to operate properly; therefore an ethics of selfishness was appropriate for rational men. Any moral or ethical problem could be approached from this perspective. Was a person acting independently? Were his or her actions based on reason and consistent with his or her premises? That was the true determinant of right, Rand taught. Even more than her fiction or the chance to befriend a famous author, Rand's philosophy bound the Collective to her. She struck them all as a genius without compare. On Saturday nights they argued and debated the fine points and applications, but never questioned the basics Rand outlined. During these marathon sessions, Rand was indefatigable, often talking until the morning light. The Collective marveled at how the opportunity to talk philosophy rejuvenated her, even after a long day of writing. The obvious was also the unthinkable. To keep up with her younger followers, Rand fed herself a steady stream of amphetamines.[40]

Always by her side at these occasions, Frank was a silent paramour, an ornamental and decorative figure. As the conversation wore into the evening, he served up coffee and pastries but contributed little to the discussion, sometimes dozing silently in his chair. The move to New York had been profoundly disruptive for Frank. He made a fainthearted attempt to sell flowers to decorate building lobbies, printing up cards that identified him as "Francisco, the lobbyist." But without his own land and greenhouse, the business offered little reward and soon collapsed. Rand turned again to fiction to sort out Frank's behavior, telling the Collective, "He's on strike." She continued to value their connection, always introducing herself to strangers as "Mrs. O'Connor." When their schedules diverged as she stayed up late to write, she left him friendly notes about the apartment, always addressed to "Cubbyhole" and signed "Fluff." Rand was elated when he suggested that one of her chapter titles, "Atlas Shrugged," serve as the book's title, and she proudly informed new visitors that Frank had thought up the book's name. Such claims did little to disguise Frank's failure to emulate the active, dominant heroes Rand celebrated. The Collective knew, however, that his place by Rand's side was never to be questioned. Frank was outside the rankings, of the Collective but not in it.[41]

Although Rand disliked him at first, Alan Greenspan soon became one of her favorites. For ten months he was married to Joan Mitchell, Barbara's closest friend, and through her met Rand a few times. Once their marriage was amicably annulled, the former couple grew closer as friends, and Greenspan began joining Rand's circle on a regular basis. Even Joan's subsequent marriage to Allan Blumenthal, Nathan's cousin, did little to disturb Greenspan or discourage his interest in Rand's group. At early meetings he was quiet and somber, earning the nickname "the Undertaker" from Rand. Heavily influenced by logical positivism, Greenspan was unwilling to accept any absolutes. He became legendary for his confession that he might not actually exist—it couldn't be proved. Hearing this, Rand pounced: "And by the way, who is making that statement?" To Greenspan it was a deep exchange that shook his relativist beliefs to the core.

By many accounts Rand excelled at the kind of verbal combat that impressed Greenspan. Hiram Haydn, an editor at Bobbs-Merrill and later Random House, marveled at Rand's ability to conquer sophisticated

New Yorkers in any argument: "Many are the people who laughed at my description of her dialectical invincibility, only later to try their hands and join me among the corpses on the Randian battlefield." Rand began with the basics, establishing agreement on primary axioms and principles. She came out on top by showing how her opponent's ideas and beliefs contradicted these foundations. This approach was particularly effective on those who prided themselves on logic and consistency, as did Greenspan. He remembered that "talking to Rand was like starting a game of chess thinking I was good, and suddenly finding myself in checkmate." Greenspan was hooked.[42]

Greenspan's attraction to Rand was fairly standard for those drawn into her orbit. As she had for Rothbard, Rand exposed Greenspan to previously unknown intellectual treasures, "a vast realm from which I'd shut myself off." Before meeting Rand, Greenspan was "intellectually limited…": "I was a talented technician, but that was all." Under Rand's tutelage he began to look beyond a strictly empirical, numbers-based approach to economics, now thinking about "human beings, their values, how they work, what they do and why they do it, and how they think and why they think." His graduate school mentor, Arthur Burns, had given Greenspan his first exposure to free market ideas. Rand pushed him further, inspiring Greenspan to connect his economic ideas to the big questions in life. Now he found that morality and ethics had a rational structure that could be analyzed and understood, just like the economy or music, his first passion. Primed to accept Rand's system by his devotion to mathematical thought, Greenspan was soon an enthusiastic Objectivist. His friends noticed the change immediately, as he began flavoring his conversations with Objectivist vocabulary and the Randian injunction "check your premises."[43]

Unlike most members of the Collective, who were students, Greenspan stood out as an established professional with a successful economic consulting business. He was in the rare position of being able to teach Rand something. While she dominated the others, when it came to Greenspan "it was the reverse, he was the expert, she was learning from him," remembered a friend.[44] His firm, Townsend-Greenspan, charged huge sums for the information it synthesized about all aspects of economic demand. Greenspan was legendary for his ability to comb statistical data, analyze government reports, and ferret out key figures from industry contacts.

Ayn Rand's husband of fifty years,
Frank O'Connor, Hollywood, 1920s.
(The Ayn Rand® Institute)

Isabel Paterson, a well known
conservative columnist from the
New York Herald Tribune, helped
cement Rand's political thinking in
the early 1940s. (Courtesy Stephen
Cox)

This author's photograph, taken for the 1943 publication of *The Fountainhead*, was Rand's favorite picture of herself. (The Ayn Rand® Institute)

The Illustrated *Fountainhead*
by
Ayn Rand

Rand's second novel, *The Fountainhead*, published in 1943, was so popular it was made into a film and a comic book. (©King Features Syndicate)

In 1947, Rand volunteered to testify before the House Un-American Activities Committee about Communist infiltration of the motion picture industry. (Getty Images)

The O'Connors purchased a 13 acre ranch in Chatsworth, California, with a house designed by the modernist architect Richard Neutra. (J. Paul Getty Trust. Used with permission. Julius Shulman Photography Archive, Research Library at the Getty Research Institute (2004.R.10))

The 1953 wedding of Barbara Weidman and Nathaniel Blumenthal, soon to be known as Barbara and Nathaniel Branden. The couple were Rand's closest confidants for nearly twenty years. (Courtesy Barbara Branden)

Rand in New York in 1957, eagerly anticipating the release of her opus, *Atlas Shrugged*. (The Ayn Rand® Institute)

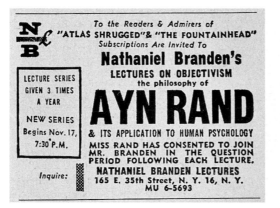

After *Atlas Shrugged* was widely panned by reviewers, Nathaniel Branden started a lecture series to promote Rand's ideas. (Courtesy Nathaniel Branden)

Nathaniel Branden at the NBI podium. His goal was to "omnisciate and inflam-minate," he told a friend. (Courtesy Nathaniel Branden)

Businessmen have always been among Rand's most avid fans. Ten years after *Atlas Shrugged* was published, young entrepreneur Ted Turner erected more than 200 billboards throughout the southern United States asking "Who is John Galt?" Turner went on to found the cable television network CNN.

By the 1970s, Rand had largely retreated from public life, though she continued to publish *The Ayn Rand Letter* sporadically. (The Ayn Rand® Institute)

Rand turned to him for information about the steel and railroad industries, using his knowledge to make *Atlas Shrugged* more realistic. The two shared a fascination with the nuts and bolts of the economy, the myriad daily processes that meshed into a functioning whole.

The position of Leonard Peikoff was more precarious. He met Rand while visiting Barbara, his older cousin, in California. Their first meeting was revelatory. Torn by his family's desire that he study medicine, a field he found unappealing, Leonard asked Rand if Howard Roark was moral or practical. Both, Rand replied, launching into a long philosophical discussion about why the moral and the practical were the same. Her answer spoke directly to Peikoff's conflict, and "opened up the world" for him. He left thinking, "All of life will be different now. If she exists, everything is possible." Within a year he had abandoned medicine for philosophy and moved to New York to be near Rand. She took a motherly tone toward "Leonush," one of her youngest fans. But Peikoff's occasionally incurred Rand's wrath when he showed interest in ideas she disapproved of. Over time, as Peikoff's expertise grew, Rand came to depend on him for insight into modern philosophy.[45]

Rand saw nothing unusual in the desire of her students to spend each Saturday night with her, despite most being more than twenty years her junior. The Collective put Rand in the position of authority she had always craved. She initiated and guided discussion, and participants always deferred to her. It was a hierarchical, stratified society, with Rand unquestionably at the top. Closely following her in stature was Nathan, then Barbara, with the other students shifting status as their relationship with Rand ebbed and flowed. Rand carefully watched the balance of power, openly playing favorites and discussing her preferences with Nathan and Barbara. Because conversation revolved around Rand's ideas and the novel-in-progress, the Collective was valuable fuel for her creative process; she could rest from the rigors of writing without truly breaking her concentration. The Collective was becoming a hermetically sealed world. Within this insular universe dangerous patterns began to develop.

Murray Rothbard caught a glimpse of this emerging dark side in 1954. In the years since their first meeting, Rothbard had gathered to himself a subset of young libertarians who attended Mises's seminar and carried on discussion into the early hours of the morning, often at Rothbard's apartment. Energetic, polymathic, and erudite, Rothbard dazzled his retinue, mostly young men who were students at the Bronx High School of Science. This group called themselves "the Circle Bastiat," after the nineteenth-century French economist Frederic Bastiat, and looked to Rothbard as an intellectual leader. When the Circle Bastiat discovered he knew the famous Rand, they clamored to meet her. Rothbard reluctantly agreed. First he went to her apartment with two students, and then a week later brought the whole gang.

Both visits were "depressing," Rothbard told Richard Cornuelle in a lengthy letter. The passage of time, and the presence of reinforcements, did not help. Rand argued vigorously with George Reisman, one of his group, subjecting him to a barrage of vitriol. According to Rothbard, Reisman was the only one to "realize the power and horror of her position—and personality." The rest of the high school students were captivated by Rand and eager for more contact. Rothbard, however, was secretly relieved that Reisman's battle with Rand provided the perfect excuse to avoid seeing her again. Even better, he would no longer have to deal with the Collective, a passive, dependent group who "hover around her like bees."[46]

Rand was bad enough, but Rothbard was truly horrified by the Collective. "Their whole manner bears out my thesis that the adoption of her total system is a soul-shattering calamity," he reported to Cornuelle. Rand's followers were "almost lifeless, devoid of enthusiasm or spark, and almost completely dependent on Ayn for intellectual sustenance." Rothbard's discomfort with the Collective masked his own conflicting emotions about Rand and her circle. After all, Rothbard had also gathered to himself a set of much younger students over whom he exercised unquestioned intellectual authority. He freely used the word "disciple" to refer to both his and Rand's students, a word she eschewed. Now some of Rothbard's own students were feeling the magnetic pull of Rand. Even Rothbard, as he later confessed, was subject to the same response. Many years later, speaking of this time, he told Rand, "I felt that if I continued to see you, my personality and independence would become overwhelmed by the tremendous power of your own."[47] Rand was like a negative version of himself, a libertarian Svengali seducing the young.

Rothbard fortified his emotional distaste for Rand with intellectual disagreement. By the time of his second encounter with her, Rothbard was close to finishing his doctorate and increasingly certain about his ideas. He explained to Richard Cornuelle, "my position—and yours too, I bet—is not really the same as hers at all." The strength of Rand's system, he argued, was that it treated ethics as a serious field, in contrast to the void of utilitarianism, positivism, and pragmatism. Apparently after his first meeting with Rand, Rothbard had credulously accepted her claims to originality. Now he discovered that "the good stuff in Ayn's system is not Ayn's original contribution at all." There was a whole tradition of rational ethics, and "Ayn is not the sole source and owner of the rational tradition, nor even the sole heir to Aristotle."[48] Moreover, Rand's interest in liberty was only superficial, Rothbard believed. A few of his disciples continued to meet with Rand and reported back that she claimed Communists should be jailed. They also introduced Rand to Rothbard's anarchism, and his idea of privately competing courts and protective agencies that could replace the state. Rand responded swiftly that state action was necessary to hold society together. For Rothbard, an anarchist who believed the state itself was immoral, all this merely confirmed his differences with Rand.

More seriously, Rothbard teased apart Rand's system and discovered that it meant the very negation of individuality. Rand denied both basic instincts and the primacy of emotion, he wrote Cornuelle. This meant, in practice, that "she actually denies all individuality whatsoever!" Rand insisted that all men had similar rational endowments, telling Rothbard, "I could be just as good in music as in economics if I applied myself," a proposition he found doubtful. By excising emotions, asserting that men were only "bundles of premises," and then outlining the correct rational premises that each should hold, Rand made individuals interchangeable. Therefore, Rothbard concluded, in an eerily perceptive aside, "there is no reason whatever why Ayn, for example, shouldn't sleep with Nathan." The proof of Rothbard's analysis lay in the Collective, a group of lifeless acolytes who frightened Rothbard in their numb devotion to Rand.[49]

Always a charismatic and dominant personality, Rand now began to codify the rules of engagement. Richard Cornuelle was among the first to experience this treatment. He enjoyed the certainty he found in Rand, the sense that he "suddenly had an answer for practically anything that might come up." He was both drawn to Rand and unsettled by her. Pecking away at his Calvinist shell, Rand would ask him psychologically probing questions about sexuality and his feelings. "I think she might have been wanting to help me, I think…and wanted to contribute to my relaxing about that kind of thing," he reflected later. But at the time he felt "terribly uncomfortable." Another violent clash between her and Mises spelled the end of their relationship. Rand and Mises argued over conscription, which Rand saw as tantamount to slavery. Mises, his eyes on history, argued that only conscription could prevent the rise of dangerous mercenary armies. After the argument Rand telephoned Cornuelle. She wanted him to make a choice:

> "You have to make a decision. You're either going to continue to be my disciple or his." I said, I'd rather duck. She said, "you can't." And that was it. I never spoke to her again after that….She didn't want me to agree with her. She wanted me to discontinue my relations with von Mises as a way of showing I was on her side.[50]

Rand now began to demand allegiance from those around her. She had made "the most consistent arguments" on behalf of a fully integrated system and cast out those who did not acknowledge her achievement.

The Collective, and Nathaniel Branden in particular, were her replacement. The bond between the two had grown fast and thick. In New York Branden became not only Rand's "brain mate" but her teacher, as he began to push her philosophical ideas into the realm of psychology. Branden's major innovation was the theory of "social metaphysics." He developed this concept to describe a person whose frame of reference was "the consciousness, beliefs, values, perceptions of various other people."[51] Branden translated the qualities Rand had celebrated in her novels into psychological terms. In *The Fountainhead* Howard Roark's stoic disregard for the opinions of others could be understood as a dramatized ideal, a standard that could inspire despite its unreality. Recast as a psychological syndrome, the same idea became dangerous, because it suggested that the abnormal should be normal. Essentially, "social metaphysics" made everyday human concern with the thoughts and opinions of others problematic and pathological. It was a judgmental and reductive concept, a pejorative label that both Branden and Rand began using freely.

Branden's new idea was doubly destructive because he employed it during therapy sessions with members of the Collective and other interested patients. Indeed, Branden had first derived the idea after

conversations with fellow Collective members whom he deemed insuf-
ficiently independent. His credentials in the area of counseling psychology were slim, to say the least; he had only an undergraduate degree.
But with Rand's system behind him, Branden felt qualified to promote
himself as an expert. Rand had always enjoyed talking to people about
their personal problems, urging them to apply rationality to any problem in life. Now Branden picked up this habit, his authority buttressed
by Rand's obvious respect for him. In tense therapy sessions, during
which he paced the room "like a caged tiger," as one patient remembered, Branden demanded that members of the Collective check their
premises and root out all traces of irrationality from their thinking.[52]

Rand was delighted by Branden's psychological innovations. She began
to openly acknowledge him as her teacher as well as her student, her intellectual heir who would carry her work forward. Even though her novels
dwelled at length on the internal motivations and conflicts of characters,
she had always dismissed psychology as "that sewer."[53] Now she could
learn about the field without actually reading Freud, or the other psychologists whom she freely castigated. Armed with Branden's theories
she became even more confident in her judgments about other people.
Still fascinated by his mentor, Branden listened with rapt attention to
her memories of the past, her tales of struggle, her frustrations with the
world. He offered her what her passive, withdrawn husband could not:
both intellectual stimulation and emotional support. Rand began to talk
of him as her reward, the payoff for all she had gone through.

Although it started innocently enough, there had always been a current of flirtation between the two. Rand made no secret of her esteem
for Nathan, openly identifying him as a genius. His face, she said, was
her kind of face. The Brandens' marriage only briefly papered over the
growing attraction between Ayn and Nathan. The subtext of their relationship spilled into the open during a long car ride to Canada in the
fall of 1954. The two couples and another friend had taken a road trip to
visit Barbara's family. On the ride home Barbara watched her husband
and Rand holding hands and nuzzling in the backseat of the car. Sick
with jealousy and anger, she confronted him afterward. Nathan denied
everything. He and Rand had a special friendship, nothing more. His
sentiment was genuine. Nathan worshipped Rand, but it was Barbara he
had chosen, or so he consciously believed.

Like Barbara, Ayn had registered a shift. The next day she summoned Nathan to her apartment, where she waited alone. It was a scene out of the best romantic fiction. After some delay, Rand became urgent and direct. She and Nathan had fallen in love, yes? Nathan, overwhelmed, flattered, excited, confused, responded in kind. They kissed hesitantly. There would be no turning back.

But this was still the founder of Objectivism, believing in rationality above all else. They must be honest with their spouses, Rand decided. She called them all to a meeting at her apartment. As Barbara and Frank listened incredulously, Rand's hypnotic voice filled the room and stilled their protests. The spell she had cast was too strong to break now. At meeting's end she and Nathan had secured what they requested: a few hours alone each week. Their relationship would be strictly platonic, they assured their spouses. Privacy would allow them to explore the intellectual and emotional connection they could no longer pretend did not exist.

When the inevitable happened, Rand was again honest with both Barbara and Frank. She and Nathan wished now to be lovers, she explained. But it would naturally be a short affair. She had no wish to hold back Nathan, twenty-five years her junior. Her explanation came clothed in the rational philosophy she had taught them all. By giving their feelings full expression, Nathan and Ayn were simply acknowledging the nature of reality.

For all her iconoclasm, Rand had a streak of cultural conventionality deep within. Afraid of what the outside world would say, she insisted the affair be kept a secret. Her work and her reputation would be smeared if anyone found out, she told the others. Uncomfortable with the idea of literally disrupting her marriage bed, Nathan proposed that they rent a small apartment in her building, ostensibly an office, that could be used for their meetings. Rand refused. On the surface everything would continue as usual. Even members of the Collective could have no inkling of the new arrangements between the Branden and O'Connor households.

The officially sanctioned yet secret affair sent all four parties spinning into perilous emotional territory. For all the passion they shared, relations between Nathan and Ayn were not smooth. Ayn was an insecure, jealous lover, constantly pushing Nathan to express his feelings. Not a naturally emotive person, Nathan struggled to please. They spent many of their assignation hours deep in psychological and philosophical discussion, atonement for Nathan's latest perceived slight or indifference. Although he was thrilled by the affair, Nathan felt pressured to meet the depth of her romantic feeling for him, a task that became more difficult as the novelty of their relations wore off. He was also pulled away by his loyalty to Barbara, who began suffering intense panic attacks. Nathan, who styled himself a psychologist, could find no reason for Barbara's anxiety. Neither of them imagined the affair, and the deception it engendered, could be a source of her inner turmoil. Perhaps the hardest hit was Frank, who was displaced from his apartment twice a week when Nathan arrived to rendezvous with his wife. His destination on many of these afternoons and evenings was a neighborhood bar.[54]

Rand's liaison with Branden came just as she began writing the most crucial part of *Atlas Shrugged*. The early stages of the book had been fairly trouble-free. She had created a cast of characters that made for pleasant company. There was Hank Rearden, a conflicted industrialist whose new steel alloy is appropriated by the collectivists. Between appearances at the latest jet-set parties, Francisco D'Anconia, a brilliant aristocratic playboy, destroys his family company lest it fall to the enemy. Most fun of all was Dagny Taggart, who gave Rand the chance to present the ideal woman. An engineer like Kira in *We the Living*, Dagny is a proto-feminist heroine, a powerful businesswoman who moves easily from one lover to the next. Like all Rand heroines, Dagny is beautiful as well as brilliant, and socially well born. A glamorous and striking blonde, she is the granddaughter of a pioneering railroad tycoon whose empire she now controls. The book's driving force is John Galt, a character Rand variously identified as a fictional version of Frank or Nathan. The leader of the strike and the mouthpiece for Rand's philosophy, Galt is a physicist who invents groundbreaking technologies while working as a menial laborer.

Rand's difficulties came to a head around Galt's speech, which occurs toward the very end of the 1,084-page book. Whereas the rest of *Atlas Shrugged* is a fast-paced narrative, full of the tightly plotted twists and turns that Rand loved to write, Galt's speech is something different altogether. Rand finally had answers to the first questions the novel had raised, indeed the questions that had driven her for years. Objectivism was the rational, error-free system Rand had not found in the wider world. It began with A = A, her nod to Aristotle's law of identity. From this basic axiom of existence, it built to a towering edifice that addressed the most important issues of life: economics, morality, sex, knowledge itself. Its centerpiece was Galt's speech, a philosophical defense of the rational, fully autonomous individual. Not only was man free to choose; he *had* to choose, and the preservation of life itself was not involuntary, but a choice. As Galt explains, "His mind is given to him, its content is not.... Reason does not work automatically; thinking is not a mechanical process.... [Man] has no automatic knowledge of what is good for him or evil."[55] Rand did not mean this existentially, but literally. Objectivism denied the existence of instincts or innate knowledge that propel humans toward food, shelter, sex. Instead, she held that the choice to live was a rational choice, to be consciously made by man's mind. What was the role of the mind in man's existence? Mind was everything.

The catch was that Rand had chosen to express all these ideas in the context of a fictional story. Although she spoke fluidly about her philosophical accomplishments to her young followers, translating her system into fiction was a daunting task. To integrate her ideas into the flow of the story she had to present arguments without arguing, for Galt's speech is a monologue, not a dialogue. It would have been easy to do, Rand thought, if she were writing a treatise. But how could Galt convincingly express these ideas in the context of a dramatic story? She toggled back and forth uncertainly between clashing genres, feeling her mind "working on two tracks."[56] Every time the words began to flow, Rand realized she was writing as a philosopher, not a novelist. Angrily she would cut herself off and start again. Until Galt's speech was finished she was unwilling to secure a publisher, making it feel as if the entire project was on hold. Frank, who had watched her write for more than two decades, thought it was the worst time she had ever endured.

Rand's difficulties cut to a deep problem of self identification. "I seem to be both a theoretical philosopher and a fiction writer," she noted to herself with some pleasure as she began planning the novel nearly ten years before.[57] At first it had seemed a winning combination. But given its long gestation, *Atlas Shrugged* caught Rand once more in the transition from one mode of thinking to another. *The Fountainhead* was marked by Rand's first encounter with American political life. *Atlas Shrugged* was formed in a different crucible, the clash between fiction and philosophy, the romantic and the rational. Rand drained herself to finish the book, and when it was over she would never write fiction again.[58]

During the two years she struggled to write Galt's speech, Rand's pronounced nervous tension wreaked havoc on those closest to her. The emotional center of Nathan's, Barbara's, and Frank's lives, she set the mood for all. She was irritable, angry, and tense. Nathan's attentions did little to soothe her. No matter how welcome, he was a distraction to her writing. When he let her down, the price seemed too much to pay. Rand flayed him in private for his inattention, while praising him extravagantly to others. She erupted at Frank for small transgressions, sometimes drawing Nathan into their arguments. She was also infuriated by Barbara's persistent anxiety attacks and her accompanying pleas for help.

In frustration, Rand developed a new theory of "emotionalism" to explain Barbara's behavior. Like the idea of social metaphysics, emotionalism was a psychological rendering of the ideals conveyed in Rand's fiction. Emotionalists were those who, contrary to Objectivist teaching, allowed their emotions, rather than their rationality, to guide them through the world. Rand speculated that emotional repression might be one source of emotionalism; that is, repression might eviscerate the rational faculty altogether. By not acknowledging emotions, the emotionalist was subject to their sway. Certainly this theory did provide some insight into Barbara's suffering. However, in Rand's and Nathan's hands, the idea of emotionalism was not a tool for understanding, but rather a method of judgment. Neither suggested that Barbara's emotional repression came from her acceptance of the "rational" affair between her husband and her closest friend.

Rand's new interest in psychological ideas reflected Nathan's influence. He was now studying for a master's degree in psychology and continued to expand Objectivism into new areas, with Rand following suit. Emotionalism led Rand to further musings on human psychology, captured under the terms "sub basement" and "superstructure," her words for the subconscious and conscious mind. The opposite of an emotionalist would be a rationalist, whose emotions would always be explicable and on the surface. Rand began defining various members of the Collective by their psychology, and she scribbled an excited note to Nathan after a series of musings on emotionalists, rationalists, sub-basement, and superstructure: "My stomach (and brain) is screaming that this is the right track....I am sure that the role of psychology is to discover, identify, and then be able to cure all the essential 'epistemological' errors possible to a human consciousness."[59] Psychology offered Rand yet another way to apply Objectivist principles to daily life.

Her changing language also indicated the growing authority she accorded Leonard Peikoff as his studies in philosophy continued. Rand's vocabulary now included technical terms such as "epistemology" and "metaphysical," to which she often appended her own prefixes, creating neologisms like "psycho-epistemology." It was a sharp departure from her previous interests. In place of writers like Paterson, Lane, and Mises, who worked within an established intellectual tradition and drew on a rich social context, Rand's ideas now came from young men who cited her as their primary inspiration. She was no longer working with terms or concepts that were accessible to outsiders, but instead lived in an Objectivist echo chamber. She read little beyond a daily newspaper, preferring conversation with her associates. She had turned a corner into her own private intellectual world.

Rand was now unreachable by anyone but the Collective. At Nathan's urging she had stepped out of the conservative movement at its most critical hour. In these years came the founding of *National Review,* the rejuvenation of *The Freeman,* the rise and fall of Senator McCarthy. Rand was disconnected from all these events. Occasionally she saw one of her friends from earlier years, but the Brandens and their circle occupied the bulk of her free time. Whereas *The Fountainhead* and Rand's first ideas for *Atlas Shrugged* had been shaped by Rand's immersion in the libertarian world of the 1940s, Objectivism was shaped by the concerns and interests of the Collective. They were with her to celebrate when she wrote the last pages of Galt's speech in the fall of 1956, and were the only ones who understood its significance to her.

With Galt's speech finally finished, Rand could relax at last, and so could her three closest friends. The rest of the writing flowed. Barbara's anxiety abated, her panic attacks fading as fast as they had come on.

Nathan completed his master's degree and began working as a full-time therapist. Frank underwent the most dramatic transformation. One evening, spurred by a philosophical disagreement, several members of the Collective tried painting. The results quickly disproved Rand's assertion that artistic skills could be easily taught to anyone, for Frank outstripped the others immediately. As his background in floral design suggested, Frank was a natural. Soon he was drawing at every turn, filling sketchbooks with his work.

Rand too was rejuvenated and relieved. She was finally prepared to begin shopping the manuscript around, and with *The Fountainhead* still selling briskly, had her pick of eager publishers. Bobbs-Merrill, which had first right of refusal on her next book, pronounced an early version of *Atlas Shrugged* "unsaleable and unpublishable," setting her free on the market. She mentioned the book to Hiram Haydn, who had left Bobbs-Merrill for Random House. Despite Random House's liberal reputation, Rand was impressed that they had published Whittaker Chambers's *Witness* and was willing to give them a hearing. She was also interested in having her old editor, Archie Odgen, onboard. Ogden was no longer employed by a publishing house but had agreed to work with Viking as the editor of her novel, should they publish it. Rand was unsure if this ad hoc arrangement would be right for her prized creation.

Haydn and his boss, the legendary Bennett Cerf, played their cards perfectly. They proposed a lunch with Rand simply to learn more about the book. When Rand's agent torpedoed the plan for being unfair to other publishers, they had another suggestion to make. What if Rand had lunch with every seriously interested publisher? They were even amenable to a dual submission, should Rand choose. At lunch Haydn, Cerf, and a third editor quizzed Rand about the implications of her book. One ventured that if the novel was an uncompromising defense of capitalism, it would necessarily contradict Christian morality. Rand was pleased with the observation. Random House was offering her respect and understanding, if not agreement. By the end of the lunch she had essentially made up her mind. It took Random House a similarly short time to make an offer on the manuscript. Haydn himself found Rand's philosophy repugnant, but could tell that *Atlas Shrugged* had "best-seller" stamped on it. He and Cerf were sure it would be an important and controversial book and told Rand to name her terms.[60]

The months from the completion of *Atlas Shrugged* in March to its publication in October 1957 were a rare idyll for Rand. Random House treated her reverently. Cerf asked her to speak personally to the sales staff about the book, a special honor for an author. When she refused to accept any editorial changes whatsoever the house acquiesced. No longer "with novel," Rand was relaxed, happy, and triumphant.[61] She and Branden continued their affair, settling into their blended roles as lovers and intellectual collaborators. It was the calm before the storm.

PART III

Who Is John Galt? 1957–1968

CHAPTER SIX

Big Sister Is Watching You

$ WHEN *THE FOUNTAINHEAD* was published Rand was an obscure author, unknown to the literary world. By contrast, legions awaited *Atlas Shrugged*. Buzz had been building about the book. *The Fountainhead*'s astounding sales, still strong a decade after publication, seemed to guarantee that her next work would be a blockbuster. Rand herself was becoming a mythological figure in New York, a vivid and memorable character rarely seen by those outside the Collective. Random House fed the beast with a series of teaser ads, a press conference, and a prominent display window on Madison Avenue. The word was out: a major new novel was on the way.

Rand and the Collective too were breathless with anticipation. Rand told her followers she would face criticism: she steeled herself for attack. The Collective did not take her warnings seriously. Carried away by the power of Rand's words, they were convinced it would only be a matter of years before Objectivism conquered the world. Robert Hessen, a new member of Rand's circle, remembered the feeling: "We were the wave of the future.... Objectivism would sweep everything in its path."[1] With such a buildup, Rand and those closest to her were utterly unprepared for the fierce condemnation that greeted the book. "Is it a novel? Is it a nightmare?" *Time* magazine asked in a typically snide review.[2] A few right-leaning magazines and newspapers praised *Atlas Shrugged*, but taken as a whole the harsh verdict was clear. Rand was shattered. More than anything else, she wanted a defender, an intellectual equal who would trumpet her accomplishment to the world. None appeared.

As it turned out, there was not one *Atlas Shrugged*, but many. Hostile critics focused relentlessly on Rand's treatment of human relationships, her anger, her bitterness. Business owners and capitalists saw instead her celebration of industry, her appreciation for hard work and craftsmanship, her insight into the dynamics of free markets. Students and younger readers thrilled to her heroic characters and were overjoyed to discover the comprehensive and consistent philosophy of Objectivism. The aftermath of the book's publication taught Rand that she was truly on her own. Her path to intellectual prominence would not be typical, conventional, or easy. In retrospect, it seems obvious: Rand would do it her way.

Taken at the level of a story, *Atlas Shrugged* is a moral fable about the evils of government interference in the free market. The novel is set in a dystopian world on the brink of ruin, due to years of liberal policymaking and leadership. The aggrandizing state has run amok and collectivism has triumphed across the globe. Rand's decaying America resembles the Petrograd of her youth. The economy begins to crumble under the pressure of socialist policies, and food shortages, industrial accidents, and bankruptcies become commonplace. Gloom and dread pervade the country. Fatalistic and passive, citizens can only shrug and ask the empty question, a catchphrase of the novel, "Who is John Galt?"

Rand shows us this world through the eyes of two primary characters, Dagny Taggart and Hank Rearden. Both are gifted and inventive business owners who struggle to keep their enterprises afloat despite an ever-growing burden of government regulation. Starting off as business partners, the single Dagny and married Hank soon become lovers. Strong, handsome, and dynamic, Dagny and Hank contrast sharply with Rand's villains, soft and paunchy government bureaucrats and corrupt business owners who seek favors from the politicians they have bought. Dagny and Hank's enemies begin with laws that restrict competition, innovation, and cross-ownership of businesses, and by the end of the novel have nationalized railroads and the steel industry. In a detail reminiscent of Soviet show trials, when the government expropriates private property it forces the owners to sign a "gift certificate" framing the action as a patriotic donation.

Rebelling against this strangulation by the state, the creative minds of America go "on strike," and throughout the course of the story all competent individuals in every profession disappear. Until they are granted complete economic freedom and social respect, the strikers intend to withhold their talents from society. To Dagny and Hank, who do not understand the motivation of the strikers, the mysterious disappearance of their counterparts in every industry is yet another burden to bear. The man masterminding this strike, John Galt, does not appear as a main character until more than halfway through the 1,084-page novel. Although Galt is only a shadowy figure for most of the book, he is the culmination of Rand's efforts to create a hero. Like Howard Roark, Galt is a man of physical beauty, outsize genius, and granite integrity. He has created a motor run by static electricity that will revolutionize science and industry, but keeps it a secret lest it be captured by the collectivists. Once Galt enters the story, he begins pursuing Dagny and Hank, the last two competent industrialists who have not joined the strike. He wants to lure them to his mountain hideaway, Galt's Gulch, where the strikers have created a utopian free market society.

The dramatic tension in *Atlas Shrugged* comes from Rand's underlying belief that evil is impotent unless aided by the good. Galt must teach Dagny and Hank that by refusing to join the strike, they are aiding and abetting the collectivist evils that have overcome their country. Without "the sanction of the victim"—the unwitting collaboration of exceptional individuals—Rand's collectivists would be powerless.[3] The book tips into philosophical territory as Galt makes his case to Dagny and Hank, aided by a cast of colorful secondary characters such as Francisco Domingo Carlos Andres Sebastián D'Anconia, a renegade aristocrat. Here the novel becomes more than a parable about capitalism. Rand's characters learn to reject the destructive sacrificial ethics and devotion to community they have been taught, and instead join the ethical selfishness of Galt's strike.

As in *The Fountainhead*, Rand redefined morality to fit her vision. It was moral to make money, to work for oneself, to develop unique talents and skills. It was also moral to think, to be rational: "A rational process is a moral process," Galt lectures his audience. "Thinking is man's only basic virtue, from which all the others proceed" (944). It is immoral to ask for anything from others. Galt's strikers swear an oath that encapsulates Rand's ethics: "I swear by my life and my love of it that I will never live for the sake of another man, nor ask another man to live for mine" (680).

Throughout the novel Hank Rearden serves as Rand's object lesson, her example of philosophy in the real world. Although rational in his business dealings, in his personal life he is crippled by guilt and a feeling of obligation toward his parasitic family. These feelings also keep him toiling in an economy controlled by his enemies rather than joining the strike. Only when Rearden realizes that rationality must extend to all spheres of his life, and that he does not owe either his family or the wider society anything, can he truly be free. Withdrawing the "sanction of the victim," he joins Galt's Gulch. Dagny is a harder case, for she is truly passionate about her railroad. Even after embarking on an affair with Galt, she resists joining the strike. Only at the end of the novel does she realize that she must exercise her business talents on her own terms, not on anyone else's. When she and Rearden finally join the strike, the ending is swift. Without the cooperation of the competent, Rand's bad guys quickly destroy the economy. Irrational, emotional, and dependent, they are unable to maintain the country's vital industries and use violence to subdue an increasingly desperate population. At the novel's end they have ushered in a near apocalypse, and the strikers must return to rescue a crumbling world.

Outside of the academic and literary worlds *Atlas Shrugged* was greeted with an enthusiastic reception. The book made Rand a hero to many business owners, executives, and self-identified capitalists, who were overjoyed to discover a novel that acknowledged, understood, and appreciated their work. The head of an Ohio-based steel company told her, "For twenty-five years I have been yelling my head off about the little realized fact that eggheads, socialists, communists, professors, and so-called liberals do not understand how goods are produced. Even the men who work at the machines do not understand it. It was with great pleasure, therefore, that I read 'Atlas.'"[4] Readers such as this welcomed both the admiring picture Rand painted of individual businessmen and her broader endorsement of capitalism as an economic system. *Atlas Shrugged* updated and formalized the traditional American affinity for business, continuing the pro-capitalist tradition Rand had first encountered in the 1940s. She presented a spiritualized version of America's market system, creating a compelling vision of capitalism that drew on traditions of self-reliance and individualism but also presented a forward-looking, even futuristic ideal of what a capitalist society could be.

Throughout the novel Rand demonstrated a keen appreciation for capitalism's creative destruction and a basic comfort with competition and flux. A worker on Taggart Transcontinental admires the prowess of a competitor, stating, "Phoenix-Durango is doing a brilliant job" (16). By contrast, her villains long for the security of a static, planned economy. One bureaucrat declares, "What it comes down to is that we can manage to exist as and where we are, but we can't afford to move! So we've got to stand still. We've got to stand still. We've got to make those bastards stand still!" (503). Rand lavished loving attention on railroad economics, industrial processes, and the personnel problems of large companies. She had conducted extensive research on railroads while writing the book, and her fascination with and respect for all industry shone through the text. As she described the economy, Rand avoided the language of science or mechanism, employing instead organic metaphors that present the economy as a living system nurturing to human creativity and endeavor. To her, money was "the life blood of civilization" (390) and machines the "frozen form of a living intelligence" (988). The market was the repository of human hopes, dreams, talents, the very canvas of life itself.

Ignoring the daily drudgery of economic life, Rand portrayeds capitalism and capitalists as creative, even glamorous. Dagny and Hank rush from one crisis to the next, the fate of their companies always hanging on a single decision that only they can make. Every company mentioned in *Atlas Shrugged,* from the smallest concern to the largest multinational corporation, is eponymous, signifying the link between individual and firm. Rand also tied corporate capitalism to individuals through her focus on inventions and discoveries. Many of her protagonists have an entrepreneurial bent and accumulate wealth through an ingenious invention or by making a scientific breakthrough. Even Dagny, whose railroad is the emblematic old-economy business, is successful because she has an outstanding conceptual grasp of the marketplace and is the only executive who understands the potential of new technologies to improve her operations.

With its blend of old-fashioned economic individualism and modern corporatism, *Atlas Shrugged* is simultaneously nostalgic and visionary.[5] Rand drew a clear connection between her ideal of capitalism and the imagined American past. When the competent go on strike, they retreat to Galt's Gulch, a refuge nestled deep in the mountains of Colorado, where they re-create a nineteenth-century world. Residents of the valley are on a first-name basis with each other and attend Chautauqua-type lectures at night. The former head of Sanders Aircraft is a hog farmer; a federal court judge supplies the eggs and butter. Rand's heroes are a diverse band of "producers," including industrialists, artists, and scientists, whom she intended to embody moral truths. These producers lead moral lives because they do not extract resources from others, but depend on their own talents and ingenuity to advance. Once gathered together in the strike, they represent the pure and honest West, set against the corruption and overweening power of Washington.

Rand made clear that these individualist principles underlay not only Galt's Gulch, but industrial corporate capitalism, properly understood. In books like *The Organization Man, White Collar,* and *The Lonely Crowd* contemporary social scientists bemoaned the large company as a place of soulless conformity. By contrast, Rand presented corporate capitalism as the ultimate field for expression of self. She was able to offer this alternate vision because she focused entirely on heroic individuals like Taggart and Rearden, who are able to shape great organizations in their own image.

For those who could plausibly self-identify as the "producers" that Rand celebrated, the novel was a powerful justification of their livelihood. Rand's defense of wealth and merit freed capitalists from both personal and social guilt simultaneously. A businessman who reprinted five hundred copies of her speech "Faith and Force" for distribution at his own expense made this clear in his cover letter: "Dear Friend: Is success wrong? Is it evil to earn a profit—as much profit as you can make honestly? Why should the morality of the successful person be criticized because of his success? ... You may not agree with Miss Rand's answers, but I don't think you will ever forget her basic message."[6]

A potent source of Rand's appeal was "The Meaning of Money," a speech from *Atlas Shrugged.* "So you think that money is the root of all evil?" asks dissolute copper magnate Francisco D'Anconia, misquoting the biblical injunction against love of money. He draws a direct correlation between money and merit, identifying wealth as the product of virtue, and concludes, "money is the root of all good." This message spurred many corporations to spread the good news, and Rand granted several requests to reprint the speech. The Colorado Fuel and Iron Corporation asked permission to reproduce the speech "for internal distribution to supervisory personnel." The company explained, "We feel that this material is very much in line with some of the economic principles we have been disseminating."[7]

Businessmen were attracted both to the content of Rand's ideas and their unification into a cohesive, integrated whole. One executive told the management of his company that Rand could help them "probe deeper into the philosophic and economic causes of the decline of freedom.... Miss Rand explains completely the inseparability of right moral action, private property, free economic activity and rational action. Each is proven to be inextricably woven into the others. And as one reads and grasps the proofs she offers as the absolute, and always superiority of a free society, he begins to see why so many of our efforts to thwart collectivism, welfare ism, etc., fail so miserably."[8] Rand offered both an explanation for any antibusiness sentiment and an action plan for the future. This combination bowled over Clement Williamson, president of Sealol Incorporated in Providence, Rhode Island, who told her, "after years of trying to arouse business leaders to conviction and action in the field of government and politics, I feel that I now have the key which will eventually unlock the tremendous potential available in this group. Nowhere in my literature researching have I found the one answer except in this philosophy of yours."[9] Rand's readers felt that she had penetrated to the root causes of the regulatory and social environment that bedeviled them.

In Rand business had found a champion, a voice that could articulate its claim to prominence in American life. Invitations to symposia and conferences began to stream in. Rand was recruited to speak at a meeting of the National Industrial Council on the "Ethics of Capitalism," and three times presented at the week-long seminar of the President's Professional Association, an organization affiliated with the American Management Association. Two professors at the Columbia Business School excerpted *Atlas Shrugged* in a textbook and invited her to address a course on the conceptual and institutional foundations of modern business. Business could even offer Rand an intellectual platform of sorts. The *Atlantic Economic Review,* published by a Georgia business school, invited Rand to contribute to a symposium on *The Organization*

Man, asking her to write about "A Faith for Modern Management."[10] The many executives who distributed excerpts from *Atlas Shrugged* or sent copies to their friends further spread her message.

When professional reviewers looked at *Atlas Shrugged,* they tended to overlook this celebration of business and the tight philosophical system that Rand had woven into her story. Instead they focused on her bitter condemnation of second-handers, looters, moochers, and other incompetents. *Atlas Shrugged* inspired a shocking level of vituperation. Reviews were often savage and mocking commentaries rather than literary assessments. The *New York Times Book Review,* which had generously praised *The Fountainhead,* featured a scathing article by the former Communist Granville Hicks, who declared, "Loudly as Miss Rand proclaims her love of life, it seems clear that the book is written out of hate." For the most part, reviewers did not primarily object to Rand's political or moral views, or even her adulation of the superior man. What they focused on instead was her tone and style. "The book is shot through with hatred," wrote the *Saturday Review.* Others complained about Rand's repetition, grim earnestness, and utter lack of humor.[11]

Reviewers were right to notice that alongside its reverent depiction of capitalist heroes, *Atlas Shrugged* had a decidedly misanthropic cast. In many ways the novel was the final summation of the theory of resentment Rand had first formulated in Crimea. It was also a return to the mood of her earliest unfinished fiction. Once again Rand let loose all the bile that had accumulated in her over the years. Particularly when John Galt takes center stage, Rand's text seethes with anger and frustration and yields to a conspiracy theory that sees the world as a battleground between competence and incompetence. Galt tells his radio audience, "What we are now asked to worship, what had once been dressed as God or king, is the naked, twisted, mindless figure of the human Incompetent.... But we—we, who must atone for the guilt of ability—we will work to support him as he orders, with his pleasure as our only reward. Since we have the most to contribute, we have the least to say" (688). Rand's Manichaean worldview comes through in Galt's speech, with a competent elite facing off against an ineffectual commons.

Beyond the idea of conspiracy, Rand's ethical revolution led her to see natural human sympathy for the downtrodden as an unacceptable stricture on those she designated "at the top of the pyramid." Through Galt Rand reversed the typical understanding of exploitation, arguing:

> The man at the top of the intellectual pyramid contributes the most to all those below him, but gets nothing except his material payment, receiving no intellectual bonus from others to add to the value of his time. The man at the bottom who, left to himself, would starve in his hopeless ineptitude, contributes nothing to those above him, but receives the bonus of all of their brains. Such is the nature of the "competition" between the strong and weak of the intellect. Such is the pattern of "exploitation" for which you have damned the strong. (989)

In these passages Rand entirely drops the populism and egalitarianism that characterized her earlier work, reverting to the language used by earlier defenders of capitalism. Although she did not use explicit biological metaphors, her arguments were like a parody of social Darwinism. *Atlas Shrugged* was an angry departure from the previous emphasis on the competence, natural intelligence, and ability of the common man that marked *The Fountainhead*.

Why such a dramatic shift in thirteen years? Partly Rand was simply tending back to the natural dynamics of pro-capitalist thought, which emphasized (even celebrated) innate differences in talent. These tendencies were exaggerated in Rand's work by her absolutist, black-and-white thinking. Her views on the "incompetent" were particularly harsh because she was so quick to divide humanity into world-shaking creators and helpless idiots unable to fend for themselves. This binarism, coupled with her penchant for judgment, gave the book much of its negative tone. Because she meant to demonstrate on both a personal and a social level the result of faulty ideals, Rand was often merciless with her characters, depicting their sufferings and failings with relish. In one scene she describes in careful detail the characteristics of passengers doomed to perish in a violent railroad crash, making it clear that their deaths are warranted by their ideological errors (566–68). Such spleen partially explains the many negative reviews Rand received. After all, by renouncing charity as a moral obligation she had voluntarily opted out of any traditional expectations of politeness or courtesy. *Atlas Shrugged* demanded to be taken on its own merits, and most book reviewers found little to like.

Politics undoubtedly played a role, too. Rand's book was a full frontal assault on liberal pieties. She liked nothing more than to needle her antagonists and was often deliberately provocative, even inflammatory. One character declares Robin Hood the "most immoral and the most contemptible" of all human symbols and makes a practice of seizing humanitarian aid intended for poor countries, giving it instead to the productive rich. Another hero proudly assumes the nickname "Midas" Mulligan, while the discourse upon "money, the root of all good" continues for several pages (387–91). Then there were the hopelessly hokey parts of *Atlas Shrugged*, which even Rand called "those gimmicks": mysterious dollar-sign cigarettes smoked by the cognoscenti, a death ray machine operated by the government, the gold dollar-sign totem that marks Galt's Gulch, the repetition of the question, "Who is John Galt?"[12] Criticized for her lack of humor, Rand was actually having plenty of fun with *Atlas Shrugged*. But liberals did not get the joke.

Conservatives were no less offended. The most notorious review of *Atlas Shrugged* was written by Whittaker Chambers and published in *National Review*, the most influential conservative magazine of the time. Chambers had become a household name through his testimony against Alger Hiss in a Soviet espionage case and his subsequent best-selling memoir, *Witness*. Once a dedicated Communist, Chambers had shifted far to the right, becoming a mentor to William F. Buckley Jr., who asked him to review *Atlas Shrugged* as his first assignment for *National Review*. Buckley, who disliked Rand, surely knew what the outcome of such an assignment would be. In *Witness* Chambers had written movingly about his religious conversion and his belief that only God could rescue mankind from the evils of Communism. It was not hard to predict how he would react to Rand, an avowed atheist. Chambers was uninterested in the book and reluctant to write such a negative review, yet at Buckley's request he plunged into battle with an article entitled "Big Sister Is Watching You."[13]

In his vitriolic review Chambers noted Rand's popularity and her promotion of conservative ideals such as anti-Communism and limited government, but argued that because she was an atheist her underlying message was faulty and dangerous. According to Chambers, Rand's triumphal secularism was hopelessly naïve and fundamentally unable to combat the evils of collectivism. In fact, by criticizing collectivism without the guidance of religion, Rand's work verged into the very territory of absolutism, Chambers maintained. He found *Atlas Shrugged* marked by strong fascist elements and ultimately pointing to rule by a "technocratic elite." The review was marked by a strong personal animus. Rand's writing was "dictatorial" and had a tone of "overriding arrogance"; she was not sufficiently feminine, hinted Chambers, speculating that "children probably irk the author and may make her uneasy."[14] In a stunning line, Chambers intoned, "From almost any page of *Atlas Shrugged*, a voice can be heard, from painful necessity, commanding: 'To a gas chamber—go!'"[15] At base it was a clash of two radically different versions of human nature. Rand's novel showed mankind, guided by rationality alone, achieving heroic deeds. Chambers, traumatized by Communism, saw rational man as a damned and helpless creature trapped in dangerous utopian fantasies of his own creation.

Chambers was also unsettled by Rand's godless capitalism, which might be even worse than godless Communism. Where Rand saw the free market as an essentially spiritual realm and competition as the meaning of life itself, Chambers saw only a heartless machine world. In the 1940s Rand had been one of many intellectuals seeking a plausible grounding for individual rights and democracy. By the 1950s conservatives had found an answer in religion. Defining Communism as essentially atheistic, they were able to frame Christianity and capitalism as natural partners in the fight against government regulation. If the two impulses were paradoxical or contradictory at base, that was the very point, for conservatives wanted the free market set within an explicitly Christian society. Only religion could balance the "materialism" of free enterprise, with the Christian emphasis on charity, humility, and equality blunting the harsher edges of laissez-faire. But now Rand appeared to be tacking back to the earlier nineteenth-century vision of Darwinian capitalist competition, absent the soothing balm of Christian egalitarianism.

Atlas Shrugged represented a fundamental challenge to the new conservative synthesis, for it argued explicitly that a true morality of capitalism would be diametrically opposed to Christianity. By spinning out the logic of capitalism to its ultimate conclusion *Atlas Shrugged* showcased the paradox of defending free market capitalism while at the same time advocating Christianity. Rand's ideas threatened to undermine or redirect the whole conservative venture. Even worse, given her popularity, there was the significant danger that Rand would be seized on by liberals as a spokesperson for conservatism. She might then confirm the liberal stereotype that conservatism was nothing more than an ideological cover for the naked class interests of the haves. For all these reasons, Rand would have to be cast out of the respectable right. More than just a literary judgment, the *National Review* article was an exercise in tablet keeping. The review signified Buckley's break with the secular libertarian tradition Rand represented and his efforts to create a new ideological synthesis that gave religion a paramount role. It was as Nathan had foreseen: Rand and the conservatives were not on the same side.

Chambers's review sent shock waves across the right. Rand herself claimed to have never read it, but her admirers were horrified. The Collective chafed at the injustice of assigning a former Communist to review her work and barraged the magazine with a number of incendiary letters angrily comparing *National Review* to the *Daily Worker*.[16] Isabel Paterson resurfaced from her own misanthropic isolation to chide Buckley for publishing such an "atrocious" review and warned him that Rand was likely to sue for defamation (she never did). The letters column of *National Review* hummed with controversy for weeks afterward. One high-profile defender was John Chamberlain, who had given Rand rare favorable reviews in *The Freeman* and the *Wall Street Journal*.[17] In an "Open Letter to Ayn Rand" Chamberlain praised her "magnificent" exposition of freedom and averred that he would continue "the lugubrious task of persuading people to read it in spite of themselves." Chamberlain thought that much of the outcry against *Atlas Shrugged* was based on religion and lamented that Rand had not "chosen to admit just one vocal and practicing Christian in her Fellowship of the Competent."[18]

Chamberlain was right to highlight religion as fundamental to the controversy over Rand, for it was religious conservatives who most disliked her book. William Mullendore, who had long enjoyed warm relations with Rand, was repelled by the harshness of *Atlas Shrugged*. In the years since Rand had left California, Mullendore had undergone a sort of religious awakening, and he now found Rand's work disturbing. After reading the book he sent a concerned three-page letter to his children, telling them, "This is no defense of free enterprise. This is the promotion of the egotism and wrong understanding of one Ayn Rand. I am sorry she wrote it; and I am doubtful that I should have given her as much 'praise' as I did in my letter to her. It is really an evil book." Mullendore was concerned lest his children look to Rand for guidance and carefully explained the many errors he found in *Atlas Shrugged*. Similarly, many of the *National Review*'s religious readers shuddered at Rand's atheism and her depiction of capitalism. Rand's "attempt to portray characters as living only by economic principles is preposterously impossible and dangerous," wrote one, and another applauded the magazine's attempt to draw firm boundaries, for "only when the ideological perverts are removed from the camp, will true (ergo, Christian) conservatism make the gains which are imperative for the survival of our way of life."[19]

By contrast, secular and agnostic libertarians were more likely to tolerate or even embrace Rand. Murray Rothbard jumped into the fray on Rand's side. Rothbard was deeply impressed by *Atlas Shrugged*, and his earlier reservations about Rand vanished. He began attending weekly meetings at her apartment and enrolled in therapy with Nathaniel Branden. As if to prove his loyalty, Rothbard began a letter-writing campaign on behalf of Rand and her book. He sent querulous letters to Whittaker Chambers and others who had negatively reviewed *Atlas Shrugged* and began recommending it to many of his correspondents. Ludwig von Mises also hailed the book, writing Rand to tell her how much he enjoyed reading it. The novel meshed well with his deep-seated elitism. He told Rand admiringly, "You have the courage to tell the masses what no politician told them: you are inferior and all the improvements in your conditions which you simply take for granted you owe to the effort of men who are better than you."[20] He invited Rand to attend his seminar as an honored guest.

Robert LeFevre, a radical libertarian and founder of the anarchistic Freedom School, watched the controversy with amusement. He wrote to Rose Wilder Lane, "'Atlas' has demonstrably agitated the complacent. Perhaps it's the size. Perhaps it's the daring. Perhaps it's the sex angle. Perhaps it's the anti-religious approach. Although I'll probably not like it when I read it, but not reading it (as yet) I like it." Once he finished the book LeFevre told friends he found Chambers's review unfair. Rose Wilder Lane was still dubious about Rand's contribution. She worried

"that this current 'return to religion' is a most dangerous tendency.…
But the alien atheism of Ayn Rand, with its worship of Reason and
of an Elite of Noble, Productive Men, and its contempt of human
beings, the 'masses,' is no answer to the Kirks."[21] Rand's work accen-
tuated the sharp differences that still separated libertarians from
conservatives.

As controversy raged in the letters section of *National Review,* Rand
suffered through her darkest days yet. She sank into a deep depression,
crying nearly every day in the privacy of her apartment. Some form
of letdown was probably inevitable after the long buildup to publication, and Rand's continued use of Benzedrine may have further contributed to her emotional fragility. What she dwelled upon was the painful
absence of intellectual recognition. Rand longed to be publicly hailed
as a major thinker on the American scene. The Collective had satisfied
her need to be a teacher and an authority, but it left unquenched her
desire for accolades from intellectual peers. Rand enjoyed being a dominant figure, but she also wanted to admire, to lift her gaze upward like
Howard Roark. Nathan and Alan Greenspan elicited her favor precisely
because they could teach her about psychology and economics, fields
about which she knew little. Mises's endorsement was welcome, but not
enough. She had already counted him among her supporters, and he
held little sway outside libertarian circles. Rand directly confessed her
disappointment only to Frank, Nathan, and Barbara, but her anguish
was palpable to the rest of the Collective.

Rand's quest for intellectual recognition was doomed from the out-
set. It was not simply that her political views were unpopular. Five years
after the publication of *Atlas Shrugged* Milton Friedman advanced similarly controversial ideas in his *Capitalism and Freedom,* with little loss to
his academic reputation. Friedman's association with the University of
Chicago and his technical work in economics insulated him against the
type of attacks Rand endured.[22] She had neither a formal academic post
nor any academic training beyond her Soviet undergraduate degree. Yet
it was her choice of style rather than form which inhibited her work's
reception. Rand's romantic fiction, with its heavy political messages
and overdrawn contrasts between good and evil, was hopelessly out of

fashion as a vehicle for serious ideas. *Atlas Shrugged* was a throwback to Socialist realism, with its cardboard characters in the service of an overarching ideology.

But the most significant obstacle to Rand's joining the ranks of the intelligentsia was her antagonistic attitude. The caricatures of *The Fountainhead* had made her feelings clear. In *Atlas Shrugged* she rarely missed a moment to attack "those parasites of subsidized classrooms, who live on the profits of the mind of others" (941). With her focus on the mind, Rand blamed contemporary intellectuals for every evil in the world, particularly the expanding welfare state. It was true that many prominent intellectuals had supported Communism and socialism, but Rand went far beyond standard conservative rhetoric about traitorous eggheads. She was particularly enraged by college professors, the "soft, safe assassins of college classrooms who, incompetent to answer the queries of request for reason, took pleasure in crippling the young minds entrusted to their care" (923). She seemed particularly offended that Aristotelian logic and rationality were no longer dominant in American classrooms. Even scientists, in the form of Robert Stadler, came in for criticism. It was not clear if there were any living intellectuals whose endorsement Rand would have accepted.

Rand was fighting against a powerful current, not so much politically as intellectually. *Atlas Shrugged* was published just as a great era of system building had passed. Weary from Communism, fascism, and two world wars, intellectuals were above all uninterested in ideology. Daniel Bell's book *The End of Ideology: On the Exhaustion of Political Ideas in the 1950s* captured the mood well. Rand's Objectivism, a completely integrated rational, atheistic philosophical system delivered via a thousand-page novel, was simply not what most established intellectuals were looking for in 1957.[23] Those curious enough to investigate it were repelled by her attacks on college professors and the intellectual classes.

Desperate for anything to cheer her up, Nathan convinced Rand to endorse a series of public lectures about her philosophy. If universities would not teach Objectivism, then Nathan would establish his own sort of Objectivist University. If intellectuals scorned Rand's ideas, then he would raise up a new generation fluent in her thought. His creation of the Nathaniel Branden Institute (NBI) was intended to circumvent the intellectual establishment that was so hostile to Rand's ideas. Not incidentally, NBI also promised to advance Nathan's career. He had already begun to establish himself as a therapist on Rand's coattails, drawing patients primarily from those who found her work interesting. Now he started a second business drawing on Rand's ideas.

Nathan's organization drew on earlier Objectivist efforts at education. Immediately following the publication of *Atlas Shrugged* Rand had conducted informal classes in fiction writing in her apartment. The invitation-only classes were her first foray into cultural criticism. As she taught students the basics of her style, which she called "Romantic Realism," Rand criticized the work of such authors as Thomas Wolfe for writing stories without a plot or moral meaning. Just as there was an Objectivist view on sex, there was also an Objectivist theory of literature. These fiction classes also formed the nucleus of a "Junior Collective," whose members enjoyed less frequent contact with Rand than the original insiders. If a student showed particular promise he or she would be invited for a one-on-one audience with Rand. From there a friendship might blossom. Or Nathan might suggest that an aspiring Objectivist write Rand a letter, expressing appreciation for her philosophy; if Rand was suitably impressed a closer relationship could develop. When *Time* magazine published a negative review of *Atlas Shrugged*, Nathan instructed all members of the Junior Collective to cancel their subscriptions as an exercise in living up to their principles.[24]

There was also a precedent for someone other than Rand to teach the basics of her philosophy. Before *Atlas Shrugged* was published, Leonard Peikoff had given a series of lectures on Objectivism. His informal talks attracted a few members of the Collective and Murray Rothbard's Circle Bastiat. But Leonard was too junior, and his status with Rand too insecure, for him to front an organization devoted to her philosophy. It was the charismatic and confident Nathaniel Branden who would become the public face of Objectivism, second only to Rand.

Rand was initially skeptical of the entire venture. She doubted Nathan could change the culture and worried he would be hurt trying. But she was willing to endorse his work and lend her name in support. She took no financial stake in the organization, which would remain Nathan's exclusive possession. After creating a series of twenty lectures on "Basic Principles of Objectivism," Nathan mailed information to a select list of area fans who had written letters to Rand. In 1958 he offered the first course to twenty-eight New Yorkers in a rented hotel room. Confounding the opinions of almost all who had weighed in on the topic, he discovered a ready market of people willing to spend time and money on philosophy lectures given by an unaccredited, newly established institution. Undoubtedly Rand was the primary draw. In the beginning she attended the question-and-answer session at the end of each lecture. The Brandens soon discovered additional demand. Barbara began offering a similar course in Philadelphia, with Rand an occasional visitor, and developed her own curriculum on "Principles of Efficient Thinking."

It was Barbara who suggested the tape transcription idea that led to the rapid expansion of Nathaniel Branden Lectures, soon incorporated as the Nathaniel Branden Institute (NBI). The idea seemed preposterous at first: Branden would record his New York lectures and send them to approved representatives across the country. These representatives would then charge an admission fee for the twenty-week series. Enrolled students would gather around a tape recorder to listen to Branden and take notes. Again, the unlikely idea had wings. Soon Barbara had quit her publishing job and was working full time for NBI.

These new ventures strained the already stressful relationships in Rand's inner circle. Despite their new business partnership Nathan and Barbara's marriage was deteriorating fast. Weepy and lethargic, Rand called an effective stop to her sexual relationship with Nathan. She had no appetite for love but hoped their affair might resume in the distant future. The return to platonic relations was a relief to Nathan, whose ardor for Rand had dimmed considerably. No longer her lover, he now became her psychologist. Swamped by melancholy, Rand turned to Nathan as her lifeline. Following her own philosophy she strained to rationally understand the source of her negativity. John Galt wouldn't have felt this way, she was sure. More often Rand focused on the deficiencies of the culture around her, working with Nathan to find explanations for the state of the world. She was in a state of crisis, her home a "hospital atmosphere," as Nathan remembered it.[25]

Unable to help Rand shake off her darkness, Nathan compensated by becoming her bulldog. He began answering Rand's correspondence from persons who offended or attacked her, making himself a buffer between her and the world. He wrote angry letters to magazines and newspapers that reviewed her work unfavorably. The rest of the Collective followed suit, leaping to the defense of their leader. But Collective members themselves were on uncertain ground. In Galt's speech Rand had made judgment into a virtue, telling her readers, "To withhold your contempt for men's vices is an act of moral counterfeiting" (946). Now if a member of the Collective offended, Nathan would "invite that person to lunch, and, in a quiet but deadly voice, I would inform him or her of the nature of the transgression."[26] Serious offenses could mean an appearance before the entire Collective, a sort of show trial with Branden or Rand presiding. Defendants who promptly confessed their guilt and promised to work harder at living Objectivist principles were let back into the fold.

Murray Rothbard was again one of the first outsiders to witness this new direction. He had reconnected with Rand after reading *Atlas Shrugged*, a work he considered "not merely the greatest novel ever written, it is one of the very greatest books ever written, fiction or nonfiction." In an extraordinarily frank letter Rothbard not only sang the praises of Rand's novel, an "infinite treasure house," but apologized for avoiding her in the past. Trusting that the author of *Atlas Shrugged* would receive his confession in the proper spirit, he told her how their previous meetings had left him depressed. It was not her fault, but his. He admitted, "I have come to regard you like the sun, a being of enormous power giving off great light, but that someone coming too close would be likely to get burned." Although his words revealed some lingering trepidation, Rothbard was eager to close the gap he had created between himself and Rand. "Please let me know if there's anything I can do to promote the sale of the novel," he wrote, and enclosed as a peace offering a letter attacking one of the book's unfavorable reviews.[27] Within weeks the Collective and the Circle Bastiat were back in close contact.

Once again Rothbard tried to keep his intellectual distance from Rand but was psychologically vulnerable to her powers. After an all-night session between the two groups he reported to a friend, "As clear and rational as she is in so many matters, she is clearly muddled as a legal and political theorist, where the Circle takes primary rank."[28] Still, Rothbard was being drawn into the Objectivist universe. For years he had suffered from a variety of phobias, the most crippling being a fear of travel that kept him from leaving New York. When Nathan promised that he could cure this phobia in a manner of months, Rothbard eagerly signed up for therapy. As a condition of his therapy Rothbard was required to take the Principles of Objectivism course. He and his wife, Joey, began socializing on a regular basis with Rand and the Collective.

Before long Rothbard tired of the Randian routine. He was annoyed when others questioned him after he skipped an occasional Objectivist gathering. He began to doubt Nathan's effectiveness as a therapist, especially after Nathan criticized his marriage to Joey, a Christian. A union of two people who held conflicting premises was inherently unstable, Nathan lectured Rothbard. He should seek a partner who held rational premises instead. Still hoping that his travel phobia could be overcome, Rothbard stayed in therapy even as he wondered whether Nathan could really help him. Nathan promised the two of them would venture outside city limits together, but the trip never materialized. Meanwhile Rothbard signed up to deliver an academic paper in Georgia, believing he would be cured by the time of the conference.

Instead, the academic conference became the grounds for a bitter final breakup between Rothbard and the Rand circle. Tensions had been building over Rothbard's stubborn allegiance to anarchism. After almost six months of regular contact Rand and the Collective expected Rothbard to be convinced that anarchism was unworkable. In July 1958 a special Saturday night session was scheduled for Rothbard and Rand to debate. By then Rothbard had realized, "I hated the guts of [Nathan] and Ayn and the rest of the gang." After a stormy appointment with Nathan he decided to terminate therapy and all relations with Rand's group. The next day Nathan called to summon him to another meeting, this time with Rand alone. At issue was the paper Rothbard had written for his upcoming conference, which Nathan accused him of plagiarizing from both Rand and Barbara Branden. Outraged, Rothbard hung up the phone "on that tin Jesus."[29] That evening's mail brought a special delivery letter from Rand's lawyer, outlining in detail the accusation of plagiarism and threatening a lawsuit against both Rothbard and the conference organizer, the German sociologist Helmut Schoeck.

The confrontation soon spilled out into open warfare between the Collective and the Circle Bastiat. George Reisman and Robert Hessen, formerly Rothbard loyalists, took Rand's side in the plagiarism dispute. After a tense showdown Rothbard kicked Reisman out of his apartment. Angry phone calls flew back and forth between Rand, Nathan, and the remaining members of Circle Bastiat. When the dust settled, Rothbard had lost both Reisman and Hessen to the Collective. In a gesture of high drama Joey Rothbard mailed each a torn dollar bill, symbolizing their broken connection. Filled in on the accusations, outsiders like Schoeck, the *National Review* editor Frank Meyer, and Richard Cornuelle dismissed Rand and her group as "crackpots." They found her accusations of plagiarism groundless. The ideas that Rand claimed as her own, Schoeck noted, had been in circulation for centuries. Still constrained by his phobia, Rothbard was unable to attend the conference as planned.[30]

The incident left Rothbard with a deep hatred of Rand and her followers. He was profoundly traumatized by the hostility of Nathan, with whom he had shared deeply private information during therapy. Just as bad was the defection of Reisman and Hessen, longtime friends who now accused him of immorality and intellectual dishonesty. Rothbard was shaken to the core. He scrawled a lengthy memo to himself, outlining nine "flaws of Randianism" and a separate list of Randian heresies. He consoled himself with the idea that Nathan's letter was so unreasonable his accusations would never be taken seriously. "It is now obvious to me and everyone else what a contemptible clown Branden is," he wrote his parents, concluding, "I'm certainly glad I'm free of that psycho." Looking again at Whittaker Chambers's review of *Atlas Shrugged*, Rothbard discovered that he had been warned. He sent Chambers a second, appreciative letter, apologizing for his first attack and marveling at Chambers's ability to identify Rand's dictatorial nature. Later he would write a satirical play about Rand, *Mozart Was a Red*, and a pamphlet titled *The Sociology of the Ayn Rand Cult*.[31] He was a powerful enemy who did everything possible to turn fellow libertarians against Rand.

Despite her longing for recognition, Rand found intellectual interchange hard to manage. When she did have contact with those prominent enough to enhance her reputation, she rarely made a positive impression. It did not take long for her to repel Sidney Hook, a prominent anti-Communist philosopher at NYU. Hook first heard of Rand through Barbara Branden and Leonard Peikoff, two of his students. He was suspicious of the great power Rand held over her followers, who seemed "*begeistered*" or hypnotized by her ideas. Then Peikoff, teaching an introductory philosophy course as part of his Ph.D., caused a furor by replacing a unit on Immanuel Kant with a unit on Objectivism. Rand was embarrassed by the uproar but used the occasion to strike up a correspondence with Hook. She professed to admire his views and was clearly interested in establishing a rapport, but he declined her request to meet. When the two were finally introduced in person at the University of Wisconsin as co-panelists at an ethics symposium, Hook was unimpressed. He later told Barbara, "It seemed to me that when I spoke she did not so much as listen as wait for me to cease talking, in order to resume the thread of what she was saying. At the time she did not appear very analytical in her responses."[32] Rand's desire for complete agreement with her ideas and her single-minded focus on consistency were distasteful to Hook.

During this time Rand continued reaching out to professional philosophers, trading books and brief complimentary letters with Brand Blanshard, a Yale professor and leading interpreter of Aristotle. Later she would also connect with the head of the Philosophy Department at Hobart College, George Walsh, who became a dedicated NBI student in the late 1960s.[33] But neither had the promise of John Hospers, a young rising professor with a doctorate from Columbia. Rand and Hospers met when she spoke at Brooklyn College, where Hospers was teaching. A specialist in ethics, Hospers was struck by her unusual perspective and the two spent the night deep in philosophical conversation. When Hospers relocated to California they corresponded in long letters. He was smitten by Rand's work and cried upon reading *The Fountainhead*.

This appreciation kept him tethered to Rand even as she denigrated his profession. Hospers found Rand's blanket condemnation of all modern philosophers difficult to take. He told her, "I see on the students' faces that it is all beginning to jell in their minds, that the 'integration—experience' is now theirs, thanks to my careful presentation and probing questions. And then I go home and get a letter from you, for which I AM very grateful, but in it you condemn all modern philosophy—which presumably includes everything that I have been laboriously doing throughout so many of my waking hours."[34] Still, Hospers found Rand a stimulating sparring partner. Although they often disagreed, he remembered that "I wasn't so concerned with what conclusion we ended up with, as with the route by which we got there: no circularity of reasoning, no begging the question, no smuggling in a premise under another name, and so on."[35] Rand helped him clarify his political views, moving him to a libertarian position.

Rand's attack on modern philosophy was inspired by Leonard Peikoff, who for years had been telling her it was still the age of "pre-reason." This was not a message she wanted to hear while toiling on her rationalist novel. After its publication, however, Peikoff seemed to have a point. He identified Kant as the source of all error in modern thought, an opinion Isabel Paterson had also held. To Peikoff, Kant's argument that the means of perception structured humans' sense of reality undermined objective reality, reason, and all absolutes. Kant's ideas had opened the philosophical gates to destructive ideas like relativism and existentialism, which created the poisonous atmosphere that greeted *Atlas Shrugged*. Rand began to listen more seriously to Peikoff's opinions about philosophy.

In a pivotal conversation, Peikoff argued that she had a significant contribution to make. He told her that no philosopher had claimed her rendering of "existence is identity," an idea she considered a self-evident update of Aristotle. The deciding factor was her meeting with Hospers. Conversations with him convinced Rand that there were indeed enormous holes in the contemporary approach to philosophy. She decided that her ideas about the proper approach to universals and concept formation were new and valuable. If she were to work them out systemically she could prove "why conceptual knowledge can be as absolute as perceptual evidence." She had the feeling of "taking on a big assignment." Imagining herself as an intellectual detective, chasing down the logical errors and frauds perpetrated over the ages, she became increasingly interested in meeting professional philosophers.[36]

Hospers scheduled a meeting with Rand that included Martin Lean, a Wittgenstein expert and chair of the Philosophy Department at Brooklyn College. It was a rowdy session, with Rand even calling Lean a "shyster" when he made a favorable comment about the USSR. Lean enjoyed their combat immensely, telling Rand afterward in a lengthy letter, "For my part I cannot recall having argued with anyone as intellectually dynamic, challenging, and skilled as you since my...Fulbright year at Oxford." He admitted to some pretensions about his own dialectical ability, yet acknowledged Rand as his equal, perhaps even his superior: "The combination of intellectual vigor and native logical acuity which you possess are truly awesome. It is academic philosophy's loss that you did not choose this as the field of your concentration."[37] He went on to express disagreement with Rand's political and economic position, noting that her arguments were thought-provoking, if not convincing.

Lean also touched on what he called "communication difficulties." Some of their disagreement, he thought, stemmed "from the fact that certain words and statements have a customary technical meaning among contemporary professional philosophers that differs from the historical use." Rand and he had different understandings of such terms as "volition" and "volitionality," he noted. Lean also suggested that Peikoff had mischaracterized Wittgenstein and other linguistic philosophers and offered to make a formal presentation to clear up the confusion. Throughout 1961 Lean and Rand corresponded occasionally and had at least one more meeting of their "small discussion group." Lean declined an invitation to attend the opening of an NBI lecture series but did deliver the promised presentation of Wittgenstein in a session that proved to be, in Rand's words, "indecisive."[38]

As Lean noticed, it was undoubtedly true that Rand had her own unique definitions for common philosophical terms. In a designation that must have shocked Rand, he even joked that he was "not as much of a Kantian" as Rand.[39] Instead of believing all questions could be resolved by fact and deductive logic, a position he attributed to Kant, Lean suggested that subjective factors might play a role. Hospers had the same experience with Rand: "I had to be careful that she not misinterpret or oversimplify what a philosopher was saying; she was so 'out of the loop' of the give-and-take of contemporary philosophers that she found even the basics to be elusive."[40] If she truly wanted to make an impact on the field, Hospers told her, she should publish in an academic journal and respond to her critics; a dialogue would start, and she would be on her way. But the normal push and pull of academic life was alien to Rand.

Her friendship with Hospers ended dramatically when he invited her to present at the 1962 American Aesthetics Association meeting, held at Harvard University. Rand must have felt she was finally getting her due, speaking to Ivy League philosophers as an equal. But after her presentation Hospers took the floor and made a critical commentary on her presentation. In his role as commentator he held forth as an authority, commending Rand in some areas, tweaking her in others, suggesting avenues of further inquiry or points to clarify. This was not the kind of treatment Rand had expected, and she was deeply hurt. At the reception afterward neither she nor the Collective would acknowledge Hospers's presence. By criticizing her in public Hospers had committed an unforgivable error, made all the worse by Rand's sensitivity to her status among intellectuals. He tried to heal the breach, but Rand would never again speak to him. Hospers continued to acknowledge Rand as an influence, including a discussion of her work in his textbook, *Introduction to Philosophical Analysis*. But he alone could do little to transform Rand's reputation in the academy. Later he even came to believe his identification with Rand cost him a job at UCLA and a Guggenheim fellowship.[41]

The long years of labor on *Atlas Shrugged*, the stress of her relationship with Nathan and her disappointment in Frank, regular drug use and unhealthy personal habits, all had culminated in a mental rigidity that increasingly defined Rand. She was even unwilling to acknowledge her own intellectual development, releasing an edited version of *We the Living* in 1959 that erased any passages at odds with Objectivism.[42] For years she had sealed herself off from all outside influences save Nathan and Leonard, and it was now impossible for her to communicate with contemporaries. The woman who had written long demonstrative letters to Isabel Paterson and Rose Wilder Lane, trying her best to understand and be understood, had vanished forever.

CHAPTER SEVEN

Radicals for Capitalism

S"I AM COMING back to life," Rand announced as the Nathaniel Branden Institute entered its second year of existence. Watching Nathan's lectures fill, Rand began to believe she might yet make an impact on the culture.[1] Roused from her despair, she began once more to write. In 1961 she published her first work of nonfiction, *For the New Intellectual,* and in 1962 launched her own monthly periodical, *The Objectivist Newsletter.* Over the course of the decade she reprinted articles from the newsletter and speeches she had given in two more books, *The Virtue of Selfishness* and *Capitalism: The Unknown Ideal.* Although she occasionally talked of a fourth novel, Rand had abandoned fiction for good. Instead she reinvented herself as a public intellectual. Gone were the allegorical stories, the dramatic heroes and heroines, the thinly coded references to real politicians, intellectuals, and events. In *The Objectivist Newsletter* Rand named names and pointed fingers, injecting herself directly into the hottest political issues of the day. Through her speeches and articles she elaborated on the ethical, political, and artistic sides of Objectivism.

Rand's ideas were particularly attractive to a new generation of campus conservatives, who saw rebellion against a stifling liberal consensus as a basic part of their identity. Unlike older conservatives, many right-leaning college students were untroubled by her atheism, or even attracted to it. As Rand's followers drew together in campus conservative groups, Ayn Rand clubs, and NBI classes, her ideas became a distinct stream of conservative youth culture. Through her essays on government, politics, and capitalism Rand herself encouraged the politicization of her work. In 1963 she even endorsed a new Republican on the scene, Barry Goldwater, a move that situated her as the leader of a growing political and intellectual movement.[2]

At first look Objectivism may appear a freakish outgrowth of the turbulent 1960s, but it had significant parallels in American history. Nearly a century before, similar reading clubs and political activism had sprung up around Edward Bellamy's *Looking Backward,* a book uncannily similar to *Atlas Shrugged,* if diametrically opposite politically. Bellamy's futuristic book, written in 1887 but set in 2000, imagined a bemused time traveler awakening in a socialist utopia and marveling at the rampant selfishness and greed that had characterized his own time. In Bellamy's most famous metaphor, a character describes late Victorian society as a carriage pulled by toiling masses, on top of which decadent capitalists live a life of luxury and ease. Inspired by Bellamy's vision of a planned, egalitarian society, organizations sprang up across the country to advocate for his plans.[3] Now, similarly enraptured by Rand's utopia, came forth a new cohort of well-educated, affluent reformers, this time eager to defend the carriage-pulling capitalists against the mob who rode atop their effort.

Rand made her network television debut in 1960, appearing on Mike Wallace's celebrated interview show. Her dark eyes flashing, she refused to be intimidated by the liberal Wallace and expertly parried his every question and critique. Her performance caught the eye of Senator Barry Goldwater, who wrote Rand a letter thanking her for defending his "conservative position." Rand had not mentioned the senator by name, but he immediately recognized the similarity between their views. Goldwater told Rand, "I have enjoyed very few books in my life as much as I have yours, *Atlas Shrugged.*" He enclosed an autographed copy of his new book, the best-selling *Conscience of a Conservative.* Shortly thereafter the two met briefly in New York. Rand followed up this encounter with a lengthy letter urging Goldwater to support capitalism through reason alone.[4] Although she considered him the most promising politician in the country, Rand was distressed by Goldwater's frequent allusions to religion. *The Conscience of a Conservative* had been written primarily by L. Brent Bozell, William F. Buckley's brother-in-law, and accordingly reflected the fusionist consensus of *National Review.*

In her letter to Goldwater Rand hammered on the need to separate religion and politics, a theme that would animate her for decades. She singled out *National Review* for special criticism because it was a sup-posedly secular magazine that surreptitiously tried "to tie Conservatism to religion, and thus to take over the American Conservatives." If such an effort succeeded, Rand asked, what would become of religious minori-ties or people like herself who held no religion? Goldwater's response, which reiterated his Christian religious beliefs, was brief yet polite.[5] Rand had a powerful admirer, but not a convert.

As her depression lifted, Rand began to explore different ways she might exercise cultural influence. She was newly interested in politics because of her esteem for Goldwater and her dislike of the dashing presidential contender, Jack Kennedy, to her a glamour candidate who offered no serious ideas. She made her first venture back into politi-cal commentary with a scathing attack on Kennedy, "JFK: High Class Beatnik," a short article published in the libertarian journal *Human Events*.[6] In the summer of 1960 she even dispatched Nathan to investi-gate the possibility of founding her own political party. It was unclear if Rand saw herself as a potential candidate or simply a gatekeeper for others. Nathan sounded out a few of Goldwater's political advisors, who told him that Rand's atheism severely limited her prospects. Abandoning that idea, Rand returned once again to intellectual pursuits. She sent her attack on JFK to the head of the Republican National Committee to be used as needed in Republican publications.

Shaking off her lethargy, Rand now began paying attention to the new following she had gained through *Atlas Shrugged*. The book was an instant best-seller despite the largely negative reviews it received. As with *The Fountainhead* enormous quantities of enthusiastic fan mail poured in. Although Rand could not respond personally to every letter, she was interested in her readers, particularly those who wrote especially perceptive or ignorant letters. Nathan often interposed himself between Rand and the most objectionable writers, but in the early 1960s it was entirely possible to send her a letter and receive a personal response. Sometimes she even engaged in a lengthy correspondence with fans she had not met, although her more usual response was to refer the writer to work she had already published.

The Nathaniel Branden Institute both capitalized on and fostered Rand's appeal. Nathan used the addresses from her fan mail to build NBI's mailing list and advertise new courses. As the lectures expanded into new cities, he took out newspaper advertisements describing Objectivism as the philosophy of Ayn Rand. In 1962 he and Barbara published a hagiographic biography, *Who Is Ayn Rand?*, which included an essay by Nathan on the fundamentals of her philosophy. Slowly public perception of Rand began to shift, establishing her as a philosopher, not just a novelist. The NBI ads and lectures made Objectivism into a movement, a larger trend with Rand at the forefront.

Rand's first published work of nonfiction, *For the New Intellectual*, set forth the creed her young fans would follow in the coming decade. Most of the book consisted of excerpts from Rand's already published fiction, except for the title essay, which called for a cadre of "New Intellectuals" who would work together with business to celebrate the achievements of industrialism and capitalism. In the essay Rand identified three categories of men who had clashed throughout history: Atillas (despotic rulers), Witch Doctors (priests and intellectuals), and Producers (spiritual forerunners of American businessmen). The first two terms, she noted, had been coined by Nathaniel Branden, whom she formally thanked for his "eloquent designation."[7] She traced their conflicts through Western history until the Industrial Revolution, when two new social types were born: the modern businessman and the modern intellectual. According to Rand, the two were supposed to work in tandem to manage, direct, and explain the changes stemming from the Industrial Revolution. But intellectuals had committed "treason" in the face of this grave responsibility, choosing instead to hold down Producers by promoting altruism as an ethical imperative.

Rand's essay mixed history, philosophy, and polemic into a bewitching brew. While her typologies bore a clear resemblance to traditional divisions between proletariat, capitalist, and revolutionary vanguard, she centered these differences in mental outlook, not economic position. Producers were different from Witch Doctors and Atillas because they were independent and rational rather than mystical. Even though she avoided the language of economic determinism, Rand saw history as a kind of spiritualized class struggle. She took readers on a rapid tour of Western intellectual history, quickly summarizing and critiquing several major schools of philosophy.

Rand then paused to clarify her most misunderstood and controversial idea, her attack upon altruism, or "moral cannibalism," as she liked to call it. She explained that she used the word as did the French philosopher August Comte, to mean "self-sacrifice." This usage was philosophically precise, but potentially very confusing. Most of Rand's critics took the word in the more colloquial sense, as broadly meaning concern for or caring about other people. This meant that Rand seemed to be attacking even kindness itself. Once again, as she had with selfishness, Rand was redefining words to match her philosophical concepts.[8] It was not, she thought, her fault that she was sometimes misunderstood, and in any event she relished her iconoclastic persona. If her audience thought she was violating all standards of human decency, so much the better.

Rand presented herself as a serious philosophical thinker and analyst of American history, but could not fully escape her innate penchant for provocation and emotional invective. Her high-minded discussion of philosophy was punctured by colorful and occasionally bizarre metaphors. She described contemporary intellectual discourse as "a sticky puddle of stale syrup" and referred to "chickens hiding their heads in the sand ('ostrich' is too big and dignified a metaphor for this instance)."[9] Still, she effectively charged her readers with a world-historical task: her New Intellectuals must challenge and replace the left-leaning supporters of socialism and the welfare state.

For the New Intellectual drew a terrific blast from Sidney Hook in the *New York Times Book Review*. Hook observed archly, "Despite the great play with the word 'Reason,' one is struck by the absence of any serious argument in this unique combination of tautology and extravagant absurdity." Like the reviewers of *Atlas Shrugged*, Hook focused as much on Rand's tone as her ideas. He granted that nonprofessionals could write interesting work on philosophy, but not by "substituting denunciation for analysis and mouthing slogans instead of considering problems... The language of reason does not justify references to economists with whom one disagrees as 'frantic cowards,' or to philosophers as 'intellectual hoodlums who pose as professors.' This is the way philosophy is written in the Soviet Union." Hook could conceive of no possible reason why Rand should be taken seriously as a thinker. Still, his scorn did little to dent Rand's popularity or the book's sales.[10]

Other reviewers made similarly vain attempts to stem the tide of Objectivism. Gore Vidal seconded Hook's opinion in *Esquire*, calling Rand an unreadable novelist who "has a great attraction for simple

people who are puzzled by organized society." His censure was mingled
with anxiety about Rand's influence, for Vidal recalled that in his campaign for the House of Representatives she was the one writer "people
knew and talked about."[11] Having been earlier scored by leading conservative thinkers, Rand now took a drubbing at the hands of establishment liberals. *Newsweek,* the *New Republic, America,* and the *Christian
Century* all piled on, publishing harshly negative reviews of *For the New
Intellectual.*

The reaction to Rand fell neatly into a pattern established years
before. Since the advent of Joseph McCarthy, Wisconsin's famously anti-
Communist senator, liberals had trouble treating conservative ideas as
legitimate. A prominent 1955 volume, *The Radical Right,* set the tone
by treating libertarianism and anti-Communism as psychological syn-
dromes, an expression of paranoia or status anxiety.[12] Accordingly liberal
commentators derided Rand and her following as a fringe element with
little to contribute to the nation's intellectual life. But Rand's popularity
appeared impervious to attack by the most esteemed members of the
establishment. The more the guardians of respectability criticized Rand,
the more irresistible she became to conservatives who loved thumbing
their noses at the ascendant liberal order.[13]

Accustomed by now to negative press, Rand plunged forward with
two new projects in 1962: *The Objectivist Newsletter* and a syndicated
column for the *Los Angeles Times.* The newspaper column lasted barely
a year, when it was canceled by mutual agreement. Rand found it difficult to meet the column's weekly deadline. Its frequency did, however,
encourage her to explore a range of topics that might otherwise have
escaped her comment. The *Times* column inspired some of her first
writing on American popular culture, an interest of hers since arriving in Hollywood. She wrote a touching obituary of Marilyn Monroe,
calling her an "eager child" who projected "glowing innocent sexuality…uncorrupted by guilt."[14] According to Rand, Monroe's suicide signified a hatred of values that was the dominant style of the century. The
theme of America's bankrupt culture was becoming ever more prominent in her writing, fed by her new interest in modern philosophy and
the lingering trauma of *Atlas Shrugged*'s reception.

Unlike NBI, which was wholly owned by Nathan, *The Objectivist
Newsletter* was a joint undertaking between Ayn and Nathan. The two

ventures were deeply intertwined, sharing the same office space and staff. Barbara was the managing editor, and Nathan's sister, Elayne Kalberman, came aboard as circulation manager. The newsletter established a path of upward mobility for aspiring NBI students who could now be published as Objectivist writers. Its primary contributors were Ayn and Nathan, but others chimed in with book reviews, essays, and cultural commentary. Rand had final say over all articles and enjoyed editing and shaping submissions. The newsletter fulfilled a dream that dated from her days on the Willkie campaign. Back then she had imagined a publication that would serve to unite opponents of the New Deal and inspire them to fight for capitalism. Twenty years later she achieved that goal.

The introduction of *The Objectivist Newsletter* marked Rand's redefinition of herself as a public intellectual ready to comment on current events. In the first issue she announced the arrival of Objectivism as a philosophical movement with a unique political viewpoint. "Objectivists are *not* 'conservatives.' We are *radicals for capitalism*," she declared.[15] The newsletter was a slim publication that typically ranged from four to eight pages in length. Most issues included a lead article by Ayn or Nathan, a book review, a feature titled "Intellectual Ammunition Department," where reader queries about the application of Objectivist principles to real-life situations were answered, and an Objectivist calendar making note of pertinent activities. Almost all of the books reviewed had a right-wing slant or tended to reinforce Objectivist biases, although the magazine gave a glowing review to Betty Friedan's *The Feminine Mystique,* calling it "brilliant, informative, and culturally explosive."[16] Other covered titles included the Aristotelian philosopher Brand Blanshard's *Reason and Analysis* and Ludwig von Mises's *Human Action*. Reviews were generally evenhanded, mixing praise and criticism, and each concluded with a section that evaluated the book according to Objectivist standards. Through the longer articles by Rand, often reprints of her speeches, subscribers got a firsthand look at her elaboration of Objectivism beyond the outline presented in her novel.

Unapologetic and extreme, the new Rand had a talent for getting headlines. As her ideas spread she became both a media punching bag and a media darling. Mike Wallace was among the first to understand that Rand was one of the "people other people are interested in." After her appearance on his TV show, several of his staff members converted to Objectivism. A coworker remembered the transformation of Edith Efron, who "began speaking in a very, very strange way about psychology, art, politics—in a way that I'd never heard before and certainly not from a New York Jewish intellectual. I thought she was going out of her mind." Soon other outlets recognized Rand's audience appeal. She began a radio program on the Columbia University station, "Ayn Rand on Campus," and appeared on CBS's discussion series *The Great Challenge*. In 1964 she reached what was then a lofty summit of journalism, the *Playboy* interview. In the mid-1960s *Playboy* was at the height of its cultural influence, publishing serious essays and commentary alongside photos of its famous playmates. Hugh Hefner had long been a fan of Rand, and his magazine ran a long and probing piece by the future futurist Alvin Toffler, who treated Rand with care and respect. She even visited a Playboy Club, which she pronounced "a wonderful place and a brilliant undertaking."[17]

Despite all the attention she attracted Rand was an unwilling celebrity. Even NBI events disconcerted her. She normally made a dramatic entrance from the back of the room, receiving applause as she made her way to the stage. An NBI student seeing her off was surprised when Rand muttered, "I hate doing this. Every time I walk down that long aisle, I feel like a bride getting married." When she traveled to distant places she preferred to have the Collective with her, or at least Frank and Nathan. Her husband raised eyebrows among outsiders like Mike Wallace, who called him "her gelded companion."[18] The Collective had grown used to Frank's silence, but to others his passivity was a troubling suggestion of Rand's need for dominance. Few understood how vital Frank's presence was to Rand. If it could benefit Objectivism, she would go through the rituals and forms of being famous and expose herself to the public eye. But she needed Frank there with her, a comforting shield against the world.

Nowhere was Rand more popular than on college campuses. Her first appearance before a student audience, at Yale University, was a tour de force. A reporter at the event described the overflow audience Rand drew, a motley assemblage with "ladies in fur hats or stoles, students in sneakers and shirt-sleeves. There were crew cuts and long-hairs, and beards of various lengths and colors hiding young faces. No smoking signs were disregarded." Rand spoke forcefully and confidently to her Ivy League audience and particularly relished the question-and-answer session that followed. When an audience member questioned her "slur" of the New Deal, "'It was not a slur' Rand shot back. 'I intended it to be a damnation.'"[19] She concluded to a standing ovation. The speech put Rand back in a role she had last enjoyed in her Willkie days: the featured speaker, holding forth against all comers.

After Yale she began to regularly accept invitations to visit on college campuses. By all accounts a fascinating and effective public speaker, she regularly drew above-capacity crowds. In public Rand cultivated a mysterious and striking persona. Her dark hair was cut in a severe pageboy style, and she wore a long black cape with a dollar sign pin on the lapel. Decades after emigration she still spoke with a distinct Russian accent. At parties afterward she chain-smoked cigarettes held in an elegant ivory holder, surrounded by her New York entourage. Before long Rand was receiving far more speaking invitations than she could possibly accept; in 1965 alone she turned down more than twenty requests from colleges and universities. She accepted only the most coveted invitations, preferring to speak at Ivy League schools and selective public universities like the University of Wisconsin and the University of California, Berkeley. After the publication of *For the New Intellectual* she established a relationship with Boston's Ford Hall Forum, where she delivered an annual address for the next twenty years. One of her greatest triumphs came in 1963, when Lewis and Clark College invited her to campus for its annual Reading Week, assigned *Atlas Shrugged* (among other novels) to all students and faculty, and awarded her an honorary doctorate in humane letters.[20]

Although Rand was not included in most colleges' official curricula, she inhabited a shadow world of intellectual resources that students shared among themselves. One young man described his first encounter with Objectivism: "A stunningly beautiful studymate, who had read *Atlas,* asked me a stunning question: 'is it just that my father, a surgeon, is forced to pay a greater percentage of income in taxes than do other people?' I had no answer." Secure in her affluence, this student used

Rand as a defense and vindication of her social position. Rand's campus speeches were a gateway into Objectivism for many. Her provocative stance electrified audiences and stood in contrast to the more prosaic, measured presentation of ideas students normally heard. After Rand spoke at the University of Virginia, one student said that her speech was the first thing "he'd gotten really excited about in three years in college." Interest in Rand was contagious. A female student at Brown University was crossing campus when she "ran into a yelling, enthusiastic mob of girls surrounding somebody." The cause of the excitement was Rand, fresh off her speech "The Intellectual Bankruptcy of Our Age." Curious, the student began reading Rand and over summer vacation brought her two brothers into the fold.[21]

Rand's student followers were drawn to her because she offered an attractive alternative to the mainstream intellectual and political culture of the 1960s. Rand was a system builder in the old style, an unabashed moralist, an ideologue, and an idealist. Objectivism contrasted sharply with the dominant ideas in universities, where most intellectuals had become skeptical of claims to objective truth, preferring to emphasize multiple perspectives, subjectivity, and the conditioned nature of reality. They were, as Rand put it, "opposed to principles on principle." Philosophy had become insular and esoteric, with mathematical discussions of logic and linguistics dominating professional discourse. By contrast, Rand wrote in a casual style and addressed the ethics of everyday life, the conundrums of money, sex, work, and politics.[22] Her ideas spoke powerfully to students who hoped that in college they would study the great questions of existence, and instead found their idealism stifled by a climate of skepticism and moral relativity. As one Objectivist remembered, "I thought that philosophy and psychology held the key to understanding the 'meaning of life.' When I took those courses, I found myself studying instead the meaning of words and the behavior of rats in mazes."[23] Objectivism filled in the gaps universities left unattended.

Another student outlined myriad complaints in a letter to Rand. He was particularly bothered by a pervasive cynicism in the two universities he had attended: "Anyone who seeks, or makes a statement on, truth and/or beauty is (a) ignored, (b) the recipient of a vague, benevolent smile, (c) scorned, (d) politely laughed at and called 'unsophisticated,' or (e) treated as a refugee from some quaint spot, which, fortunately, is now 'lost.'"[24] Rand, though, was interested in both truth and beauty. She defined herself as a leader of the nearly lost Romantic school and attacked Naturalistic writers and artists as "the gutter school." Alluding to Vladimir Nabokov's *Lolita*, Rand criticized modern intellectuals and writers: "They feel hatred for any projection of man as a clean, self confident, efficacious being. They extol depravity; they relish the sight of man spitting in his own face."[25] She preferred the popular mystery novels of Mickey Spillane, featuring a hard-boiled detective who doggedly tracked down evildoers.

Objectivism was also appealing because it promised sure footing on the slippery terrain of right and wrong. Rand insisted that ethics could be scientifically derived from the nature of man, properly understood. Man was a rational being and therefore, that which served his life, *qua* man, was the good. More important than her elevation of selfishness was Rand's insistence that her ethics could be proven and defended objectively. Remembering his turn to Objectivism, a radio host explained, "I think the biggest change that occurs is that you recognize that there are absolutes, that there are guidelines as criteria, that you can know and understand." The absolutist and rationalistic form of Rand's ethics appealed as much as their content. "Above all, Dagny is sure of herself, and lots of young people want to be sure of themselves," one college fan told an interviewer.[26]

It was not certainty alone that Rand offered, but the idea that things *made sense,* that the world was rational, logical, and could be understood. Order was the particular reward of *Atlas Shrugged,* which portrayed a world in which politics, philosophy, ethics, sex, and every other aspect of human existence were drawn together into a cohesive narrative. Just as Rand had provided businessmen with a set of ideas that met their need to feel righteous and honorable in their professional lives, she gave young people a philosophical system that met their deep need for order and certainty. This aspect of her appeal rings through again and again in accounts of her influence. One young fan told Rand that before finding her work, he was "a very confused person" but "You gave me the answers, and more important, a moral sanction for existing." Often the lure of Rand's intelligible world was enough for readers to trade in long-standing beliefs overnight. A self-described former "altruist and socialist" started her books skeptically but soon found in Rand the "consistent philosophy that ignored no aspect of life" he had always sought. Sharon Presley, one of the few women to become active in the libertarian movement, remembered *Atlas Shrugged* as a revelation: "It wasn't until Rand that I had some kind of explicitly articulated theory or set of principles that made sense to me…so that was a major, major influence on my life."[27] Objectivism seemed immediately superior to her previous habits of thought because Rand's ideas interlocked and supported one another.

In many ways the overwhelming impact of Rand's ideas mimicked Marxism's influence. Arthur Koestler's memory of his conversion to Communism echoes the sentiments expressed by Rand's readers: "The new light seems to pour from all directions across the skull; the whole universe falls into pattern like the stray pieces of a jigsaw puzzle assembled by magic at one stroke. There is now an answer to every question; doubts and conflicts are a matter of the tortured past." Only a small portion of Rand's readers became as feverishly devoted to her ideas as Koestler did to Marxism, but the basic dynamic was similar. A twenty-four-year-old woman told Rand, "you have combined all my stray thoughts into an orderly, workable pattern—this alone is worth many years of my life."[28] Rand's perspective could bring refreshing clarity to the unfocused, replacing doubt and uncertainty with passion and conviction.

No matter how they came to Rand, some basic similarities seemed to underlie those who were attracted to her. In his 1963 study of young conservatives, *They'd Rather Be Right,* Edward Cain designated Rand the primary "theorist" of conservative youth and described the type who was drawn to her. According to Cain, the follower of Rand was limited in number "but qualitatively very important. He is very likely to picture himself as someone whom John Galt might call to his mountain retreat. Bright, alert, and conscious of his capacity, he would admire the boldness of heroic action. Having something to offer, he feels there should be appropriate reward for a job well done, and has probably long despised the 'second handers,' or drones, who have had to crib from his chemistry reports or term papers."[29] Although Cain's emblematic Objectivist was male, the presence of Rand herself, along with her independent, intelligent female heroines, made Objectivism attractive to female students in search of role models. Whatever their gender, Rand drew students who were self-consciously intellectual and willing to read outside their assigned coursework. No one who quailed at a novel in the thousand-page range would get very far into the Objectivist world.

Once engaged with Rand, students often attempted to bring her into the classroom, with uniformly disastrous results. A Brown University student described how his grades plummeted after he began relying heavily on Rand for his schoolwork. First came the term paper on Franklin Roosevelt, analyzing him as a "social metaphysician" under the authority of Nathaniel Branden. Then followed his turn toward Romanticism after reading Rand's essay "The Goal of My Writing." The student recounted: "It just hadn't occurred to me, until then, that I had been writing rather realistic, naturalistic stuff. Ayn Rand made that sound like part of the international Communist conspiracy. Treason to Tarzan. I was just bowled over." Formerly the star of his creative writing class, the student now began to churn out derivative, Rand-style Romantic stories on the level of "C grade movies." His instructor despaired at seeing his prize pupil's creativity and talent disappear overnight, but the student remembered: "It never occurred to me that what was happening to me was anything but Howard Roark banished by the Dean."[30] Feeling marginalized or discriminated against was no burden to Objectivists; indeed it indicated that they were acting as honorable, independent individualists.

Students pressed onward in their quest to share Rand's ideas, often becoming the bane of their college instructors in the process. One student at Montclair State in New Jersey described his battle with a political science professor: "One day after class I recommended your books and repeated the Oath of Self Allegiance. He winced."[31] Rand bedeviled college professors of all stripes. Some took preemptive action: *The Objectivist Newsletter* reported on a philosophy professor who automatically failed any student who wrote a paper on Objectivism. Arriving at Wellesley College, Nora Ephron was whisked to an orientation seminar where the evils of Rand's philosophy were stressed. "How pleased I was to read your excellent book review!" a professor of French at Columbia University told Sidney Hook, recounting a recent run-in with a student who had "exuberant enthusiasm about Ayn Rand's 'philosophy.'" Exhausted and exasperated by the effort "to make this student realize that logical analysis ought to be applied when judging Ayn Rand's statements properly," the professor was grateful to Hook for offering a definitive rebuttal of her ideas in the nation's most respected newspaper.[32]

A writer for *New University Thought* captured the mood among university professors. Robert L. White grudgingly admitted Rand's influence, calling her "a genuinely popular ideologue of the right" and identifying a "genuine grass-roots fervor for her ideas." According to White, Rand was the only contemporary novelist his students consistently admired, and he found it "dismaying to contemplate the possibility that Ayn Rand is the single writer who engages the loyalties of the students I am perhaps ineffectually attempting to teach." White thought Rand was "a horrendously bad writer," and, condescendingly, he thought his student's identification with her heroic characters "pathetic." But White was also scared. Even though he couldn't take Rand seriously as a thinker or a writer, he worried that when his students outgrew her, "some of Ayn Rand's poison is apt to linger in their systems—linger and fester there to malform them as citizens and, possibly, deliver them over willing victims to the new American totalitarians."[33] Like many of Rand's critics it was difficult for White to imagine Rand as simply another purveyor in the marketplace of ideas.

Professorial opposition to Rand was undoubtedly fed by her reputation as a right-wing extremist. On college campuses those interested in Rand typically gravitated toward conservative student groups, soon making Objectivists into a visible segment of the conservative youth population. *Atlas Shrugged* had been roundly denounced by Rand's conservative and libertarian contemporaries, but a new generation greeted the book with enthusiasm. A 1963 *National Review* survey of student conservatives noted that "a small but appreciable headway is being made by the Objectivists" and estimated that they composed less than 10 percent of the student right.[34] The survey included Sarah Lawrence, Williams, Yale, Marquette, Boston University, Indiana, South Carolina, Howard, Reed, Davidson, Brandeis, and Stanford. The highest percentage of self-identified Objectivists were at Stanford and Boston University (7 percent and 5 percent, respectively). In California she had a significant following at both public and private schools.

From its founding days, Rand's ideas haunted Young Americans for Freedom (YAF), one of the first conservative youth organizations. The brainchild of William F. Buckley, the group drew up its founding principles, "The Sharon Statement," during a meeting at Buckley's Connecticut estate in 1960. Like Rand, Buckley wanted to form a cadre of young activists who would influence the country's political future. Buckley's new intellectuals, however, would swear allegiance to God and country, rather than reason and capitalism. Although Buckley intended the new organization to reflect the fusionist consensus of *National Review,* not all members of YAF were willing to go along. The organization's first student head, Robert Schuchman, a Yale Law student, had written Rand a gushing fan letter a year earlier, telling her, "*Atlas Shrugged* was a fulfillment of a literary promise I only began to see in *The Fountainhead:* the promise of a logical view of existence, based on experience, a view which I had always held but had never been able to verbalize."[35] Now he and a few others fought to make Rand's secular libertarianism a prominent part of YAF. In a dispute over the proposed organization's name, they prevailed against the suggested "Young Conservatives" and ensured that the Sharon Statement had a libertarian cast. For Schuchman and other secular libertarians, Rand's pro-capitalist philosophy was exciting and her atheism unremarkable.

Another prominent young conservative, Karl Hess, was attracted to Rand specifically by her atheism. Formerly a practicing Catholic, his faith began to waver after he started reading Rand. He remembered, "My previous armor of ritual and mystery were insufficient to the blows dealt it by an increasing interest in science and by the unshakeable arguments of Ayn Rand." Similarly Tibor Machan, a young Hungarian refugee who would become a libertarian philosopher, found Rand while he was in the throes of a religious crisis. Machan struggled against the ethical imperatives of Christianity, which filled him with guilt, shame, and confusion. Reading *The Fountainhead* convinced him to abandon religion altogether in favor of Rand's rational morality. A year later he told Rand, "The change in me has been so drastic that only one who himself has gone through it could fully understand." He enclosed a letter he had written to his priest, drawing a thoughtful and encouraging response from Rand.

Although Objectivism appeared a way to escape religion, it was more often a substitute, offering a similar regimentation and moralism without the sense of conformity. Rand's ideas allowed students to reject traditional religion without feeling lost in a nihilistic, meaningless universe. But from the inside Objectivists threw off the shackles of family and propriety by defining themselves anew as atheists. "Last spring I discarded my religion, and this past Fall I took the Principles course in Washington. Two better choices can hardly be imagined," one Georgetown student reported proudly to Rand.[36]

Like most conservatives, Rand was energized and excited by Barry Goldwater's battle for the 1964 Republican nomination.[37] She saw his leading opponent, New York Governor Nelson Rockefeller, as another Eisenhower, a dangerous moderate who would dilute the differences between the two parties. In a boxed note set off from the rest of the October 1963 *Objectivist Newsletter,* Rand suggested that "all those who are interested in political action and specifically all those who advocate capitalism" should register as Republicans in order to vote for Goldwater in the primary. She was initially cautious in her praise of Goldwater, writing, "At present, he is the best candidate in the field." Six months later she was more enthusiastic. In "How to Judge a Political Candidate" she appeared to be convincing herself that Goldwater's religion was not significant. She told her readers it was not necessary to endorse a candidate's total philosophy, only his political philosophy. On this basis Goldwater was still the best candidate, "because freedom is his major premise....Some of his specific steps may be wrong; his direction is right." Even better, he was "singularly devoid of power lust." As far as his policies, Rand was most impressed by Goldwater's aggressive foreign-policy stance, his invocation of national honor, his assertion of "America's self interest and self-esteem." Once Goldwater won the nomination she actively sought a role in his presidential campaign through their shared contacts, offering her help in any capacity.[38]

Goldwater and Rand drew from the same wells of libertarian enthusiasm. During Goldwater's campaign, subscriptions to *The Objectivist Newsletter* boomed, rising from five thousand in 1963 to fifteen thousand by the end of the following year.[39] The Arizona senator hailed from the libertarian sunbelt region where Rand's books were favorites, and both were popular among small business owners. In Washington State, the Draft Goldwater Committee ordered two hundred copies of *Atlas Shrugged* for potential supporters. Goldwater, like Rand, talked about profits, production, and the burden of taxation and regulation. "Profits are the surest sign of responsible behavior," he said on the Senate floor, almost echoing Rand's ideas about money as the root of all good.[40]

His belief in the power and efficacy of free markets endeared him to the independent business owners who formed the backbone of his organization.

Young Goldwater enthusiasts quickly noticed that he seemed to perfectly embody Rand's iconography of the independent, manly hero. Jerome Tuccille, an avid libertarian, remembered, "More important than his message was the fact that Goldwater managed to *look the part* as though he had been made for it.... One look at him and you knew he belonged in Galt's Gulch, surrounded by striking heroes with blazing eyes and lean, dynamic heroines with swirling capes." The campaign's student arm was saturated with Rand fans, as one MIT student remembered. He joined YAF and Students for Goldwater, only to find that "Most of the key people in both groups (which mostly overlapped) were Objectivists, and I kept getting into discussions of Rand's ideas without having read the books." The connection between Rand and Goldwater's campaign was cemented by Karl Hess, a dedicated NBI student and one of Goldwater's chief speechwriters. Hess sprinkled Randian parlance liberally throughout his boss's speeches. "There were strong echoes from the novelist of romantic capitalism, Ayn Rand," the *Washington Star* noted of one Goldwater speech.[41]

As the campaign wore on, Rand was outraged to see Goldwater caricatured as a racist by the mass media. It was true that both she and Goldwater opposed the 1964 Civil Rights Act, a litmus test of liberal acceptability, but neither she nor Goldwater was truly prejudiced. Rand inveighed against racism as "the lowest, most crudely primitive form of collectivism," and Goldwater had integrated his family's business years before and was even a member of the NAACP. But Goldwater's libertarianism trumped his racial liberalism. He was among a handful of senators who voted against the bill, a sweeping piece of legislation intended to address the intractable legacy of racial discrimination in the South. Goldwater's vote was based on principles he had held for years. A firm supporter of state's rights, he was alarmed at the expansive powers granted the federal government under the act. Following the analysis of his friends William Rehnquist and Robert Bork, he also believed the act was unconstitutional because it infringed on private property rights. In the scrum of electoral politics such distinctions were academic. Goldwater's vote went down as a vote for segregation.

Rand understood his action differently because she shared his individualistic perspective on rights and his belief that private property was sacrosanct. Unlike Goldwater, Rand was unimpressed with the doctrine of state's rights, which "pertains to the division of power between local and national authorities.…It does not grant to state governments an unlimited, arbitrary power over its citizens." But she was equally appalled by the act's clauses II and VII, which forbade discrimination in public accommodations and employment. If the act passed it would be the "worst breach of property rights in the sorry record of American history," she wrote. Early civil rights activists who struggled against government-enforced segregation drew Rand's approval. Now she criticized "Negro leaders" for forfeiting their moral case against discrimination by "demanding special race privileges." Rand considered race a collectivist fiction, a peripheral category to be subsumed into her larger philosophy. Her rendering of American history did not ignore race, but neatly slotted it into her larger vision of capitalism. Slavery simply proved her point about the country's "mixed economy," and the Civil War demonstrated the superiority of the capitalistic North against "the agrarian-feudal South."[42]

In the pages of *The Objectivist Newsletter* Rand vigorously defended Goldwater against the widespread perception that he represented "the Radical Right," a dangerous fringe element said to be imperiling American democracy. The charges stemmed from Goldwater's popularity among members of the John Birch Society (JBS), a secretive anti-Communist group. Members and the group's founder, the candy manufacturer Robert Welch, tended to anti-Semitism and bizarre conspiracy theories. In a much ballyhooed comment Welch once told supporters he believed Dwight Eisenhower to be a Communist agent. Members of the society, which kept its roster confidential, were found in every segment of the political right. But its oddities, once uncovered by the mass media, were fast making the JBS a political hot potato. Richard Nixon denounced the group in 1962 while running for governor of California. It was a move intended to advance his appeal among moderates, but instead it cost Nixon a sizable chunk of his base and he lost the election. Goldwater was unwilling to take such a step, for he understood how vital the JBS was to his campaign. Society members were as common among adult volunteers as Objectivists were among his campus following. Goldwater walked a careful line, making use of JBS volunteers who did not publi-cize their membership.[43]

Rand was not bothered by the charges against the JBS, which she char-acterized as "an artificial and somewhat unworthy strawman." She had lunch with Welch in Boston before her first Ford Hall Forum appearance; apparently it was a successful encounter despite their differences. Welch followed up with a copy of Grace Lumpkin's anti-Communist religious autobiography, noting that Rand might disagree with the theme but still find it of interest. The JBS even had a form letter of sorts for Objectivists who inquired about membership. "Since Miss Rand is an avowed atheist, she would certainly not follow the Society in its insistence that its mem-bers believe in God," the letter read, continuing, "Any support, however, which you might be able to give to the principles of less government, more individual responsibility, and a better world, outside membership in the Society, would certainly be appreciated." To Rand the JBS was simply another group of misguided religious conservatives. She didn't understand the extent to which the society had become synonymous in the popular mind with incipient fascism and totalitarian mob rule. The JBS had even been widely—and falsely—linked with the Kennedy assassination. It struck fear into the hearts of liberal commentators, ever alert for demagogues after an era of totalitarianism. By contrast Rand wondered, "What, exactly, is the evil of the so-called 'radical right?'" It couldn't be racism, she argued, for "the main, active body of racists in this country" were southern Democrats.[44]

Rand viewed the charge of racism as a smokescreen for liberal oppo-sition to capitalism. In her mind Goldwater's defense of capitalism explained his popularity, for the main issue of the age was capitalism versus socialism. In a postmortem on the Republican convention she wrote, "Now consider the term extremism. Its alleged meaning is: 'intol-erance, hatred, racism, bigotry, crackpot theories, incitement to vio-lence.' Its real meaning is: 'the advocacy of capitalism.'"[45] To some degree Rand had a point. Liberal commentators appeared especially incredu-lous at the mention of libertarian ideas, and support for the Liberty Amendment, a proposal to ban the income tax, ran high among Birchers. But free markets were only a piece of the larger JBS worldview, which included staunch opposition to civil rights and anti-Communism à la McCarthy. With her single-minded focus on capitalism, Rand missed the political realities unfolding on the ground. The violence and unrest of 1964, including the Watts riot, stoked racial anxieties. Goldwater had staked out his territory as an opponent of the Democratic approach to civil rights; whether he liked it or not, he was becoming a central figure in the political clash over integration and desegregation, and these issues, far more than capitalism, underlay his political fortunes.

An eager booster of Goldwater up to his triumphant nomination at San Francisco's Cow Palace, Rand became disillusioned as he moved into the general election. It was the same mistake Willkie had made. Goldwater began to retreat from his pro-capitalist stance, repackaging himself as a moderate who could appeal to a broad swath of voters. Afterward Rand dissected his campaign angrily: "There was no discussion of capitalism. There was no discussion of statism. There was no discussion of the blatantly vulnerable record of the government's policies in the last thirty years. There was no discussion. There were no issues." A month before the election Rand warned her readers that Goldwater was moving toward defeat, and she urged them to prepare for the "bitter disappointment." Perhaps hoping to reverse the tide, as the campaign drew to a close Rand sent him a speech to be used without attribution.[46] Her speech, like her letter to Goldwater, recast conservatism along purely economic lines, celebrating the power of the free market. The campaign, by now past the point of rescue, ignored her contribution.

In truth Goldwater faced a nearly impossible task. He was running against the master politician Lyndon Baines Johnson, who pulled the mantle of the deceased John F. Kennedy close around his shoulders. And Goldwater's irreverent, shoot-from-the hip, folksy style, so attractive to straight-talking libertarians, was a huge liability. Caricatured as a racist fanatic who would drag the United States into nuclear war, Goldwater lost by a landslide in the general election. Besides Arizona the only states he won were in the Deep South, filled with the very southern Democrats Rand cited to disprove his racism. Yet Goldwater's decisive defeat held within it the seeds of political transformation, for his positions had made the Republican Party nationally competitive in the South for the first time since the Civil War. It was an augury of the first national political realignment since FDR's New Deal.[47]

"It's earlier than we think," Rand told the *New York Times* the day after Goldwater's loss. Advocates of capitalism had to "start from

scratch" and concentrate on culture rather than practical politics.[48]
This was the same conclusion she had reached after the Willkie campaign—that a popular consensus on the virtues of capitalism had to
be established before electoral success could be achieved. Laissez-faire
capitalism belonged to the uncharted future rather than the past. The
senator himself seemed to accept Rand's explanation for his defeat,
quoting her in his syndicated column.[49] In *The Objectivist Newsletter*,
her private forum, Rand openly blamed Goldwater for his loss. She was
appalled that the only voters he had drawn to his banner were southern whites: "As it stands, the most grotesque, irrational and disgrace-
ful consequence of the campaign is the fact that the only section of
the country left in the position of an alleged champion of freedom,
capitalism and individual rights is the agrarian, feudal, racist South."[50]
The only glimmer of hope had been Ronald Reagan's principled and
philosophical speech on behalf of Goldwater, but it had been too little,
too late.

Despite her enthusiasm for Goldwater, Rand was blazing a trail distinct
from the broader conservative movement, as indicated by the title of her
second nonfiction book, *The Virtue of Selfishness*. Whereas traditional
conservatism emphasized duties, responsibilities, and social intercon-
nectedness, at the core of the right-wing ideology that Rand spearheaded was a rejection of moral obligation to others. As one reader told
her after finishing *Atlas Shrugged*, "I accepted the principle that I was
my brother's keeper, asking only why those who told me this did not
keep their brothers. I felt a moral obligation to renounce wealth, success,
love until the downtrodden masses were cared for. I wondered why I felt
resentment if I gave a bum a quarter and guilt if I didn't. I was bewil-
dered at these contradictory emotions and thought, 'there is something
wrong with me.' There was something wrong all right, but not with me,
but with my code."[51] Rand shared with the fusionist conservatives of
National Review a fear of socialism and a suspicion of the state, but her
thought rested on a fundamentally different social basis. Her vision of
society was atomistic, not organic. Rand's ideal society was made up of
traders, offering value for value, whose relationships spanned only the
length of any given transaction.

The Virtue of Selfishness was the brainchild of Bennett Cerf at Random House, who was eager to add to the Rand franchise. She was a veritable golden goose for the house, which had published *For the New Intellectual* and the Brandens' biography, *Who Is Ayn Rand?* Combined sales were well into the hundreds of thousands and showed no signs of leveling off. Cerf suggested that some of Rand's speeches and articles from her newsletter could be repackaged as a stand-alone volume. In response Rand proposed a new book, titled *The Fascist New Frontier,* after her essay of the same name. Originally enthusiastic about the project, Cerf grew increasingly uncomfortable with the book's title as he tried unsuccessfully to rouse the interest of his sales staff.

The title was intentionally provocative but also reflected Rand's deep revulsion at the Kennedy administration. The famous line from Kennedy's inaugural speech, "Ask not what your country can do for you, but what you can do for your country," inflamed Rand.[52] (Milton Friedman also found this sentiment objectionable, attacking Kennedy's statement in the very first sentence of *Capitalism and Freedom.*) In the title essay she juxtaposed excerpts from speeches by Kennedy and Hitler to demonstrate their similarity; to her, both were collectivists who demanded that men live for the state. Such a comparison was too much for Cerf, who requested that she delete the passages and select a new title. Rand angrily rejected both suggestions and accused Random House of breach of contract. She had chosen the publisher because they promised not to censor her work; from her perspective, Cerf's request proved their agreement was a sham. She split from Random House and published the book instead with the New American Library, a division of Penguin.

Cerf was slow to understand what had transpired. Not only had his prize author left the house, but she had taken her friendship away too. After an initial testy exchange of letters he waited in vain for further communication from Rand. Even Kennedy's assassination brought no comment. He pleaded, "Truly, a profound but honest difference about a publishing matter cannot have affected our relationship this deeply! Please do write to me." Rand finally relented with a brief note wishing him well. Cerf was bemused and saddened by Rand's attitude. He continued to follow her career with interest. "How wonderful it must be to be so sure you are right!" he commented to the circulation manager as he renewed his subscription to Rand's magazine.[53] Cerf had wandered into a danger zone with Rand, who never reacted well to criticism. Even Nathan could not budge her on this point. He argued against her replacement title, *The Virtue of Selfishness,* claiming that it would obscure her meaning and alienate readers, but Rand disagreed.

When it appeared in 1964 *The Virtue of Selfishness* brought the political and philosophical ideas expressed in Rand's newsletter to a much wider audience. Most of the book reprinted articles that had already been published, but it did include one significant new essay, "The Objectivist Ethics," first delivered to a symposium at the University of Wisconsin. The piece reflected Rand's new understanding of herself as an innovative philosopher. Much of the essay was heavy slogging, with Rand carefully defining such key terms as "percept," "concept," and "abstraction." From there she quickly translated her ideas into a common idiom: "The principle of trade is the only rational ethical principle for all human relationships, personal and social, private and public, spiritual and material. It is the principle of justice."[54] Her elevation of the trader echoed the older libertarian idea of the contract society, in which individuals were finally liberated from feudal hierarchies. As she had in the 1940s, Rand was revitalizing the inherited wisdom of libertarian theory for a new generation.

Two other chapters, "Man's Rights" and "The Nature of Government," outlined Rand's political philosophy and helped situate her relative to the rapidly evolving right wing. In "Man's Rights" she began by linking capitalism, private property, and individual rights, which each depended on the other. She then drew a careful distinction between economic and political rights. According to Rand, all rights were political rights, because rights pertained to actions, not results. "A right does not include the material implementation of that right by other men; it includes only the freedom to earn that implementation by one's own effort." Looking at the 1960 Democratic platform, which listed rights to housing, a job, education, and so forth, she asked, *"At whose expense?"*[55] The Democrats were attempting to redefine rights in economic terms, a move Rand rejected. She argued that the United States had thrived because it recognized the supremacy of individual rights, which served to limit and constrain government, the most dangerous threat. Shifting to economic rights would empower the state to seize the private property of some for distribution to others. In its basic outline Rand's discussion of rights was similar to her "Textbook of Americanism," which she had shared with FEE decades earlier. Now her discussion was much more sophisticated, grounded in both a developed Objectivist philosophy and concrete examples taken from history and politics.

Similarly "The Nature of Government" expanded on the noninitiation principle that Rand had included in "Textbook of Americanism." She repeated the idea in *Atlas Shrugged* and *For the New Intellectual*, making it a basic tenet of her ethics: "No man has the right to *initiate* the use of physical force against others."[56] Physical force was a core concern of Rand's political philosophy, for she held that rights could only be violated by physical force. The role of government was to protect individual rights by establishing a monopoly on the use of physical force. Citizens would forgo the use of force knowing they would be protected by the government, itself constrained by objectively defined laws. To protect men from criminals and outside aggressors, the government would exercise its monopoly through police and armed forces.

Although it sounded straightforward, Rand's definition of force was nuanced. She defined fraud, extortion, and breach of contract as force, thus enabling government to establish a legal regime that would create a framework for commerce. Critically, Rand also considered taxation to be an "initiation of physical force" since it was obtained, ultimately, "at the point of a gun." This led her to a radical conclusion: that taxation itself was immoral.[57] In a separate essay, "Government Financing in a Free Society," Rand considered the implications of taxation as force. In a truly free society, one without taxes, how would the government have any money to perform its proper functions? She suggested a few examples, such as a fee tied to each contractual transaction, including credit transfers, or a government lottery. Such schemes "would not work today," Rand emphasized, delegating the details to "the field of the philosophy of the law."[58] Though the proper arrangements had yet to be developed, the basic principles behind voluntary financing were the only ones compatible with true freedom, she maintained.

Like most of Rand's books, *The Virtue of Selfishness* sold briskly, going through four editions that totaled more than four hundred thousand copies in its first four months. It also had an important impact on her public profile. At the suggestion of Robert Hessen, a Collective member in the bookselling business, the book included a small tear-out card that readers could send back to receive additional information about Rand's philosophy. Readers drawn to her ideas would find a thriving Objectivist universe, complete with foundational texts, celebrities, and opportunities for advanced study. Even those who did not return the card now learned there was a community and a movement centered around Rand.[59]

Taken together, NBI and Rand's willingness to directly engage current events suggested a new way to be on the right. In 1955 William F. Buckley's *National Review* had brought together a variety of competing ideas, blending libertarianism, religious traditionalism, and anti-Communism into a creed he called "American conservatism." For close to a decade Buckley had monopolized discourse on the right, suggesting that his synthesis was the only respectable and responsible way to oppose the liberal order. Now he faced a formidable challenge from Rand. In the wake of *Atlas Shrugged* Rand had come to see herself as an abstract philosopher who might make important contributions to human knowledge. But it was as a political philosopher that she would leave her mark on history.

CHAPTER EIGHT

Love Is Exception Making

$ BY THE MIDDLE of the 1960s Rand's popularity among young conservatives, her open support of Goldwater, and the continued appeal of her books had pushed her to a new level of mainstream visibility. As a backlash unfolded against Lyndon Johnson's Great Society and the war in Vietnam, Rand's ideas seemed ever more relevant and compelling. In 1967 she was a guest on Johnny Carson's *Tonight Show* three times in five months. Each time she explained to Carson the fundamentals of her philosophy, the audience response was so great she earned another invitation.[1] Ted Turner, then a little-known media executive, personally paid for 248 billboards scattered throughout the South that read simply "Who is John Galt?"[2] Ten years after the publication of *Atlas Shrugged* she was at the apex of her fame.

With success came new challenges. Most troubling of all was her relationship with Nathan. Rand had designated him her intellectual heir, openly and repeatedly. She had dedicated *Atlas Shrugged* to him (and Frank), allowed his name to be publicly linked with Objectivism, entered business arrangements with him. The Nathaniel Branden Institute had blossomed into a national institution, with around thirty-five hundred students enrolled each year in more than fifty cities.[3] The institute had heavy concentrations of followers in southern California, New York, and Boston. In New York City Objectivism became its own subculture, complete with sports teams, movie nights, concerts, and annual dress balls. An NBI student could socialize, recreate, and study exclusively with other Objectivists, and many did. At the top of this society stood Nathan and Ayn, living embodiments of her philosophy. They were bound by a thousand ties, personal and professional, private and public, past and present. But more than a decade after they first became lovers, the two were further apart than they had ever been.

The success of NBI and Rand's new fame transformed the Collective from a small band of intimates into a much admired and watched in-group. New York NBI students knew them all by sight. Nathan was "tall, striking, his hair cascading in blonde waves over his forehead and his eyes sparkling like blue ice." (Less flatteringly, other Objectivists remembered Nathan's "Elmer Gantry" style and called him a "great showman.")[4] Barbara, cold and remote in her bearing, looked the part of a Rand heroine with her delicate features and pale blonde hair. Alan Greenspan, nebbish and awkward, was an occasional lecturer, offering a course in the Economics of a Free Society, and Leonard Peikoff, hover-ing in Nathan's shadow, taught the History of Philosophy.

When new NBI tape transcription courses debuted in far-flung cities, Nathan would fly in like a rock star to deliver the first lecture. When Ayn accompanied him once to Los Angeles, an overflow audience of eleven hundred crowded several rooms to hear them talk. Their tours on behalf of NBI not only energized the faithful, but helped Nathan maintain con-trol over his sprawling empire. The institute's business representatives were carefully vetted; they served as the official representatives of NBI to the vast majority of Rand's students, who would never see her or Nathan in person. The tours gave Nathan a chance to hire, meet with, and supervise the work of this core stratum. Paid by the number of stu-dents they enrolled, NBI's business representatives, already enthusiastic Objectivists, had further incentive to spread Rand's ideas.[5]

Relationships among the Collective were now codified by residence and employment. The O'Connors, the Brandens, and the Blumenthals had all moved into the same building on East Thirty-fourth Street, which also housed the NBI offices and Nathan's private office. Many of Rand's inner circle worked for her or an Objectivist enterprise. In addition to the magazine, NBI launched a book service and sold reproductions of romantic art. Barbara Branden, NBI's executive director, oversaw opera-tions and taught her class on efficient thinking. Lecturing gigs at NBI paid well, as befit a capitalist establishment. Nathan and Allan Blumenthal received the bulk of their therapy clients from NBI students. Robert Hessen, then a graduate student in history at Columbia, became Rand's secretary. Members of the Collective were not only friends, they were neighbors; they were not only neighbors, they were coworkers. Breaking into this tight circle was impossible for most NBI students.

Saturday nights at Rand's apartment remained the most coveted invitation in Objectivist society. Most of Rand's original group continued to attend the weekly sessions, and they always tried to be together on New Year's Eve, one of Rand's favorite holidays. As the clock turned, Rand made a great show of retreating to her bedroom with Frank, who would emerge later with lipstick smeared on his face. Rand extended her favor to those who boasted extraordinary professional success or intellectual or artistic talent, but the Collective remained primarily a family affair. The only outsiders successfully adopted married in, such as Charles Sures, the husband of Mary Ann Rukavina, an art student who had worked as Rand's typist when she wrote *Atlas Shrugged*. Around the Collective orbited several loose bands of more dedicated Objectivists, who might occasionally be invited to a Saturday night gathering at Rand's apartment or a private party hosted by one of the Collective.

Newcomers to NBI were directed to start with Nathan's twenty-week lecture series, "Basic Principles of Objectivism," the prerequisite for all further study. It was by far the most popular of NBI's offerings, with some students even taking it twice. Most Objectivists took the course via tape transcription in the city where they lived, but Branden delivered the lectures live in New York City, where he consistently attracted an enrollment of nearly two hundred students each time it was offered. Although Branden sprinkled his own psychological theories through the curriculum, his course was primarily dedicated to a broad summary of Rand's ideas, covering her positions on reason, altruism, economics, art, and sex.

The first lecture situated Objectivism within the history of philosophy and covered the "bankruptcy of today's culture." The next two lectures were more technical, covering philosophical topics such as reason, abstraction, concept formation, identity, and causality. A third lecture was devoted to "the destructiveness of the concept of God." The course then began to focus on proper cognitive processes, mixing philosophical and psychological concepts. It branched next into a focus on Rand's ethics, including a discussion of economics and capitalism. The last lectures tackled free-standing topics such as the nature of evil, art, and sex, including a lecture on "the nature and purpose of art" given by Rand. The final lecture promised to answer the question of why "human beings repress and drive underground, not the worst within them, but the best." In New York lectures were followed by a question-and-answer period in which Rand often participated.[6]

Rand was unquestionably the dominant influence and comprehensive frame of reference at NBI. Whatever subject they taught, NBI lecturers were, by definition, members of her inner circle who had passed muster and acknowledged her as their primary teacher. The Objectivist intellectual world was developed in deliberate opposition to what Rand saw as the dominant method (or lack thereof) in American universities. She harshly criticized universities for their opposition to system building and the "arbitrary, senseless, haphazard conglomeration of most curricula, the absence of any hierarchical structure of knowledge, any order, continuity, or rationale."[7] By contrast, Objectivism was to be a carefully ordered system. Initiates began with the basics and moved up to more advanced classes as they mastered different concepts. Particularly ambitious students in the New York area could aspire to meet with Rand personally and participate in philosophical discussions with the Collective.

As Objectivism grew, Rand became increasingly sensitive about her public profile. Immediately after *Atlas Shrugged* was published she had sparred with liberals in televised forums, in print, and at academic symposiums. Now she refused to appear with others, telling an inquirer she did not do debates because the "epistemological disintegration of our age has made debate impossible."[8] Stung by years of bad publicity, by the mid-1960s she had composed a release form to be used for media appearances. The form required that her appearance be "a serious discussion of ideas" and that disagreements, "if any, will be expressed politely and impersonally." Rand insisted that no references be made to her critics and reserved the right to approve the exact wording of her introduction. She was also touchy about the unexpected side effects of her literary fame, telling an eager fan, "I am sorry that I cannot let you take snapshots of me. I have discontinued this practice because I photograph very badly." When an NBI student violated this policy at a lecture Nathan confronted the student and exposed her film.[9]

Far from welcoming the swelling in Objectivist ranks, Rand was increasingly suspicious of those who claimed to speak in her name. Even the Ayn Rand campus clubs, which germinated spontaneously at many of the nation's top colleges and universities, including Boston University, Dartmouth, MIT, Stanford, and Columbia, began to bother her, for they used her name without her supervision. In May 1965 Nathan issued a rebuke and a warning to the campus clubs in *The Objectivist Newsletter*. He and Rand were particularly concerned about the names these organizations might choose. Nathan explained that names such as the Ayn Rand Study Club were appropriate, whereas names such as the John Galt Society were not. "As a fiction character, John Galt is Miss Rand's property; he is *not* in the public domain," Nathan argued.[10]

He also spelled out the proper nomenclature for those who admired Rand's ideas. The term Objectivist was " intimately and exclusively associated with Miss Rand and me," he wrote. "A person who is in agreement with our philosophy should describe himself, not as an Objectivist, but as a student or a supporter of Objectivism." At a later date, when the philosophy had spread farther, it might be possible for there to be more than two Objectivists. Further, any campus club that wished to issue a newsletter should indicate their agreement with Objectivism but make clear that they were not official representatives of the philosophy. Nathan closed with a strong attack against another group of Rand readers, the "craven parasites" who sought to use Objectivism for non-Objectivist ends. Into this category fell anyone who advocated political anarchism and anyone who tried to recruit NBI students into schemes for a new free market nation or territory.[11]

Nathan's unease gives some indications of how the student right was developing in the wake of Goldwater's failed campaign. Goldwater had been a unifying factor, a figurehead who drew together diverse groups on the right and channeled their political energy into preexisting institutions. With the collapse of Goldwater's prospects, his young followers scattered into different groups. Objectivists were no longer found in Students for Goldwater, but began to form their own clubs. Anarchism too was beginning to circulate among the more radical students, primarily through the efforts of Murray Rothbard. In 1962 Rothbard published his two-volume *Man, Economy, and the State*, an exegesis of his mentor Ludwig Von Mises's thought. The book was written with a concluding set of chapters advocating anarchism, which Rothbard's sponsors at the Volker Fund quietly excised. Rothbard took his ideas to a more receptive audience, founding a magazine called *Left and Right* that hoped to attract student rebels from both ends of the political spectrum.[12] Although anarchism was a minority position, to say the least, the very idea of it infuriated Rand. But some students saw anarchism as the logical next step after Objectivism. Others, infatuated with Rand's idea of a capitalist utopia, hatched elaborate plans for a new libertarian Atlantis. A truly free market society could be founded in uninhabited lands or even established on offshore floating platforms, they believed. Rand found these schemes ludicrous.

She was more troubled by the New Left. Leftist campus activism had started small, with a few dedicated students protesting against mandatory anti-Communist loyalty oaths for faculty. It gathered steam in tandem with the Civil Rights movement. Soon the locus of concern shifted to students themselves, their rights on campus, their place within the university structure. Later the Vietnam War and the draft would become central issues. Rand made her clearest statement against the New Left in a 1965 essay directed at UC Berkeley's Free Speech movement, "Cashing In: The Student Rebellion." Characteristically, she blamed Berkeley's troubles on modern philosophy. According to her, "the man most responsible for the present state of the world" was Immanuel Kant, whom she identified as the spiritual "father" of Berkeley's student rebel leader, Mario Savio. Rand's invocation of the villainous Kant was one aspect of Objectivism's kooky side. Yet it was also a source of its appeal, for the demonization of Kant spoke to Objectivism's earnest intellectualism and deep reverence for the power of ideas.

Rand's focus on the philosophical roots of the campus disturbances also highlighted a basic theoretical difference between left and right. Unlike their counterparts on the left, Objectivists saw the problems of society in entirely abstract terms. The left certainly had theorists analogous to Rand, namely Herbert Marcuse and Jean-Paul Sartre. But students on the left tended to see injustice as firmly embedded in the material world, be it racism, sexism, militarism, or class oppression. Conversely, contrast Rand and her followers identified the ills of the world in purely philosophical terms. This was a tendency that permeated the right more broadly. Conservatives had long believed that "ideas have consequences," as the title of Richard Weaver's 1948 book put it. Similarly, in *The Conscience of a Conservative* Barry Goldwater identified a critical distinction between left and right: "Conservatives take account of the whole man, while the Liberals tend to look only at the material side of man's nature.... In the name of a concern for 'human beings' [liberals] regard the satisfaction of economic wants as the dominant mission of society."[13] This idea was anathema to conservatives because it could provide a justification for altering the outcomes of market capitalism. Conservatives instead wanted to shift emphasis to the more abstract, "spiritual" side of human nature. Although she was an atheist, Rand's ideas followed the same dynamic, for she too was untroubled by the idea of "economic wants" going unsatisfied. Indeed, Rand understood society as simply a function of its dominant ideas.

Rand's essay on the New Left did, however, come back to earth long enough to urge clear-headed action against the philosophically misguided. She told readers, "The first step is to make oneself heard, on the campus and outside. There are many civilized ways to do it: protest meetings, speeches, pamphlets, letters-to-editors." The key was that students must "fight intellectually, on moral-intellectual grounds," since "ideas cannot be fought except by means of better ideas."[14] She encouraged "civilized" protest to highlight the violent and coercive nature of the protestors. Her followers threw themselves eagerly into the campus fray. Columbia University, a hotbed of left protest, was also home to one of the most dedicated Objectivist organizations, the Committee for the Defense of Property Rights. A photo in the *Columbia Owl* captured well the Objectivists' mission: two serious young men with neat hair, shaven faces, ties, and overcoats stand proudly over a chair with a large banner declaring "Abolish SDS."[15]

The antiwar protests were the perfect chance for Objectivists to practice what they preached, and they eagerly presented themselves as a lone outpost of order and rationality in a sea of mysticism and irrationality. For all Rand's criticism of American universities, student Objectivists were still eager to defend the university's academic mission. A student at Washington University wrote, "The students and faculty are here on a voluntary contractual basis to learn and teach (or engage in research), respectively. We are not here to run the university."[16] The Committee for Defense of Property Rights claimed it was formed "to work for the nonviolent atmosphere which scholarly progress requires" and warned that Columbia, "a center of learning," was endangered by "a handful of drugged, bearded Brown Shirts."[17] Objectivist protestors revealed their essential orientation toward studying, learning, and personal advancement. Objectivists were excited by ideas, not political programs (although eventually the ideas were to cause political change). Their version of rebellion was fundamentally scholastic: reading philosophy rather than taking over buildings.

Still, student Objectivists had to be careful how they used Rand's ideas or they would incur her wrath. The University of Virginia Ayn Rand Society planned an ambitious three-day conference, with speakers, discussion groups, a banquet, and several cocktail parties. Eager to draw Rand's blessing and interested in her advice, the organizers shared their plans for an event intended to "provide what neither our colleges nor our culture provides—an exciting intellectual experience and a social event." What Rand noticed instead was that the club used a phrase from John Galt's oath on its stationery. Her lawyer dispatched a blistering letter ordering removal of the offensive quote. The club's president was apologetic and ashamed: "I have cut the bottoms from all of our stationery I have, and have issued instructions and anyone else who has any of our stationery shall do likewise."[18]

A similar fate befell Jarrett Wollstein, a dedicated student of Objectivism. Wollstein offered a course on Rand's thought at the University of Maryland's "free university," hoping to balance the overtly leftist content of the other courses. He was careful to identify himself as an independent operator who had not been sanctioned by Rand. But his disclaimer was to no avail. The local NBI representative soon visited his class to read aloud a legalistic statement announcing that he was not an approved teacher, in the process scaring off several students. Next Wollstein's application for an NBI class was rejected and his registration fee refunded. Rand then publicly disowned his project in *The Objectivist*, writing, "I wish to put it on record that I repudiate and unequivocally disapprove of Mr. Wollstein's entire undertaking."[19] Lengthy letters to Rand and Branden brought no reply.

When Wollstein attended an Objectivist-sponsored conference on the draft his presence caused a storm of controversy. Although the conference was not an official NBI event, Leonard Peikoff was the keynote speaker. Peikoff refused to speak if Wollstein was permitted to attend even a single session of the conference, throwing the day's proceedings into jeopardy. After a tense confrontation with two NBI-affiliated lawyers, Wollstein accepted a refund and left the conference. He later received a brief letter from Nathan banning him from all NBI lectures. Even such treatment could not wean Wollstein off Rand or dampen his enthusiasm for her message. He wrote an article for YAF's *New Guard* criticizing Rand and her associates as "the founders of a new orthodoxy" but also asserted, "The value of Objectivism will stand for all time."[20]

Rand's attack on the campus clubs was part of her increasing impatience with NBI students, whom she now regularly assailed during her question-and-answer sessions. The chance to hear from Rand in person had originally been one of NBI's greatest draws. In the beginning she was a regular attendee at the New York classes and occasionally delivered a lecture herself. Although she was normally generous in her responses to general audiences, NBI students were held to higher standards. Rand was likely to denounce anyone who asked inappropriate or challenging questions "as a person of low self-esteem" or to have them removed from the lecture hall. In front of journalists she called one questioner "a cheap fraud" and told another, "If you don't know the difference between the United States and Russia, you deserve to find out!" These were moments of high drama, with Rand shouting her angry judgments to the widespread applause of the audience. But this antagonism toward his paying customers made Nathan extremely uncomfortable, and he began discouraging her from attending lectures.[21]

Always quick to anger, Rand now erupted regularly. She even began to clash with Frank. Since that first fateful evening with the Collective, Frank had continued to paint. His work was impressive, and one of his best paintings, a gritty yet etherial composition of sky, sun, and suspension bridge graced the cover of a 1968 reissue of *The Fountainhead*. But Ayn forbade him to sell his paintings, saying she couldn't bear to part with any of them. When she offered unsolicited advice about his work, he blew up at her. Frank preferred the Art Students League to NBI. He kept a low profile, never telling anyone about his famous wife. He stood out nonetheless. Before either became fashionable, Frank wore a navy blue cape and carried a shoulder strap bag. His fellow students described him as "always just very chic, very elegant without overdoing it." In 1966 they elected him vice president of the League. This vote of confidence came just as Frank's artistic career was cut short by the decline of his body. Stricken by a neurological disorder, by the end of 1967 his hands shook so badly he could paint no more.[22] Once playful and witty, Frank now became sharp and snappish. He withdrew to the sanctuary of his studio, where he drank his days away.

Besides Frank's decline, Rand was further disconcerted by the dete-rioration of her connection to Nathan. Aside from a few brief episodes just after *Atlas Shrugged* appeared, their relationship had been platonic for years. Rand had halted the affair during the depths of her depression. After recovering her spirits she became eager to rekindle their romance. Nathan, however, was reluctant and uninterested. He offered one excuse after another. It was the strain of betraying Barbara; the stress of cuck-olding Frank; the pressure of lecturing at NBI, deceiving his students and public audience. What Nathan kept from Rand was the most obvi-ous explanation of all: he had fallen in love with one of his NBI students, a twenty-three-year-old model named Patrecia Gullison.

Nathan first noticed Patrecia when she enrolled in his Principles class. Strikingly beautiful in the manner of Dominique Francon or Dagny Taggart, Patrecia was far more lighthearted than any Rand her-oine. Carefree and gay, she teased Nathan about his serious bearing, even as she made her dedication to Objectivism clear. She struck up a romance with another Objectivist and invited both the O'Connors and the Brandens to the wedding, where Nathan brooded at the sight of her with another man. Soon the two began meeting privately under the aegis of her interest in Objectivism. Their conversations in his office grew longer. Nathan's feelings for Patrecia, which developed into an intense sexual affair, lit the fuse that would blow Objectivism sky high.

Unaware of Nathan's new dalliance but anxious to maintain Objectiv-ist rationality, Barbara petitioned her husband for permission to renew relations with an old boyfriend who was now working at NBI. First Nathan forbade it, then he relented. Barbara's new sanctioned liaison forced the Brandens to admit that their marriage had been a hollow shell for years. Mismatched from the beginning, the pair had no natural chemistry and little in common besides mutual admiration for Rand. In 1965 they decided to separate. Just months later Patrecia and her husband split up.

All this was more than enough to make Rand uneasy and ill-tempered. She had counseled Barbara and Nathan through each step of their relationship and endorsed their marriage. The separation was a sign that she had failed. Even more significantly, the Brandens' marriage, however troubled, meant Nathan was taken by a woman Rand liked and even controlled; their secret was safe with Barbara. Now Nathan could once again become a single man. And he had lost the one believable excuse that could explain his reluctance to begin relations with Rand anew. Rand worried that her deepest fear had come true: Nathan did not love her anymore. She was still his idol, but no longer his sweetheart.

After his separation from Barbara, Nathan began a lame effort to integrate Patrecia into his public life, even as their affair remained a secret to all. He told Patrecia about his past with Rand, swearing her to silence. Nathan assumed that if Rand discovered his new romance she would banish him forever. Still, he allowed himself to hope that if she got to know Patrecia first, she would be less hurt when their relationship came to light. He began to drop Patrecia's name into conversation, and he included her regularly in Collective events.

At first Rand did not suspect Patrecia of being a rival. By now she was a high-profile member of the Junior Collective, by dint of her good looks and eager interest in Rand's philosophy. At an Objectivist fashion show she wowed the audience in a glamorous wedding gown. Following Nathan's lead, Patrecia worked to develop a friendship with Rand. She was solicitous and respectful, telling her in a letter, "When I read *The Fountainhead* and *Atlas Shrugged*, when I first saw you, when I think of you and see you now, and when I look at this picture of you—my head is always bowed."[23] When Patrecia decided to pursue an acting career she took the stage name "Patrecia Wynand," after a character in *The Fountainhead*. Before her *Tonight Show* appearances Rand asked Patrecia for help with her makeup. Rand liked Patrecia and admired her beauty. She had even asked for one of her professional headshots, which she kept in her desk drawer. But she could not understand why Nathan kept bringing her up in their private conversations.

Ayn and Nathan were both trapped by Objectivist theories of love, sex, and emotion, which allowed them no graceful exit from a failed affair. From the start Rand had integrated sexuality into Objectivism. In *Atlas Shrugged* she argued that sexual love was a response to values and a reflection of self-esteem. Love was not mysterious, mercurial, or emotional, and desire was never a mere physical response. "Tell me what a man finds sexually attractive and I will tell you his entire philosophy of life. Show me the woman he sleeps with and I will tell you his valuation of himself," declares Francisco D'Anconia.[24] So it was that Dominique loved Howard, Dagny loved Galt, and Nathan loved Ayn. According to Objectivism, Nathan's love for Ayn was natural, even expected, because he held her as his highest value. To repudiate her was to repudiate all his values; to deem her unattractive was to reject her on the deepest level. Yet Nathan was still an Objectivist, still considered Rand a genius. He could find no way to reconcile his esteem for Rand with the seeming contradiction that he no longer wished to be her lover. Even worse, how could he value the young and winsome Patrecia over her? What did that say about him?

Nathan's problems were compounded by his development of Objectivist psychology, which denied the autonomy and importance of emotions. Working with the base materials of Rand's novels, Nathan constructed an airtight model of the psyche that downgraded emotions to a subordinate position. Rand trumpeted her distrust of emotion in almost all her writing. In *For the New Intellectual* she declared, "Emotions are not tools of cognition," a statement that would resurface repeatedly in all Objectivist writing. To Rand an emotion "tells you nothing about reality" and could never be "proof" of anything. In his radio speech Galt declares, "Any emotion that clashes with your reason, any emotion that you cannot explain or control, is only the carcass of that stale thinking which you forbade your mind to revise."[25] It was Rand's loss that her primary intellectual collaborator did little to broaden her outlook, shake her loose from her inherent emotional repression, or introduce her to the teachings of modern psychology. Instead, captive to Rand's mind since meeting her almost twenty years before at age nineteen, Nathan pushed her philosophical ideas into the realm of psychology, with devastating results.

Nathan saw Objectivism's deviation from the accumulated wisdom of psychology as evidence of pathbreaking innovation, rather than a denial of widely recognized human truth. Unlike all other schools of psychology, Branden boasted, Objectivism did not "regard desires and emotions as irreducible primaries, as the given." Rather, emotions sprang from thought and "are the product of the thinking [a man] has done or has failed to do."[26] Therefore, the way to handle painful or unpleasant emotions was to uncover and change the thinking that had created them. Objectivist psychotherapy was not unusual in its rational investigation of emotional patterns. What made Nathan's form of therapy truly destructive was its emphasis on judgment, another inheritance from Rand. The emotions that Objectivist therapy uncovered were to be judged and changed rather than accepted and understood. Objectivist psychology was not even psychology as such, Nathan admitted. He told Rand, "My whole interest in psychology is not to cure patients, but to justify our view of man."[27] At the time he began his liaison with Patrecia Nathan was working to apply these ideas in the realm of romantic love.

Nathan's own life provided the perfect example of his psychological system in action. Unable to accept, change, or rationally understand his feelings for Patrecia, he went into denial. Their affair was only temporary, he told himself, and would fizzle out before long. Nor was he able to pull away from Rand, despite his faltering desire. Instead he tried to explain his behavior in rational terms. And he began to lie. He told Rand he suffered from a mysterious sexual block; something was wrong with him. Ever eager to help her prize student, Rand met with him for long therapy sessions. She held out some hope that he and Barbara would reunite, seeing them together for additional meetings. Rand even allowed herself to confront the unacceptable: that Nathan, now in his early thirties, had no sexual or romantic desire for a woman who was nearly sixty. When she asked directly, Nathan denied that his feelings had changed. He at once prevaricated and hinted at the truth, hoping for a miracle that would deliver them all. Maybe Rand would decide of her own accord their affair was over and set him free. But Rand, never one for subtlety or nuance, could not read between the lines.[28]

Rand was also blinded by her idea of man worship, a corollary to her sex theory. Men and women are equal, Rand emphasized, but nonetheless a woman should look up to her man's superior masculinity. When *McCall's* called Rand for a puff piece about a woman president, she told the magazine, "A woman cannot reasonably want to be a commanderin-chief." Many readers of *The Objectivist* were astounded by the assertion and asked Rand for clarification. She elaborated in a longer essay, "An Answer to Readers: About a Woman President." According to Rand, a woman should never be president, not because she was unqualified for the task, but because a woman president would be too powerful. As commander in chief she would be unable to look up to any man in her life, and this would be psychologically damaging. Any woman who would consider such a position, Rand claimed, was unfit for it, for "a properly feminine woman does not treat men as if she were their pal, sister, mother—or *leader*."[29] Rand's theory of man worship was an abstract projection that kept her ignorant of both Frank's and Nathan's inner emotional states. Although she called Frank a hero, in truth he was a passive and withdrawn man whose brief renaissance as an artist had been snuffed out by alcohol and old age. The idea of man worship was a wishful fancy, as unattainable for her as the svelte physiques and Aryan features of her heroines. Still, it was a fantasy that satisfied. Rand identified Nathan as a hero, a paragon of morality and rationality. Such beliefs made it impossible for her to let go of him as a lover or to suspect him of duplicity. "That man is no damn good!" Frank stormed after one of their counseling sessions.[30] But Rand continued to take Nathan's words at face value.

As these tensions simmered under the surface, Objectivism continued to grow rapidly. Ayn and Nathan renamed the newsletter *The Objectivist* in 1966, adopted a more professional magazine format, and saw paid subscriptions surge to a high of twenty thousand.[31] The new format marked Rand's deepening interest in philosophy, as demonstrated by a series of articles titled "Introduction to Objectivist Epistemology," later released as a book. Rand's disillusionment with Goldwater, and her ongoing conversations with Leonard Peikoff, shifted her interest away from politics and cemented her new identity as a philosopher. Over time her most loyal students would identify *Introduction to Objectivist Epistemology* as her most significant work. In the short run, however, she remained far better known for her politics than for her philosophy.

Rand's intellectual stature was enhanced during these years by the widespread sense that *Atlas Shrugged* was a prophetic work. She made few public comments about President Johnson and the Great Society, but many of her readers thought *Atlas Shrugged* had predicted the rapidly expanding welfare state. A Texas newspaper quoted Rand's statist villain, Wesley Mouch, and observed, "Readers of Ayn Rand's prophetic novel, 'Atlas Shrugged,' have seen increasing signs recently of the conditions predicted in the novel"; the *Orange County Register* chimed in with an editorial querying, "Atlas Shrugged Coming True?" This sense of the novel's predictive power stretched from the grassroots to national financial magazines. A circular letter distributed by the Michigan-based Muskegon Manufacturers Association told its readers, "The book, published seven years ago, took 12 years to write. Yet in it, the steel incident occurs, the international mess we have come to accept as the norm is developed, the very words that bureaucrats and politicians are today uttering as excuses and reasons, appear in its pages." *Barron's,* a leading New York financial newspaper, began a lead story on oil import quotas with mention of *Atlas Shrugged,* commenting, "To judge by what has happened since early 1959, when the decree took effect, Miss Rand deserves high honor as a prophet."[32]

In 1966 Rand added to her nonfiction quiver with *Capitalism: The Unknown Ideal,* a collection of speeches and previously published articles. In addition to work by Rand and Nathan, the book also featured essays by Alan Greenspan and Robert Hessen. The book reflected the symmetry and hierarchy of Objectivism, for it was intended to explain the ethical theory Rand had depicted in her novels and outlined in *The Virtue of Selfishness.* She called her new book a "nonfiction footnote to *Atlas Shrugged*" that rested upon the "necessary foundation" of her earlier work. Accordingly it was tuned to applications and extensions rather than basic philosophy. The first section, "Theory and History," addressed specific economic issues such as monopoly, regulation of the airwaves, and copyright law. "Current State" collected Rand's thoughts on contemporary political issues. Rand now had an equal number of fiction and nonfiction books in print but still garnered little respect as a philosopher from the outside world. *The New Republic* jabbed at her in a sarcastic review: "With engaging self-confidence, [Nathaniel Branden] hits out at Dr. Erich Fromm. Mr. Alan Greenspan has a go at the antitrust laws....But, unquestionably, Miss Rand remains Top Bee in the communal bonnet, buzzing the loudest and zaniest throughout this all but incredible book."[33] Reviews like these ignored the growing strength of Objectivism but also indicated the limitations of Rand's appeal. She had failed to storm the temples of high culture, yet the mandarins did not notice that outside the gates she was inspiring a rising generation of politicized youth.

The paperback edition of *Capitalism: The Unknown Ideal,* released a year later, included one of Rand's most important political statements, her major argument against the Vietnam War and the draft. In "The Wreckage of the Consensus," first delivered as a speech to Boston's Ford Hall Forum, Rand denounced the Vietnam War, calling it a "hideous mess" that "does not serve any national interests of the United States."[34]

Her critique had little to do with colonialism, fascism, imperialism, or the other evils leftists laid at the feet of the United States. Rather, she argued that the only justification for war was national self-defense, and Vietnam did not meet this criterion. Although she was opposed to Communism, Rand did not buy the domino theory that guided policymakers, whereby any nation that became Communist was seen to potentially topple its neighbors in the same direction. In the fashion of the prewar right, Rand saw hostilities in Vietnam as unrelated to life in the United States. To her, the more potent threat lay at home, where statists and socialists disguised as liberals might destroy the freedoms of America.

Rand saw the draft as a sure sign that freedom was already in grave danger. She was deeply opposed to the draft and its implications for society. "Of all the statist violations of individual rights...the military draft is the worst," she told her audience. "It negates man's fundamental right, the right to life, and establishes the fundamental principle of statism—that a man's life belongs to the state, and the state may claim it by compelling him to sacrifice it in battle. Once that principle is accepted, the rest is only a matter of time."[35] Rand coupled her attack on the statist draft with an impassioned defense of young lives wasted by the war. If potential inductees turned to drugs or "the beatnik cult" in response to state enslavement, who could blame them? She was incensed that none on the right had joined her offensive; instead, she observed incredulously, it was only "the extreme *left*" who had demanded repeal of the draft. Rand argued that opposition to the draft should be the province of conservatives, "the alleged defenders of freedom and capitalism."[36] Framed as a statist violation of rights, conscription fit seamlessly into her larger opposition to coercion and the initiation of force.

Before long, opposition to the draft became a key part of the Objectivist worldview, despite Rand's active discouragement of draft resistance. She had little sympathy for those who publicly protested the draft, favorably quoting *Persuasion,* a magazine published by NBI students, "One does not stop the juggernaut by throwing oneself against it."[37] Her position was nuanced, or some might say contradictory: against the draft, and against the war, and against the protestors too. Some of this was merely cultural. Raised in the high European tradition, Rand viscerally objected to the messiness of the bohemian student protestors. Their strident demands, socialist rhetoric, and street action reminded her all too much of the Bolsheviks. Objectivists instead sought to protest the draft through legal means. Rand's personal lawyer, Henry Mark Holzer, began representing clients who had been drafted. He and several other Objectivists organized an antidraft road show that visited several cities, presenting the Objectivist argument against the draft as a violation of individual rights.[38]

Rand's opposition to the draft cemented her popularity on campus and separated her further from conservatives. Increasingly the Vietnam War was making the differences between libertarians and conservatives clear. Conservatives saw the war as an important conflict in the worldwide struggle against Communism; if anything, they urged that the war be pursued more vigorously. By contrast, libertarians doubted the war's relevancy to U.S. interests, and like Rand they saw the draft as an unacceptable violation of individual rights. In 1966 several professors at the University of Chicago called a conference to discuss the Selective Service System. A number of libertarians, including the economist Milton Friedman, made principled arguments against the draft. Rand publicized similar ideas to her student following. One young follower recalled, "It was not necessary to accept the antiquated bourgeois baggage of respect for one's elders, support for an unwinnable war, or abstention from sex. Instead, liberty could be justified, youthfully and gloriously, by the triumphant words of John Galt to a mediocre world, resonating through the campus rebellion: 'Get the hell out of my way!'"[39] Goldwater's 1964 campaign for president had given Rand her first surge of popularity among conservative youth. Now her opposition to the draft created a second rush of enthusiasm for her ideas.

A good index of her popularity came in October 1967, when *National Review* featured Rand on its cover, rendered as a stained glass window complete with dollar sign insignia, under the wry headline "The Movement to Canonize Ayn Rand." The article was essentially a hit piece commissioned by William F. Buckley, who had grown concerned with Rand's perennial appeal among young conservatives. Buckley told his chosen author, M. Stanton Evans, that he wanted a "definitive" piece on Ayn Rand that would "demonstrate to people of commonsense that her ideological and philosophical presumptions make her an inadequate mentor." Whittaker Chambers's message bore repeating to a new generation of conservatives. Evans, an activist since his student days and then an editor at the *Indianapolis News,* was to draw the line.[40]

But the message had shifted, and Evans's prominent cover story revealed how many of Rand's beliefs had become conventional conservative wisdom even as she remained, officially, persona non grata. Unlike Chambers, Evans was untroubled by her defense of capitalism and her attack on government regulation. She had, Evans wrote, "an excellent grasp of the way capitalism is supposed to work, the efficiencies of free enterprise, the central role of private property and the profit motive, the social and political costs of welfare schemes which seek to compel a false benevolence."[41] He also admired her polemical fire and consistency, and defended her against Chambers's accusation that she was an unconscious Nazi. Evans went on to argue that despite these features, Rand remained a dangerous figure for conservatives because she mixed her good qualities with the bad, namely, atheism. Her work raised several "central dilemmas of the era": "Can faith in God be reconciled with liberty for man? Is Christian belief compatible with libertarian attachment? Is Capitalism anti-Christian?" Evans seemed confident that a general consensus on each had already been reached. The only problem was that Rand answered all of these questions incorrectly. Christianity was an essential part of the conservative and capitalist agenda. Rand, an atheist, would never quite fit in. Evans urged that conservatives make judicious use of Rand, all the while being careful not to swallow her arguments whole.[42]

While Rand's inner circle continued to fray, Objectivism in New York was reaching fever pitch. With much fanfare, in May 1967 NBI signed a fifteen-year lease on offices in the Empire State Building, then the world's tallest building. Even though their offices were in the basement, it was still an ideal address. The lease also contained an auditorium, perfect for large lectures and the movie showings, performances, and dances that were becoming a regular part of the Institute's offerings. New York NBI now coordinated Objectivist baseball games, art shows, concerts, a movie series titled "The Romantic Screen," an annual NBI Ball, even an Objectivist European tour. For California Objectivists there was an NBI Ball West. *The Objectivist* announced that the new auditorium would also host seven informal, casual dress social evenings targeted toward singles.[43] Though much of this social activity stemmed from student demand, it was also linked to Rand's belief that she lived in a "dead culture." It was axiomatic to Objectivists that they lived in a state of crisis, a world uniformly opposed to their values and interests. This came through most clearly in Rand's devotion to Romantic art and her attack on contemporary art, literature, and movies. Since the mainstream contained nothing of value for Objectivists, it was necessary to create an alternative world, where NBI students could find the cultural nourishment they needed. The institute's new quarters were a testament to the durability and power of the universe Rand had forged. Few noticed that Nathan escaped to California for two months to personally teach the Basic Principles course in San Francisco and Los Angeles.

For all the successes of the New York NBI, the organization was developing an unsavory reputation. The idea that Objectivism was a weird pseudo-religion had wide currency in the mass media. Some of this sprang from the obvious passion Rand inspired in her readers. Religious metaphors were often used to describe her: she was a "prophetess" or "she-messiah," and her audience was "a congregation" or "disciples."[44] Much of the religious imagery, however, stemmed from eyewitness reports of NBI classes. *Life* quoted a student who described an NBI class as "almost liturgical: an immaculate white cloth altar with a tape-recorded tabernacle." "As a newcomer," the student said, "I was asked three times if I were a 'believer.'" Similarly, Jerome Tuccille wrote of his time as an NBI student, "My first reaction to all of this was awe, the stunned awe of the true believing convert as devout now in my atheistic capitalism as I had ever been in the Baroque Catholicism of the 1950s." At NBI Rand's writings were like holy writ. In his lectures and articles Branden used Rand's characters to make his arguments, citing John Galt's reaction during a particular scene in *Atlas Shrugged* as an example of "psychological maturity." Rand's creative world was cited as an alternative to reality, and passages from her novels were taken as proof of various trends and problems affecting the contemporary world.[45] At critical stages of argumentation Rand and others tended to insert passages from *Atlas Shrugged* to carry the point.

Visitors to NBI lectures were alarmed by the exalted place Rand held at NBI and the conformity of the students Nathan taught. "When

Miss Rand entered the room and sat down, an awed hush fell over most of the people who were gathered," remembered the psychologist Albert Ellis, the founder of rational emotive behavior therapy (REBT). Ellis's therapeutic technique was based on rational examination and understanding of emotions. He proposed a debate with Branden after hearing about Objectivism from many of his clients. The debate was a raucous affair, with Rand shouting from the sidelines and the Objectivist audience clapping for Branden and booing Ellis. Afterward Ellis was deeply disturbed. A year later he published a slashing attack on Rand and Branden, *Is Objectivism a Religion?* Even those friendly to Objectivism were disconcerted by the NBI lectures. Before their break, John Hospers sent Rand an unusually frank letter describing his experience: "I felt as if I were in a strange church where I didn't belong, where all the other people were singing the chants they were expected to and only I did not conform, and where to deny a single thing was considered heresy....And the attitude of the audience in the lecture hall shocked me even more. Rational? Good heavens—an Army of the Faithful, repeating the same incantations and asking questions only about details or applications, never questioning the tenets of the True Faith."[46]

But this was as Rand wanted it, she responded angrily to Hospers. In her letter she exhibited a striking contempt for those who showed the most interest in her philosophy. "Through all the years that I spent formulating my philosophical system, I was looking desperately for 'intelligent agreement' or at least for 'intelligent disagreement,'" she told Hospers. "Today, I am *not* looking for 'intelligent disagreement' any longer, and certainly not from children or amateurs." In other parts of the letter she called participants in her classes "weaklings" and denied, predictably, that she should have any concern for their interests. She argued that neither she nor Branden should be expected to present themselves as "uncertain" for the benefit of her students: "If you think that our certainty will intimidate the poor little 'social metaphysicians' what do you think our uncertainty would do to them? Would it make them think independently?"[47] Rand was oblivious to the idea that presenting multiple sides of an issue might stimulate students to independently measure and evaluate the validity of each option, thereby exercising their reason and arriving at their own, individual conclusions.

In the letter it also became clear that Rand thought of *Atlas Shrugged* as a kind of revealed truth. She argued that for her or Nathan to assume a stance of "uncertainty" would be tantamount to pretending "that *Atlas Shrugged* [had] not been written." She also seemed to equate disagreement with ignorance, and understanding with agreement. If her ideas weren't presented as deriving from "rational certainty," it would permit the audience to make "assertions of disagreement, while evading and ignoring everything" she and Branden said. Rand was unable to conceive of a person's understanding her ideas, yet disagreeing with them. She told Hospers that the classes were offered "*only* to those who have understood enough of *Atlas Shrugged* to agree with its essentials," as if the two were synonymous. Rand also explicitly rejected any pedagogical role, telling Hospers that NBI's purposes were very different from those of a university. They had no interest in the development of their students' minds: "*we* are not and do not regard ourselves as *teachers*....We address ourselves to adults and leave up to them the full responsibility for learning something from the course."[48] Despite her emphasis on reason and independent judgment, Rand had a very narrow idea of how this reason should be used. She conceived her ideal student as an empty vessel who used his or her rationality only to verify the validity of Objectivism. At the same time, she excoriated those who did so as weaklings or cowards.

Although Objectivism claimed to be an intellectual culture, it was decidedly not one devoted to freewheeling inquiry, but rather a community in which a certain catechism had to be learned for advancement. A flyer for the Basic Principles of Objectivism class openly alerted potential students to the bias inherent in NBI. "The lectures are not given to convert antagonists," the flyer noted, but were "addressed exclusively" to those who had read Rand's major works, "are in agreement with the *essentials* of the philosophy presented in these books, and seek an amplification and further study of this philosophy." This tendency was most prominent in New York, where Rand's opinions and actions had an immediate effect on the atmosphere at NBI. Her interest in her students seemed directly proportional to their agreement with her ideas. An NBI student remembered, "When she learned that I was a physicist, she made a comment about how physics has been corrupted by bad philosophy. She was apparently expecting my agreement. But I couldn't agree, because I didn't think that physics was corrupt. I could see the interest in me dying down in her eyes."[49] Rand could turn her charisma on and off at will, charming those who paid her proper homage while freezing out those who did not.

For every NBI student who found Rand harsh or was the target of an unprovoked rage, there is another who remembers Rand's sensitivity and caring. Jan Richman, a Los Angeles NBI representative, described her first meeting with Rand: "[She] said that I should take my glasses off. I took them off, and she said, you have very beautiful eyes. You shouldn't hide them behind glasses; get contact lenses. I remember I felt like crying." Martin Anderson, the author of a controversial book that attacked federal urban renewal programs, *The Federal Bulldozer,* was a professor at Columbia Business School when he and his girlfriend attended an NBI lecture they saw advertised in the *New York Times.* There he befriended Alan Greenspan, who invited him to several smaller events with Rand. Anderson remembers Rand as a "pussycat," a warm and caring figure. It was Rand, alone out of a late-night café crowd, who noticed his trouble and helped prepare his coffee when a broken arm left him unable to open a package of cream. When Rand learned about his upcoming wedding she asked to be invited and presented the couple with a wedding gift. Older, professionally accomplished, and married, Anderson was insulated from the groupthink and gossip of younger NBI students. His engagement with Objectivism was purely intellectual. Rand helped him clarify and unify his long-standing political beliefs, shaping them into a cohesive and integrated whole that helped direct his future work in Republican politics.[50]

There seemed to be two Objectivisms: one that genuinely supported intellectual exchange, engagement, and discourse, and one that was as dogmatic, narrow-minded, and stifling as Rand's harshest critics alleged. And the closer one got to New York, the more repressive the atmosphere became, Objectivists noticed.[51] For all their emphasis on reason, Rand and NBI instructors met intellectual disagreement with invective. Sometimes the two sides of Objectivism alternated with stunning speed, leaving Rand's followers unsure where they stood. A college student who would pursue a philosophy doctorate at the University of Rochester, and then a professorial career at Tulane, took Leonard Peikoff's NBI lecture series in the summer of 1965. He and several advanced students met separately with Peikoff for "what turned out to be an excellent, exciting, open-ended, philosophical discussion." "The topic I most clearly remember," he said, "was phenomenalism—objects are really just categories of sense data." The group was then told that for their next meeting they would meet with Rand and Nathan. Seeing this as a promotion based on their enthusiasm and expertise, the students were shocked when at the meeting, Nathan "began a long harangue about how grotesque it was for people to claim to have read Rand's works and still raise the sorts of philosophical [questions] Peikoff had reported to them. This went on for quite a while and we were all thoroughly abused."[52] It was a sudden reversal of fortune for the class, which did not understand Nathan's characterization of their questions as villainy.

The conformity engendered by NBI stretched beyond the classroom. Objectivism was a comprehensive philosophy, and Objectivists strove to apply the principles they learned at NBI to daily life. Rand's cast of mind saw all of reality as integrated by a few fundamental principles. Therefore adoption of these principles would radiate out infinitely into every aspect of a person's life. Following her reasoning, it became possible to gauge the validity of an Objectivist's commitment by the smallest details of his or her personal life and preferences. One NBI student remembered, "There was more than just a right kind of politics and a right kind of moral code. There was also a right kind of music, a right kind of art, a right kind of interior design, a right kind of dancing. There were wrong books which we could not buy, and right ones which we should....And on everything, absolutely everything, one was constantly being judged, just as one was expected to be judging everything around him....It was a perfect breeding ground for insecurity, fear, and paranoia."[53]

Striving to become good Objectivists, Rand's followers tried to conform to her every dictate, even those that were little more than personal preferences. Rand harbored a dislike of facial hair, and accordingly her followers were all clean shaven. Libertine in her celebration of sex outside marriage, she described homosexuality as a disgusting aberration. The playwright Sky Gilbert, once an enthusiastic Objectivist, remembered, "As a young, self-hating gay man, I welcomed Rand's Puritanism. I imagined I could argue myself out of homosexuality. I labored over endless journal passages, arguing the advantages and disadvantages of being gay, always reminding myself that gay was 'irrational.'"[54] If Objectivism was a religion to some people, it was a notably dogmatic and confining one. Led to Rand by a quest for answers and a need for certainty, her followers could find themselves locked into the system she had created.

The presence of Rand, a charismatic personality, was enough to tip Objectivism into quasi-religious territory, but Objectivism was also easy to abuse because of its very totalizing structure. There were elements deep within the philosophy that encouraged its dogmatic and coercive tendencies. Although Rand celebrated independence, the content of her thought became subsumed by its structure, which demanded consistency and excluded any contradictory data deriving from experience or emotion. Rand denied any pathway of knowledge that did not derive from rational, conscious thought and did not lead to the conclusions she had syllogistically derived. Thus Objectivism could translate quickly into blind obeisance to Rand. One former Objectivist remembered, "If you think to yourself, I have to be able to go by rational arguments, and you're unable to refute them, then you're really in a bind, which is where we all were." At NBI balls dozens of women appeared in slinky, one-shouldered gowns, like Dagny wore in *Atlas Shrugged*. When Ayn and Frank purchased a new piece of furniture, the Objectivist dining table became all the rage.[55]

Roy Childs, an active Objectivist and later advocate for anarchocapitalism, remembered that many did not simply read *Atlas Shrugged* but were "dominated" by it. Rand's fan letters reflected this truth. "Your philosophy has affected me to such a depth that I can longer think outside its context, nor can I picture myself in any other activity, save the discussion of it," one man wrote to her. Another college student reported cheerfully, "About a month ago I noticed how much I was talking about your books to my teachers and classmates. As a result of my enthusiasm I have lost two friends. I am beginning to realize how unimportant these people are.[56] Just as her fans mimicked Rand's language and rhetorical structures, so too could they come to imitate her psychology, including the rejection of friends who did not measure up to Objectivist standards. Principled schisms and breaks were commonplace in the Objectivist subculture as fans followed Rand's cues about proper human relationships.

The Collective bore the brunt of Objectivism's shadow side. Saturday nights at Rand's apartment often came with a price. One night Robert Hessen and his wife arrived fresh from a movie they had both enjoyed, *Topaz*. Rand's brow darkened when she heard them describe a scene in which a Russian defector is confronted with the bounty and splendor of Western goods: "[She became] literally furious, and started screaming at us how stupid we were." The room fell silent as Rand spoke. Didn't they realize this was propaganda, intended to make all defectors seem like materialistic opportunists rather than people motivated by a desire for freedom? To focus on this scene without understanding its meaning meant the Hessens were immature, superficial, naïve. The evening was ruined, the Hessens feeling "beaten and battered, humiliated."[57]

Members of Rand's inner circle saw her outbursts as a danger they would willingly brook in exchange for what she offered. Henry Holzer, Rand's lawyer, remembered that nights at her apartment involved a trade-off of sorts: "Ayn would hold court mostly, and every word, every sentence was magic. It was a revelation.... But, on the other hand, I think it's fair to say that most people were walking on egg shells." He described Rand's reaction if one of her friends said something she did not like: "She'd look at you with those laser eyes and tell you that you have a lousy sense of life, or what you said was really immoral, or you didn't see the implications, or it was anti-life."[58] Such tongue-lashings did little to deter Rand insiders. She offered them a "round universe" and a comprehensive philosophy that seemed to clear an easy path through life's confusions. Once they made a psychic investment in Rand, it was nearly impossible to pull away.

Many victims accepted that they had done something wrong, even as they were cast out of Rand's world. The worst offenders were publicly rebuked in group discussions and analyses that resembled trials. It mattered little if the accused was also a patient of Branden's who had exposed personal information as part of treatment and expected confidentiality or support. This official rejection by friends, therapist, and intellectual idol was crushing. The journalist Edith Efron, excommunicated when her sharp wit displeased Rand, wrote an ingratiating letter after her trial, thanking Rand for the gift of *Atlas Shrugged* and her other work: "I fully and profoundly agree with the moral judgment you have made of me, and with the action you have taken to end social relations.... I have repaid you for this greatest of gifts [*Atlas Shrugged*] with hurt and disappointment. Do me, if you wish, the courtesy of understanding that my self-condemnation is ceaseless."[59] Efron's expulsion was accompanied by a notice in *The Objectivist*, a harbinger of splits to come.

As Murray Rothbard knew, trials had a long pedigree in Objectivist society. They took on new importance as Nathan and Ayn's relationship crumbled. Trials were a way for Nathan to reassure Ayn of his dedication to Objectivism. They were also one of the few ways they could again act as one. Barbara Branden remembered that both Rand and her husband played a pivotal role: "She more than went along. She approved. But Nathan was the instigator of those terrible sessions."[60] Fearing he or she might be next, no one in the Collective dared to question the judgments being meted out.

Through all the purges and breaks, Rand was suffering as much as anyone. During 1967 her relationship with Nathan became purely therapeutic, as he continued to seek her help for his sexual problems. Nathan claimed that he still loved her and wanted to resume an affair with her; he simply couldn't. Four years into his clandestine affair with Patrecia he claimed to be asexual, unattracted even to desirable eighteen-year-olds, practically a celibate. Rand, for her part, was now reluctant to take Nathan back. His behavior was too confusing, his indifference too hurtful. She plied him with questions: Was she too old for him? Should they call the whole thing off? Convinced that Rand would disown him and destroy NBI if he rejected her explicitly, Nathan professed his love. The two considered every option to help him. Maybe an affair would help rejuvenate him sexually, they wondered. Rand vacillated on this point, telling him at one point that she could tolerate him taking another lover, then saying it was unacceptable. Nathan vacillated too. One day he talked of Rand as his ideal woman, the next he described a future in which he had a spiritual and sexual relationship with her yet lived his daily life in partnership with a woman of his own age. Patrecia came up frequently, but Nathan denied having romantic feelings for her.

Their discussions were incomprehensible to Rand on any level, but she knew something was terribly wrong. Nathan, once remarkably rational and clear in his conversations with her, was like a different person.

He spoke in circles, contradicted himself, and was unable to state his thoughts clearly. Most distressing of all, when Rand asked Nathan how he felt about her, he responded, "I don't know." Nor could he explain his feelings for Barbara or Patrecia. The man Rand hailed as her teacher of psychology was utterly divorced from his inner state. After a year of this Rand was losing hope. "He makes me *feel dead*," she wrote in her journal.[61] Then in June 1968 Nathan presented Rand with a letter in which he stated clearly that their age difference made it impossible for him to resume an affair with her.

Nathan's letter was a devastating rejection not only of Rand, but of the Objectivist philosophy itself. Objectivism taught that sex was never physical; it was always inspired by a deeper recognition of shared values, a sense that the other embodied the highest human achievement. Not only was Rand emotionally crushed, she now worried that Nathan was an inadequate representative of her life's work. He was caught in the snare of physical attraction, which spoke volumes to his emotional and spiritual confusion. And he had struck hardest at Rand's deepest insecurities by telling her she was no longer attractive to him.

Even after the letter, Rand clung to the hope of some relationship with Nathan. So quick to break with others who angered her, she went to extraordinary lengths to preserve their connection. "Love is exception making," she had written in *The Fountainhead,* and now she carved out an exception for the man to whom she had dedicated *Atlas Shrugged.*[62] She and Nathan would continue as business associates, understanding that they would never recapture the personal closeness of their early years. NBI and *The Objectivist* would continue unchanged. Nathan would work on his inability to live by Objectivist principles, and he would agree to give up seeing Patrecia, the source of his emotional troubles. Rand still believed that their relationship was platonic but suspected that Nathan had buried feelings for Patrecia. It was yet another instance of his failing to check his premises or think rationally.

This unstable accord held together, barely, for most of the summer. Ayn and Nathan continued to edit articles together, but the long therapy sessions were over. Nathan began seeing Allan Blumenthal instead. Blumenthal had a medical degree but no formal training in psychology beyond what Nathan taught him. Now he served as Nathan's confessor. Nathan admitted his love for Patrecia, but not the affair. Rand grew increasingly frosty after this revelation, which Blumenthal immediately transmitted to her. Still she said nothing publicly. She and Nathan appeared on their way to refiguring a new and more distant relationship as colleagues and business partners. The Collective could sense the tension, but none understood the full dimensions of what was happening in their upper stratum.

It was Barbara Branden who finally called off the charade. The letter of half-truths had done little to ease the pressure under which both Brandens lived. Haggard and sickly, Nathan was deteriorating daily under the weight of his lies. He had told Barbara about Patrecia, making her complicit in both his affair and his rationalizations to Rand. As Rand began to shift her allegiance to Barbara, she was struck by a deep guilt. In August, when Rand announced she planned to make Barbara her legal heir in place of Nathan, she could stand it no more. Barbara gave Nathan an ultimatum: it was time Ayn knew the whole truth, including the complete history of his relationship with Patrecia. If he couldn't tell her, she would. With a sense of fatalistic relief, Nathan gave his ex the go-ahead.

It was the worst and most violent of Rand's many breakups. When Barbara told her the full story of Nathan's relations with Patrecia, Rand was white-hot with fury. She summoned Nathan, cowering in his apartment several floors above. Barbara, Frank, and Allan Blumenthal waited with her. When Nathan arrived, Rand blocked him from the living room, seated him in her foyer, and unleashed a torrent of abuse. He was an impostor, a fake. She would destroy him and ruin his name. In a crescendo of rage she slapped him hard across the face, three times. Nathan sat motionless, absorbing her words and her blows. Years later he and Barbara remembered her parting words verbatim: "If you have an ounce of morality left in you, an ounce of psychological health— you'll be impotent for the next twenty years! And if you achieve any potency, you'll know it's a sign of still worse moral degradation!"[63] Then she ordered him out of her apartment. It was the last time the two would meet.

Rand's anger was boundless. She would never forgive, never forget. More than the fury of a woman scorned, it was the fury of a woman betrayed. For nearly five years, Nathan had lied to Rand about his feelings for her and his relationship with Patrecia. Their hours of intense conversation and counseling, so painful and taxing to Rand, had been a pretense and a ruse to distract her from his deceptions. In the meantime, NBI had grown from a small lecture series to a national institution. Nathan had become famous and wealthy speaking in Rand's name. He had a book contract with her publisher and a therapy practice filled with followers of her philosophy. As Rand saw it, he passed himself off as John Galt or Howard Roark—but was worse than any villain she could have conjured. The public face of Objectivism and the one who would carry her legacy forward was nothing more than a contemptible second-hander, unable to practice the principles he preached. He had struck deeply at Rand's heart and her philosophy, and made a mockery of both.

In the days after Nathan's confession, Rand moved swiftly to dismantle his businesses and strip him of all association with her and Objectivism. She sent her lawyer to demand that he sign over control of *The Objectivist* to her and deed NBI to Barbara. By week's end she was no longer speaking to Barbara either because she had attempted to defend Nathan against Rand's onslaught. Now Rand insisted that NBI be dismantled altogether. Word of the crisis spread rapidly through Objectivist circles. Nathan appeared, ashen-faced, before his staff and announced his resignation, explaining that he had committed grave moral wrongs and Rand had justifiably severed their relationship. Rumors flew wildly. New Yorkers willing to hear the gossip quickly divined the full story of Nathan and Rand's affair and its aftermath.[64]

In the NBI offices factions quickly emerged. Some Objectivists found the situation absurd and refused to repudiate Nathan without more information about his transgressions. Others were willing to take Rand at her word. Leonard Peikoff emerged as Rand's staunchest defender, asking rhetorically if anyone "could *possibly* believe that the author of *Atlas Shrugged* had done anything fundamentally wrong." Nathan quickly found himself isolated and alone, with Barbara his only prominent supporter. Over the years his arrogant reign over NBI and his aura of superiority had created a deep reservoir of resentment. Now he was shunned by some of his closest friends and relatives.[65] He and Barbara began the dreary work of liquidating NBI, splitting the leftover money between them.

The coup de grâce came in the next issue of *The Objectivist*, published in October but datelined May. In a letter addressed "To Whom It May

Concern," Rand attacked both Brandens. Rand's statement was rambling and vague, accusing Nathan of financial misdeeds, unspecified deception and manipulation, and failing to live up to Objectivist principles. Her overarching message, however, was clear: "I have permanently broken all personal, professional and business associations with [Nathaniel and Barbara Branden]....I repudiate both of them, totally and permanently, as spokesmen for me or Objectivism."[66] The letter was signed by Leonard Peikoff, Alan Greenspan, Allan Blumenthal, and Mary Ann Sures.

His name was mud where before he had been an admired leader, Nathan fought back with "In Answer to Ayn Rand," a letter sent to all *Objectivist* subscribers, appended with a postscript from Barbara. Nathan's letter refuted Rand's allegations point by point, detailed his dedication to Objectivism, and quoted from earlier statements she had made praising both Brandens. He concluded with a final, breathtaking paragraph in which he explained the true reason for their break: "[I attempted] to make clear to her why I felt that an age distance between us of twenty-five years constituted an insuperable barrier, for me, to a romantic relationship."[67] Even at the end, his Objectivist career ruined and his separation from Rand complete, Nathan skirted the issue, hinting that sexual jealously played a role in the break but failing to acknowledge the full extent of his actions or the relations between him and Rand. Sent out in tandem with Barbara's statement, his letter suggested that it was Rand alone who had acted inappropriately.

The scandal did much to tarnish Rand's reputation. George Walsh, then a professor at Hobart College, was organizing an Ayn Rand Caucus within the American Philosophical Association when the breach happened. He explained, "The people that I was gathering together to form the discussion group all fell away. They simply disappeared! They didn't answer my further letters or they explained that this was too much for them, that it seemed to be something other than it appeared to be, and that personal matters were apparently mixed up in it and they didn't want to touch it with a 10 foot pole."[68] To Rand's critics the dramatic collapse of NBI vindicated all they had been saying over the years: her philosophy was fundamentally flawed and morally corrupt. Her longtime antagonists on left and right were delighted. In *National Review* William F. Buckley crowed, "Remember, these were the people who were telling the rest of the world how to reach nirvana. By being like them."[69]

It was no coincidence that emotion cracked open Rand's world. By the time he met Patrecia, Nathan had created a monster out of NBI. Under Nathan's hand the institute drew forth and magnified the worst tendencies of Objectivism: its dogmatism, encouragement of judgment, rationalization of sexuality, suppression of emotion. Of all these tendencies, it was the last that would boomerang most sharply on Rand herself.

For the dedicated, the break was tantamount to a divorce between beloved parents. Ayn, Nathan, and Barbara had stood as exemplars and role models for their Objectivist flock. They suggested that the ideals of Rand's fiction could be lived in the ordinary world and that true love and deep friendship were possible. When Ayn and Nathan broke apart many Objectivists were shattered too. One fan sent Rand a heartfelt missive: "Today, when I received a copy of the issue 'To Whom it May Concern' I cried."[70] The rationally ordered universe NBI students sought and found in Rand was no more.

PART IV

Legacies

In 1974, Alan Greenspan invited Ayn and Frank to the White House to attend his swearing in a chairman of President Ford's Council of Economic Advisers. Courtesy Gerald R. Ford Library.

CHAPTER NINE

It Usually Begins with Ayn Rand

$THE SCHISMS OF 1968 were a disaster for Rand but a boon for
many of her readers. Afterward she retreated into private life,
emerging only once every year to address the Ford Hall Forum, an
event that became known as the "Objectivist Easter." But the ideological
energy amassed by Rand and her followers was too strong to disappear
overnight, as had NBI. The break even had an invigorating effect on the
spread of Objectivism, broadly considered, because the shuttering of
NBI coincided with a new wave of right-wing activity on campus. As
young conservatives began to mobilize against an increasingly radical
New Left, Rand's ideas became an important source of inspiration and
guidance. And now, without the dictats of NBI, there was ample room
for interpretation. No longer "students of Objectivism," those who liked
Rand were free to call themselves Objectivists or libertarians. They
could follow the logic of their antistatism all the way to the newly popular position of anarchism or, with a nod to Rand, anarcho-capitalism.[1]
Rand's works were too potent and too popular to be confined or controlled, even by their creator.

Once unleashed, Rand's ideas helped power an ideological explosion
on the right that culminated in an independent libertarian movement.
These new libertarians distinguished themselves proudly from traditional conservatives, who in turn greeted the movement with dismay.
At times, libertarians talking fervently about revolution seemed to have
more in common with the left than the right. For a brief moment it
even seemed that libertarianism or anarchism might become the latest
addition to the New Left's rainbow of ideologies.[2] But since Rand had so
deeply imprinted capitalism upon the face of the libertarian subculture, this latent potential never fully developed. Instead, libertarians
remained fierce defenders of the free market and apologists for all the

social consequences thus engendered. The greatest contribution of Rand's Objectivism was to moor the libertarian movement to the right side of the political spectrum. In turn, libertarians kept Rand's ideas actively circulating in the years after NBI's demise. Rand denounced libertarian appropriation of her work, never accepting that with her success came a commensurate loss of control. Objectivism, *Atlas Shrugged*, John Galt—they no longer belonged to Rand exclusively. She had set them loose in the world, and their fortunes were no longer tied to hers.

After the deluge, Rand's first priority was to produce the year's remaining issues of *The Objectivist*, now nearly five months behind schedule. Her main preoccupation was with Nathan and his betrayal. In long philosophic discussions with the remains of the Collective—the Blumenthals, the Kalbermans, and Leonard Peikoff—Rand strove to identify the root of Nathan's corruption, to find the seed of evil that had transformed him from trusted friend to sworn enemy.[3] Rand did what she could to erase the past, removing his name from future editions of *Atlas Shrugged* and repudiating him in a postscript to her nonfiction collections. She sabotaged his book contract with New American Library, her publisher, refusing to release copyright to *Objectivist* articles he intended to use and convincing the firm to drop his contract after a missed deadline. Her letter in *The Objectivist* was intended to ruin his reputation and prevent him from capitalizing on her work.

It was too late. Nathan was already beyond her reach, relocated to Los Angeles with Patrecia, whom he soon married. California Objectivists cared little about the crisis in New York, and before long he had another flourishing psychotherapy practice. Rand had built Nathan up to great heights among her readership; it was impossible now for her to tear him down. All but the most orthodox remained interested in his activities. In 1969 he found a different publisher for *The Psychology of Self Esteem*, which launched him on a new career as a leader of the self-esteem movement. Nathan's early work remained highly derivative of Rand, notwithstanding the photo on the book's back cover, which showed him towering over a headless statue of a winged goddess. Over time, as he continued to benefit from his earlier affiliation with Rand, Branden would repudiate many of her ideas. His Biocentric Institute strove to reconcile, as he and Rand never had, the connections between mind and body, sexuality and intellect.[4] Barbara Branden was in California too, but she stayed far from Nathan. Neither wanted to re-create the world they had just escaped.

Frank, who had witnessed the cataclysmic ending of her extramarital affair, became Rand's primary source of comfort. As her relationship with Nathan disintegrated, she came to newly appreciate her husband. In May 1968 she wrote a preface to the twenty-fifth anniversary edition of *The Fountainhead* that sang his praises. "Frank was the fuel," she wrote, describing his support in her darkest days of writing.[5] Her discovery of Frank's essential virtues came just as his hold on reality began to slip. He had been softening for years, and when life after the break settled into a new normal it became obvious that he was growing senile. By the early 1970s he was homebound, no longer able to visit galleries or participate in art classes. With her firm belief in free will and the power of rationality, Rand found it difficult to understand Frank's deterioration. In vain she tried to help him through his confusions with lengthy rational explanations. When he could no longer communicate, she asked his doctor if he could be mentally retrained so he could learn how to speak again. His obvious need for care stirred Rand's motherly side, and she fussed and worried over his every move. After almost fifty years of marriage Rand still loved her husband, or the shell of him that remained.[6]

Rand was also cheered by the unfailing loyalty and attention of Leonard Peikoff, one of the last remaining insiders from the years before *Atlas Shrugged*. During Objectivism's glory days Leonard had been a valued but decidedly second-tier member of the Collective. Now, bolstered by a new appointment as a philosophy professor at the Polytechnic Institute of Brooklyn, he emerged as Nathan's successor. Excerpts from his manuscript in progress, *The Ominous Parallels*, a comparison of Nazi Germany and contemporary America, filled the pages Nathan had claimed in *The Objectivist*, and he began to offer private courses in Objectivism. He and Rand were wary of recreating NBI, so his courses were not offered by tape transcription, only in person. Students had to sign a consent agreement stating that they would not associate with Nathan or Barbara Branden. Eventually *The Objectivist* would advertise a smattering of courses led by Rand's remaining associates, including several that had been recorded, but the level of activity never approximated NBI's. Nathan's transgressions had profoundly damaged Rand's willingness to popularize her work.

Instead Rand restricted her teaching to a small group of students, most of whom were pursuing graduate degrees in philosophy. These students were primarily interested in Rand's theory of concepts, which she laid out in *The Objectivist* in 1967 and would publish in 1979 as *Introduction to Objectivist Epistemology*. In these smaller courses Rand often discussed topics she did not write about, leading to the development of an Objectivist "oral tradition" carried forth by this remnant of the larger movement. Her lectures and Peikoff's extension of her ideas provided fertile ground for later Objectivist philosophers, but Rand had little new published work to offer. In 1971 she released her last two nonfiction books, *The New Left: The Anti-Industrial Revolution* and *The Romantic Manifesto,* both collections of previously published articles.[7]

In the outside world the "Objecti-schism" diminished Rand's authority considerably. In the year following her split with Branden subscriptions to *The Objectivist* dropped sharply, from twenty thousand to fourteen thousand. Stepping into the vacuum, entrepreneurial Rand enthusiasts began to redefine her philosophy to suit their interests. Objectivism had always been more than NBI, for the institute's rigidity repelled many a would-be student. Anne Wortham was a devoted reader of Rand when she visited the New York NBI, but she was disappointed by the "big-wigs" on stage and Rand herself, who "seemed cold, dogmatic, authoritarian, without that benevolent sense of life that she wrote so eloquently about." Although she never enrolled in an NBI course, Wortham continued a "private" relationship with Objectivism and used Rand's ideas to inform her later academic work in sociology.[8] Similarly, after Jarrett Wollstein was ejected from NBI for daring to teach a course on Objectivism at the local free university, he continued to identify Rand as a major influence on his thought. Wollstein started one of the most successful neo-Objectivist organizations, the Society for Rational Individualism, which published *The Rational Individualist,* a journal "in basic agreement with Objectivism."[9]

Despite its stated orientation, *The Rational Individualist* published the first serious challenge to Rand's hegemony, an "Open Letter to Ayn Rand" by Roy Childs Jr., a student at the State University of New York,

Buffalo. Childs admired Rand but questioned her stance on govern-ment as he gravitated toward an anarchist position. With his letter, sent to Rand on July 4, 1969, Childs repudiated Objectivism and debuted as the enfant terrible of anarcho-capitalism. Boldly Childs opened with a straightforward declaration: "The purpose of this letter is to convert you to free market anarchism." Relying heavily on Objectivist concepts and Randian words and phrases, Childs argued that Rand's advocacy of a limited state was contradicted by her own philosophy. Her told her, "Your political philosophy cannot be maintained without contradiction, that, in fact, you are advocating the maintenance of an institution—the state—which is a moral evil." Beyond offering an ethical critique, Childs also turned Rand's terminology against her, arguing that her idea of a limited government that did not initiate force was a "floating abstrac-tion." According to Childs, all governments must initiate force to survive as governments and maintain their monopoly on coercion. And if the initiation of force was forbidden in both the Objectivist and libertar-ian worlds, then the state itself must be opposed. Childs lectured Rand, "Your approach to the matter is not yet radical, not yet fundamental: *it is the existence of the state itself which must be challenged* by the new radi-cals. It must be understood that the state is an *unnecessary evil*."[10] Rand was unimpressed by Childs's logic. Her only response was to cancel his subscription to *The Objectivist*.

Although Rand vehemently opposed anarchism, many adherents insisted that anarchism was a logical outgrowth of Objectivism. Surveying the student right, the *Western World Review* observed, "Her philosophy and ethic appear to be functioning as a campus way sta-tion or half-way house on the road to the anarchism she opposes."[11] In many ways, the new vogue for anarchism had the quality of an Oedipal revolt against Rand. Anarchism was a way to resolve the contradictions that many found in Rand's political philosophy. How was it possible to oppose the initiation of force (a key Randian tenet), yet still defend a minimal state? R. W. Bradford, later an editor of *Liberty* magazine, remembered, "A few were willing to accept her obfuscations on the issue, but the overwhelming majority were unwilling to evade the problem. Virtually all these people became anarchists."[12] To many libertarians tutored in Rand's absolutist style of thought, the steps were simple: the state was bad, so why not abolish it entirely? Childs put it this way: "As in ethics there are only two sides to any question—the good and the evil—so too are there only two logical sides to the political question of the state: either you are for it, or you are against it."[13] Describing the origin of radical libertarianism and the new anarcho-capitalism, Jerome Tuccille called *Atlas Shrugged* "the seeds of this latest eruption."[14] Even more tellingly, he titled his memoir of libertarian activism *It Usually Begins with Ayn Rand*.

To some degree, Rand was proud of her role as an intellectual counterpoint to the New Left. In the first *Objectivist* published after her break with Nathan she praised a group at Brooklyn College, the Committee against Student Terrorism, for protesting a leftist rebellion with a leaflet that "condemned the violence, named the philosophical issues involved, and demonstrated that the antidote to the problem was to be found in the works of Ayn Rand and the literature of the Objectivist philosophy."[15] At the same time, she emphasized that students of Objectivism "cannot be and must not attempt to be the theoreticians of the subject they are studying." She repeated a guideline from two years earlier: "It is our job to tell people *what* Objectivism is, it is your job to tell them *that* it is." Such limited horizons did little to satisfy right-wing students, particularly those chafing with enthusiasm for anarchism.

The demise of NBI, if anything, accelerated the transformation of Objectivism into a bona fide movement, rife with competing schools who all cited Rand in support of their position. Anarchists were challenged by "minarchists," supporters of a minimal state, who closely followed Rand's arguments about government in "The Nature of Government," an essay from *The Virtue of Selfishness*. In this essay Rand argued that government performs a vital social function by "*placing the retaliatory use of physical force under objective control*—i.e., under objectively defined laws" (italics in original). Governments permitted individuals to live in peace and to form long-term contracts, knowing they would be objectively enforced. Rand was adamant that anarchism, "which is befuddling some of the younger advocates of freedom," could not work. To claim that man could live without a state was naïve, she insisted. Even a society of completely rational and moral men would still require "*objective* laws" and "an arbiter for honest disagreements among men." Nonetheless, both sides of the anarchist-minarchist debate insisted only they understood the true implications of Rand's political philosophy.[16]

Rather than seeing these debates as a sign of intellectual health and fertility, a testimony to the excitement and energy her ideas engendered, Rand was violently opposed to any unapproved usage of her work. Even as she laid down an official party line, she insisted, "Objectivism is not an organized movement and is not to be regarded as such by anyone." But such stern warnings did little to stop her readers from calling themselves Objectivists and creating lectures, parties, social clubs, and newsletters devoted to her thought. Rand's principled opposition to the draft had endeared her to politically aware students who sought a rational justification for their opposition to the war. Beyond that, *Atlas Shrugged* had indelibly etched the idea of a stateless capitalist utopia onto the right-wing psyche. Anarchists were right to recognize that Rand's ideas had first opened them to the possibility of radical antistatism. By denying the morality of both conscription and taxation, Objectivism de-legitimized two fundamental functions of any state. At the same time Rand's fiction suggested that an alternative world was within reach. Once imagined, Galt's Gulch could never be forgotten.

Rand's ideas became a powerful current in the fast-running tides of the student right, referenced by a popular new symbol, the black flag of anarchy modified with a gold dollar sign. A broad reference to radical libertarianism, the flag had multiple meanings. The dollar sign, the totem of John Galt and *Atlas Shrugged*, was a clear allusion to Rand. Its juxtaposition on the flag of anarchy, however, indicated allegiances beyond Rand, usually to anarchism. Whatever its exact meaning, the black flag looked menacing to conventional conservatives as it spread beyond the Objectivist subculture into the wider conservative movement. Reporting on a southern California Young Americans for Freedom conference held in conjunction with Robert LeFevre's radically libertarian Rampart College, Gary North, a writer for the conservative newsletter *Chalcedon Report*, was dismayed by what he found. Instead of studious conservatives affirming faith in God and country, the conference was filled with eccentrics waving the black dollar-sign flag. Enthusiastic libertarians debated proposals to create offshore tax havens and argued over the finer points of Objectivist doctrine. "When the talk drifted into a debate over whether or not Rearden was the true hero of *Atlas Shrugged*, given the world in which we live, I left," North reported. He concluded, "I think it is safe to say that YAF is drifting."[17]

North's reaction was representative. Many conservatives simply could not understand the new vogue for libertarianism, to them a bizarre tendency that might become dangerous if not nipped in the bud.

YAF was indeed drifting, particularly in California. By the late 1960s a significant number of chapters and the state director identified as libertarian rather than conservative. In early 1969 the Californians and their allies in other states organized a Libertarian Caucus to increase their influence within YAF. Libertarians committed to aggressive anti-statism now questioned YAF's reflexive patriotism, cultural traditionalism, and explicit identification as a conservative group. A cultural gap was opening between libertarians and the clean-cut, anti-Communist YAF majority, whom libertarians derided as "trads," short for traditional conservative. Sporting long hair, beards, and bell bottoms, libertarians delighted in shocking trads with proposals to legalize marijuana and pornography. Calling the United States a fascist state, they openly swapped draft evasion tips. The YAF National Office kept an uneasy eye on these developments. The libertarian upsurge came at a critical time for the organization, as it was positioning itself to wealthy donors as the one group that could effectively challenge SDS and other student activists. But now some YAF members looked and sounded like the dreaded New Left itself.

How much of this new wave of libertarianism in YAF drew from Rand's work? In 1970 an informal survey published in the *New Guard*, YAF's magazine, listed 10 percent of members as self-proclaimed "Objectivists." It is likely, however, that Rand influenced a broader group than those willing to identify as official followers of her philosophy. If exact lines of influence are hard to quantify, they are easy to trace. From the outside, at least, many saw Rand and libertarianism as interchangeable and used Rand as shorthand for all libertarians. Running for the national board on a unity platform, Ron Docksai published a campaign pamphlet that suggested, "Let us waste no energy in intramural debate over each other's credentials, but let us combat those Leftist merchants of death who will burn a book irrespective of whether it was written by Russell Kirk or Ayn Rand." Writing to the Libertarian Caucus prior to the national convention, Don Feder asked, "Are you saying to the Traditionalists in YAF, 'Either become Objectivists or leave the organization'? This seems to be the case." According to Feder, "an avowed Objectivist" ran the Boston

University delegation. Berle Hubbard, the mastermind of security for the Libertarian Caucus, queried a friend about *For the New Intellectual:* "Could you dig it? Or was it too heavy for you?" Rand was far from the only source of libertarianism in YAF; others mentioned Robert LeFevre, Milton Friedman and his son David, the novelist Robert Heinlein, and Ludwig von Mises as key influences. But she was an essential part of the libertarian stew.[18]

In 1969 this combustible mixture of anarchism, Objectivism, and traditionalist conservatism erupted in full display at the YAF annual conference in St. Louis.[19] The Libertarian Caucus brought an ambitious program to the convention. Their goals included making all seats on the national board elective, developing a resolution on YAF's direction in the 1970s, and amending the Sharon Statement, YAF's founding credo. Libertarians wanted to remove the Sharon Statement's opening reference to "young conservatives" and add domestic statism to international Communism as a "twin menace" to liberty. In short, they were proposing major changes to the YAF's governance, goals, and values.[20] It was a bold agenda for the three hundred activists in a population of more than a thousand delegates. Not surprisingly, most of their alternative planks were soundly rejected by the convention, including those that advocated draft resistance, an immediate withdrawal from Vietnam, and the legalization of marijuana.

On the third day of the conference libertarian frustration bubbled over when their antidraft resolution went down to defeat. Not only did the convention reject the libertarian plank, but in the plank that passed they included a pointed clause condemning draft resistance and the burning of draft cards. The convention's decision to endorse abolition of the draft, but not resistance to it, was critical. It signaled that there were definite limits to YAF's antistatism. The organization would remain firmly within the political establishment. Rhetorical support of limited government was fine, but anarchism and radical libertarianism were beyond the pale.[21]

In the face of this insult, the libertarians could no longer resist their innate impulse to challenge authority. A small pack of students gathered in a conspiratorial knot. One of the group had a facsimile of his draft card. (Apparently the conservative within him lived still, for he was unwilling to sacrifice the actual card.) Another dissident seized a microphone and announced to the assembly that any person had a right to defend himself against violence, including state violence. Then "he raised a card, touched it with a flame from a cigarette lighter, and lifted it over his head while it burned freely into a curling black ash."[22] The symbol of YAF, a hand holding the torch of liberty, had been deftly satirized and openly mocked.

After a few moments of shocked silence, pandemonium erupted on the convention floor. "Kill the commies" yelled the patriotic majority. Amid shouts, shoving, and fisticuffs, the traitorous facsimile draft card burners were ejected from the convention floor. Around three hundred of their ideological brethren followed the rebels out of the convention, and out of Young Americans for Freedom. A chasm now separated the libertarians and the traditionalists. By the end of the year a substantial number of YAF chapters had either left the organization or had their charters rescinded. California alone lost twenty-four chapters.[23]

This libertarian secession was the culmination of a dynamic that had plagued modern American conservatism since its emergence earlier in the century. Postwar conservatives had crafted a careful synthetic ideology with a productive contradiction at its core: the tension between free market capitalism and cultural traditionalism. Clashes over the balance of power had broken out regularly ever since, with Rand's excommunication by *National Review* among the most prominent. The cultural upheavals of the late 1960s were a watershed, for they made stark the difference between laissez-faire libertarians and tradition-bound conservatives. Taking inspiration from the revolutionary language of the New Left, libertarians finally had enough confidence and strength to identify themselves as a distinct political movement. They were no longer conservatives, but following in Rand's footsteps they would remain part of the right.

Immediately after the convention Murray Rothbard and his new comrade Karl Hess attempted to pull the exodus of libertarians to the left, but it was Rand who emerged as a more decisive influence. Rothbard's call for a pan-ideological movement was soundly rejected by Libertarian Caucus organizers. In an open letter to Rothbard distributed in St. Louis, Don Ernsberger scoffed at Rothbard's "small group in New York" and told him, "Join the Left if you will Dr. Rothbard, but don't try to hand us that crap about the forces of freedom being there.

Your view is pure negation."[24] Rothbard and Hess pulled together a few left-right conferences in the year following St. Louis, but their Radical Libertarian Alliance was short-lived. More durable were the many neo-Objectivist groups that emerged in the fall of 1969. In open revolt against YAF the UCLA chapter began putting out "some real volatile stuff," one California libertarian informed the deposed state director. "It has black flags with dollar signs and quotes from Rand yet."[25] At the University of San Diego another student reported that the local YAF leader "has changed her chapter into an open Objectivist group and has been holding extensive and intensive study groups in the area and has been sponsoring speakers on campus."[26]

The largest and most influential organization to emerge from the libertarian secession, the Society for Individual Liberty (SIL), grew out of Objectivist roots. The group was formed by a merger between YAF's Libertarian Caucus and the Society for Rational Individualism, publisher of *The Rational Individualist*. One of the organization's first press releases, "S.I.L. Asks Release of Imprisoned Radical," blended fiction with reality by objecting to the imprisonment of John Galt. The group rallied in protest on November 22, the date given in *Atlas Shrugged* for Galt's delivery of his famous sixty-page speech. The small band of libertarians waving black flags with dollar signs in front of the Philadelphia Federal Courthouse was largely misunderstood, with several passersby accusing them of Communist sympathies.[27] Even a reading of Galt's individualist oath did little to clarify the protest's intent.

However inscrutable to outsiders, SIL quickly emerged as the central clearinghouse for the libertarian movement by dint of its free-form membership structure and the enthusiasm of its founders. Immediately after its birth SIL claimed 103 chapters, and at its first-year anniversary boasted thirteen hundred members, three thousand persons in contact with the organization, and 175,000 pieces of literature distributed.[28] The 1972 directory of SIL was fat with libertarian organizations. Subdivided into multiple categories, the directory provides a snapshot of the early libertarian movement: 36 Libertarian Action Organizations are listed, along with 98 local SIL chapters, 33 institutes, 4 foundations, 29 booksellers, 31 libertarian-friendly publishers, 6 education endeavors, 24 enterprises, and 13 new community projects. The directory also identified a range of issue groups and political action groups, including nine antidraft groups and others dedicated to antiwar, antitax, abortion rights, mental health, gun control, women's liberation, gay liberation, legal defense, and marijuana legalization.[29]

SIL was supported in its mission by hundreds of libertarian magazines that mushroomed in the early 1970s, many of them Objectivist in orientation. During the early years libertarian periodicals essentially *were* the movement. Grassroots magazines and newsletters helped create a dense, thriving network out of far-flung local groups, fledgling business enterprises, and scattered efforts at political activism. As essential as magazines were, however, they were far from glamorous. Most were little more than mimeographed leaflets started by college students. The *A Is A Directory,* an annual libertarian index named for Rand's favorite Aristotelian principle, warned readers of the magazines it listed "to be prepared for inconsistency" and admitted, "Writing, editing, and printing are apt to be poor."[30] Many magazines took their cue from Rand's publications, including political commentary, cultural analysis, and romantic fiction in their offerings. Of the 128 magazines listed in the 1972 *A Is A Directory,* more than thirty had an explicit Objectivist or Objectivist-friendly orientation. Objectivism was by far the most popular affiliation, with generic anarcho-capitalism running a distant second with nine periodicals.[31]

Rand had little appreciation for her new fan base. During her annual public appearances she called libertarians "scum," "intellectual cranks," and "plagiarists." Because she defined Objectivism as her personal property, she viewed libertarian use of her ideas as theft. What others would see as tribute or recognition of her work, Rand defined as "cashing in" or plagiarism. "If such hippies hope to make me their Marcuse, it will not work," she wrote sourly.[32] Her comment was not far off the mark, for Rand's writings were a sort of ur-text for the libertarian movement. They could be challenged, interpreted, reinterpreted, adopted, celebrated— but never ignored. Whether she liked it or not, libertarians would always consider Rand a vital part of their intellectual heritage.

The source of Rand's appeal to the new libertarian movement was multifold. On the most basic level, her ideas and fictional characters served as an easy shorthand and a way to cement bonds between likeminded individuals. No matter their current political allegiance, Objectivist, anarchist, minarchist, or somewhere in between, reading Rand had been a rite of passage for most libertarians. Trading jokes about John Galt, fondly reminiscing over one's first encounter with *Atlas Shrugged,* and employing specialized Rand references such as "second-hander," "stolen concept," and "package deal" created a sense of group cohesion and identity. This feeling of togetherness and unity was particularly important in a movement that claimed individualism as its mantra and was phobic of conformity. As the joke went, "If you put half a dozen libertarians into a room together, you will eventually end up with four factions, 2 conspiracies, 3 newsletters, 2 splinter groups and 4 withdrawals of sanction!"[33] Or, as the editors of *New Libertarian Notes* warned, "Everyone in this publication is in disagreement!"[34] Rand helped libertarians create a cohesive subculture without sacrificing autonomy or independence.

Rand's emphasis on capitalism also helped libertarians remain distinct from the New Left. To outsiders, libertarian symmetry with the counterculture was among the movement's most salient characteristics, but careful observers understood that similarities between libertarians and the left were only skin deep. A writer for the gentleman's magazine *Swank* stumbled across a Greenwich Village coffee house identified only by a dollar sign on the door, where waiters handed out a petition endorsing Rand for president. Here he found not beatniks but "buckniks," a species of disenchanted youth who "hates everything about our society...but who believes in free enterprise on the individual level and wants to 'make good' in a business sense as deeply as any Horatio Alger hero."[35] It was true that Objectivists did have a tendency toward sartorial experimentation, but their rebellion was always in the service of capitalism. Some NBI students liked to dress like Rand, sporting dollar-sign insignia, flowing capes, and elongated cigarette holders. At the Radical Libertarian Alliance conference a "Randian superhero" appeared, with a gold cape, "black stretch suit with an enormous gold dollar sign embroidered on his chest and a gold lame belt cinching his waist."[36] There were even beaded and bearded Randian "heads," lovers of both LSD and logic. However long their hair and outlandish their dress, however, few libertarians were interested in a durable alliance with the New Left.

Indeed, hippie styles only created trouble by luring lefties to the cause under false pretenses, as libertarian writers noted uneasily. Writing in *Protos* Don Franzen identified a key sticking point: "It is not exaggeration to say that in selling libertarianism to Leftists, many libertarians are slightly embarrassed or hesitant to openly advocate capitalism. 'Freedom' is the bill of goods we try to sell to the flower children and the leftists." Continuing in a Randian vein, he noted, "If we wish to advocate capitalism, we must advocate it from a moral stand—we must assert that production is right for man, that rational self-interest is right for man, that aside from (and in addition to) the fact that man should be free, he should also be selfish and productive."[37] Here the restrictions that Rand put on libertarianism were clear. Rand had made capitalism a sacrosanct ideal for most libertarians, an allegiance that rapidly marginalized leaders like Karl Hess who hoped to draw libertarians to the left.

Rand's insistence on capitalism lay at the core of her appeal to libertarians, for it was part of a larger morality that many libertarians asserted was essential to their movement. By itself libertarianism spoke only of freedom, of minding your own business, there ain't no such thing as a free lunch. As *SIL News* asked in one of its first issues, "The essence of the philosophy is the radical advocacy of freedom....At this point a very serious question must be raised. After freedom...what?"[38] It was this philosophic hole at the center that made libertarianism such an excellent partner to conservatism. Tradition and religion filled in where libertarianism was silent. When libertarians rejected conservatism, they needed something to take its place.

For many this role was filled by Objectivism. Rand's moralism grounded and bounded libertarian freedoms by emphasizing rationality, self-interest, individual rights, and capitalism. *SIL News* asserted, "Certain values are right for man, and certain values are wrong. Certain actions benefit him, and certain destroy him. Turning man loose to follow his own whims...a 'do your own thing' approach...will not by itself achieve human well-being."[39] Echoing the magazine's stance, the budding journalist Robert Bidinotto electrified the second annual East Coast Libertarian Think-In with an inflammatory speech attacking hippies and drug use. Bidinotto, then an anarchist, nonetheless argued that Rand's rationalist morality was the proper basis for libertarianism. Objectivism helped him cast stones at others on moral grounds, even while he advocated complete political freedom.[40]

This is not to say that Objectivism and Rand were without controversy in libertarian circles. Rand's ubiquity made her a convenient target for disgruntled and sarcastic libertarians. In a disapproving article *SIL News* noted a new phenomenon, "the Anti-Randian Mentality," or the growing practice of libertarians "gaining apparent psychological enjoyment and esteem from making publicly a disparaging snide or comical innuendo about Ayn Rand or certain Objectivist jargon." Although there indeed might be "humorous aspects" to Objectivism, the newsletter declared that it was harmful to single out Rand for ridicule since she remained "the fountainhead" of libertarianism.

More substantively Rand's patriotism and her reverence for the Founding Fathers were controversial in a movement that considered the Constitution a coercive document (because it claimed jurisdiction over even those who had not signed).[41] Rand's account of the Apollo 11 launch crystallized this difference for many. In the *Objectivist* she described how she had been invited to a VIP viewing of the rocket launch. Shepherded past the masses to within three miles of the take-off, Rand was awe-struck. Apollo 11 was "the concretized abstraction of man's greatness," and as she saw the rocket rise she had "a feeling that was not triumph: but more: the feeling that that white object's unobstructed streak of motion was the only thing that mattered in the universe."[42] It was a masterful piece of writing that became one of Rand's personal favorites.

Reading her account, Jerome Tuccille was incredulous. In *The Rational Individualist* he asked, "Has Ayn Rand been co opted into the system by her new role as White House 'parlor intellectual'?" To Tuccille NASA was a bunch of "bandits operating with billions of dollars stolen from the taxpayer—'rational' bandits, perhaps, achieving a superlative techno-logical feat—but bandits nevertheless."[43] Libertarians might make peace with Rand's endorsement of limited government, but singing the praises of NASA made Rand's antistatism seem superficial, a belief to be cast aside when convenient. Nor was the article an isolated incident. Apollo 11 became an encouraging sign of the times for Rand, who referred to the launch repeatedly in the years that followed.

What libertarian critics of the "moon jaunt" missed was how Rand's appreciation of Apollo 11 was tied to her ever-present worry that the United States was going backward, regressing to Petrograd circa 1920. Her fears were stirred anew by the emergence of the environmental movement, which she viewed as a virulent atavism that would drag mankind back to primitive existence. In her 1970 lecture to the Ford Hall Forum she attacked environmentalism as "the Anti-Industrial

Revolution." She imagined a grim future where a middle-class every-man made his morning coffee on a gas stove, electric percolators and ovens having been banned, and endured a two-and-a-half-hour com-mute on the city bus, cars now likewise forbidden. "His wife washes dia-pers for hours each day, by hand, as she washes all the family laundry, as she washes the dishes—by hand, as there are no self-indulgent luxuries such as washing machines or automatic dishwashers." As usual Rand was unwilling to accept the claims of a political movement at face value, convinced that hidden agendas drove the environmental movement. "Clean air is not the issue nor the goal of the ecologists' crusade....it is *technology* and *progress* that the nature-lovers are out to destroy," she told her listeners.[44]

Nature was not benevolent to Rand, but a force to be kept at bay by man's reason. Petrograd under the Communists had fallen to nature, regressing from a citadel of European culture to a city stalked by starva-tion, where survival was a daily struggle. Now environmentalists seemed to be questioning the basic achievements of industrialization and com-merce, the discoveries that had lifted man above the beasts. Collectivists, previously focused on inequality and injustice, were "now denouncing capitalism *for creating abundance*." In this context Apollo 11 stood out for Rand as a bright sign of hope; it was not the powers of the state that she celebrated, but the wonders of technology and human achievement.[45]

Rand missed the fact that environmentalism was yet another arena of thought powered by selective appropriation of her work. She focused relentlessly on what historians call conservation environmentalism, which emphasized the dangers of technology and was resolutely anti-growth. But another strain of environmental thought had discovered Rand's celebration of human creativity and the power of markets. Pragmatic or countercultural environmentalism focused on invention and innovation, rather than regulation, as solutions to the environmental crisis. The survivalist *Whole Earth Catalog*, a hippy-techno-geek bible, was an important node of this movement. "We are as gods and might as well get good at it," the catalogue announced, striking a vaguely libertarian note with its intention to support "a realm of intimate, personal power" and "the power of the individual." Not surprisingly the catalogue's founder, Stewart Brand, thought Rand was an exciting thinker.[46]

In 1968 Brand noted in his diary, "I'm reading *Atlas Shrugged* these days, again, on quite a different level—keeping some watch on myself, but mostly letting the notions run on." He returned to Rand during a period of deep thinking, aided by his near daily consumption of nitrous oxide. For more than a month his journal made occasional references to Rand and showed unmistakable traces of her thought. He wrote after a discussion of Arthur Koestler's views on abstract and emotional thought, "Don't sever 'em, connect 'em up better. Then your abstract advances will be accompanied by emotional joy, and so forth. Which sounds Ayn Randish."[47] In the *Last Whole Earth Catalog*, a countercultural classic that sold more than a million copies and won a National Book Award, Brand offered a cryptic one-line review of *Atlas Shrugged*, "This preposterous novel has some unusual gold in it," followed by a short excerpt. Brand's ability to freely mingle Rand's ideas with futuristic themes like moon colonization foreshadowed the emerging culture of cyberspace, which was strikingly libertarian from the beginning.[48]

Looking at another new movement of the 1970s, feminism, Rand was similarly critical. Like feminists Rand had always emphasized the importance of paid, professional work for both men and women, and her proto-feminist heroines rejected traditional female roles. She was also fiercely against any legal restrictions on abortion, calling it "a moral right which should be left to the sole discretion of the woman involved." When New York State considered liberalizing its abortion laws, Rand broke from her typical position of detached analysis and urged *Objectivist* readers to write letters in support of the proposed change. Watching the pro-life movement take shape, Rand was aghast. "An embryo *has no rights*," she insisted. The principle was basic: restrictions on abortion were immoral because they elevated a potential life over an actual life. It was essential that women be able to choose when, and whether, to become mothers.[49]

Despite this common political ground, Rand regarded the feminist movement as utterly without legitimacy. In a 1971 article, "The Age of Envy," she declared, "Every other pressure group has some semiplausible complaint or pretense at a complaint, as an excuse for existing. Women's Lib has none." To Rand, feminism was simply another form of collectivism, a variation on Marxism that replaced the proletariat with women, a newly invented oppressed class.[50] The proof was in feminist calls for government to redress discrimination, when it was not government itself that had created the problem. She wrote, "The notion that a woman's place is in the home...is an ancient, primitive evil, supported and perpetuated by women as much as, or more than, by men." What infuriated Rand the most was that feminism, as she saw it, was a claim based on weakness, a rebellion "against strength as such, by those who neither attempt nor intend to develop it." Feminists elevated their gender above their individuality and intelligence and then expected unearned success, to be enforced by government quotas and regulations. Rand was also withering in her personal scorn for feminists, "sloppy, bedraggled, unfocused females stomping down the streets."[51] Feminists reminded her of Comrade Sonja, a brash, masculine Communist from *We the Living*.

In turn, Susan Brownmiller attacked Rand as "a traitor to her sex" in her feminist classic *Against Our Will: Men, Women, and Rape*. Brownmiller considered Rand alongside the psychologists Helene Deutsch and Karen Horney as women who contributed to "the male ideology of rape." She argued *The Fountainhead*'s infamous rape scene "romanticized" the rape victim through its depiction of Dominique, who reveled in Roark's sexual attack on her. By portraying rape as "grand passion," Rand cast an unrealistic patina over sexual violence and furthered the dangerous idea that women desired to be raped. The worst of it was that Rand could even convince other women that rape was romantic. Brownmiller remembered, "*The Fountainhead* heated my virgin blood more than 20 years ago and may still be performing that service for schoolgirls today."[52] When she visited the library to check out Rand's novel Brownmiller was discouraged to find its pages fell open to the rape scene, effectively indexed by other readers. Like the conservatives of *National Review*, Brownmiller recognized Rand's work was both appealing and ideologically dangerous.

Similarly, a writer for *Ms.* magazine warned women against Rand's influence, calling her work "fun-bad." *Ms.* noted that Rand's call to self-ishness and independence might justifiably appeal to women, who had been taught to always place others before themselves. In reality, though, her work offered a seductive, destructive fantasy: "a strong dominant women who is subdued by an even stronger, more dominant male...the independent woman who must, to preserve her integrity, capitulate to a more powerful man."[53] There was a puzzling duality to Rand. Her characters were iconic strong women, and in her personal life Rand lived many feminist tenets. All of this was contradicted, however, by her theory of "man worship" and her consistent depiction of women sexually submitting to men. What made the messages particularly confusing was Rand's insistence that her views on men and women were rational conclusions rather than emotional responses. In truth, Rand's fiction was part projection, part identification, part fantasy, and accurately reflected the tangled sexuality of her life. Setting these contradictions aside, other women focused simply on the positive messages in her fiction. Former Objectivists became active in several organizations dedicated to "individualist feminism," and Rand's work, particularly the character of Dagny Taggart, was lauded as inspirational by the pioneering tennis greats Billie Jean King, Martina Navratilova, and Chris Evert.[54]

Rand's excoriation of feminism was reflective of her general distemper throughout the 1970s, a mood that began to alienate even her most loyal fans. At the end of 1971 she terminated publication of *The Objectivist*, announcing a new fortnightly, *The Ayn Rand Letter*. The *Letter* was a shorter publication, written exclusively by Rand with occasional guest appearances by Leonard Peikoff. Again Rand had trouble sticking to the ambitious publication cycle she set for herself, and the magazine's appearance was erratic. As the volume of her new writing decreased, her annual speeches to the Ford Hall Forum became an increasingly important conduit between her and the many readers who continued to track her every move. The question-and-answer sessions she held after each lecture were a particular flashpoint.

Prompted by her fans, Rand offered a number of controversial stances that particularly outraged libertarians. Her statements after the "Age of Envy" speech in 1972 were particularly disturbing. Asked about amnesty for draft dodgers, Rand told her audience that "bums" who didn't want to fight in Vietnam "deserve to be sent permanently to Russia or South Vietnam at the public's expense." She praised labor unions and Congressman Henry "Scoop" Jackson, an ardent militarist. Her praise for Jackson was based on his aggressive stance toward the Soviet Union. Previously Rand tended to downplay the Russian threat, believing its command economy could never match the military prowess of the United States. Now she became implacably opposed to disarmament or arms control, for she believed the USSR could never be trusted. In other appearances she attacked Native Americans as savages, arguing that European colonists had a right to seize their land because native tribes did not recognize individual rights. She extended this reasoning to the Israel-Palestine conflict, arguing that Palestinians had no rights and that it was moral to support Israel, the sole outpost of civilization in a region ruled by barbarism. Rand revealed that Israel was the first public cause to which she had donated money. And she continued to flay anarchists and libertarians as "worse than anything the New Left has proposed."[55] Without NBI or significant new publications, Rand had nothing positive to offer that could offset her negativity or support her sweeping judgments on current events.

By the end of 1972, even SIL had had enough. On the front page of *SIL News* the directors announced, "We are not in sympathy with or identified with all of the political applications that Ayn Rand cares to make based on her philosophy of Objectivism," citing her positions on draft resistance, the Vietnam War, the space program, civil liberties, amnesty for draft evaders, and support for collectivist politicians. "The basic works of Rand continue to be the most powerful influence on our membership," the directors admitted. "However, moral men cannot stand quiet."[56] Only a year earlier SIL had published an article defending Rand against the "anti-Rand mentality." Now they too wished to draw a distinction between Rand's beliefs and their own. As Rand became ever more jingoistic, libertarians remained deeply suspicious of all state action. They were also sympathetic to the cultural changes sweeping the nation that Rand found so alarming. The political spectrum was shifting, and Rand was moving to the conservative side of the right.

The real rift between Rand and the libertarians came with the founding of the Libertarian Party in 1971. The party's founder, David Nolan, was an MIT graduate and Rand fan. He was galvanized to action by Nixon's announcement of wage and price controls, intended to curb inflation. (By contrast Rand endorsed Nixon twice, regarding him as the lesser of two evils.) Nolan and a few friends announced plans for a libertarian national convention, held in Denver the following year. At the convention libertarians organized themselves into a loose network of state parties, coordinated by an elected central committee. They adopted organizational bylaws and a platform calling for withdrawal from Vietnam, draft amnesty, and abolition of victimless crimes and the Federal Communications Commission. The Party's statement of principles declared, in hyperbolic language, "We, the members of the Libertarian Party, challenge the cult of the omnipotent state and defend the rights of the individual."[57] By libertarian standards the Party was a smashing success. At the June convention the Party claimed one thousand members and doubled its numbers by election day. By the end of 1973 it had three thousand members, with organizations in thirty-two states.

In the early years there was a distinctly Objectivist flavor to the Party. Nolan remembered that many early members were "fans, admirers, students of Ayn Rand…heavy Objectivist influence." The *Colorado Libertarian Newsletter*, published by the founding chapter of the Party, was studded with Randian ideas and references. Authors and advertisers took for granted that readers would know what was meant by "the Randian sense-of-life" or that they would be interested in seminars held by Nathaniel Branden. A survey of Californian Libertarian Party members revealed that 75 percent of members had read *Atlas Shrugged*, more than any other book. The third most popular book was *The Virtue of Selfishness*. Party members were "required to sign a pledge against the initiation of physical force as a means of achieving social and political goals," thus enshrining a principle Rand had articulated more than thirty years earlier in her "Textbook of Americanism."[58]

Like Rand, the Libertarian Party was controversial within libertarian movement circles. Some libertarians worried about hypocrisy. How could a movement opposed to the state become part of the formal electoral system? Don Ernsberger, one of SIL's founders, took the Randian line that the formation of a Libertarian Party was premature: "My negativism stems from the fact that social change never results from politics but rather politics stems from social change."[59] He also worried that libertarians would become morally tainted by their venture into the political world. The *Southern Libertarian Review* and the *Libertarian Forum*, among other publications, made similar arguments against the Party. Party supporters countered that their electoral campaigns were a form of education and an effective way to reach the masses.

This contention was borne out by the 1972 election, when the new party nominated candidates for both president and vice president. After an unsuccessful attempt to draft Murray Rothbard, the convention settled on Rand's old friend John Hospers, a philosophy professor at the University of Southern California, and Tonie Nathan, a broadcast journalist and businesswoman based in Oregon. Hospers and Nathan were on the ballot in only two states, Colorado and Washington, and had a campaign budget under seven thousand dollars. Although the Party earned only 3,671 votes, it gained one electoral vote—and national media coverage—when a renegade Virginia elector, Roger MacBride, cast his vote for Hospers-Nathan.[60] The nominally Republican MacBride had been tutored in the fundamentals of libertarianism by no less a luminory than Rose Wilder Lane, who considered him her adopted grandson and made him her literary heir. His rebellion made Nathan the first woman to receive an electoral college vote, an event that drew television news trucks to the normally staid Richmond Capitol Building where electors voted. The Party's quixotic decision to run candidates had turned out to be a savvy move, garnering national news coverage far beyond what was warranted by the campaign. MacBride became an instant hero to Party members and sympathizers and would go on to be the Party's next presidential candidate.

After the election the Party usurped Rand as a basic commonality among libertarians. Every libertarian had heard of the Party, and every libertarian had an opinion about it. The group even began to attract new members from the Democrats and Republicans, particularly after Watergate created widespread disillusion with politics-as-usual. One of these new converts was the future interior secretary Gale Norton, who found her way to the Party through an early interest in Rand.[61]

Undaunted, Rand hammered away at the Libertarian Party in her yearly Boston speeches. The party was a "cheap attempt at publicity," and libertarians were "a monstrous, disgusting bunch of people." Her primary theme was that libertarians had plagiarized her ideas. "It's a bad sign for an allegedly pro-capitalist party to start by stealing ideas." Later, she expanded on this idea, telling a questioner that the party stole her ideas and then "mixes them with my exact opposite."[62]

Besides their supposed plagiarism, what Rand objected to was libertarian laissez-faire in morals and the Party's acceptance of anarchism. After contentious infighting anarchists and minarchists had established a mutually agreeable party platform, so many members of the Party claimed to be working for the ultimate abolition of the state, a position Rand found irresponsible and absurd. Even worse was that libertarians had no guiding philosophy, and were proud of it. Rand supported abolition of the drug laws and the draft, but libertarians went beyond these positions, celebrating drug culture, draft dodging, and general rebellion against law and order. This tendency toward chaos had made Rand's morality appealing to libertarians who sought boundaries and guides to their rebellion. Now the Libertarian Party offered the same kind of structure. Unlike Rand, the Party also offered a positive program for the future, even a promise of political influence. By opposing the Party so vehemently, Rand undermined her vaunted position among libertarians.

No longer star-struck teenagers, libertarians were now ready to challenge Rand's authority and even her intellectual contribution. A Libertarian Party organizer, Edward Crane III, responded specifically to Rand's allegation that the Party existed on "borrowed" ideas. "Sure, we've 'borrowed' some of the concepts used by Miss Rand," wrote Crane. "But the myth that she *invented* those ideas should long since have been dispelled," he added, citing a number of earlier libertarian writers who had influenced Rand, including Rose Wilder Lane and Isabel Paterson. Crane surmised that Rand was most troubled because she did not control the Libertarian Party. Despite his harshness Crane tempered his criticism, noting in a foreword, "I am a great admirer of Rand and had mixed emotions about writing the piece. I am inclined to believe that the Ayn Rand I was writing about is not quite the same Ayn Rand of a decade ago."[63] Framing Rand as a new and different person helped ease the sting. And to some degree it was true: Rand had become increasingly unpleasant, querulous, and rigid as the years progressed. But libertarians had also changed. Their worldview, goals, and ambitions had shifted, as would their intellectual horizons.

Libertarian ambitions were fed by the ascendancy of Rand's protégé, Alan Greenspan, to the president's Council of Economic Advisers. Anarchists and purists regarded him as a statist sell-out; others wondered if he would subtly pull the administration in an Objectivist direction. He and Rand were still close, although they met infrequently. Greenspan had largely stayed above the fray in 1968 but had not hesitated to publicly support Rand in her disavowal of Nathan. This action cemented Rand's appreciation of his friendship, and he in turn made no secret of his involvement with her philosophy. Greenspan's rise within Republican circles had been meteoric, aided by his alliance with Martin Anderson, whom he had met through the New York NBI. Once a regular at NBI lectures and a visitor to Rand's private salons, Anderson had been swept out of the Objectivist orbit when he joined Richard Nixon's first presidential campaign. But he remembered both his Objectivist principles and friends, bringing Greenspan on board the campaign and urging Nixon to oppose the draft on libertarian grounds.[64] Anderson and Greenspan were both appointed to the Gates Committee, which eventually recommended abolition of the draft. From there Greenspan's economic expertise made him a valued consultant to the president and set him on the path toward his eventual chairmanship of the Federal Reserve.

Greenspan was only the first of many high-profile economists to break out of the libertarian ghetto, broadening the libertarian focus beyond Rand. After decades of honing their approach, academic libertarians were ready to take advantage of opportunities created by the economic doldrums of the 1970s. The long struggle for acceptance paid off when both F. A. Hayek and Milton Friedman were awarded Nobel Prizes in economics in 1974 and 1976, respectively. Their ascent to the top of the economics profession reflected a major intellectual shift away from Keynesianism. The failings of socialist economies and the appearance of "stagflation," which Friedman had famously predicted, made economists and policymakers alike more interested in libertarian arguments. Although Rand despised Hayek, his classical liberal views were a species of libertarianism to all but the purists, and his public recognition was an index of the increased respectability of antistatism. Hayek's prize also brought attention and prestige to his overlooked mentor, Ludwig von Mises, who remained a favorite of Rand's, and gave a boost to the fourth-generation Austrian School clustered around NYU. During this time the libertarian-inflected law and economics movement, an outgrowth of the Chicago School, made inroads at several important law schools.[65]

In 1975 libertarians won another coveted prize when Harvard Professor Robert Nozick was awarded the National Book Award for *Anarchy, State, and Utopia,* a philosophic defense of the limited state. Nozick had been introduced to libertarianism through Murray Rothbard and cited both Rothbard and Rand in his pathbreaking book. Typically understood as a response to the egalitarianism of his Harvard colleague John Rawls, *Anarchy, State, and Utopia* must also be recognized as the fullest intellectual flowering of the libertarian subculture. Even while attacking the argument Rawls had propounded in *A Theory of Justice*, Nozick was equally concerned with responding to Murray Rothbard and the ongoing minarchist/anarchist debate. He intended to establish that a state could be compatible with "solid libertarian moral principles." Nozick was an enthusiastic member of the Libertarian Party, appearing at the 1976 conference to argue on behalf of a VP candidate who had been rejected due to his homosexuality.[66]

This libertarian move into the mainstream eroded the distinction between academic and popular libertarianism, and with it Rand's reputation among libertarians. The gap between academic and popular (or "movement") libertarianism first developed in the 1940s, when organizations such as the Foundation for Economic Education, the Volker Fund, and the Mont Pelerin Society began concentrating their funding on professional economists, to the exclusion of popular writers like Rand, Isabel Paterson, and Rose Wilder Lane. As Rand developed Objectivism, professors supported by libertarian organizations began to make their way into academia, many becoming associated with the University of Chicago. Rand's claim to a comprehensive philosophy and her refusal to recognize other libertarians besides Ludwig von Mises had kept many of her followers ignorant of the strides libertarianism had made in the academy. Accordingly the early libertarian movement was shaped largely by popularizers like Rand, Robert LeFevre, and Murray Rothbard. Now grassroots publications such as *A Is A Newsletter* began paying attention to the latest publications from Chicago, and Friedman and other luminaries likewise reached out to the movement. Friedman was viewed with suspicion by many libertarians for his involvement in designing compulsory tax withholding, but his son David, an anarchist, was active in several organizations. Tipped off to the existence of a growing popular movement, the elder Friedman addressed an SIL convention via telephone and began promoting the group to his college audiences.[67]

The barriers between movement libertarians and the broader intellectual and political world were beginning to collapse. In 1973 a wave of consolidation swept over the movement, spearheaded in large part by SIL. After years of irregular publication SIL severed its connection to Wollstein's *Individualist,* offering members in its place a subscription to *Reason* magazine. Originally started as a handmade mimeographed Objectivist newsletter out of Boston University, by 1973 *Reason* had almost six thousand subscribers, making it the most successful libertarian magazine by far. *Reason* was the first libertarian magazine since Rand's *Objectivist* to garner a subscription base in the thousands. As *Reason* developed, fewer and fewer small homegrown libertarian magazines appeared. Professionally produced and designed, *Reason* charted a careful course away from libertarian extremism toward greater mainstream visibility and respectability.

Reason owed much of its circulation to a coup scored in 1971, when it published Nathaniel Branden's first post-Rand interview. As Branden well knew, the libertarian movement offered him a chance to refurbish his reputation among the Objectivist rank and file. Branden was coy about his experiences with Rand, but clearly indicated his growing differences with her philosophy. He still considered her "one of the greatest minds in history" and claimed, "[She is] the greatest novelist I have ever read," but he spoke frankly about the flaws he saw in her personality and her philosophy. Branden was contrite about his own role in what he called the "intellectual repressiveness" of NBI, and he offered his latest book, *The Disowned Self,* as a way to "undo some of the damage" he admitted to "caus[ing] students of Objectivism in the past." Though he still considered himself an expert on psychology, Branden had lost some of his overbearing moralism. When the magazine asked if sex without love was moral he responded, "What, am I your mother?"[68] The interview's overall tone reflected the general libertarian stance toward Rand, who was now seen as a figurehead or a respected elder rather than a source of direct guidance. She was a totem and ideal to be admired, but not worshipped. *Reason* was interested in Rand but not beholden to her.

By 1973 *The Ayn Rand Letter* was slipping badly. Issues were often months behind schedule and Rand's standards of discourse had plunged. In a review of John Rawls's *Theory of Justice* Rand dropped the pretense that she had read his work, announcing, "Let me say that I have not read and do not intend to read that book."[69] Instead, she offered a review of the reviews Rawls had received in the *New York Times*. Aside from Leonard Peikoff, Rand had no other contributors to her publication, and between Frank's declining health and her own it was impossible for her to produce a fortnightly publication unaided.

Rand was occupied primarily by personal events, particularly the discovery of her long-lost sister Nora. In the spring of 1973 Rand was shocked to receive word from Nora, whom she had presumed dead decades ago. At a U.S.-sponsored art show in Leningrad, Nora picked up a booklet on American authors and discovered her sister's picture. She wrote to the group sponsoring the exhibit, who in turn contacted Rand. It was the first news she had received of her family in more than thirty years. The two women had a tearful phone conversation and arranged for Nora and her husband to pay a visit. Rand was overjoyed. Here, after the hard years of disappointment and betrayal, was a reward to brighten her old age. Despite declining health she threw herself into preparations, renting an apartment for the couple in her building and investigating Russian communities in the area where they could settle. She would sponsor Nora and Victor to stay in the United States, supply them with whatever they needed to make their lives near hers.

But Nora's visit was a disaster, a sad reprise of Rand's last failed days with Isabel Paterson. At first the two sisters connected ecstatically. Nora, though, was paranoid and suspicious, suspecting Rand's driver, cook, and Leonard Peikoff of being American spies. Shaped by years of propaganda, she refused to believe they were not being watched. Rand was frustrated by her sister's inability to understand the freedoms of America. Nora pushed back, criticizing the messiness and clamor of Rand's beloved New York. She showed little interest in her sister's books, instead devouring a volume by Alexander Solzhenitsyn, banned in the USSR. Rand considered Solzhenitsyn the worst kind of Russian mystical collectivist, but Nora praised his work. The two began to argue nonstop. Rand canceled the parties she had planned for Nora as their six-week visit devolved into a clash of wills. Nora was jealous of her sister's fame and fortune perhaps, or maybe she was just overwhelmed by the differences between their lives. But she could not, would not reject Russia as Rand expected her to. Equally stubborn and righteous, neither sister could let go of her disagreement and reach for common ground. By the close of the visit, both knew it was impossible for Nora to settle in the United States. When Nora and Victor returned to Russia Rand was deeply disappointed. She had offered her sister freedom, and Nora had chosen dictatorship. Nora was not like her at all—and so much like her yet.

Not long after Nora left, Rand was diagnosed with lung cancer. She had smoked two packs of cigarettes a day for decades, resolutely insisting that statistics about their health risks were not reliable evidence. Now the proof was in her own labored breathing and fading energy. Before undergoing surgery on her left lobe she accepted an invitation to speak at the West Point commencement ceremony. Facing an enthusiastic audience of cadets Rand gave a rousing speech, "Philosophy, Who Needs It?, later reprinted in the West Point curricula. That summer she scheduled her operation. It was a success, but her recovery was painful and slow. *The Ayn Rand Letter* fell almost a year behind its supposed publication schedule. Rand mailed the August 1974 issue in May 1975, telling readers that the letter would soon become a monthly. After two more issues she knew it was no use. The November–December issue, she announced, would be the final one.

In the final *Ayn Rand Letter,* her effective exit from public life, Rand sounded somber yet familiar themes. It was sad to cease publication, she told her readers, but also a relief. Month after month she found herself saying the same things: "I do not care to go on analyzing and denouncing the same indecencies of the same irrationalism." She had lost the sense that she was leading an effective crusade that could reverse the drift toward collectivism. Gone was the optimism that had led her to endorse Goldwater, to rouse campus audiences across the country, to dissect the popular culture and media. Now she was "haunted by a quotation from Friedrich Nietzsche: 'It is not my function to be a fly swatter.'" Rand recognized her own weariness, and also her own circularity. For all the distance she had traveled in her life, a few fundamentals still guided her thought. Russia haunted her still, an object lesson in what might happen if the wrong ideas triumphed. The injustice served her father resonated in the welfare state she opposed, both starkly demonstrating the evils of altruism. Capitalism dragged under the weight of compromise and contradiction. For all the emotional upheavals she had suffered, rationality was still her only guide and source of wisdom, individualism her favored theme. "Well, I told you so," she sighed. "I have been telling you so since *We the Living*, which was published in 1936."[70]

Rand had one last word of warning to issue. Referring to the upcoming Republican primaries she wrote, "I urge you, as emphatically as I can, not to support the candidacy of Ronald Reagan." Reagan was a conservative in "the worst sense of the word," she told her readers.[71] Not only did he support a mixed economy, a compromise between laissez-faire and government controls, but his opposition to abortion demonstrated a dangerous disregard for individual rights. Reagan represented the triumph of all the political trends on the right Rand had fought throughout her long career. He blended libertarianism with religion, submerging a rational defense of capitalism under altruistic ethics. His position on abortion was the clearest indicator that he did not understand the free society he claimed to defend. Like Willkie and Eisenhower before him, Reagan was a false friend, a conservative who would destroy the very principles he claimed to uphold.

Although Rand would never appreciate their efforts, her political beliefs were shared by the Libertarian Party, who worked vigorously to provide an alternative to the majority party stars Reagan, Ford, and Carter. But like Rand, the Libertarian Party was subject to sudden political enthusiasms and dashed hopes. Party activists vacillated between a genuine belief that they could create immediate political change and a more realistic understanding that their campaigns were little more than public relations events. After a disappointing showing in the 1976 election several Party leaders swung back to the Randian position that education must precede action. In partnership with the Koch brothers, wealthy libertarians who had bankrolled most of the campaign, Party Chair Ed Crane started the Cato Institute, dedicated to spreading libertarian ideas. Born from the early libertarian ethos of education, Cato nonetheless became deeply involved in policy and politics. From the start it strove for respectability among the intellectual elite, publishing *Inquiry*, a magazine that offered serious, well-researched, and quietly libertarian articles for an educated readership. As the years passed Cato would develop into a true player within the beltway think-tank world. Along with *Reason* magazine, Cato injected a consistent libertarian voice into national political debates. The institute relocated to Washington,

D.C., shortly after its founding and became an influential think-tank as the capitol tended rightward. By the mid-1980s Cato had replaced the Libertarian Party as the institution of choice for libertarians who hoped to create meaningful social change.[72]

Rand was left largely isolated in New York. One by one she drove away the last remnants of the Collective. She stopped speaking to the Hessens after their Palo Alto Book Service offered for sale a novel by Kay Nolte Smith, whom Rand had exiled years before.[73] The Blumenthals, who had nursed her so tenderly through her cancer surgery, broke with Rand after she harangued them endlessly about their artistic tastes. Next to go were the Kalbermans, unable to tolerate Rand's diatribes against the now despised Blumenthals. Mary Ann and Charles Sures, who lived in Maryland, were occasional visitors. But only Frank and Leonard Peikoff, loyal to the last day, remained by her side.

Orthodox Objectivism continued to draw a small audience, and a core group of serious students clustered around Leonard Peikoff. Rand was too faded to hold the famed all-night sessions of yore, but Peikoff helped form another cadre eager to carry her ideas forward. Rand approved two new magazines, *The Objectivist Forum* and *The Intellectual Activist,* run by her last philosophy students. In the late 1970s she was captivated by the idea of *Atlas Shrugged* as a television mini-series. Numerous proposals to dramatize the work had landed on her desk, but this was the first time producers were willing to give her full script control. She began working on the adaptation, which was to be broadcast on NBC, and had completed most of the script when the project was canceled. In her spare time she collected stamps avidly and began taking algebra lessons with a private tutor.[74]

The hardest blow came in 1979, when Frank died. The two had been married for fifty years. As difficult as their union had been, Frank had never betrayed Rand, never broken her trust or abandoned her in a time of need. He had been a silent and at times sullen paramour, but he was unfailingly consistent—and consistency was something Rand valued above almost anything else. She was disconsolate after his loss, weeping in her apartment and pestering his niece, her last remaining family contact, for reminiscences about him as a young man. Making a final television appearance on Phil Donahue's show, Rand was sanguine about the prospect of her own end. She did not believe in life after death, she told

Donahue, otherwise she would have committed suicide by now in order to join Frank.

His death brought a renewed connection with Barbara Branden, who reached out to Rand after more than a decade of silence. Rand welcomed Barbara's overture. She had a ready excuse for Barbara's past behavior; like her, Barbara had been tricked and traduced by Nathan. It was an interpretative frame that glossed much of the truth but allowed the two women to draw together for a final peaceful visit in New York one afternoon. Nathan remained an untouchable. His third wife, Devers, whom he married after Patrecia's tragic death in a drowning accident, attempted a reconciliation between the two. She arrived on Rand's doorstep one day, urging her to speak with Nathan and heal the past. Torn between suspicion and curiosity, Rand let Devers inside her apartment for a few hours. Later she hardened against her, and still she refused to speak to Nathan. He called her once, hoping in some way to smooth over their history. She hung up immediately.[75]

In the aftermath of Frank's death, Rand had few projects and almost no energy. She became obsessed with Hans Gudagast, a German-born movie actor who resembled Frank. While writing the *Atlas* script she had envisioned him playing the role of Francisco D'Anconia. Then Gudagast, now using the name Eric Braeden, grew a moustache, ruining his resemblance to Frank. Ayn pined for a photo of him without facial hair. When she discovered one in a magazine she had the idea to derive a full-size photo from the small thumbnail. Ignoring the pleas of her solicitous housekeeper Eloise, Rand plunged out into the rain to a photo studio in Times Square. Without a coat or umbrella she was caught in a downpour on her way back home. She fell ill with a cold, a dangerous malady for a woman of seventy-six with a history of lung cancer.[76]

Only a few days later she addressed the annual meeting of the National Committee for Monetary Reform, a group dedicated to the restoration of the gold standard. The NCMR's founder was a devoted fan of Rand's work, and he lured her to the group's New Orleans conference with the promise of a private rail car. With Leonard and Cynthia Peikoff, Rand traveled down the eastern seaboard of the United States in executive luxury, much as Hank Rearden and Dagny Taggart would have done. She spoke to a roaring audience of three thousand hard money enthusiasts, defending the morality of profit and production. By the time the return train reached New York Rand's cold had transformed into pneumonia. The Peikoffs took her directly to the hospital.

Death was not something Rand feared. As her condition worsened she accepted the inevitable. All she wanted was to die at home. In the final weeks of February 1982 she gave her work in progress to Peikoff, now her designated legal and intellectual heir. A hired nurse was in her apartment twenty-four hours a day, and it was the nurse who sat by her bedside in early March when Rand slipped away.

Her funeral was an event to rival the great Objectivist gatherings of the past. Close to a thousand mourners paid her final tribute, waiting for hours outside the funeral home on Madison Avenue. Her last battles, breakups, and flights of inspiration behind her, Rand lay facing the world in an open casket. Next to her coffin was an enormous topiary, shaped into the sign of the dollar.

EPILOGUE:
AYN RAND IN AMERICAN MEMORY

When Rand died in 1982, her old enemies were quick to declare victory. "Ayn Rand is dead. So, incidentally, is the philosophy she sought to launch dead; it died still born," William F. Buckley Jr. announced in a mean-spirited obituary that once again set the letters column of *National Review* abuzz. Buckley's dismissal of Rand was overconfident by any standard. Only a year before, George Gilder had recognized Rand as an important influence in *Wealth and Poverty,* a book soon known as the bible of the Reagan administration. Two years after her death another of her admirers, Charles Murray, would light the conservative world aflame with his attack on welfare, *Losing Ground.* Along with *A Time for Truth,* written by former Treasury Secretary William Simon and former Collective member Edith Efron, these books suggested that Rand's influence was just beginning to be felt in policy circles. The *New York Times* would even dub Rand the "novelist laureate" of the Reagan administration, citing her influence on Alan Greenspan, Martin Anderson, and several others.[1]

Yet as Buckley's obituary suggested, Rand's reputation was captive to the events of her lifetime. In 1986 Barbara Branden lifted the curtain on Rand's private affairs with the publication of her memoir cum biography, *The Passion of Ayn Rand,* followed three years later by Nathaniel Branden's own lurid memoir, *Judgment Day: My Years with Ayn Rand.* Sparing no detail, the Brandens disclosed the full story of her relationship with Nathan and emphasized the dark side of Rand, including her harsh treatment of the Collective, her anger and depression, and her habitual use of amphetamines. Although both Brandens lauded Rand's intellectual accomplishments, the revelations about her personal life overshadowed their assertions of her worth as a thinker.

The news that Rand and Nathaniel Branden had been lovers stunned the broader Objectivist community. Many of Rand's fans had unquestioningly taken her side and had been content to let lie the mystery of Nathan's depredations. Upon learning the truth, one defender of Rand recounted a deep sense of betrayal: "and all those years I had thought Frank was a model for Francisco. My blood literally ran cold at the extent of Rand's deceit."[2] To those who had known Rand intimately or seen her attack questioners at an NBI lecture, the revelations of her personal failings were less shocking. But to the outside world Rand emerged a deeply unsavory figure, manipulative, controlling, self-deceived, and wildly emotional despite her professed rationality. This impression was further reinforced when Barbara Branden's memoir was transformed into an HBO television movie starring Helen Mirren and Eric Stolz. Complete with scenes of a mink-clad Ayn making furtive love to Nathan in her foyer, the movie destroyed the vaunted image of Rand as an intellectual paragon who lived by rationality alone.

Barbara Branden's memoir also precipitated another great schism across Objectivist ranks. After Rand's death a small but active orthodox Objectivist community had emerged, led by Leonard Peikoff, who inherited Rand's estate and whom she publicly proclaimed her "intellectual heir." In 1985 Peikoff institutionalized the orthodox approach by creating the Ayn Rand Institute (ARI), a nonprofit dedicated to spreading Objectivism. Peikoff and the other philosophy students who had clustered around Rand in her final years combined their Objectivist studies with work in academic philosophy departments, giving them the grasp of contemporary philosophical discourse that Rand had so sorely lacked. This network bore fruit in 1988 with the publication of David Kelley's *The Evidence of the Senses*. One of Objectivism's rising young stars, Kelley had a doctorate in philosophy from Princeton, where he studied under the eminent pragmatist philosopher Richard Rorty. Opening with a tribute to Ayn Rand, Kelley's book presented a philosophically rigorous defense of her approach. Educated in a top-ranked philosophy department and by a mentor who stood in opposition to all Rand taught, Kelley was the first Objectivist philosopher to grapple seriously with opposing points of view rather than dispensing with them in the loaded language that Rand typically employed. As such his volume opened a new range of possibilities for Rand's presence within contemporary philosophy.[3]

But shortly after the book's publication Kelley fell from grace when he agreed to address two libertarian forums. Rand had made clear that libertarians were beyond the pale, and the Ayn Rand Institute followed her lead. To Peter Schwartz, writing in the *Intellectual Activist,* Kelley's appearance amounted to "moral sanction" of Rand's enemies, and he urged that anyone who collaborated with libertarians be shunned. Kelley defended himself with a short pamphlet circulated among friends, which drew a further response from Peikoff, "Fact and Value."[4]

The two sides articulated clear differences. To Kelley, Objectivism was "a magnificent system of ideas. But it is not a closed system." His outreach to libertarians was essential, he maintained, if Objectivism was ever to grow beyond its small circle of adherents. To Peikoff, spreading Objectivism was nonsensical if the truth and validity of Rand's ideas was lost in the process. "Please drop out of our movement: drop Ayn Rand, leave Objectivism alone," he wrote. Hovering in the background was the unacknowledged issue of Kelley's failure to publicly repudiate Barbara Branden's memoir. Unlike the ARI top brass, Kelley considered its contribution meaningful. And then he was on the outs, the latest casualty of Rand's penchant for judgment.[5]

Unlike Rand's earlier victims, Kelley was largely unperturbed by his ejection from the Objectivist inner circle. After being denied tenure at Vassar he reconstituted himself as the leader of an independent Objectivist movement, founding the Institute for Objectivist Studies in 1990. His break with ARI energized emerging groups such as the magazine *Full Context,* whose subscribers appreciated Rand but quailed at the demand that they accept her philosophy uncritically. Kelley's activities also helped reunite Objectivists with libertarians, many of whom remained attentive to Rand despite their dissatisfaction with the developments of her last years.

Thenceforth ARI and the Institute for Objectivist Studies (later renamed the Objectivist Center and then the Atlas Society) developed along parallel tracks. Both transformed themselves into advocacy think tanks, seeking funding from wealthy capitalists who admired Rand's works. They launched newsletters, websites, and online discussion forums and held annual summer seminars on Objectivism, drawing strength from a newly vibrant Randian subculture that rekindled itself on the Internet. Although dogged by the same poor reputation that had shadowed Rand and NBI, the Ayn Rand Institute benefitted greatly from its legal connection to Rand's estate. It used Rand's personal papers as a source of revenue, releasing several new fiction and nonfiction books under her name. As it became more established, ARI relocated to Irvine, California, a region historically receptive to free market ideas. The institute's most successful initiative, an annual essay contest on Rand's novels for students, awards prizes of up to ten thousand dollars and has done much to stimulate reading of her works. In the 1990s it established an archive to house Rand's papers and began supporting the work of scholars interested in Rand, thereby raising her profile within the academy.

As internecine warfare erupted between her followers, Rand's standing in the outside world plummeted. Ignored by most literary critics and professional philosophers, Rand passed into the lexicon of American popular culture, a signifier of ruthless selfishness, intellectual precocity, or both. "Some people matter, and some people don't," one character tells another, brandishing a copy of The Fountainhead, in the hit 1987 film Dirty Dancing. On TV's The Simpsons Marge Simpson deposits her infant Maggie in the Ayn Rand School for Tots, where her pacifier is confiscated and she learns "A Means A." In a second Rand-themed episode, "Maggie Roark" ends up under Ellswoorth Toohey's fist in the Mediocri-Tots day care center. These cultural references persisted decades beyond her death and became ever more substantive. In 1999 Rand found her way onto a thirty-three-cent postage stamp. In 2008 the designer of Bioshock, a popular video game, modeled his future dystopia on Objectivism, complete with the art deco styling that Rand loved and propaganda banners attacking altruism. The game's ideological backdrop was intended as "a cautionary tale about wholesale, unquestioning belief in something," explained its creator, who nonetheless professed a sympathy for Rand's individualism.[6]

Rand also remained part of the underground curriculum of American adolescence, beloved particularly by the accomplished yet alienated overachiever. Arriving at a summer school for gifted high school students in the early 1990s one participant remembered, "We were all either Rand or post-Rand."[7] Tobias Wolff spoofed this affinity in his 2004 novel Old School, in which his adolescent narrator becomes briefly obsessed with Rand: "I was discovering the force of my will. To read The Fountainhead was to feel this caged power, straining like a damned-up river to break loose and crush every impediment to its free running. I understood that nothing stood between me and my greatest desires— nothing between me and greatness itself—but the temptation to doubt my will and bow to councils of moderation, expedience, and conventional morality, and shrink into the long, slow death of respectability. That was where the contempt came in."[8] Wolff was not the only writer to find Rand an irresistible target for parody. The cape, the ivory cigarette holder, the dollar-sign pin—she is a satirist's dream come true. In Mary Gaitskill's *Two Girls, Fat and Thin,* she is the stern Anna Granite, founder of "Definitism," while Murray Rothbard mocked her as Carson Sand in *Mozart Was a Red.*[9]

That Rand had spawned a veritable genre of parodists spoke to her continued appeal. Twenty years after her death she was selling more books than ever in her life, with *Atlas Shrugged* alone averaging sales of more than one hundred thousand copies per year. These figures kept her from fading out of public memory, as did her connection to Alan Greenspan, her most famous protégé. As Greenspan's star rose, so did Rand's. Profiles and biographies of Greenspan inevitably lingered over his time spent by her side, and enterprising reporters even exhumed Greenspan's *Objectivist Newsletter* articles for clues about his intellectual development.

The financial crisis of 2008 ushered in a new Rand, one stripped of historical context and at times mythic in stature. She suddenly became a favored citation of the left, who saw in her ideas about free markets and selfishness the roots of economic devastation. Greenspan's startling admission that he "found a flaw" in his ideology offered the ultimate proof for this line of reasoning. To these criticisms Rand's followers had a ready answer, the same one she herself would have proffered. True capitalism has never been known, the Objectivists cried, and it is the statist economy that collapsed, not the free one. Rather than cause libertarians and Objectivists to recant their beliefs overnight, for many the financial meltdown simply confirmed the predictive powers of Rand's work. Yaron Brook, ARI's director, summarized the reaction: "We're heading towards socialism, we're heading toward more regulation. *Atlas Shrugged* is coming true." This understanding was not confined to Objectivist circles. Sales of *Atlas Shrugged* spiked in 2008 after the U.S. Treasury bought stakes in nine large banks and again in 2009 when the

Democratic administration announced its stimulus plan. A new vogue emerged for "going Galt," or restricting production so as to avoid higher taxes. Her novels touted anew by Rush Limbaugh, Rand was once more a foundation of the right-wing worldview.[10]

Even as she was reclaimed by her most avid fans, Rand's work transcended contemporary politics. One of the many ironies of Rand's career is her latter-day popularity among entrepreneurs who are pioneering new forms of community. Among her high-profile fans is Wikipedia's founder Jimmy Wales, once an active participant in the listserv controversies of the Objectivist Center. A nonprofit that depends on charitable donations, Wikipedia may ultimately put its rival encyclopedias out of business. At the root of Wikipedia are warring sensibilities that seem to both embody and defy Rand's beliefs. The website's emphasis on individual empowerment, the value of knowledge, and its own risky organizational model reflects Rand's sensibility. But its trust in the wisdom of crowds, celebration of the social nature of knowledge, and faith that many working together will produce something of enduring value contradict Rand's adage "All creation is individual."

Similar contradictions undergird the response to Rand of Craig Newmark, the founder of the online advertising site Craigslist. Like Wales, Newmark was once an active member of the libertarian subculture, reading "a few things by Ayn Rand, even making a pilgrimage to her offices," and later becoming a member of the Society for Individual Liberty. Like so many others, Newmark drifted away from Rand after a period of intense engagement but still identified himself as someone who prefers market solutions, a "hybrid libertarian."[11] Something of Rand remained in his insistence that people are rational and markets work. Even as Craigslist feeds on a Randian iconoclasm against established ways of doing business and her faith in human rationality, it also undercuts Rand's individualism through its emphasis on collaboration and mutuality. In both cases Newmark and Wales built on Rand's ideas but married them to a very different theory of human nature, one in which community and connection are paramount.

It is precisely these contradictions and complexities that make Rand a source of perennial fascination. Rand insisted that she had held the essentials of her philosophy since she was a child, and she presented her ideas as fixed and unchanging by their very nature. But her work proved remarkably malleable, as underscored by the radically divergent reactions to her novels. One fan wrote to her in 1957, "It appears that there must be two books entitled *Atlas Shrugged*. I know that I never read the book which some claim to review. Very happy that I was able to get the one you had written."[12] The many ways Rand has been reinvented, remade, and reimagined are both an index of her popularity and a reason for it. Though later in her life Rand insisted that her ideas were not subject to interpretation, this imperative clashed with her earliest beliefs. As she wrote in 1935, "The worst of all crimes is the acceptance of the opinions of others."[13] Many of her readers learned this firsthand from Rand herself. In falling sway to her system and then casting it aside, they learned how to think for themselves.

What remains of Rand, once the context and politics are stripped away, is a basic ethical truth that continues to attract admirers of every ideological persuasion. Be true to yourself, Rand's books teach, sounding a resonant note with the power to reshape lives. One of her readers made the point in a brief fan letter. Lee Clettenberg was forty three and living in Detroit when he wrote to Rand. He had only a seventh-grade education, a twist of fate that left him consumed with anger, confusion, and self-hatred. He struggled to improve his life, discovering, "Every time I tried to claim a piece of me, I felt like a thief, a robber of the dead." But then came Rand. He stumbled across *The Virtue of Selfishness*, and there he found "the" question: "'Why does man need a code of values?' BANG! Everything I have read and learned fell into place, just like that. BANG! AND...just like that...YOU...gave ME...back to...MYSELF!"[14] Though his letter was unusually evocative in its folksy directness, the intensity of his reaction to Rand was typical. It is this enthusiastic response that has made Rand's prodigious novels, dismissed uniformly by literary critics, into modern classics.

In a 1968 introduction to *The Fountainhead*, Rand was forthright about the religious energies that pulsed through her work. She described the book's Nietzschean roots and registered both her disagreement with the German philosopher and her desire to convey his exalted sense of life in her novel. Rand argued, "Religion's monopoly in the field of ethics has made it extremely difficult to communicate the emotional meaning and connotations of a rational view of life." According to Rand, the primary emotions that religion had usurped were exaltation, worship, reverence, and a sense of the sacred. She maintained that these emotions were not supernatural in origin, but were "the entire emotional realm of man's dedication to a moral ideal." It was these emotions she wanted to stir with *The Fountainhead*, "without the self-abasement required by religious definitions."[15] Rand intended her books to be a sort of scripture, and for all her emphasis on reason it is the emotional and psychological sides of her novels that make them timeless. Reports of Ayn Rand's death are greatly exaggerated. For many years to come she is likely to remain what she has always been, a fertile touchstone of the American imagination.

ACKNOWLEDGMENTS

This project would never have been possible without the assistance of Jeff Britting, archivist at the Ayn Rand Institute. From my first exploratory trip down to Irvine eight years ago, Jeff was unfailingly professional, endlessly informative, and always willing to go the extra mile. Through his efforts the archive has become a hospitable place indeed for scholars interested in Ayn Rand. Numerous other librarians and archivists gave me valuable assistance. Deserving of particular mention are archivists at the Herbert Hoover Presidential Library in West Branch, Iowa, the Stanford University Library Special Collections, Yale University, the Foundation for Economic Education, and the Ludwig von Mises Institute.

I am grateful to all the individuals and organizations that granted me use of copyrighted material in this work. Permission to include excerpts from the writings of Rose Wilder Lane has been granted by the copyright owner, Little House Heritage Trust. The Rothbard Papers are cited courtesy of the Ludwig Von Mises Institute, Auburn, Alabama. Material from Leonard Read is used with permission of the Foundation for Economic Education (www.fee.org). The Department of Special Collections and University Archives, Stanford University Libraries, granted me permission to use material from the Stewart Brand Collection (M1237). Barry Goldwater is quoted with the permission of the Arizona Historical Foundation. Barbara Branden and Nathaniel Branden, Ph. D, kindly granted use of photographs and documents. Permission to quote from Ayn Rand's unpublished material was granted by the Estate of Ayn Rand, and other material is used courtesy of the Ayn Rand Archives. The Ayn Rand Archives at the Ayn Rand Institute is a reference source. Use of its materials by this author does not constitute endorsement or recommendation of this work by the Ayn Rand Institute.

The early stages of this project were supported by grants from the University of California, Berkeley, History Department. I received travel funding from the Institute for Humane Studies and the Herbert Hoover Presidential Library and a summer stipend from the National Endowment for the Humanities. The Mises Institute generously offered me room and board during my stay in Auburn. A W. Glenn Campbell and Rita Ricardo-Campbell National Fellowship, awarded by the Hoover Institution, Stanford University, gave me a full year to write and research. In the last critical stages of writing I received support through the University of Virginia Excellence in Diversity Fellowship, Professors as Writers Program, summer grant, and the Digital Classroom Initiative.

In the eight years I worked on this project I have benefited from the support, advice, and friendship of many people. Apologies in advance to anyone I may have left out. I alone am responsible for all interpretations, arguments, errors, or omissions in this book.

At the University of California, Berkeley, my advisor, David Hollinger, guided me expertly from seminar paper to finished dissertation. I will never forget the gleam in his eye when I proposed the topic of Ayn Rand. His confidence in me has been inspiring and his guidance indispensible. I also benefited immensely from the critical skepticism of Kerwin Klein and the prompt attentions of Mark Bevir. As I finished writing, Eitan Grossman and Kristen Richardson provided valuable editorial support. From the beginning of the project, Eitan urged me to think carefully about the nature, significance, and depth of Rand's intellectual appeal.

The rich secondary literature on Rand, which I describe more fully in my concluding Essay on Sources, provided an invaluable starting point for my inquiry. I am grateful to the broader community of scholars and writers interested in Rand who paved the way before me.

Many historians have read all or part of the manuscript. I benefited from the insightful comments and questions of Joyce Mao, Jason Sokol, and members of David Hollinger's intellectual history discussion group, especially Nils Gilman and Justin Suran. Nelson Lichtenstein, Charles Capper, Thomas Bender, Louis Masur, anonymous readers for *Modern Intellectual History,* and the editorial board of *Reviews in American History* helped me perfect parts of the dissertation for publication. Michael Kazin, Daniel Horowitz, and Don Critchlow read the entire dissertation and suggested fruitful ways to reconceptualize it as a book.

Paula Baker gave the manuscript two terrific readings at different stages in the project. James Kloppenberg's comments and questions fortified my final revisions.

I am also grateful to the many audiences who listened to me present various pieces of my research, starting with attendees at the Capitalism and Its Culture Conference at the University of California, Santa Barbara. Gregory Eow arranged a visit to the Rice University History Department, where I learned from Thomas Haskell's probing questions. Audience members, panelists, and commentators at meetings of the American Historical Association, the Organization of American Historians, the Policy History Conference, and the Davis Center for Russian Studies Sixtieth anniversary symposium shaped and strengthened my interpretations. Thanks to David Farber and Michelle Nickerson for sparking memorable discussion at the AHA. Kathleen Frydl, Abena Osseo-Asare, Jo Guldi, and Daniel Immerwahr helped polish my postdoctoral work.

David Kennedy offered valuable advice on publishing. Though I am not a client of hers, Susan Rabiner generously offered her counsel at several points.

At the Hoover Institution Martin Anderson and Tibor Machan supported my work and offered me their insight into Rand, as did Bob Hessen. I am also grateful to Kenneth Jowett. Andy Rutten and Katherine Mangu-Ward guided me through the world of modern libertarianism. Ron Unz gave me access to his database of libertarian periodicals, and Andrew Kirk helped me track down an elusive Rand citation. During a critical hour John Judis turned up at Stanford and gave me three unforgettable words of writing advice.

My greatest discovery was Jane Barnes, who pushed me to excel with tact and verve. This book is immeasurably better for her hard work and sharp insight. Will Schulman gamely played the role of informed general reader and offered excellent feedback as the manuscript developed. Shoshana Milgram shared her Rand expertise with me on several occasions. Joan Rosenberg offered me lodging in Irvine numerous times, making my research trips infinitely more pleasant, as did Jasmine Kerrissey. In Charlottesville my colleagues in the History Department provided a wonderfully supportive atmosphere for the last days of writing. Guy Ortolano and Carmen Pavel critiqued my drafts and cheered me on. With unfailing good humor and scrupulous accuracy, Stephen

Macekura helped me track down stray citations, books, and facts as my deadline loomed.

At Oxford University Press Susan Ferber immediately grasped the essence of the project. I have benefited greatly from her keen editorial advice, comprehensive vision, and tactical insight. The rest of the team at Oxford, particularly Susan Fensten, Andrew Varhol, Christian Purdy, and Jessica Ryan, has done a spectacular job readying the book for publication.

I am thankful for the many friends who helped me both work hard and play hard, especially Anna, Halton, Chris, Lilly, Natalie, Merry Jean, and the Booty Karma crew. Many a physicist brightened my day in Palo Alto, and new friends welcomed me to Charlottesville. Old friends Alexis and Jerome and Elizabeth were particularly supportive as the end drew near.

My immediate and extended family have been there for me in myriad ways. Christine and Steve listened to several presentations of my research and offered their home as a much valued writing getaway, and Blake, Chase, and Brooke kept me in touch with my inner child. Tim started this whole thing by giving me *The Fountainhead* many years ago. He also read the dissertation from top to bottom, pulling out key details that suggested a path forward for the book. Several Burnses tackled their first Ayn Rand novels on my behalf, a much appreciated labor of love. My parents gave me generous financial support, but more important encouraged my ambitions without becoming overbearing. This book is dedicated to my father, but it is my mother who perhaps best understands what it means to me. Gail, Chuck, and Sara welcomed me to their family with open arms and quickly learned when to ask and not ask about the book. My husband, Nick Cizek, has heightened my highs and lessened my lows, both personal and professional. His courage, compassion, and honesty are my version of the heroic.

ESSAY ON SOURCES

PUBLISHED WORKS BY RAND

The scholar of Ayn Rand has an enviable problem: a surfeit of published sources. Rand's enormous corpus of fiction and nonfiction, including bound volumes of her newsletters, is readily available in libraries and bookstores across the country. Many of her speeches have been reprinted in her nonfiction books. In addition to work that Rand herself published, posthumously her estate has released a steady stream of material, including her earliest efforts at fiction, her question-and-answer sessions at public speeches, transcripts from writing courses, and volumes of her letters and journals.

Unfortunately, there are grave limitations to the accuracy and reliability of the putatively primary source material issued by Rand's estate. Discrepancies between Rand's published journals and archival material were first publicized by the Rand scholar Chris Sciabarra, who noticed differences between the *Journals of Ayn Rand* (1999) and brief excerpts published earlier in *The Intellectual Activist*.[1] After several years working in Rand's personal papers I can confirm Sciabarra's discovery: the published versions of Rand's letters and diaries have been significantly edited in ways that drastically reduce their utility as historical sources.

The editor of the *Letters of Ayn Rand* (1995) acknowledges that "some of the less interesting material within letters" and "the routine opening and closing material" have been deleted.[2] These omissions are of high interest to the historian, for it is here that Rand notes details of her schedule, makes offhand comments on recent events in her life, and includes unique touches that personalize her communication. Looking at the originals of Rand's letters has helped me reconstruct the web of contacts she maintained and track shifts and developments in key relationships. I did not discover any changes to the body of her correspondence. The letters as published have not been altered; they are merely incomplete. Scholars can benefit from this material, but historians in particular should note that important insights can be gleaned only from the originals.[3]

The editing of the *Journals of Ayn Rand* (1997) is far more significant and problematic. On nearly every page of the published journals, an unacknowledged change has been made from Rand's original writing. In the book's foreword the editor, David

Harriman, defends his practice of eliminating Rand's words and inserting his own as necessary for greater clarity. In many cases, however, his editing serves to significantly alter Rand's meaning.

Many of the edits involve small words that carry great weight, such as "if" and "but." Sentences that Rand starts with the tentative "if" are rewritten to sound stronger and more definite. Separate sentences are joined with "but." Changes are sometimes made for what seem to be unarticulated aesthetic preferences, such as replacing Rand's "heated-over" with "warmed-over."[4] Rand's original wording here is significant, for it provides evidence of her lingering difficulty with idiomatic and vernacular English. These rough patches have been edited out of her fiction and published writing but remain in her private notes as a valuable testimony to her origins and linguistic development.

The editing also obscures important shifts and changes in Rand's thought. Early in her career Rand idolized the architect Frank Lloyd Wright, whom she used as inspiration for Howard Roark. Even in this early phase of infatuation, however, there were seeds of Rand's later disillusionment with Wright's "mysticism." Reading his book *The Disappearing City* she noted to herself, "More of Wright's ideas. Some beautiful, a great many too many not clear." That hint of disappointment is muted in the published journals, which render Rand's sentiments more positively as "Some beautiful, a great many not clear."[5] Gone too is the Nietzschean-style repetition of "many too many," which marks Rand's continued attraction to the German philosopher.

Even more alarming are the sentences and proper names present in Rand's originals that have vanished entirely, without any ellipses or brackets to indicate a change. While arguing in her notebooks against a specific point of view, Rand would often attack by name an exponent of that view. For example, she mentions two libertarians, Albert Jay Nock and James Ingebretsen, while disagreeing with ideas she attributes to them. The erasure of these names from the published diary changes the nature of Rand's intellectual work, making her ideas entirely self-referential instead of a response to the larger social and political world in which she operated.[6]

Other omissions serve to decontextualize Rand entirely. Gone is a pessimistic musing about the degeneration of the white race, as well as casual slang like "nance" (homosexual).[7] It is not surprising that Rand's diaries reflected the prejudices and prevailing ideas of her time; indeed, it would be more surprising had she remained unaffected.

Considered individually, many of the changes to Rand's diaries are minor, but taken as a whole they add up to a different Rand. In her original notebooks she is more tentative, historically bounded, and contradictory. The edited diaries have transformed her private space, the hidden realm in which she did her thinking, reaching, and groping, replacing it with a slick manufactured world in which all of her ideas are definite, well formulated, and clear. Even her outlines for her major novels have been rewritten, with different drafts collapsed into one another. Given Rand's titanic clashes with editors who sought to modify her work, it is not hard to guess what her reaction would be to these changes.

The *Journals of Ayn Rand* are thus best understood as an *interpretation* of Rand rather than her own writing. Scholars must use these materials with extreme caution. They serve as a useful introduction to Rand's development and a guide to the available archival material, but they should not be accepted at face value. Accordingly, I quote from the published diaries only the sections that I have personally verified as accurate with the archival records, and I note where important discrepancies exist. (The only exception is in the case of Rand's earliest philosophical journals, which were lost after publication, so that no originals remain.) Similar problems plague *Ayn Rand Answers* (2005), *The Art of Fiction* (2000), *The Art of Non-Fiction* (2001), and *Objectively Speaking* (2009). These books are derived from archival materials but have been significantly rewritten.

ARCHIVAL SOURCES

In light of the bowdlerization of Rand's published papers, the starting point for rigorous historical and philosophical inquiry into her work must be archival. The Ayn Rand Archives, which holds original versions of the materials described above, is the definitive resource for scholars. Material here ranges from the mundane to the spectacular, from household ephemera to the most wrenching of Rand's diary entries during the agonies of her break with Nathaniel Branden. The archive consists of two related collections, the Ayn Rand Papers and Special Collections. Together they encompass more than two hundred document cartons, which hold manuscripts, fiction and nonfiction notes and outlines, screenplays, business and personal correspondence, fan mail, research files, personal photographs, daily calendars, address books, memorabilia, press clipping files, Objectivist periodicals, materials from Objectivist organizations, and Russian academic and legal documents. There are more than three thousand handwritten pages and several hundred hours of interviews with Rand and persons who knew her, and more than eleven hundred pages of letters sent to her from Russia by the Rosenbaum family. The archive has an active acquisitions program and has taken steps to digitize and preserve its ever-expanding holdings.

Of particular note are transcripts of more than forty hours of interviews Barbara Branden conducted with Rand in 1961, which formed the basis of Branden's 1962 biographical sketch, *Who Is Ayn Rand?*, and her later *Passion of Ayn Rand*. The biographical interviews reveal details about Rand that cannot be found elsewhere, particularly concerning her early life and her creative process. Later research indicates that Rand's recollections of her life in Russia are of questionable accuracy, and the listener must always keep in mind Rand's novelistic inclination to embellishment. Nevertheless they are an invaluable resource for understanding both the younger Rand and her self-presentation at midcareer. These interviews are also held in the private collection of Barbara Branden.

Although it is affiliated with the Ayn Rand Institute, an explicit advocacy organization, the Ayn Rand Archive has evolved into a professional institution on par with any university collection. The papers are well organized and include a detailed finding aid. During the course of my research I was afforded full access to Rand's papers and benefited enormously from the knowledge and efforts of the Archives staff. Since 2001 the Archive has been open to serious scholars, but does occasionally restrict access to avoid conflict with sponsored projects. Researchers known to be hostile to Rand, or with a history of involvement in Objectivist controversies, may find their entry limited or denied.

Fortunately, primary source material on Rand's life can be found in numerous other venues. The Ayn Rand Papers at the Library of Congress include drafts, typescripts, and galleys of *Anthem, We the Living,* and *Atlas Shrugged* and miscellaneous administrative material. The collection also contains seventy-two handwritten essays written between 1971 and 1974 for the *Ayn Rand Letter*. Also at the Library of Congress, the William Rusher Papers contain material on the Rand-inflected young conservative movement.

The Herbert Hoover Presidential Library in West Branch, Iowa, holds several important collections, including the papers of Isabel Paterson and Rose Wilder Lane, which contain extensive correspondence from Rand. Relevant items in the papers of William Mullendore can also be found here. Other important material is in the Rothbard Papers at the Ludwig von Mises Institute, the Leonard Read papers at the Foundation for Economic Education, the Sidney Hook papers at the Hoover Institution, Stanford University, and the William F. Buckley papers at Yale University.

Numerous primary source materials on Rand are also scattered among private individuals. Barbara Branden retains personal correspondence, sundry materials, and transcripts of the interviews she conducted with Rand in the 1960s, as well as tapes of interviews used in her 1986 biography of Rand. A large swath of Rand's papers was sold at auction by Barbara Branden and Robert Hessen in the mid-1980s. Some of this material was purchased by the Ayn Rand Estate, but the bulk was purchased by manuscript dealers who have resold the individual pieces. More material undoubtedly lies in the attics and basements of former Objectivists. Recordings of lectures by Rand, Peikoff, and the Brandens are also available through several Objectivist and libertarian organizations.

The Objectivist community retains a strong sense of its own history and is a rich source of material on Rand's cultural impact. The Objectivist Oral History Project, sponsored by the Atlas Society, has interviewed many of the major players of Objectivism and sells DVDs of their interviews. The now defunct *Full Context* magazine for many years ran a series of interviews with former Objectivists that give a vivid picture of the Objectivist subculture.

I also made use of unedited interview transcripts and edited video recordings of nearly a hundred individuals who knew Ayn Rand. These interviews were either conducted by me, uncovered in archives, created by the Objectivist Oral History Project, or recorded as part of a similar initiative at the Ayn Rand Institute. They contain the usual liabilities of oral history, that is, distorted memory and personal bias, but used in tandem with archival documents they are an invaluable resource. A full listing of interviews used is given in the bibliography.

For research on the libertarian movement that grew out of Rand's ideas, the best sources are archival collections at the University of Virginia and Stanford University's Hoover Institution. The University of Virginia holds a large but as yet largely unprocessed accession from Roger MacBride, Rose Wilder Lane's heir and the second Libertarian Party presidential candidate. At the Hoover Institution the papers of Williamson Evers, Patrick Dowd, Roy Childs, and David Walter illuminate early libertarianism. Material of interest can also be found in the Gordon Hall and Grace Hoag Collection of Dissenting and Extremist Printed Propaganda, John Hay Library, Brown University, and the William Rusher Papers at the Library of Congress.

SECONDARY SOURCES

There is a large body of secondary scholarship on Rand, much of which has enhanced and sharpened my own ideas, and only a fraction of which I can mention here. Scholarship on Rand has gone through roughly three overlapping waves. The first books written about Rand attempted to either vindicate or denounce her philosophy. Into the critical camp fall works like William O'Neil's *With Charity towards None: An Analysis of Ayn Rand's Philosophy* (1971) and Sidney Greenberg's *Ayn Rand and Alienation* (1977). Books that defend Rand, many written by her former students, include Douglas J. Den Uyl and Douglass B. Rasmussen's *The Philosophic Thought of Ayn Rand* (1984), Leonard Peikoff's *Ominous Parallels: The End of Freedom in America* (1982), and David Kelley's *Evidence of the Senses* (1986). These works were largely consumed by the Objectivist community itself, a world riven with breaks and schisms dating from Rand's day. These dynamics are described in Kelley, *Truth and Toleration* (1990) and *The Contested Legacy of Ayn Rand: Truth and Toleration in Objectivism* (2000).

The 1986 publication of Barbara Branden's *Passion of Ayn Rand*, followed by Nathaniel Branden's *Judgment Day: My Years with Ayn Rand* (1989), decisively shifted the terms of debate by bringing Rand's personal life front and center, at the same time attracting a broad popular audience. As a historical source, Barbara Branden's biography has both strengths and weaknesses. Like the material issued by Rand's estate, it does not adhere to rigorous standards of accuracy. Sentences that are presented in quotes as if they were spoken verbatim by Rand have been significantly edited and rewritten, as anyone who listens to or reads the original interviews Branden used will quickly detect. Rand never lost either her Russian accent or her awkward sentence structure, and her actual words are full of circumlocutions and jarring formulations. Like the editors of Rand's journals, Branden has created a new Rand, one far more articulate than in life.

Moreover, Branden's biography is marred by serious inaccuracies and tales that do not stand up to historical investigation, including the now debunked story that Rand named herself after her typewriter. Too often Branden takes Rand's stories about herself at face value, reporting as fact information contradicted by the historical record. Although Branden's biography was the first book to describe Rand's early life, it should be used with caution and in conjunction with volumes like Jeff Britting's short biography, *Ayn Rand* (2004) and Anne Heller's *Ayn Rand and the World She Made* (2009). Shoshana Milgram's forthcoming authorized biography should become another resource of note.

Nonetheless, as Rand's closest friends for nearly twenty years, the Brandens' memoirs remain important as accounts of Rand's personal life. Barbara and Nathan were privy to Rand's inner doubts, triumphs, and insecurities as were no others. Both memoirs are marked by a certain amount of score settling, often between the Brandens themselves. Responding to postpublication criticism, Nathaniel Branden released a revised *My Years with Ayn Rand* (1999), notable primarily for its softened portrait of Barbara Branden and an addendum describing Rand's encounter with his third wife. All three of the Brandens' books concur in the fundamentals of their first meeting with Rand, the progress of their relationship with her, and the events surrounding the rise and fall of NBI. Still the scholar of Rand must be careful with these sources. Clearly colored by personal bias, they also exert a more subtle interpretative power, for instance glorifying the Brandens' importance to Rand at the expense of other significant figures such as Leonard Peikoff and Frank O'Connor. Though it often goes overboard in its attacks on the Brandens, James Valliant's *The Passion of Ayn Rand's Critics* (2005) subjects both books to intense scrutiny and offers an alternative account of Rand's break with Nathaniel Branden. Jeff Walker's *The Ayn Rand Cult* (1999), based on interviews with former Objectivists, follows the Brandens' emphasis on Rand's personal life.

Accounts that attempted to return discussion to Rand's ideas include ARI scholar Alan Gotthelf's *On Ayn Rand* (2000), published as part of the Wadsworth philosophy series, and Ronald E. Merrill's *The Ideas of Ayn Rand* (1991). Louis Torres's *What Art Is* (2000) explores Rand's aesthetic theory. Leonard Peikoff's *Objectivism: The Philosophy of Ayn Rand* (1991) offers the orthodox Objectivist exegesis of her thought.

Yet another distinct cycle of writing about Rand began in the mid-1990s, when scholars began to draw on documentary and archival material to craft increasingly sophisticated analyses of Rand's philosophy and writings. The first author to integrate Rand's life and thought was Chris Sciabarra, who situated Rand within the tradition of dialectical philosophy in *The Russian Radical* (1995). Though written without access to Rand's personal papers, Sciabarra's book employed original research and brought to light hitherto unknown information about Rand's educational background. Along with Mimi Reisel Gladstein, Sciabarra attempted to draw Rand scholarship out of the Objectivist ghetto by assembling a broad range of contributors for the volume *Feminist Interpretations of Ayn Rand* (1999). Sciabarra and several collaborators also launched the *Journal of Ayn Rand Studies,* a publication that touts its independence from any group, institution, or philosophical perspective. The prolific libertarian philosopher Tibor Machan, once an acquaintance of Rand's, added to the academic literature with his study *Ayn Rand* (1999).

In recent years there has been an explosion of scholarship on Rand, much of it fed by the newly opened Ayn Rand Archives and funded by the Ayn Rand Institute. Modeled on other libertarian advocacy groups, such as the Institute for Humane Studies, the now defunct Volker Fund, and the Liberty Fund, ARI has launched an Objectivist Academic Center that runs seminars and conferences on Rand's thought and supports a journal, *The Objective Standard*. The newly active Anthem Foundation, an affiliated organization, offers grants and other financial support to university professors interested in Rand. These efforts have yielded *Facets of Ayn Rand* (2001), a sympathetic memoir by Charles and Mary Ann Sures; *Ayn Rand* (2004), a short and factually accurate biography of Rand written by the head archivist, Jeff Britting; and Valliant's *The Passion of Ayn Rand's Critics* (2005). The Institute has also sponsored a series on each of Rand's major novels, edited by Robert Mayhew, which includes *Essays on Ayn Rand's* We the Living (2004), *Essays on Ayn Rand's* Anthem (2005), *Essays on Ayn Rand's* The Fountainhead (2007), and *Essays on Ayn Rand's* Atlas Shrugged (2009). Although they are clearly written by partisans of Rand and thus lack a critical edge, the essays in Mayhew's books are based on historical evidence and carefully argued. They represent a significant step forward in Objectivist scholarship.

Another major source of funding for Objectivist scholars is the charitable foundation of BB&T, one of the country's largest banks. Run by John Allison, an avowed Objectivist, BB&T has stirred controversy with its grants to universities that require the teaching of *Atlas Shrugged*. Most of the scholars supported by BB&T are also affiliated with ARI in some capacity, including the Aristotelian scholar Alan Gotthelf and the philosopher Tara Smith, who holds the BB&T Chair for the Study of Objectivism at the University of Texas, Austin, and is the author of *Ayn Rand's Normative Ethics* (2006). The success of Smith's book, which received generally positive reviews from her peers, suggests that Objectivism may finally be granted a hearing by the guild of professional philosophers.

Though orthodox Objectivist scholarship has taken important steps to engage in dialogue with the broader academic community, it remains hampered by a spirit of faction. Rand's emphasis on judgment and moral sanction remains important to many ARI-funded scholars, who have attacked independent outposts like the *Journal of Ayn Rand Studies* and are often unwilling to acknowledge the work of independent scholars. Until these disputes evolve into the more routine, measured, and impersonal disputation of scholarly life, Objectivists will remain stigmatized within the intellectual world.

Finally, Rand has begun to find her place within the literature about conservatism and the American right that has flourished of late in the historical profession. When historians first turned their attention to the success of conservative politics and ideas, many have noted Rand's presence among the thinkers who inspired a rising generation. Earlier work on conservatism tended to make perfunctory acknowledgment of Rand or situate her as an irrelevant outcast from mainstream conservatism. George Nash's seminal *The Conservative Intellectual Movement in America Since 1945* (1975) framed Rand as an extremist outsider effectively silenced by Buckley's *National Review,* an interpretation Buckley himself promoted in his fictional *Getting It Right* (2003). Still, for much of this early work Rand remained a cipher. For example, Lisa McGirr's excellent study, *Suburban Warriors: The Origins of the New American Right* (2001), inadvertently quotes Rand several times as she describes the libertarian worldview of Orange County activists. In one of the few academic discussions of the student libertarian movement, Jonathan Schoenwald's essay in the edited volume *The Vietnam War on Campus: Other Voices, More Distant Drums* (2001) ignores Rand and identifies Murray Rothbard as the sole source of right-wing radicalism. Rand and libertarianism more generally are given a thorough, albeit brief, treatment by John Kelley in *Bringing the Market Back In: The Political Revitalization of Market Liberalism* (1997).

As historians have begun to locate the origins of conservatism in reaction against the New Deal and thereby accord more weight to business libertarianism, Rand has emerged as a figure of greater consequence. In *Invisible Hands: The Making of the Conservative Movement from the New Deal to Reagan* (2009), Kimberly Phillips-Fein asserts the centrality of libertarian businessmen to the conservative renaissance, an important new line of interpretation that is being followed by a host of emerging scholars. Phillips-Fein notes Rand's popularity among businessmen and describes her early political activism. Although not academic in nature, Brian Doherty's celebratory *Radicals for Capitalism:*

A Freewheeling History of the Modern American Libertarian Movement (2007) also recognizes Rand as a foundational thinker of libertarianism, alongside F. A. Hayek, Milton Friedman, and Murray Rothbard. Taken together, these books indicate a new interest in the history of libertarianism and a dawning understanding that political conservatism draws from both secular and religious roots. As historians continue to explore the importance of economic individualism, Rand will take her deserved place within the right-wing firmament.

NOTES

Introduction

1. Jan Schulman, Ayn Rand Institute (hereafter ARI) Oral History, Ayn Rand Papers (hereafter ARP); Craig Singer to AR, December 9, 1969, ARP 161–37–05; Roy Childs, *Liberty against Power,* ed. Joan Kennedy Taylor (San Francisco: Fox and Wilkes, 1994), xiii.

2. Ayn Rand, *For the New Intellectual* (New York: New American Library, 1961), 12, 14.

3. Ayn Rand Institute, "Interest in Ayn Rand Soaring," *ARI Impact,* 15, no. 4 (2009). A significant number of these purchases were made by the Ayn Rand Institute itself, but even excluding the approximately 300,000 copies the Institute distributed for free, the figures are impressive

4. Ayn Rand, *The Fountainhead,* 50th anniversary ed. (1943; New York: Signet, 1993), 24–25; "Mike Wallace Asks Ayn Rand," *New York Post,* December 12, 1957.

Chapter 1

1. Ayn Rand, Biographical Interview 11, February 15, 1961, by Barbara and Nathaniel Branden, tape recording, New York, December 1960–May 1961, Ayn Rand Papers, a Special Collection of the Ayn Rand Archives, Irvine, California. Henceforth cited as Biographical Interview with corresponding number and date.

2. Yuri Slezkine, *The Jewish Century* (Princeton, NJ: Princeton University Press, 2004), 116–17. St. Petersburg was renamed Petrograd in 1914 and Leningrad in 1925.

3. Lissette Hassani, Ayn Rand Oral History Project, Ayn Rand Papers. Subsequently cited as Oral History, ARP.

4. Biographical Interview 11.

5. Rand attended the Stoiunin Gymnasium, a progressive and academically rigorous school for girls. Chris Matthew Sciabarra, *Ayn Rand: The Russian Radical* (University Park: Pennsylvania State University Press, 1995), 69. Although few Jewish girls were formally educated, they were more likely than boys to attend Russian primary schools. The proportion of Jewish students in St. Petersburg schools was strictly limited to 3 percent. See Benjamin Nathans, *Beyond the Pale: The Jewish Encounter with Late Imperial*

Russia (Berkeley: University of California Press, 2002), 222; Zvi Gitelman, *A Century of Ambivalence: The Jews of Russia and the Soviet Union, 1881 to the Present* (Bloomington: Indiana University Press, 2001), 10. According to Anne Heller, the Stoiunin Gymnasium was able to circumvent these restrictions, meaning about a third of Alisa's classmates were Jewish. Anne C. Heller, *Ayn Rand and the World She Made* (New York: Doubleday, 2009), 18.

6. Biographical Interview 11.

7. Ibid.

8. Interview with Nora Drobysheva, Oral History, ARP.

9. Biographical Interview 11.

10. Ibid.

11. Ibid. Alisa's coolly rational rejection of religion also marked other intellectuals of Jewish origin who later became prominent conservatives or right-wing activists. See George H. Nash, "Forgotten Godfathers: Premature Jewish Conservatives and the rise of *National Review,*" *American Jewish History* 87, nos. 2–3 (1999): 123–57. Nash notes that his subjects prided themselves on their individuality and independence, which may account for their distance from Judaism.

12. Ayn Rand, *We the Living* (1936; New York: Signet, 1959), 44, 26.

13. Sciabarra, *Ayn Rand: The Russian Radical,* chapter 3.

14. AR to Isabel Paterson, May 8, 1948, in *Letters of Ayn Rand,* ed. Michael S. Berliner (New York: Penguin, 1995), 214. Henceforth cited as *Letters.*

15. In *Ayn Rand: The Russian Radical,* Chris Sciabarra argues that Rand should be considered a thinker in the Russian dialectical tradition, an argument that falls outside the purview of this work. Sciabarra argues that Rand was influenced by the work of N. O. Lossky, a prominent dialectical philosopher affiliated with Petrograd (Leningrad) State University, whom she claimed to have studied under. However, evidence connecting her to Lossky remains fragmentary, inconclusive, and contradictory. Sciabarra's research has provided valuable and hitherto unknown details of Rand's education. His findings are described in *Ayn Rand: The Russian Radical;* Sciabarra, "The Rand Transcript," *Journal of Ayn Rand Studies* 1, no. 1 (1999): 1–26; Sciabarra, "The Rand Transcript, Revisited," *Journal of Ayn Rand Studies* 7, no. 1 (2005): 1–17. Sciabarra's findings suggest inaccuracies in Rand's recollection of her time at the university, which accordingly must be treated with care. My discussion of Rand's education draws on Sciabarra and Rand, Biographical Interview 6, January 2, 1961.

16. Barbara Branden, *The Passion of Ayn Rand* (New York: Random House, 1986), 45.

17. Rand's movie diary and the two pamphlets have been published in Rand, *Russian Writings on Hollywood,* ed. Michael S. Berliner (Irvine, CA: Ayn Rand Institute Press, 1999).

18. Ibid., 76.

19. Rand, *We the Living,* 52.

20. Preparations for Alisa's departure are described in Jeff Britting, *Ayn Rand* (New York: Overlook Press, 2004), 29–33, and multiple letters in the Russian Family Correspondence, ARP.

21. Britting, *Ayn Rand,* 30, 32; Russian Family Correspondence, ARP.

22. Rand's change of name was fairly typical of Jewish writers and actors making their living in Hollywood. See Neal Gabler, *An Empire of Their Own: How the Jews Invented Hollywood* (New York: Crown, 1988), 301, 372. Contrary to legend, Rand did not name herself after her Remington-Rand typewriter, nor is her name an abbreviation of the diminutive "Ayneleh," as William F. Buckley Jr. claimed. Nicknames were common in the Rosenbaum household, and letters from Russia confirm that Alisa had experimented with a range of possible pennames, including "Lil Rand," before settling on "Ayn Rand." See Nora Rosenbaum to AR, March 23, 1926 and April 11, 1926, letters 21a and 24d, Russian Family Correspondence, Ayn Rand Archives. Rand gave differing accounts of her name throughout the 1930s. She told a reporter, "My first name is Ayna, but I liquidated the 'A,' and Rand is an abbreviation of my Russian surname." In a letter to a fan she wrote, "I must say that 'Ayn' is both a real name and an invention," and she indicated that her first name was inspired by a Finnish writer (whom she declined to identify) and her last an abbreviation of Rosenbaum. Michael Mok, "Waitress to Playwright—Now Best Seller Author," *New York Post*, May 5, 1936; AR to W. Craig, January 30, 1937, ARP 041–11X.

23. Biographical Interview 7, January 15, 1961; Harvey Goldberg, Oral History Interview, ARP. Decades later, members of Rand's extended family still smarted at what they considered her failure to properly acknowledge or appreciate their help. More seriously, they charged that had she fully explained the Rosenbaum's dire circumstances in Russia, the family would have brought them all to America, thus saving their lives. Heller, 61.

24. Rand, *Russian Writings on Hollywood*, 77.

25. F. Scott Fitzgerald, *The Love of the Last Tycoon* (1941; New York: Scribner, 1993), 11; Nathanael West, *Miss Lonelyhearts and The Day of the Locust* (New York: New Directions, 1962), 132.

26. B. Branden, *The Passion of Ayn Rand*, 73.

27. Marcella Rabin, Oral History outtakes, ARP; Ayn Rand, *Journals of Ayn Rand*, ed. David Harriman (New York: Penguin, 1999), 48, henceforth cited as *Journals*.

28. *Journals*, 48.

29. Anna Borisnova to AR, January 22, 1926, and September 22, 1926, letters 9a and 89a, Russian Family Correspondence, ARP.

30. These stories, which Rand never attempted to publish, were released by her estate in *The Early Ayn Rand*, ed. Leonard Peikoff (New York: Penguin, 1986).

31. Lynn Simross, "Studio Club Closes Door on Past," *Los Angeles Times*, February 9, 1975, L1.

32. *Journals*, 38. Rand's willingness to celebrate a criminal anticipates the work of later writers such as Norman Mailer, Truman Capote, and Cormac McCarthy, who all to some degree portray the murderer as a person of unusual strength, sensitivity, or both. A more immediate parallel for Rand would have been a book she knew well, Fyodor Dostoevsky's *Crime and Punishment*, a serious novel of ideas built around the psychology of a murderer.

33. Ibid., 27, 37, 36.

34. Ibid., 32.

35. Popular American understandings of the Superman are outlined in Jennifer Ratner-Rosenhagen, "Neither Rock nor Refuge: American Encounters with Nietzsche and the Search for Foundations," PhD diss., Brandeis University, 2003, 231.

36. Rand, *Journals,* 23.

37. Ibid., 29, 42.

38. Ibid., 48.

39. Anna Borisnova to AR, October 2, 1930, letter 228a, Russian Family Correspondence, ARP.

40. Nora Rosenbaum to AR, September 15, 1931, letter 245a, Russian Family Correspondence, ARP; Rosalie Wilson, Oral History, ARP.

41. The sale of *Red Pawn,* without mention of Morris, is covered in Robert Mayhew, *Essays on Ayn Rand's* We the Living (Lanham, MD: Lexington Books, 2004), 259. Morris described his role to the columnist Lee Shippey, "The Lee Side o' L.A.," *Los Angeles Times,* March 11, 1936, A4.

42. "Russian Girl Finds End of Rainbow in Hollywood," *Chicago Daily News,* September 26, 1932.

43. Edwin Schallert, "Night of January 16th: Unique Courtroom Drama," *Los Angeles Times,* March 2, 1926, 17. Rand's first title for the play was *Penthouse Legend.*

44. *Journals,* 68.

45. Ibid., 68, 69.

46. Ibid., 73, 72.

47. Ibid., 69, 70.

48. Docky Wolfe, Oral History, ARP.

49. Rand, *We the Living,* 216.

50. Ibid., 387.

51. Ibid., 446, 425.

52. Rand, *Journals,* 58.

53. Rand, *We the Living,* 80.

54. The connections between Rand's characters and people she knew in Russia are detailed in Scott McConnell, "Parallel Lives: Models and Inspirations for Characters in *We the Living,*" in Mayhew, *Essays on Ayn Rand's* We the Living, 47–66.

55. AR to Jean Wick, October 27, 1934, and June 19, 1934, both in ARP 077–12A. Portions of these letters are reproduced in Mayhew, *Essays on Ayn Rand's* We the Living, 139, 135. Mencken's views are described in Terry Teachout, *The Skeptic: A Life of H. L. Mencken* (New York: Harper Collins, 2002).

56. Biographical Interview 14, March 3, 1961.

57. Jean Wick to AR, June 29, 1934, ARP 077–12A.

58. David C. Engerman, *Modernization from the Other Shore: American Intellectuals and the Romance of Russian Development* (Cambridge, MA: Harvard University Press, 2003).

59. Ted Morgan, *Reds: McCarthyism in Twentieth-century America* (New York: Random House, 2003), 166–67.

60. Whittaker Chambers, *Witness* (New York: Random House, 1952), 269. For leftist New York in the 1930s, see Michael Denning, *The Cultural Front: The Laboring of American Culture in the Twentieth Century* (New York: Verso, 1997).

61. Quoted in Morgan, *Reds,* 171.

62. Dina Garmong, "*We the Living* and the Rosenbaum Family Letters," in Mayhew, *Essays on Ayn Rand's* We the Living, 72.

63. B. Branden, *The Passion of Ayn Rand,* 122–23.

64. "Russian Triangle," *Cincinnati Times-Star,* July 5, 1936; Ben Belitt, "The Red and the White," *The Nation,* April 22, 1936; "Days of the Red Terror," *Toronto Globe,* May 9, 1936. Discussion of the novel's reviews can be found in Michael S. Berliner, "Reviews of *We the Living,*" in Mayhew, *Essays on Ayn Rand's* We the Living.

65. Elsie Robinson, "Listen World: So This Is Communism!," *Philadelphia News,* July 8, 1936.

66. M. Geraldine Ootts to AR, April 5, 1937, ARP 073–06x.

67. O. O. McIntyre, "New York Day by Day," syndicated column, June 9, 1936. *We the Living* did better overseas and in 1942 was even pirated by an Italian filmmaker, who made it into a two-part movie, *Noi Vivi* and *Addio Kira.* Rand was originally outraged by the theft but then pleased to learn the film had been banned by Italian authorities as antifascist. R. W. Bradford has cast doubt on this claim, suggesting Rand embellished the story for dramatic effect or misunderstood the film's history. After suing for lost royalties she eventually recovered a print of the film, which she partially edited and rewrote. In 1988 a posthumous "author's version" with English subtitles was released as *We the Living.*

68. Roosevelt quoted in Alan Brinkley, *The End of Reform: New Deal Liberalism in Recession and War* (New York: Knopf, 1995), 10, and David Kennedy, *Freedom from Fear: The American People in Depression and War, 1929–1945* (New York: Oxford University Press, 1999), 104.

69. AR to Ruth Morris, July 2, 1936, ARP 98–03C.

70. Rand's letter is quoted in John Temple Graves, "This Morning," *Citizen* (Asheville, N.C.), August 26, 1936.

71. Alan Brinkley, *Voices of Protest: Huey Long, Father Coughlin, and the Great Depression* (New York: Knopf, 1982).

Chapter 2

1. Biographical Interview 11, February 15, 1961.

2. Biographical Interview 11. Rand's division of the world into two types of people closely followed the analysis of Ortega y Gasset in *Revolt of the Masses,* which Rand read during this time. Ortega y Gasset emphasized a distinction between mass-man, "who does not value himself…and says instead that he is 'just like everybody else,'" and the select individual, "who demands more from himself than do others." *Revolt of the Masses* (Notre Dame, IN: University of Notre Dame Press, 1985), 7.

3. Biographical Interview 10, January 26, 1961.

4. See discussion in Walter Kaufmann, *Nietzsche: Philosopher, Psychologist, Antichrist* (Princeton, NJ: Princeton University Press, 1974), especially chapter 3. Nietzsche's phrase is on 109. There is a long-running discussion among Rand scholars about the extent and meaning of her connection to Nietzsche. The evidence of his influence on her is incontrovertible, but many scholars focus on Rand's explicit rejection of Nietzsche's Dionysius and her dislike of *The Birth of Tragedy,* arguing that

she experienced only a brief "Nietzsche phase." According to Leonard Peikoff, "By her early thirties, AR had thought herself out of every Nietzschian element." Quoted in *Journals of Ayn Rand,* ed. David Harriman (New York: Penguin, 1997), ix. Similar arguments about Nietzsche's transient influence are found in essays by Merrill, Mayhew, and Milgram in Robert J. Mayhew, ed., *Essays on Ayn Rand's* We the Living (Lanham, MD: Lexington Books, 2004), and Chris Matthew Sciabarra, *Ayn Rand: The Russian Radical* (University Park: Pennsylvania State University Press, 1995), 103. These scholars share Rand's understanding of Nietzschean ethics as solely a call for the strong to dominate the weak. What is attributed to Nietzsche in this formulation may in fact stem from other writers Rand read during this time, including Ortega y Gasset, Oswald Spengler, Albert Jay Nock, and H. L. Mencken, Nietzsche's first American interpreter and a particular Rand favorite. I agree that there are many differences between Rand and Nietzsche, most strikingly her absolutism as opposed to his antifoundationalism. Yet I approach the question of influence from a different angle, focusing primarily on Nietzsche's transvaluation of values and his call for a new morality. From this perspective, though Rand's reliance on Nietzsche lessened over time, her entire career might be considered a "Nietzsche phase."

5. *Journals,* 77, 84, 87. Rand identified the aphorism from *Beyond Good and Evil* she intended to use in her introduction to the twenty-fifth anniversary edition of the novel: "It is not the works, but the *belief* which is here decisive and determines the order of rank—to employ once more an old religious formula with a new and deeper meaning—it is some fundamental certainty which a noble soul has about itself, something which is not to be sought, is not to be found, and perhaps, also, is not to be lost. *The noble soul has reverence for itself.*" Quoted in Rand, *The Fountainhead,* 50th anniversary ed. (1943; New York: Penguin, 1993), x.

6. *Journals,* 78.

7. *Journals,* 79, 80.

8. *Journals,* 78.

9. *Journals,* 93, 187.

10. Second-Hand Lives notebook, ARP 167. An edited and revised version of this quotation can be found in *Journals,* 80. It is notable that Rand spoke openly here about Christianity as an exemplar of the ideals she opposed, rather than altruism.

11. *Journals,* 81; AR to Newman Flower, April 12, 1938, ARP 078–14x.

12. Biographical Interview 11.

13. Rand's comments on Spengler have been excised from her published *Journals* but can be found in First Philosophical Journal, ARP 166–02X. Skepticism about democracy was common among intellectuals across the political spectrum. See Edward Purcell, *The Crisis of Democratic Theory: Scientific Naturalism and the Problem of Value* (Lexington: University Press of Kentucky, 1973).

14. This reference is deleted from page 81 of Rand's published *Journals* but can be found in notebook "Second-Hand Lives," December 4, 1935, 13, ARP 167–01B. Her reference to racial determinism was not unusual for her time and place, although it is sharply at odds with her later rejection of race as a collectivist concept.

15. *Journals,* 84, 80.

16. *Journals*, 74.

17. *Journals*, 93. In her early notebooks characters are listed by names that Rand ultimately changed (e.g., Everett Monkton Flent became Ellsworth Monkton Toohey and Peter Wilson became Peter Keating). For clarity's sake, I refer to all characters by their final, published names, just as I refer to "Second-Hand Lives" as *The Fountainhead*.

18. *Journals*, 142. As her note suggests, Rand's claim to have taken only general inspiration from Wright's life is false, for many specific incidents from his career surface in *The Fountainhead*. Roark's Stoddard Temple closely resembles Wright's famous Unity Temple, conceived as "a temple to man." As does Roark, Wright had a model for a sculpture pose on the construction site of Midway Gardens. Both incidents are described in Wright's autobiography, which Rand read while researching her novel. Frank Lloyd Wright, *Autobiography of Frank Lloyd Wright* (New York: Longmans, Green, 1932), 154, 184.

19. Laski notebook, ARP 086–20X. These politically incorrect musings about women are not included in the published versions of the notebook, found in *Journals*, 113–15; "Second-Hand Lives," March 28, 1937, 85, ARP 167–01D. Rand's use of the term "nance," contemporary slang for a homosexual man, does not appear in the published version of these notes, found in *Journals*, 109. Merrill Schleier investigates Rand's presentation of masculinity and gender in "Ayn Rand and King Vidor's Film *The Fountainhead*: Architectural Modernism, the Gendered Body, and Political Ideology," *Journal of the Society of Architectural Historians* 61, no. 3 (2002): 310–31, and *Skyscraper Cinema: Architecture and Gender in American Film* (Minneapolis: University of Minnesota Press, 2009).

20. Biographical Interview 11.

21. Biographical Interview 11.

22. Documents are in ARP 136–25b, also reprinted in Jeff Britting, *Ayn Rand* (New York: Overlook Press, 2004), 54.

23. Rand's last contact from her family came at the beginning of 1939, when they exchanged telegrams marking the New Year. Anna Borisnova to AR, January 3, 1939, postcard 475, Russian Family Correspondence, ARP.

24. According to members of the O'Connor family, Rand had an abortion in the early 1930s, which they helped pay for. Rand never mentioned this incident, but it accords with her emphasis on career and her unequivocal support for abortion rights. Anne C. Heller, *Ayn Rand and the World She Made* (New York: Doubleday, 2009), 128.

25. Biographical Interview 11.

26. Ibid.

27. See, for example, Garet Garrett and Bruce Ramsey, *Salvos against the New Deal* (Caldwell, ID: Caxton Press, 2002); George Wolfskill and John A. Hudson, *All but the People: Franklin D. Roosevelt and His Critics* (London: Macmillan, 1969). Usually termed the "Old Right," Roosevelt's political opposition is described in Sheldon Richman, "New Deal Nemesis: The 'Old Right' Jeffersonians," *Independent Review* 1, no. 2 (1996): 201–48; Murray Rothbard, *The Betrayal of the American Right* (Auburn, AL: Ludwig von Mises Institute, 2007); Leo Ribuffo, *The Old Christian Right* (Philadelphia: Temple

University Press, 1983); Justin Raimondo, *Reclaiming the American Right: The Lost Legacy of the Conservative Movement* (Wilmington, DE: Intercollegiate Studies Institute, 2008); John E. Moser, *Right Turn: John T. Flynn and the Transformation of American Liberalism* (New York: New York University Press, 2005); James T. Patterson, *Congressional Conservatism and the New Deal: The Growth of the Conservative Coalition in Congress, 1933–1939* (Lexington: University of Kentucky Press, 1969); Paula Baker, "Liberty against Power: Defending Classical Liberalism in the 1930s," unpublished paper. Recently historians have begun to trace the connections between this Old Right and the postwar conservative movement. See Gregory L. Schneider, *The Conservative Century: From Reaction to Revolution* (New York, Rowman and Littlefield, 2008); Donald Critchlow, *The Conservative Ascendancy: How the GOP Right Made Political History* (Cambridge, MA: Harvard University Press, 2007); Kimberly Phillips-Fein, *Invisible Hands: The Making of the Conservative Movement from the New Deal to Ronald Reagan* (New York: Norton, 2009); Joseph Lowndes, *From the New Deal to the New Right* (New Haven, CT: Yale University Press, 2008).

28. Although it did not become widely used until the 1950s, "libertarian" was in circulation prior to the New Deal. It emerged after Roosevelt popularized a new understanding of "liberal," the term formerly used by advocates of limited government. The first prominent figures to identify as libertarians were H. L. Mencken and Albert Jay Nock. See H. L. Mencken, *Letters of H. L. Mencken,* ed. Guy Forgue (New York: Knopf, 1961), xiii, 189; Albert Jay Nock and Frank W. Garrison, eds., *Letters from Albert Jay Nock, 1924–1945 to Edmund C. Evans, Mrs. Edmund C. Evans and Ellen Winsor* (Caldwell, ID: Caxton Printers, 1949), 40. The careers of both and their relation to conservatism are discussed in Patrick Allitt, *The Conservatives: Ideas and Personalities throughout American History* (Cambridge, MA: Harvard University Press, 2009), 141–52. Paterson's views are covered in Steven Cox, *The Woman and the Dynamo: Isabel Paterson and the Idea of America* (New Brunswick, NJ: Transaction, 2004).

29. Rand to the *New York Herald Tribune,* February 9, 1937, ARP 099–05x.

30. George Wolfskill, *Revolt of the Conservatives: A History of the American Liberty League, 1934–1940* (Boston: Houghton Mifflin, 1962), chapter 4.

31. Ultimately produced on Broadway in 1940, *The Unconquered* was a resounding flop that closed after six performances. Britting, *Ayn Rand,* 56.

32. The connection between *Anthem* and Stephen Vincent Benét's "The Place of the Gods" is well established, but there is no documented link between Rand and Zamyatin. Still, the similarities between the two are striking. For the argument that Zamyatin influenced Rand, see Zina Gimpelevich, "'We' and 'I' in Zamyatin's *We* and Ayn Rand's *Anthem,*" *Germano-Slavica* 10, no. 1 (1997): 13–23. A discussion of Rand's relationship to Benét and a rebuttal of her connection to Zamyatin can be found in Shoshana Milgram, "*Anthem* in the Context of Related Literary Works," in *Essays on Ayn Rand's* Anthem, ed. Robert Mayhew (Lanham, MD: Lexington Books, 2005), 119–171.

33. AR to Marjorie Williams, June 18, 1936, *Letters,* 33.

34. Biographical Interview 11.

35. Biographical Interview 13, February 26, 1961.

36. See AR to Knopf, June 24, 1938, and Knopf to Ann Watkins, October, 25, 1940, ARP 137–25F.

37. Charles Peters, *Five Days in Philadelphia: The Amazing "We Want Willkie!" Convention of 1940 and How It Freed FDR to Save the Western World* (New York: Public Affairs, 2005).

38. Details on Willkie's early career are from Erwin C. Hargrove, *Prisoners of Myth: The Leadership of the Tennessee Valley Authority, 1933–1990* (Princeton, NJ: Princeton University Press, 1994), especially 46–47, and Steve Neal, *Dark Horse: A Biography of Wendell Willkie* (Garden City, NY: Doubleday, 1984).

39. Charles Peters, "The Greatest Convention," *Washington Monthly* 36, no. 7/8 (2004): 16.

40. Willkie is quoted in Neal, *Dark Horse*, 74; Biographical Interview 14, March 3, 1961.

41. Ayn Rand to Gerald Loeb, August 5, 1944, *Letters*, 154.

42. Biographical Interview 10, January 1, 1961.

43. Barbara Branden, *The Passion of Ayn Rand* (Garden City, NY: Doubleday, 1986), 161.

44. *Journals*, 73.

45. Biographical Interview 14.

46. Isolationism is described in Justus Doenecke, *Storm on the Horizon: The Challenge to American Intervention, 1939–1941* (Lanham, MD: Rowman and Littlefield, 2000); Justus Doenecke and Mark A. Stoler, *Debating Franklin D. Roosevelt's Foreign Policies, 1933–1945* (Lanham, MD: Rowman and Littlefield, 2005); Wayne S. Cole, *Roosevelt and the Isolationists, 1932–1945* (Lincoln: University of Nebraska Press, 1983).

47. Biographical interview 10.

48. Biographical interview 14.

49. Bill Kauffman, *America First! Its History, Culture, and Politics* (Amherst, MA: Prometheus Books, 1995), 18.

50. "New Force?," *Time*, December 23, 1940.

51. *Journals*, 345, 347. First used during the Spanish Civil War, "fifth column" was a fairly popular term for internal subversion at the time. See Ribuffo, *The Old Christian Right*. Rand had also recently read a conservative screed about Communists in the United States, Joseph Kamp's *The Fifth Column in Washington!* (New Haven, CT: Constitutional Education League, 1940). Peikoff Library Collection, Ayn Rand Archives. Rand's usage of "totalitarianism" rather than "collectivism" followed a similar shift in the public understanding of communism and fascism. See Benjamin L. Alpers, *Dictators, Democracy, and American Public Culture* (Chapel Hill: University of North Carolina Press, 2003). This equation of Russia and Germany occurred particularly among business leaders and in corporate publications. See Les K. Adler and Thomas G. Paterson, "Red Fascism: The Merger of Nazi Germany and Soviet Russia in the American Image of Totalitarianism, 1930s–1950s," *American Historical Review* 75, no. 4 (1970): 1046–64. The bulk of Adler and Paterson's sources for this discourse are business leaders and corporate publications, although they do not comment on this.

52. *Journals*, 345.

53. Important geographic variations persisted, with the Party remaining strong in California throughout World War II. Betty Friedan and Robert Oppenheimer, for example, became close to Communists in Berkeley during this time. See Daniel Horowitz, *Betty Friedan and The Making of the Feminine Mystique* (Amherst, MA: University of Massachusetts Press, 1998), 92–94.

54. For the history of the CPUSA, including membership figures, see Harvey Klehr, *The Heyday of American Communism: The Depression Decade* (New York: Basic Books, 1984); Maurice Isserman, *Which Side Were You On? The American Communist Party During the Second World War* (Middletown, CT: Wesleyan University Press, 1982).

55. Pollock's column "This Week," ran in the supplement to the *Sunday Herald Tribune.* Pollock, "What Can We Do for Democracy," Town Hall Forum of the West, ARP 146-PO1.

56. AR to Pollock, April 28, 1941, *Letters,* 45.

57. Rand's "Manifesto of Individualism" has not been published. For an extended treatment, with particular attention to the connections among the "Manifesto," *Anthem,* and *The Fountainhead,* see Jeff Britting, "Anthem and the Individualist Manifesto," in Mayhew, *Essays on Ayn Rand's* Anthem, 70–80.

58. Rand, "Manifesto of Individualism," undated typescript with handwritten edits, 2–4, ARP, 029–90A.

59. Ibid, 6.

60. Ibid. 14.

61. Ibid., 15.

62. Ibid., 17. Rand's distinction between social classes, typically understood, and her views of the worthy echoes Ortega y Gasset, who railed against the "masses" yet emphasized that the term did not mean working class but rather "anyone who does not value himself." *Revolt of the Masses,* 7.

63. *Journals,* 90.

64. Rand, "Manifesto of Individualism," 10, 12, 33.

65. *Journals,* 84. Some of the changes Rand made to a second edition of *We the Living,* released in 1959, may also track this shift in perspective. See Robert Mayhew, "We the Living: '36 and '59," in *Essays on Ayn Rand's* We the Living (Lanham, MD: Lexington Books, 2004), 203–4; Rand, "Manifesto."

66. Biographical Interview 14.

67. Carl Snyder, *Capitalism the Creator: The Economic Foundations of Modern Industrial Society* (New York: Macmillan, 1940), 4, 363. Tellingly, Synder's work was also read by F. A. Hayek; see Hayek, "Review of *Capitalism the Creator* by Carl Snyder," *Economica* 7, no. 28. (1940): 437–39.

68. Snyder, *Capitalism the Creator,* 416.

69. Rand, "Manifesto," 21, quoted in Britting, *Ayn Rand,* 74.

70. Adam Smith, *Theory of Moral Sentiments* (1759; New York: Cambridge University Press, 2005).

71. Rand, "Manifesto," 22, 32, 33, quoted in Britting, *Ayn Rand,* 74.

72. AR to Pollock, May 1, 1941, *Letters,* 46.

Chapter 3

1. Rand, "Dear Mr.——," undated fundraising letter, ARP 146-PO4.

2. AR to Pollock, July 20, 1941, *Letters,* 33.

3. AR to Ann Watkins, May 17, 1941, reprinted in Robert Mayhew, ed., *Essays on Ayn Rand's* The Fountainhead (Lanham, MD: Lexington Books, 2007), 66.

4. Biographical Interview 11, February 15, 1961.

5. Ibid.

6. Monroe Shakespeare to DeWitt Emery, November 25, 1941, ARP 139-E2x.

7. Emery to Rand, undated, ARP 139-E1.

8. AR to Pollock, June 23, 1941, *Letters,* 53; AR to Emery, August 14, 1941, *Letters,* 57.

9. Biographical Interview 14, March 3, 1961.

10. Ibid.

11. Ibid.

12. John Maynard Keynes, *The General Theory of Employment, Interest, and Money* (Amherst, NY: Prometheus Books, 1997). Keynes's ascendency is described in David C. Colander and Harry Landreth, eds., *The Coming of Keynesianism to America* (Brookfield, VT: Edward Elgar, 1996). As the authors rightly note, Keynesianism did not have a direct effect on New Deal policymaking, nor was the adaptation of his ideas uncontroversial in academic departments. The attractiveness of Keynes to a young generation of economists, however, quickly minimized the influence of classical economics at key institutions like Harvard University.

13. Talcott Parsons, *The Structure of Social Action* (New York: McGraw Hill, 1937), 3–4. New work on Parsons considers him more progressive than previously understood. See Howard Brick, *Transcending Capitalism: Visions of a New Society in Modern American Thought* (Ithaca, NY: Cornell University Press, 2006).

14. Alfred Jay Nock, introduction to Herbert Spencer, *The Man versus the State* (Caldwell, ID: Caxton Printers, 1940), x.

15. Richard Hofstadter, *Social Darwinism in American Thought,* revised ed. (1944; Boston: Beacon Press, 1955), 52.

16. There is a rich debate about the role played by true Darwinian theory in this tradition of thought. None deny, however, that laissez-faire theorists drew heavily on scientific theory and the idea of evolution, even if they drastically misunderstood Darwin's ideas. See especially Robert C. Bannister's critique of Hofstadter, *Social Darwinism: Science and Myth in Anglo-American Social Thought* (Philadelphia: Temple University Press, 1979); Donald C. Bellomy, "'Social Darwinism' Revisited," *Perspectives in America History* 1, n.s. (1984): 1–129.

17. Channing Pollock, "What Can We Do for Democracy," Town Hall Forum of the West, undated, 16, ARP 146-P01; Ruth Alexander to AR, February 27, 1965, ARP 137-A2x. Nock apparently accepted Cram's bizarre theory as scientific truth, and it contributed to the pessimism of his later years. See Nock, *Memoirs of a Superfluous Man* (New York: Harper Brothers, 1943), 139; Charles H. Hamilton, foreword to Albert Jay Nock and Charles H. Hamilton, *The State of the Union: Essays in Social Criticism* (Indianapolis:

Liberty Press, 1991), xxi; Rand, "An Attempt at the Beginning of an Autobiography," ARP, 078–15x, reprinted in *Journals,* 65.

18. Paterson's career and thought are described in a recent a full-length biography: Stephen Cox, *The Woman and the Dynamo: Isabel Paterson and the Idea of America* (New Brunswick, NJ: Transaction, 2004). Her time at the *Herald* is also briefly described in Joan Shelley Rubin, *The Making of Middlebrow Culture* (Chapel Hill: University of North Carolina Press, 1992), 79–80.

19. Rose Wilder Lane to AR, undated, ARP 143-LN3.

20. Biographical Interview 14.

21. Details of the Rand-Paterson relationship are given in Barbara Branden, *The Passion of Ayn Rand* (Garden City, NY: Doubleday and Company, 1986), 164–66, and Cox, *The Woman and the Dynamo,* especially chapters 14, 18, 22, 24.

22. Maine first elaborated the distinction between status and contract societies in *Ancient Law* (1861; New York: Henry Holt, 1864). Spencer refers to this idea on the first page of *The Man versus the State* (1884), and Sumner highlights it in the first chapter of *What Social Classes Owe to Each Other* (1883; Caldwell, ID: Caxton Printers, 2003). In later libertarian writing this distinction would pass for common sense. Rand hurled it at religious conservatives in the 1960s, accusing them of advocating a return to the "ancient, frozen, status society." See Rand, "Conservatism: An Obituary," in *Capitalism: The Unknown Ideal* (New York: Penguin, 1967), 198.

23. Carl Ryant, *Profit's Prophet: Garet Garrett* (Selinsgrove, PA: Susquehanna University Press, 1989). Paterson's interest in Garrett is described in Cox, *The Woman and the Dynamo,* 126–28.

24. Biographical Interview 14.

25. Rand, "Dear Mr.——," undated fund-raising letter, ARP 146-PO4.

26. Ibid.

27. Channing Pollock to DeWitt Emery, September 6, 1941, ARP 146-PO4.

28. Quoted in Mayhew, *Essays on Ayn Rand's* The Fountainhead, 68. Isabel Paterson also claimed to have influenced Bobbs-Merrill to accept the book. See Anne C. Heller, *Ayn Rand and the World She Made* (New York: Doubleday, 2009), 144.

29. AR to Odgen, February 19, 1942, *Letters,* 63.

30. Biographical Interview 15, March 31, 1961.

31. Ayn Rand, *The Fountainhead,* 50th anniversary ed. (1943; *The Fountainhead.* 50th anniversary ed. 1943; New York: Signet, 1993), 675. Subsequent citations are from this edition and are referenced in the text.

32. AR to Monroe Shakespeare, June 12, 1943, ARP 004–15C.

33. Ayn Rand, *The Art of Fiction,* ed. Tore Boeckmann (New York: Penguin, 2000), 163.

34. AR to Paul Smith, March 13, 1965, ARP 39-07A; Barbara Branden, "Ayn Rand: The Reluctant Feminist," in *Feminist Interpretations of Ayn Rand,* ed. Mimi Reisel Gladstein and Chris Sciabarra (University Park: Pennsylvania State University Press, 1999), 37.

35. Phyllis Schlafly, for one, stopped reading the book when she reached this scene. Schlafly, *Feminist Fantasies* (Dallas: Spence, 2003), 23. *The Fountainhead* may be compared to romance novels, which use rape as a standard trope. In these popular works rape is essential to male character development and one of many

symbolic ways male and female characters interact. See Janice Radway, *Reading the Romance: Women, Patriarchy, and Popular Literature* 1984 Chapel Hill: University of North Carolina Press, 1991), 207. The rape scene is given extended treatment in Gladstein and Sciabarra, *Feminist Interpretations of Ayn Rand* and Andrew Bernstein, "Understanding the 'Rape' Scene in *The Fountainhead*," in Mayhew, *Essays on Ayn Rand's* The Fountainhead, 201–8.

36. Shoshana Milgram, "*The Fountainhead* from Notebook to Novel: The Composition of Ayn Rand's First Ideal Man," in Mayhew, *Essays on Ayn Rand's* The Fountainhead, 3–40, provides a perceptive reading of these changes.

37. See Sumner, *What Social Classes Owe to Each Other*, 107; Isabel Paterson, *God of the Machine* (1943; New Brunswick, NJ: Transaction, 1993), xii. This was in many ways an articulation of a producer ethic, which Michael Kazin identifies as an important component of populism. Kazin emphasizes that populism is a "flexible mode of persuasion," and not all who employ the idiom should be identified as populists in a sociological sense. Kazin, *The Populist Persuasion: An American History* (New York: Basic Books, 1995), 3.

38. Although class need not play a primary role in Rand's tale of individual heroism, its absence is telling. Her willingness to mount a critique of American society that elides class difference anticipates the later drift of political discussion in America and prefigures the right's success at shifting the grounds of political debate from class to culture. See Daniel Bell, "Afterword (2001): From Class to Culture," in *The Radical Right*, ed. Daniel Bell, 3rd ed. (1963; New Brunswick, NJ: Transaction, 2002), 447–503.

39. Paterson, *God of the Machine*, 235. As Sumner put it, "The next pernicious thing to vice is charity in its broad and popular sense" (*What Social Classes Owe to Each Other*, 135).

40. AR to John Gall, July 29, 1943, ARP 044–15-A.

41. Lorine Pruette, "Battle against Evil," *New York Times Book Review*, May 16, 1943, 7, 18; Bett Anderson, "Idealism of Architect Is Background for Book," *Pittsburg Press*, May 30, 1943; "Novel about a Young American Architect," *Providence Journal*, May 16, 1943; "Varieties of Complaint," *Times Literary Supplement*, November 15, 1947, 589; Diana Trilling, "Fiction in Review," *The Nation*, June 12, 1943, 843.

42. See Cox's discussion in *The Woman and the Dynamo*, 311–12.

43. "Varieties of Complaint," *Times Literary Supplement*, November 15, 1947, 589.

44. The total number of fan letters Rand received is impossible to determine, for at her death numerous unopened mail bags were destroyed. I have examined approximately one thousand of the surviving fan letters that are housed in her papers. About two hundred of these letters were exclusively concerned with *The Fountainhead*. (Later letters inspired by *Atlas Shrugged* also often mentioned *The Fountainhead*.) An exact breakdown of Rand's readers is impossible to determine, but a random sample of letter writers from 1943 to 1959 collected in one archival box indicates the diversity of her appeal. Out of 107 letters written to Rand, seventy-six provided biographical details, with a breakdown as follows: twenty writers identified themselves as high school students, seven as college students, and thirty-nine as married adults. Letter writers were geographically diverse and did not hail from any particular region of the country. ARP, cartons 38 and 39.

45. Jane E. Thompson to AR, August 21, 1944, ARP 036–01A; Betty Andree to AR, February 23, 1946, ARP 036–01C; AR to DeWitt Emery, May 17, 1943, *Letters,* 42.

46. Thad Horton to AR, December 18, 1945, ARP 036–01H; Louise Bailey to AR, August 15, 1950, ARP 036–01H; Jane E. Thompson to AR, August 21, 1944, ARP 036–01A.

47. Herbert A. Bulgerin, in Bobbs-Merrill to AR, August 23, 1943, ARP 102–17x; PFC Gerald James to AR, July 29, 1945 ARP 036–01B. For Rand's response to James, see *Letters,* 228. Mrs. Leo (Edna) Koretsky to AR, January 10, 1946, ARP 036–01A.

48. AR to DeWitt Emery, May 17, 1943, *Letters,* 73.

49. Ayn Rand, "Dear Mr.————," undated fund-raising letter, circa 1942, ARP 146-PO4.

50. Ruth Austin to AR, undated, 1946, ARP 036–01F. Rand's responses to Austin are in *Letters,* 287–89, 293–96, 303–4. Alden E. Cornell to AR, 1947, ARP036–01D; Edward W. Greenfield to AR, October 15, 1957, ARP 100–11x. As the historian Alan Brinkley notes, even at the height of the New Deal there was a strong popular impulse to "defend the autonomy of the individual and the independence of the community against encroachments from the modern industrial state." *Voices of Protest: Huey Long, Father Coughlin, and the Great Depression* (New York: Knopf, 1982), xi. In 1935, 60 percent of Americans told the Gallup polling organization that government relief expenditures were "too great," and during the recession of 1937, only 37 percent supported increased state spending "to help get business out of its current slump." Although these early polls must be treated with caution, the antigovernment attitudes they register, across a variety of topics and years, cannot be ignored. See Alec M. Gallup, *The Gallup Poll Cumulative Index: Public Opinion, 1935–1997* (Wilmington, DE: Scholarly Resources, 1999), especially 1–197. In his brief discussion of Rand, Michael Szalay links *The Fountainhead*'s antistatism to similar attitudes in Gertrude Stein and Ernest Hemingway. Szalay, *New Deal Modernism: American Literature and the Invention of the Welfare State* (Durham, NC: Duke University Press, 2000), 75–121.

51. Excerpt from James Ingebretsen letter to Leonard Read is included in Read to AR, December 17, 1943, ARP 139-F1x; John Chamberlain, *A Life with the Printed Word,* (Chicago: Regnery Gateway, 1982), 136.

52. Ayn Rand and Oswald Garrison Villard, "Wake Up America: Collectivism or Individualism: Which One Promises Postwar Progress?," *Cincinnati Post,* October 19, 1943. The article was part of a syndicated series developed by Fred G. Clark for the American Economic Foundation and it ran nationwide in October 1943. Ayn Rand, "The Only Road to Tomorrow," *Reader's Digest,* January 1944, 88–90. Rand was furious to discover that the published article had been altered from her original, primarily by softening her language and omitting mention of Stalin as a totalitarian dictator. See AR to DeWitt Wallace, December 8, 1943, ARP 138-C4x. Rand had sold the article to the Committee for Constitutional Government, a conservative organization headed for a time by Norman Vincent Peale. The CCG placed her article in *Reader's Digest* and split the fee with her. See Ed Rumely to AR, November 1, 1943, ARP 138-C4x. The ideological orientation of *Reader's Digest* is described in Joanne P. Sharp, *Condensing the Cold War: Reader's Digest and American Identity* (Minneapolis: University of Minnesota Press, 2000). AR to Archie Ogden, May 6, 1943, *Letters,* 67.

53. AR to DeWitt Emery, May 17, 1943, *Letters,* 73

54. Ibid., 72.

55. Biographical Interview 12, January 22, 1961.

Chapter 4

1. AR to Henry Doherty, December 13, 1947, *Letters,* 382.

2. AR to Rose Wilder Lane, December 1946, *Letters,* 356.

3. Harry Hansen, "Writers Clash over Cain's Five-man Marketing Authority," *Chicago Sunday Tribune,* September 22, 1946; "Statement by Dorothy Thompson on Behalf of American Writers Association, which was to have been delivered at the Author's League Meeting, Sunday, October 20, 1946," press release, American Writers Association, October 20, 1946, Box 110–01A, ARP; "From the Editor," *The American Writer* 1, no 2 (1946).

4. See AR to R. C. Hoiles, November 6, 1943, ARP 036–01B; R. C. Hoiles, "Common Ground," *Santa Ana Register,* December 27, 1943. Hoiles's career, influence, and political views are covered in Brian Doherty, *Radicals for Capitalism: A Freewheeling History of the Modern American Libertarian Movement* (New York: Public Affairs, 2007), 172–77.

5. Biographical Interview 16, April 19, 1961. Details on Read, Mullendore, the L.A. Chamber of Commerce, and the Pamphleteers are taken from Greg Eow, "Fighting a New Deal: Intellectual Origins of the Reagan Revolution, 1932–1952," PhD diss., Rice University, 2007. Read's influence and the libertarian climate of southern California more generally is described in Lisa McGirr, *Suburban Warriors: The Origins of the New American Right* (Princeton, NJ: Princeton University Press, 2001), 34.

6. The national business movement against the New Deal is described in Kimberly Phillips-Fein, *Invisible Hands: The Making of the Conservative Movement from the New Deal to Reagan* (New York: Norton, 2009). For state activities, see Elizabeth Tandy Shermer, "Counter-Organizing the Sunbelt: Right-to-work Campaigns and Anti-Union Conservatism, 1943–1958," *Pacific Historical Review* 78, no. 1 (2009): 81–118. Interestingly, Rand later came out in opposition to right-to-work laws, which she saw as an infringement upon freedom of contract. Barbara Branden, "Intellectual Ammunition Department," *The Objectivist Newsletter* 2, no. 6 (1963), 23. For labor's gains during the war as causative of business activism, see Nelson Lichtenstein, "The Eclipse of Social Democracy," in *The Rise and Fall of the New Deal Order,* ed. Steve Fraser and Gary Gerstle (Princeton, NJ: Princeton University Press, 1989), 122–52.

7. *Anthem* was published as the entire contents of *Pamphleteers* 3, no. 1 (1946). "Our Competitive Free Enterprise System," Chamber of Commerce of the United States, Washington, D.C., 1946; Hart to AR, January 6, 1947, and Walker to AR, January 2, 1947, ARP 003–11x.

8. Elizabeth A. Fones-Wolf, *Selling Free Enterprise: The Business Assault on Labor and Liberalism, 1945–60* (Chicago: University of Illinois Press, 1994).

9. "Balzar's Hot Bargains for Cool Meals," August 5–7, 1946, Hollywood, CA, ARP 095–49x; Ralph C. Nehls to AR, December 18, 1949, ARP 004–15A; *The Houghton Line,* April–May 1944, ARP 092–12x.

10. F. A. Hayek, *The Road to Serfdom* (Chicago: University of Chicago Press, 1944), 3. For the reception of *Road to Serfdom*, see Alan Ebenstein, *Friedrich Hayek* (Chicago: University of Chicago Press, 2001). Hayek's career and thought are described in Bruce Caldwell, *Hayek's Challenge: An Intellectual Biography of F. A. Hayek* (Chicago: University of Chicago Press, 2003).

11. It is hard to exaggerate the institutional centrality of the University of Chicago to diverse strains of conservative thought. The Volker Fund also helped sponsor the nascent law and economics movement at Chicago. See Steven Michael Teles, *The Rise of the Conservative Legal Movement: The Battle for Control of the Law* (Princeton, NJ: Princeton University Press, 2008), chapter 4. Other activity at Chicago is described in Eow, "Fighting a New Deal"; John L. Kelley, *Bringing the Market Back In: The Political Revitalization of Market Liberalism* (London: Macmillan, 1987). The university was also home to the political philosopher Leo Strauss, an important influence on neoconservatives. See Shadia B. Drury, *Leo Strauss and the American Right* (New York: St. Martin's Press, 1997).

12. AR to Rose Wilder Lane, August 21, 1946, *Letters*, 308.

13. Juliet Williams argues that Hayek was more a pragmatist than an ideologue; see "On the Road Again: Reconsidering the Political Writings of F. A. Hayek," in *American Capitalism: Social Thought and Political Economy in 20th Century America*, ed. Nelson Lichtenstein (Philadelphia: University of Pennsylvania Press, 2006).

14. Ayn Rand, *Ayn Rand's Marginalia: Her Critical Comments on the Writings of Over 20 Authors*, ed. Robert Mayhew (Oceanside, CA: Second Renaissance Books, 1995), 151, 147, 150.

15. Angus Burgin, "Unintended Consequences: The Transformation of Atlantic Conservative Thought, 1920–1970," PhD diss., Harvard University, forthcoming; Rand, *Marginalia*, 146.

16. Though essentially agnostic, Hayek was sympathetic to Catholicism, the religion of his birth. His views on religion were both ambivalent and closely held, for he wished to avoid offense to believers and found religion culturally useful. See Stephen Kresge and Leif Wenar, eds., *Hayek on Hayek: An Autobiographical Dialogue* (Chicago: University of Chicago Press, 1994), 41; Rand, *Marginalia*, 148. Hayek apparently liked *Atlas Shrugged* but skipped the philosophical parts. Roy Childs, *Liberty against Power: Essays by Roy Childs, Jr.*, ed. Joan Kennedy Taylor (San Francisco: Fox and Wilkes, 1994), 272.

17. AR to Leonard Read, February 28, 1946, *Letters*, 260; Jörg Guido Hulsmann, *Mises: The Last Knight of Liberalism* (Auburn, AL: Ludwig Von Mises Institute Press, 2007). I discuss Rand's relationship with Mises more fully in the next chapter.

18. *Journals*, 245, 258.

19. Barbara Branden, *The Passion of Ayn Rand* (Garden City, NY: Doubleday and Company, 1986), 218.

20. "A Steel House with a Suave Finish," *Home and Garden*, August 1949, 54–57.

21. My description of the O'Connors' domestic life is taken from the oral histories cited, particularly Ruth Beebe Hill and June Kurisu, Rand's secretary.

22. Evan and Micky Wright, Oral History, ARP; Jack Bungay, Oral History, ARP.

23. Rosalie Wilson, Oral History, ARP. The incident raises the issue of Rand's relationship to her ethnic origins. Though her choice of name disguised her Jewish roots, she was always quick to identify herself as Jewish if anti-Semitic statements arose. Even so, since she had not chosen her religion she viewed it as largely inconsequential to her identity. As George Nash argues, this was a fairly common attitude among secular Jewish intellectuals during a time when religious and ethnic background was not celebrated as the key to authentic selfhood. Nash, "Forgotten Godfathers: Premature Jewish Conservatives and the Rise of *National Review*," *American Jewish History* 87, nos. 2–3 (1999): 123–57. Others have found Rand's Jewish origins to be of some consequence. The conservative critic Florence King asserts, "Ayn Rand's whole shtick was a gargantuan displacement of her never admitted fear of anti-Semitism," though she offers no evidence to support this point. King, *With Charity toward None* (New York: St. Martin's Press, 1992), 127. Andrew Heinze makes the more compelling case that Rand should be considered part of the American tradition of female Jewish public moralists, akin to Joyce Brothers, Laura Schlessinger, and Ann Landers. Heinze, *Jews and the American Soul* (Princeton, NJ: Princeton University Press, 2004) 300–301. Though in later years the majority of her close friends and associates were of Russian Jewish background and Rand made her first charitable donation to the state of Israel in 1973, she said and wrote virtually nothing on the topic of Judaism, nor did she mention the fate of European Jews during World War II. (Her frequent references to Hitler always came as part of a generalized discussion about totalitarianism and were usually twinned with reference to Stalin.) Rand may have had some vestigial loyalty to her birth religion, but as she stated, it seems to have been largely unimportant to her mature self-concept.

24. Ruth Hill, Oral History, ARP.

25. Jack Bungay, Oral History, ARP; Walter Seltzer, Oral History, ARP.

26. "Actress Peggy O'Neil Dead in Writer's Home," *Los Angeles Times*, April 14, 1945, A1; Oral History interview with June Kurisu; Albert Mannheimer to Ayn Rand, undated, ARP 003–13A.

27. B. Branden, *The Passion of Ayn Rand*, 197, 250.

28. Ruth Hill, Oral History, ARP.

29. Henceforth for clarity's sake I refer to the manuscript by its published title, *Atlas Shrugged*.

30. Rand purchased the volume edited by Richard McKeon, *The Basic Works of Aristotle* (New York: Random House, 1941), a classic tome of about 1,500 pages with excerpts from the *Organon, On the Heavens, The Short Physical Treatises,* and *Rhetoric* and the complete texts of *On the Soul, On Generation and Corruption, Physics, Metaphysics, Nicomachean Ethics, Politics,* and *Poetics* in their entirety. AR to Isabel Paterson, July 26, 1945, *Letters*, 179.

31. In 1948 Niebuhr was on the cover of *Time* magazine, an indication of the widespread interest in his ideas. Richard Wightman Fox, *Reinhold Niebuhr: A Biography* (New York: Pantheon Books, 1985); Patrick Allitt, *Catholic Intellectuals and Conservative Politics in America, 1950–1985* (Ithaca, NY: Cornell University Press, 1993); Edward Purcell, *The Crisis of Democratic Theory: Scientific Naturalism and the Problem of Value* (Lexington: University of Kentucky Press, 1973), chapter 8.

32. Biographical Interview 14, March 3, 1961. "A is A" is not a phrase from Aristotle but a canonical way to explain basic laws of logic. Rand used the phrase to indicate her agreement with Aristotle's Law of Identity. Her later use of Aristotle was often inaccurate. According to Rand, Aristotle believed that "history represents things as they are, while fiction represents them as they might be and ought to be." However, as two scholars sympathetic to Rand conclude, this attribution "misquotes Aristotle and misrepresents his intent." See Stephen Cox, "Ayn Rand: Theory versus Creative Life," *Journal of Libertarian Studies* 8 (1986): 20; Louis Torres and Michelle Marder Kamhi, *What Art Is: The Aesthetic Theory of Ayn Rand* (Chicago: Open Court Press, 2000), 63. An alternative interpretation of Rand's usage is given in Tore Boeckmann, "What Might Be and Ought to Be: Aristotle's Poetics and *The Fountainhead*," in *Essays on Ayn Rand's* The Fountainhead, ed. Robert Mayhew (Lanham, MD: Lexington Books, 2007). It appears that Rand drew this concept not from Aristotle, but from Albert Jay Nock. In *Memoirs of a Superfluous Man* (New York: Harper and Brothers, 1943), 191, Nock writes, "History, Aristotle says, represents things only as they are, while fiction represents them as they might be and ought to be." In her copy of the book, Rand marked this passage with six vertical lines. Peikoff Library Collection, ARA.

33. *Journals*, 263, 246–47; Isabel Paterson to AR, December 30, 1943, ARP 145-PA2; Isabel Paterson to AR, August 30, 1945, Box 4, Isabel Paterson Papers, Hoover Presidential Library, henceforth Hoover NARA.

34. *Journals*, 281.

35. "Notes on the Moral Basis of Individualism," July 9, 1945, ARP 32–11B. These notes are not included in the published version of Rand's *Journals*.

36. *Journals*, 291, 281, 285.

37. *Journals*, 305, 299. Daryll Wright traces a similar shift in "Ayn Rand's Ethics: From *The Fountainhead* to *Atlas Shrugged*," in *Essays on Ayn Rand's* Atlas Shrugged, ed. Robert Mayhew (Lanham, MD: Lexington Books, 2009).

38. B. Branden, *The Passion of Ayn Rand*, 189.

39. Frank Lloyd Wright to AR, April 23, 1944, reprinted in *Letters*, 112. Her comments on Wright are in *Journals*, April 12, 1946, 412–15. For more on their relationship, see Donald Leslie Johnson, *The Fountainheads: Wright, Rand, the FBI and Hollywood* (Jefferson, NC: McFarland, 2005).

40. Isabel Paterson to AR, December 15, 1943, Box 4, Hoover NARA.

41. Leonard Read to Rand, July 1946, ARP 146-RE2; Leonard Read to AR, May/June 46, ND, "Monday," ARP 146-RE2. There is no written record of their original agreement, but letters between the two indicate it was a well-established understanding. Rand signed her letters to Read "your ghost" and Read referred often to her responsibilities, urging her at one point, "Please keep on considering your ghost position seriously." Leonard Read to AR, July 22, 1946, ARP 146-RE2.

42. AR to Leonard Read, February 28, 1946, *Letters*, 259.

43. Leonard Read to AR, August 22, 1946, and Leonard Read to AR, March 4, 1946, ARP 146-RE2. Read explained that he could never get foundation status for an "individualist" foundation but could for one dedicated to economic education.

44. Milton Friedman and George Stigler, *Roofs or Ceilings?*, in *Verdict on Rent Control* (London: Institute of Economic Affairs, 1972), 18–32. Quote from Milton Friedman and Rose D. Friedman, *Two Lucky People: Memoirs* (Chicago: University of Chicago Press, 1998), 151.

45. AR to William Mullendore, September 20, 1946, *Letters,* 320–237.

46. AR to Leonard Read, September 12, 1946, *Letters,* 320; AR to Rose Wilder Lane, October 9, 1946, *Letters,* 332.

47. Friedman and Stigler both described the incident at length in their memoirs. See Friedman and Friedman, *Two Lucky People,* chapter 9; George Stigler, *Memoirs of an Unregulated Economist* (New York: Basic Books, 1988), chapter 10.

48. See Ayn Rand, "Textbook of Americanism," *The Vigil,* May 1946, 1, and *The Vigil,* June 1946, 2. The full "Textbook" appeared in the May, June, and July 1946 issues of *The Vigil.*

49. Of the thirteen responses Read received, four offered a complete endorsement, one a critical rejection, and the rest varied degrees of qualified endorsement. See "To Foundation Staff from L. E. R. Re. Textbook of Americanism," undated, and attached responses, ARP 146-RE3.

50. AR to Leonard Read, November 2, 1946; Leonard Read to AR, November 5, 1946; AR to Leonard Read, November 20, 1946; Leonard Read to AR, November 23, 1946, all in ARP 146-RE3.

51. See William Holtz, *Ghost in the Little House: A Life of Rose Wilder Lane* (Columbia: University of Missouri Press, 1993), especially 273–76, 379–85.

52. Richard Cornuelle, Oral History outtakes, ARP.

53. Rose Wilder Lane to AR, October 11, 1946, ARP 142-LAx.

54. AR to Rose Wilder Lane, November 30, 1945, *Letters,* 238; AR to Rose Wilder Lane, August 21, 1946, *Letters,* 307.

55. Rose Wilder Lane to AR, August 24, 1946, ARP 142-LAx.

56. Rose Wilder Lane to AR, October 11, 1946, ARP 142-LAx.

57. AR to Rose Wilder Lane, November 3, 1946, *Letters,* 343–50.

58. Rose Wilder Lane to AR, November 6, 1946, ARP 142-LAx.

59. AR to Rose Wilder Lane, December 1946, *Letters,* 353.

60. AR to Rose Wilder Lane, November 3, 1946, *Letters,* 350.

61. AR to Marie Strachnov, August 8, 1946, *Letters,* 302.

62. Ayn Rand, "Screen Guide for Americans," *Plain Talk,* November 1947, 37–42, reprinted in *Journals,* 356.

63. Ayn Rand, "Testimony before the House Un-American Activities Committee, October 20, 1947," *Journals,* 380. Contemporary reaction is in Joseph North, "Torquemada in Technicolor," *New Masses,* November 4, 1947; Garry Wills, introduction to Lillian Hellman, *Scoundrel Time* (Boston: Little Brown, 1976), 1–2. Rand's testimony is covered in Robert Mayhew, *Ayn Rand and* Song of Russia: *Communism and Anti-Communism in 1940s Hollywood* (Lanham, MD: Scarecrow Press, 2005).

64. Mayhew, *Ayn Rand and* Song of Russia, 379.

65. Rand's notes about her testimony are reprinted in *Journals,* 381–86. AR to Edna Lonigen, March 26, 1949, ARP 111-01D.

66. AR to Isabel Paterson, February 7, 1948, *Letters,* 189–90.

67. Isabel Paterson to AR, January 19, 1944. On another occasion she threatened, "to come out there in person and spank you to a blister" if Rand kept up her habit. Isabel Paterson to AR, June 7, 1944, ARP 145-PA4. See also Isabel Paterson to AR, November 30, 1943, and November 8, 1944, ARP 145-PA2.

68. Isabel Paterson to AR, November 8, 1944, Box 4, Hoover NARA.

69. Isabel Paterson to AR, February 29, 1944, Box 4, Hoover NARA.

70. AR to Isabel Paterson, July 26, 1946, *Letters,* 176.

71. Isabel Paterson to AR, July 30, 1945, ARP 145-PA4.

72. Isabel Paterson to AR, July 30, 1945, ARP 145-PA4

73. Isabel Paterson to AR, January 19, 1944, ARP 145-PA3

74. Isabel Paterson to AR, July 30, 1945, ARP 145-PA4.

75. AR to Isabel Paterson, August 4, 1945, *Letters,* 182, 184.

76. Isabel Paterson to AR, August 9, 1945, ARP 145-PA4.

77. Ibid.

78. AR to Robert Bremer, November 2, 1946, *Letters,* 339.

79. AR to Isabel Paterson, April 11, 1948, *Letters,* 205; Isabel Paterson to AR, April 7, 1948, ARP 145-PA7.

80. Isabel Paterson to AR, April 29, 1948, Box 4, Hoover NARA; AR to Isabel Paterson, May 8, 1948, *Letters,* 212.

81. Biographical Interview 14; Isabel Paterson to AR, undated, ARP 145-PA7. Taken as a whole, Paterson's chapter does not bear the stamp of Rand in any significant way. Her style of argument is dramatically different from Rand's, for she uses specific examples drawn from history, economics, and religious thought. Nor were Paterson's conclusions the same as Rand's. While criticizing humanitarianism for its unintended consequences, she does not reject traditional morality altogether: "Nor is it suggested that the virtues of good people are really not virtues." Isabel Paterson, *God of the Machine* (1943; New Brunswick, NJ: Transaction, 1993), 236. Instead she draws attention to the neglected importance of production and the distortions of modern, state-supported philanthropy. Steven Cox reaches similar conclusions about the plagiarism allegation in *The Woman and the Dynamo: Isabel Paterson and the Idea of America* (New Brunswick, NJ: Transaction, 2004), 306–12.

82. Isabel Paterson to AR, undated, ARP 145-PA7; AR to Isabel Paterson, May 17, 1948, *Letters,* 216.

83. Biographical Interview 15, March 31, 1961.

84. Ibid.; William Mullendore to AR, June 29, 1948, ARP 144-MFx.

85. AR to Isabel Paterson, May 17, 1948, *Letters,* 215; Biographical Interview 15; William F. Buckley Jr., "RIP, Mrs. Paterson (A Personal Reminiscence)," *National Review,* January 28, 1961, 43. In later years Rand would continue to recommend Paterson's *God of the Machine,* but she did not acknowledge her publicly as an important influence.

86. AR to Isabel Paterson, July 26, 1945, *Letters,* 179; AR to Isabel Paterson, February 28, 1948, *Letters,* 197.

Chapter 5

1. The film was moderately successful at the box office but received mixed reviews, including a negative review in the *New York Times*. Bosley Crowther, "In a Glass House," *New York Times*, July 17, 1949, X1; "Ayn Rand Replies to Criticism of Her Film," *New York Times*, July 24, 1949, X4. For academic analyses of the film, see Robert Spadoni, "Guilty by Omission: Girding the 'Fountainhead' for the Cold War (Ayn Rand)," *Literature-Film Quarterly* 27, no. 3 (1999): 223–32; Merrill Schleier, "Ayn Rand and King Vidor's Film *The Fountainhead*: Architectural Modernism, the Gendered Body, and Political Ideology," *Journal of The Society of Architectural Historians* 61, no. 3 (2002): 310–31; Merrill Schleier, *Skyscraper Cinema: Architecture and Gender in American Film* (Minneapolis: University of Minnesota Press, 2009). In addition to analyzing the gender dynamics of the film and book and their relation to architectural modernism, Schleier provides deep detail on Rand's creative process, but curiously suggests that Roark dynamited Cortland Homes with the intent of erecting a skyscraper in its place (vii). For more on the making of the film, see Jeff Britting, "Adapting the Fountainhead to Film," in *Essays on Ayn Rand's The Fountainhead*, ed. Robert Mayhew (Lanham, MD: Lexington Books, 2007); Barbara Branden, *The Passion of Ayn Rand* (Garden City, NY: Doubleday and Company, 1986), 208–13; Biographical Interview 12, January 22, 1961.

2. Biographical Interview 16, April 19, 1961.

3. Ruth Hill, Oral History, ARP; Jack Portnoy, Oral History, ARA.

4. Biographical Interview 17.

5. AR to Archie Ogden, April 10, 1949, *Letters,* 374; AR to Mimi Sutton, March 20, 1948, *Letters,* 391; AR to Archie Ogden, April 23, 1949, *Letters,* 438.

6. Biographical interview 17.

7. Ake and Jane Sandler, Oral History, ARP.

8. Micky Wright, Oral History, ARP.

9. Nathaniel Branden, *Judgment Day: My Years with Ayn Rand* (Boston: Houghton Mifflin, 1989), 51.

10. Barbara Branden, Objectivist History Project DVD, volume 2, "A Movement Is Launched." This CD is sold by an organization called The Objectivist Center, www.objectivistcenter.org.

11. Nathaniel Blumenthal and Barbara Weidman, letter to the editor, *UCLA Daily Bruin,* May 8, 1950, Box 117–06C, ARP.

12. The incident is described in N. Branden, *Judgment Day,* 94–96. The importance of Matthiessen to the literary left and the controversy surrounding his suicide is covered in Arthur Redding, "Closet, Coup, and Cold War: F. O. Matthiessen's *From the Heart of Europe,*" *boundary 2* 33, no. 1 (2006): 171–201.

13. Nathaniel Branden to AR, August 24, 1950, ARP 019–01B and August 28, 1951, ARP 019–01C.

14. AR to Nick Carter, October 5, 1944, *Letters,* 165.

15. Rose Wilder Lane to Jasper Crane, March 13, 1963, March–July 1963 Correspondence, Box 4, Hoover NARA; Rose Wilder Lane to AR, undated (Sunday), ARP 143-LO3.

16. Biographical Interview 16, April 19, 1961; William F. Buckley Jr., *God and Man At Yale* (1950; Washington, DC: Regnery, 1986), lxvi; George H. Nash, *The Conservative Intellectual Movement in America Since 1945* (New York: Basic Books, 1976). The centrality of Buckley and Chambers to midcentury conservatism is described in John B. Judis, *William F. Buckley, Jr.: Patron Saint of the Conservatives* (New York: Simon and Schuster, 1988); Sam Tanenhaus, *Whittaker Chambers: A Biography* (New York: Random House, 1997). For Neibuhr, see Richard Wightman Fox, *Reinhold Niebuhr: A Biography* (New York: Pantheon Books, 1985).

17. William F. Buckley Jr. to Isabel Paterson, January 7, 1958, "Paterson, Isabel (1958)," Box 6, William F. Buckley Papers, Yale University. Buckley repeated the anecdote (with slightly different spelling) in "On the Right: Ayn Rand, RIP," *National Review*, April 2, 1982, 380.

18. These debates are covered in Nash, *Conservative Intellectual Movement*; Jennifer Burns, "Liberals and the Conservative Imagination," in *Liberalism for a New Century*, ed. Neil Jumonville and Kevin Mattson (Berkeley: University of California Press, 2007).

19. Biographical Interview 17, April 19, 1961. Rand's perspective on forgiveness is explicated in Tara Smith, *Ayn Rand's Normative Ethics* (Cambridge: Cambridge University Press, 2006).

20. Biographical Interview 16.

21. Jörg Guido Hulsmann, *Mises: The Last Knight of Liberalism* (Auburn, AL: Ludwig Von Mises Institute, 2007), 850–51.

22. Biographical Interview 16.

23. The incident is related in Hulsmann, *Mises*, 1002. Hazlitt was upset that Kirk repeated the story and chided him in a letter for spreading falsehoods. Henry Hazlitt to Russell Kirk, July 5, 1962. Kirk, Russell, S25, F1,0/1–5, Ludwig von Mises Papers, Mises Institute, Auburn, AL.

24. Biographical Interview 16.

25. *Ayn Rand's Marginalia*, 116, 142; Sylvester Petro, Oral History ARP.

26. My discussion of Mises's thought draws on Israel M. Kirzner, *Ludwig von Mises: The Man and His Economics* (Wilmington, DE: ISI Books, 2001); Eamonn Butler, *Ludwig von Mises: Fountainhead of the Modern Microeconomics Revolution* (Brookfield, VT: Gower, 1988); Karen Iversen Vaughn, *Austrian Economics in America: The Migration of a Tradition* (Cambridge: Cambridge University Press, 1994); Hulsmann, *Mises*.

27. "Issues: The Unsacrificial Self," undated notes, ARP 033–19A.

28. Moreover, Mises continued, monopoly prices, should they ever arise, were not necessarily harmful. If manufacturers restricted the production of monopoly goods, that meant resources were freed for other production. Hulsmann, *Mises*, 431–36.

29. Richard Cornuelle, Oral History, ARP. Cornuelle went on to author *Reclaiming the American Dream: The Role of Private Individuals and Voluntary Associations* (New York, Random House, 1965). Rothbard's background and career are described in Justin Raimondo, *An Enemy of the State: The Life of Murray N. Rothbard* (Amherst, NY: Prometheus Books, 2000).

30. Murray Rothbard, "Two Walters Interview Transcript," Rothbard Papers, Ludwig von Mises Institute, Auburn, AL.

31. Rothbard to AR, October 3, 1957, "Letters 1957 July–December," Rothbard Papers.

32. William F. Buckley Jr., "Reflections on Election Eve," *National Review*, November 3, 1956.

33. Biographical Interview 16.

34. Ibid.

35. Barbara's and Nathan's name change has generated almost as much mythology as Rand's. Both explain the change as simply a matter of aesthetic preference, rejecting the rumor that Branden is of Hebrew derivation ("ben Rand") or was deliberately chosen to incorporate Rand's name.

36. Robert Hessen, interview with author, December 11, 2007.

37. *Journals*, 610.

38. Edward Purcell, *The Crisis of Democratic Theory: Scientific Naturalism and the Problem of Value* (Lexington: University of Kentucky Press, 1973).

39. *Journals*, 481.

40. Rand's usage of Benzedrine in the 1940s is well documented, and according to several sources, she continued to take a similar prescription on a daily basis until the 1970s. See *Passion of Ayn Rand*, 173, and Anne Heller, *Ayn Rand and the World She Made* (New York: Doubleday, 2009), 304–305.

41. ARC, 03–58; Leonard Peikoff, Oral History Interview, ARP; Mike Wallace, Oral History Interview, ARP.

42. Alan Greenspan, *The Age of Turbulence: Adventures in a New World* (New York, Penguin, 2007), 41. Contrary to Justin Martin in *Greenspan: The Man behind the Money* (Cambridge, MA: Perseus, 2000) and Jerome Tuccille in *Alan Shrugged: Alan Greenspan, the World's Most Powerful Banker* (New York: Wiley, 2002), both of whom portray Nathaniel Branden as playing a major role, Greenspan remembers Rand herself as the most influential in establishing his relationship with Objectivism. Greenspan, personal communication to author, February 27, 2009. Hiram Haydn, *Words and Faces* (New York: Harcourt College, 1973), 259.

43. Greenspan, *The Age of Turbulence*, 53. Justin Martin, *Greenspan*, 45. The impact of Arthur Burns on Greenspan is described in Tuccille and Justin Martin, *Greenspan*.

44. Author interview with Martin Anderson, January 1, 2008.

45. Leonard Peikoff, "My Thirty Years with Ayn Rand: An Intellectual Memoir," *The Objectivist Forum*, June 1987, 2; Sylvester Petro, Oral History ARP.

46. Murray Rothbard to Richard Cornuelle, August 11, 1954, Rothbard Papers.

47. Murray Rothbard to AR, October 8, 1957, Rothbard Papers.

48. Ibid.

49. Ibid.

50. Richard Cornuelle, Oral History, ARP.

51. N. Branden, *Judgment Day*, 129.

52. Robert Hessen, interview with author, December 11, 2007.

53. Ibid., 116.

54. Frank is described as an alcoholic in his later years by Barbara Branden, *The Passion of Ayn Rand,* 272–73, 339, 366, 384, and Nathaniel Branden, *My Years with Ayn Rand,* 330, but this claim has been vigorously disputed by James Valliant in *The Passion of Ayn Rand's Critics* (Dallas, TX: Durban House, 2005), 141–47. The dispute boils down to the reliability of sources whom the Brandens cite as witnesses to Frank's drinking habits. Firm diagnoses of the dead are always tenuous, but given Frank's family history, the pressures he was under, and the testimony of observers, it is not unreasonable to conclude that Frank's use of alcohol was, at the very least, unhealthy. Anne Heller reaches a similar conclusion in *Ayn Rand and the World She Made,* 494.

55. Rand, *Atlas Shrugged,* 939. Allan Gotthelf provides a helpful breakdown of the speech in "Galt's Speech in Five Sentences (and 40 Questions)," in *Essays on Ayn Rand's* Atlas Shrugged, ed. Robert Mayhew (Lanham, MD: Lexington Books, 2009).

56. Biographical Interview 17.

57. *Journals,* 480.

58. After *Atlas Shrugged* was published Rand did write fragmentary notes for one additional novel, entitled *To Lorne Dieterling.* More a therapeutic exercise than a serious attempt at another book, *To Lorne Dieterling* was to feature a female hero struggling to retain a sense of joy against a hostile world. *Journals,* 706–715, 913–927.

59. *Journals,* 673.

60. Biographical Interview 18, April 25, 1961; Hiram Haydn, *Words and Faces* (New York: Harcourt College, 1974), 260–61; Bennett Cerf, *At Random* (New York: Random House, 1977), 249–50. Rand's account differs from Haydn's in several specific details, mostly on how actively Random House sought her as an author. I draw primarily on Rand's account since it was recorded closer in time to the actual events and because Rand was privy to negotiations with her agent and Haydn was not.

61. Mickey Wright, Oral History, ARP.

Chapter 6

1. Robert Hessen, interview with author, December 7, 2007.

2. "The Solid Gold Dollar Sign," *Time,* October 14, 1957, 128. A prime example of a reviewer having fun at Rand's expense is Donald Malcolm, "The New Rand Atlas," *The New Yorker,* October 26, 1957, 194. There were a few exceptions to the generally negative assessment of *Atlas Shrugged,* mostly from right-leaning publications. See Paul Jordan-Smith, "Ideas Fill New Work, but Still It's a Novel," *Los Angeles Times,* October 6, 1957, E7; John Chamberlain, "A Reviewer's Notebook: Atlas Shrugged," *The Freeman,* December 1957, 53–56, M. E. Davis, "Reading for Pleasure: Creeping Collapse," *Wall Street Journal,* October 10, 1957; Richard McLaughlin, "The Lady Has a Message…," *American Mercury,* January 1958, 144–46.

3. Ayn Rand, *Atlas Shrugged,* 35th anniversary ed. (1957; New York: Penguin, 1992), 429. Subsequent citations are referenced in the text.

4. R. M. Lynch, Standard Slag Company, Youngstown, OH, to AR November 20, 1957, box 098–03C, ARP.

5. This theme is developed further in Andrew Hoberek, *The Twilight of the Middle Class: Post–World War II American Fiction and White-Collar Work* (Princeton, NJ:

Princeton University Press, 2005); Joseph Colin McNicholas, "Corporate Culture and the American Novel: Producers, Persuaders, and Communicators," PhD diss., University of Texas at Austin, 1999.

6. Clement Williamson, "Dear Friend," letter accompanying "Faith and Force" reprint, October 10, 1960, ARP 105–12A.

7. Algird C. Pocius to New American Library, January 5, 1966, ARP 002–05C. The speech was also reprinted by CF&I Steel Corporation, Management Newsletter, no. 169, July 1966; in the *Cleveland Plain Dealer,* October 1, 1960 by Shaker Savings Association; in a pamphlet distributed by Shaker Savings Association, ARP 083–28x.

8. C. W. Anderson, memo to IRG executives, October 31, 1961, ARP 09–11x.

9. Clement Williamson to AR, September 9, 1960, ARP 105–12A.

10. C. W. Anderson to AR, October 2, 1961, ARP 042–02A; R. J. Duncan to AR, May 9, 1961, ARP 108–24A; Joseph Moran to AR, April 30, 1962, ARP 108–24B; AR to John Sullivan, May 18, 1962, 108–24A. The two professors were Clarence Walton and Richard Eels. Rand addressed the class in 1961. Richard Eels to AR, July 12, 1961, ARP 108–24C. The symposium was intended to address issues raised by William H. Whyte's *The Organization Man.* Rand's response to the question "What is or should be the nature of the 'faith' subscribed to by modern management?" anticipated her essay "For the New Intellectual." Ayn Rand, "A Faith for Modern Management," *Atlanta Economic Review* 8, no. 9 (1958): 1.

11. Granville Hicks, "A Parable of Buried Talents," *New York Times Book Review,* October 26, 1957, 4–5. The *Times'* positive review of *The Fountainhead* is by Lorine Pruette, "The Battle against Evil," *New York Times Book Review,* May 16, 1943, 7, 18. Helen Beal Woodward, "*Atlas Shrugged,*" *Saturday Review,* October 12, 1957, 25.

12. Biographical Interview 17, April 19, 1961.

13. On his reluctance to write the review, see Whittaker Chambers to Murray Rothbard, August 25, 1958, "Letters 1958 July–Dec," Rothbard Papers, Mises Institute. Chambers's worldview is described in Sam Tanenhous, *Whittaker Chambers: A Biography* (New York: Random House, 1997); Michael Kimmage, *The Conservative Turn: Lionel Trilling, Whittaker Chambers, and the Lessons of Anti-Communism* (Cambridge, MA: Harvard University Press 2009). I give a fuller treatment of Chambers's review in Jennifer Burns, "Godless Capitalism: Ayn Rand and the Conservatives," *Modern Intellectual History* 1, no. 3 (2004): 1–27.

14. Whittaker Chambers, "Big Sister Is Watching You," *National Review,* December 28, 1957, 596.

15. Ibid., 594.

16. See "Letters to the Editor," *National Review,* January 18, 1958, 71.

17. John Chamberlain, "Reviewer's Notebook: *Atlas Shrugged,*" *National Review,* January 18, 1958. See Isabel Paterson to William F. Buckley Jr., January 2, 1958, "Paterson, Isabel (1958)," Box 6, William F. Buckley, Jr., Papers, Yale University Library.

18. John Chamberlain, "To the Editor: An Open Letter to Ayn Rand," *National Review,* February 1, 1958, 118. Murray Rothbard also took Rand's side in the ensuing exchange of letters. See Rothbard, "To the Editor," *National Review,* January 25, 1968, 95.

19. In addition to the letter, Mullendore wrote two lengthy memos analyzing *Atlas Shrugged* of six and five pages each, dated September 15, 1957 and October 12, 1957, respectively. "Dearest Carla and Louis," September 22, 1957, Mullendore Papers, "Rand,

Ayn," Box 23, Herbert Hoover Presidential Library, West Branch, IA; Sidney Krupicka, "Letter to the Editor," *National Review,* February 13, 1960, 117; Jim Kolb, "Letter to the Editor," *National Review,* February 1, 1958, 119; Kevin Coughlin, "Letter to the Editor," *National Review,* February 1, 1958, 119.

20. Ludwig von Mises to AR, February 23, 1958, quoted in Jörg Guido Hulsmann, *Mises: The Last Knight of Liberalism* (Auburn, AL: Ludwig Von Mises Institute, 2007), 996.

21. Robert LeFevre to Rose Wilder Lane, January 10, 1958, and Rose Wilder Lane to Robert LeFevre, December 26, 1957, both in Box 27, Lane Papers, Herbert Hoover Presidential Library, West Branch, IA.

22. Even hostile reviewers tended to admit that Friedman's book was valuable food for thought. Most reviews were published in scholarly journals, which were less likely to employ ad hominen attacks than the mass-market magazines that reviewed *Atlas Shrugged.* The only popular magazine to review *Capitalism and Freedom* was *The Economist,* which gave it a largely positive review. "A Tract for the Times," *The Economist,* February 16, 1963. Other representative reviews include Abba P. Lerner, "Capitalism and Freedom," *American Economic Review* 53, no. 3 (1963): 458–60; F. X. Sutton, "Capitalism and Freedom," *American Sociological Review* 28, no. 3 (1963): 491–92. A negative review is Oscar Handlin, "Capitalism and Freedom," *Business History Review* 37, no. 3 (1963), 315–16. Friedman, who never met Rand, appreciated her work, calling her "an utterly intolerant and dogmatic person who did a great deal of good." Brian Doherty, "Best of Both Worlds: Milton Friedman Reminisces," *Reason,* June 1995, 32–38.

23. Daniel Bell, *The End of Ideology: On the Exhaustion of Political Ideas in the Fifties* (New York: Free Press, 1960); Morton White, *Social Thought in America: The Revolt against Formalism* (New York: Viking, 1949). Nor were they looking for an uncritical perspective on capitalism, with some even envisioning the future as a postcapitalist world. Howard Brick, *Transcending Capitalism: Visions of a New Society in Modern American Thought* (Ithaca, NY: Cornell University Press, 2006); Nelson Lichtenstein, ed., *American Capitalism: Social Thought and Political Economy in the Twentieth Century* (Philadelphia: University of Pennsylvania Press, 2006).

24. Kathleen and Richard Nickerson, Oral History, ARP. Rand's classes formed the basis of Ayn Rand, *The Art of Fiction: A Guide for Writers and Readers* (New York: Plume, 2001).

25. Nathaniel Branden, *Judgment Day: My Years with Ayn Rand* (Boston: Houghton Mifflin, 1989), 263.

26. Ibid., 264.

27. Murray Rothbard to AR, October 3, 1957, Letters 1957, July–Dec, Rothbard Papers, Ludwig von Mises Institute.

28. Murray Rothbard to Kenneth S. Templeton, November 18, 1957, Letters 1957, July–Dec, Rothbard Papers.

29. Murray Rothbard to "Mom and Pop," Friday afternoon 5:30, Rothbard Papers.

30. Details are taken from an interview with Robert Hessen, December 7, 2007; Murray Rothbard to "Mom and Pop," July 23, 1958, Wed night 8:30 pm, Rothbard Papers. The paper was eventually published. Murray N. Rothbard, "The Mantle of Science," in *Scientism and Values,* ed. Helmut Schoeck and James W. Wiggins (New York: D. Van Nostrand, 1960), 159–180.

31. Murray Rothbard to "Mom and Pop," Friday afternoon, 5:30, Rothbard Papers; Murray Rothbard to Whittaker Chambers, August 25, 1958, Letters 1958 Jul–Dec, Rothbard Papers. This episode is also described in Justin Raimondo, *An Enemy of the State: The Life of Murray N. Rothbard* (Amherst, NY: Prometheus Books, 2000); Murray Rothbard, "Mozart Was a Red," available at www.lewrockwell.com/rothbard/mozart.html [February 19, 2009]; Murray Rothbard, "The Sociology of the Ayn Rand Cult," available at www.lewrockwell.com/rothbard/rothbard23.html [February 28, 2009].

32. Sidney Hook to Barbara Branden, April 6, 1984, Box 154, Sidney Hook Papers, Hoover Institution, Stanford University.

33. See Brand Blanshard to AR, February 4, 1965, AR to Brand Blanshard, March 4, 1965, and Brand Blanshard to AR, May 28, 1967, ARP 100–12A.

34. John Hospers to AR, January 9, 1961, ARP 141-HO3.

35. John Hospers, "A Memory of Ayn Rand," *Full Context*, March/April 2001, 5.

36. Biographical Interview 17.

37. Martin Lean to AR, October 31, 1960, ARP 001–01A.

38. AR to Martin Lean, November 30, 1961, ARP 001–01A.

39. Martin Lean to AR, October 31, 1960, ARP 001–01A.

40. Hospers, "A Memory of Ayn Rand," 6.

41. John Hospers, *An Introduction to Philosophical Analysis*, 2nd ed. (Englewood Cliffs, NJ: Prentice-Hall, 1967), 591–94, 602–3; John Hospers to Nathaniel Branden, June 25, 1965, ARP 141-HO3. A selection of Rand's and Hospers's correspondence is published in *Letters*, 502–63. The existentialist philosopher Hazel Barnes was less impressed with Rand, calling Objectivism "based on wish fulfillment." Barnes, *An Existentialist Ethics* (New York: Knopf, 1967), 149.

42. Rand claimed that the changes were only cosmetic, but they fell into two substantive categories: she rewrote the sex scenes to make male characters dominant over female characters, and she reworked all passages that demonstrated her earlier interest in Nietzsche. For a close examination of these changes, see Robert Mayhew, "*We the Living:* '36 and '59," in *Essays on Ayn Rand's* We the Living, ed. Robert Mayhew (Lanham, MD: Lexington Books, 2004).

Chapter 7

1. Nathaniel Branden, *Judgment Day: My Years with Ayn Rand* (Boston: Houghton Mifflin, 1989), 314.

2. Rand's popularity underscores new scholarly understandings of the 1960s, an era now characterized by both conservative and liberal politics and activism, particularly among youth. See Rebecca E. Klatch, *A Generation Divided: The New Left, the New Right, and the 1960s* (Berkeley: University of California Press, 1999); John A. Andrew III, *The Other Side of the Sixties: Young Americans for Freedom and the Rise of Conservative Politics* (New Brunswick, NJ: Rutgers University Press, 1997); Gregory L. Schneider, *Cadres for Conservatism: Young Americans for Freedom and the Rise of the Contemporary Right* (New York: New York University Press, 1999). Other books that incorporate this sense of the 1960s as a politically divided time are Mary C. Brennan, *Turning Right in the*

Sixties: the Conservative Capture of the GOP (Chapel Hill: University of North Carolina Press, 1995), 1; Maurice Isserman and Michael Kazin, *America Divided: the Civil War of the 1960s* (New York: Oxford University Press, 2000), 206; David Farber and Jeff Roche, *The Conservative Sixties* (New York: Peter Lang, 2003), 2–3; Rick Perlstein, *Before the Storm: Barry Goldwater and the Unmaking of the American Consensus* (New York: Hill and Wang, 2001).

3. See Alex McDonald, introduction to Edward Bellamy, *Looking Backward 2000–1887*, ed. Alex McDonald (Ontario: Broadview Literary Texts, 2003).

4. Barry Goldwater to AR, May 11, 1960, ARP 043–05A, and AR to Barry Goldwater, June 4, 1960, ARP 043–05A, *Letters*, 565–72.

5. Barry Goldwater to AR, June 10, 1960, ARP 043–05A.

6. Ayn Rand, "JFK: High Class Beatnik," *Human Events*, September 1, 1960, 393.

7. There was also the class that Rand frankly called "human ballast," who mindlessly followed whichever of the three was ascendant. Ayn Rand, *For the New Intellectual* (New York: New American Library, 1961), 20.

8. *Webster's Third New International Dictionary of English Language, Unabridged* defines "altruism" as "uncalculated consideration of, regard for, or devotion to others' interests sometimes in accordance with an ethical principle." Rand's use of Comte's definition is debated in Robert L. Campbell, "Altruism in Auguste Comte and Ayn Rand," and Robert H. Bass, "Egoism versus Rights," *Journal of Ayn Rand Studies* 7, no. 2 (2006): 357–69.

9. Rand, *For the New Intellectual*, 11, 45.

10. Sidney Hook, "Each Man for Himself," *New York Times Book Review*, April 9, 1961, 3, 28. Other negative reviews of *For the New Intellectual* are Charles Frederick Schroder, "Ayn Rand: Far Right Prophetess," *Christian Century*, December 13, 1961,1493–95; James Collins, "State of the Question: Ayn Rand's Talent for Getting Headlines," *America*, July 29, 1961, 569; "Born Eccentric," *Newsweek*, March 27, 1961, 104; Joel Rosenblum, "The Ends and Means of Ayn Rand," *New Republic*, April 24, 1961, 28–29; Bruce Goldberg, "Ayn Rand's *For the New Intellectual*," *New Individualist Review*, November 1961, 17–24. *For the New Intellectual* went through five hardcover editions in the first year and was issued in a first paperback printing of two hundred thousand.

11. Gore Vidal, "Two Immoralists: Orville Prescott and Ayn Rand," in *Rocking the Boat* (Boston: Little, Brown, 1962), 232, reprinted from *Esquire*, July 1961.

12. Daniel Bell ed., *The New American Right* (New York: Criterion, 1955) and *The Radical Right*, 3rd ed. (1963; New Brunswick, NJ: Transaction, 2002). Once dominant, this interpretation is now universally acknowledged to reveal more about the views of midcentury liberal historians than the conservatives they analyzed. See Michael Paul Rogin, *The Intellectuals and McCarthy: The Radical Specter* (Cambridge, MA: MIT Press, 1967); Alan Brinkley, "The Problem of American Conservatism," *American Historical Review* 99, no. 2 (1994): 409–29.

13. The centrality of the rebel identity to postwar society, and conservatism specifically, is explored in Grace Hale, *Rebel, Rebel: Why We Love Outsiders and the Effects of This Romance on Postwar American Culture and Politics* (New York: Oxford University

Press, 2009); Kevin Mattson, *Rebels All! A Short History of the Conservative Mind in Postwar America* (Piscataway, NJ: Rutgers University Press, 2008).

14. Rand found the weekly column time-consuming, and syndicated sales were poor. Rex Barley to AR, December 14, 1962, ARP 045–11A. Rand's articles are collected and published under different titles in Ayn Rand, *The Ayn Rand Column,* ed. Peter Schwartz (Occanside, CA: Second Renaissance Books, 1991).

15. Ayn Rand, "Check Your Premises," *The Objectivist Newsletter* 1, no. 1 (1962): 1.

16. Edith Efron, "The Feminine Mystique," *The Objectivist Newsletter* 2, no. 7 (1963): 26.

17. Al Ramus, Oral History, ARP. Edith Efron later became a conservative journalist who focused on media bias. Efron, *The News Twisters* (Los Angeles: Nash, 1971). She was also a ghostwriter for Treasury Secretary William Simon, *A Time for Truth* (New York: Reader's Digest Press, 1978). Rand's interviews for the Columbia radio program are reproduced in Ayn Rand, *Objectively Speaking: Ayn Rand Interviewed,* ed. Marlene Podritske and Peter Schwartz (New York: Lexington Books, 2009). AR to Hugh Hefner, March 14, 1964, ARP 060–14A.

18. Mike Wallace, Oral History, ARP; Frederick Feingersh, Oral History, ARP.

19. Ed Barthelmes to Bob Parker, Time, Inc., mimeographed stringer report, February 18, 1960, Box 6, Isabel Paterson Papers, Hoover Presidential Library, West Branch, IA.

20. Some examples of Rand's influence on college syllabi: Rand's essay "Faith and Force" was reprinted in William M. Jones, *Stages of Composition: A College Reader* (Boston: D. C. Heath, 1964); see Eleanor Morris to AR, May 15, 1964, ARP 001–04A. *Atlas Shrugged* was assigned as a term paper topic in Rhetoric 102 at the University of Illinois at Navy Pier, spring 1960, syllabus, Rhetoric 102, ARP 006–02E. Her work was assigned in social and political philosophy classes at the University of Colorado in 1964; see John Nelson to AR, April 2, 1964, ARP 100–13B. In 1965 Leonard Peikoff conducted a graduate seminar at the University of Denver, "The Objectivist Theory of Knowledge."

21. Karen Reedstrom, "Interview with Murray Franck," *Full Context,* June 1992, 3; Whit Hancock to AR, April 9, 1966, ARP 040–07C; Karen Reedstrom, "Interview with Walter Donway," *Full Context,* May 1992, 3.

22. See Hilary Putnam, "A Half Century of Philosophy," and Alexander Nehamas, "Trends in Recent American Philosophy," in *American Academic Culture in Transformation: Fifty Years, Four Disciplines,* ed. Thomas Bender and Carl E. Schorske (Princeton, NJ: Princeton University Press, 1997). Rand's willingness to address a general audience and popularize her concerns marked a return to an earlier ideal of the discipline, what Bruce Kucklick calls "American public philosophy." Kucklick, *The Rise of American Philosophy* (New Haven, CT: Yale University Press, 1977), xxiii.

23. Karen Minto and David Oyerly, "Interview with Tom Bethell," *Full Context,* January/February 1999, 1.

24. Michael McElwee to AR, August 24, 1965, ARP 039–07A.

25. Ayn Rand, "The Girl Hunters," *The Objectivist Newsletter* 1, no. 10 (1962), 42. This article also ran as a column in the *Los Angeles Times.*

26. Karen Reedstrom, "Interview with Mark Scott," *Full Context*, March 1990, 3; Robert L. White, "Ayn Rand—Hipster on the Right," *New University Thought*, August 1962, 65.

27. Joe E. Prewitt to AR, May 31, 1967, ARP 005–18A; John Gelski to AR, September 8, 1964, ARP 039–06C; Sharon Presley quoted in Klatch, *A Generation Divided*, 70.

28. Arthur Koestler, chapter 1 in Richard Crossman, Louis Fischer, Andre Gide, Arthur Koestler, Silone Ignazio, Stephen Spender, and Richard Wright, *The God That Failed: Six Studies in Communism* (London: Hamish Hamilton, 1950), 32; Charlotte Hering to AR, July 27, 1964, ARP 039–06D.

29. Edward Cain, *They'd Rather Be Right: Youth and the Conservative Movement* (New York: Macmillan, 1963), 48.

30. Reedstrom, "Interview with Walter Donway," 3.

31. Michael McElwee to AR, August 24, 1965, ARP 039–07A.

32. Nathaniel Branden, "Report to Our Readers," *The Objectivist Newsletter* 2, no. 12. (1963): 48; Nora Ephron, "A Strange Kind of Simplicity," *New York Times Book Review*, May 5, 1968, 8; Lilo K. Luxembourg to Sidney Hook, April 9, 1961, Sidney Hook Papers, Box 154, "Ayn Rand," Hoover Institution Archives, Stanford University.

33. White, "Ayn Rand—Hipster on the Right," 71.

34. "A Survey of the Political and Religious Attitudes of American College Students," *National Review*, October 8, 1963, special supplement. There are no extant studies of Objectivist youth, but it is likely they shared some characteristics with conservative youth more broadly, who have been identified as being slightly below the norm for income of college students as a whole, with a significant gap between them and students on the left, who tend to come from more affluent backgrounds. See Riley Dunlap, "Radical and Conservative Student Activists: A Comparison of Family Background," *Pacific Sociological Review*, 13 (summer 1970): 171–80; David Westby and Richard Braungart, "Class and Politics in the Family Backgrounds of Student Political Activists," *American Sociological Review* 31 (1996): 690–92. Religious upbringing and family background were the most important factors in determining political orientation, researchers have found. Klatch, *A Generation Divided*; Margaret M. Braungart and Richard Braungart, "The Life Course Development of Left and Right Wing Student Activist Leaders for the 1960s," *Political Psychology* 2 (1990): 243–82.

35. For Rand's influence on YAF, see Andrew, *The Other Side of the '60s*, 61–62, 106–7; Schneider, *Cadres for Conservatism*, 156. Robert Schuchman to AR, October 15, 1959, ARP 105–12D.

36. Karl Hess, *Mostly on the Edge: An Autobiography* (Amherst, NY: Prometheus Books, 1999), 207; Tibor Machan to AR, undated letter circa 1962, ARP 020–02A. In addition to publishing widely on libertarianism, Machan later became one of the founding partners of *Reason* magazine. His involvement with Rand is described in Machan, *The Man without a Hobby: Adventures of a Gregarious Egoist* (Lanham, MD: Hamilton Books, 2004). Craig Howell to AR, March 26, 1966, ARP 040–07D.

37. Goldwater's campaign is now recognized as a formative moment in the history of the conservative movement. See Perlstein, *Before the Storm;* Lisa McGirr, *Suburban Warriors: The Origins of the New American Right* (Princeton, NJ: Princeton University

Press, 2001); Brian Doherty, *Radicals for Capitalism: A Freewheeling History of the Modern American Libertarian Movement* (New York: Public Affairs, 2007).

38. Ayn Rand, "A Suggestion," *The Objectivist Newsletter* 2, no. 10 (1963): 40. On Rand's hopes for involvement with the campaign in both 1960 and 1964, see Muriel Hall to Nathaniel Branden, June 11, 1960, ARP 040–07D; Barry Goldwater to Herbert Baus, August 14, 1964, ARP 044–05D.

39. Elayne Kalberman to AR, May 7, 1964, ARP 060–17x; Nathaniel Branden, "A Report to Our Readers," *The Objectivist Newsletter* 3, no. 12 (1964): 51.

40. Goldwater quoted in Perlstein, *Before the Storm,* 234. Washington Draft Goldwater committee, chairman, Luke Williams, November 4, 1963, to Signet Books, ARP 043–05A.

41. Jerome Tuccille, *It Usually Begins with Ayn Rand* (New York: Stein and Day, 1971), 39, 37; William Minto and Karen Minto, "Interview with Robert Poole," *Full Context,* May/June 1999, 1; Paul Richard, "Writer Rests His Pen, Turns to Blowtorch," *Washington Post,* November 21, 1967, B3; "Echoes and Choices," *Washington Star,* September 3, 1964, A10.

42. Ayn Rand, "Check Your Premises: Racism," *The Objectivist Newsletter* 2, no. 9 (1963), 35. Rand's views may be taken as an early iteration of a race-neutral discourse about individual rights that nonetheless had important consequences for federal and state racial policy, particularly in suburbia. Books that explore the discourse surrounding racial issues include Matthew Lassiter, *The Silent Majority: Suburban Politics in the Sunbelt South* (Princeton, NJ: Princeton University Press, 2006); Kevin Kruse, *White Flight: Atlanta and the Making of Modern Conservatism* (Princeton, NJ: Princeton University Press, 2007); Donald T. Critchlow and Nancy MacLean, *Debating the American Conservative Movement: 1945 to the Present* (New York: Rowman and Littlefield, 2009).

43. For details on the JBS, see Donald T. Critchlow, *The Conservative Ascendancy: How the GOP Right Made Political History* (Cambridge, MA: Harvard University Press, 2007), 56–59; Jonathan M. Schoenwald, *A Time for Choosing: The Rise of Modern American Conservatism* (New York: Oxford University Press, 2001), especially 78–93; Eckard V. Toy Jr., "The Right Side of the 1960s: The Origins of the John Birch Society in the Pacific Northwest," *Oregon Historical Quarterly* 105, no. 2 (2004), 260–283.

44. Ayn Rand, "'Extremism' or the Art of Smearing," *The Objectivist Newsletter* 3, no. 9 (1964): 38; D. A. Waite to Mrs. Theodore J. Truske, April 30, 1964, box 7, folder "64," JBS Files John Hay Library, Brown University.

45. Rand, "Extremism," 37.

46. Rand's postmortem of the campaign is in Ayn Rand, "It Is Earlier Than You Think," *The Objectivist Newsletter* 3, no. 12 (1964): 50. Rand's warning about Goldwater's loss is found in Ayn Rand, "Special Note," *The Objectivist Newsletter* 3, no. 10 (1964), 44. Rand sent her speech to Michael D. Gill of Citizens for Goldwater-Miller, with the instruction that either Goldwater or Eisenhower could use it. AR to Michael D. Gill, October 28, 1964, ARP 043–05A.

47. Goldwater's success was once understood to have inspired Richard Nixon's Southern Strategy, first articulated in Kevin Phillips, *The Emerging Republican Majority* (New Rochelle, NY: Arlington House, 1969), but the importance of the Southern Strategy

has been questioned by Matthew Lassiter, who suggests it is better understood as a suburban strategy (Lassiter, *The Silent Majority: Suburban Politics in the Sunbelt South*). Byron Schafer and Richard Johnston, *The End of Southern Exceptionalism: Class, Race, and Partisan Change in the Postwar South* (Cambridge, MA: Harvard University Press, 2007), make a similar argument. Other books that engage this critical question include Kruse, *White Flight*, 252–55; Thomas B. Edsell and Mary Edsell, *Chain Reaction: The Impact of Race, Rights, and Taxes on American Politics* (New York: Norton, 1991); Jason Sokol, *There Goes My Everything: White Southerners in the Age of Civil Rights 1945–1975* (New York: Knopf, 2006), 272–75; Dan Carter, *The Politics of Rage: George Wallace, The Origins of the New Conservatism, and The Transformation of American Politics* (Baton Rouge: Louisiana State University Press, 2000); Michael Flamm, *Law and Order: Street Crime, Civil Unrest, and the Crisis of Liberalism in the 1960s* (New York: Columbia University Press, 2005); Joseph Lowndes, *From the New Deal to the New Right: Race and the Southern Origins of Modern Conservatism* (New Haven, CT: Yale University Press, 2008); Joseph Crespino, *In Search of Another Country: Mississippi and Conservative Counterrevolution* (Princeton, NJ: Princeton University Press, 2007); Rick Perlstein, *Nixonland: The Rise of a President and the Fracturing of America* (New York: Scribner, 2008).

48. Murray Seeger, "Hope Still Found for Conservatism," *New York Times*, November 5, 1964, 20.

49. Barry Goldwater, "For a Free Society," *Herald Tribune*, June 20, 1965, 8. This reference is from Rand, "It Is Earlier Than You Think."

50. Rand, "It Is Earlier Than You Think," 50.

51. Michael P. Lecovk to AR, February 7, 1965, ARP 040–07F.

52. Milton Friedman with Rose Friedman, *Capitalism and Freedom* (Chicago: University of Chicago Press, 1962), 1.

53. See Bennett Cerf to AR, October 18, 1963, AR to Bennett Cerf, October 30, 1963, Bennett Cerf to AR November 1, 1963, November 22, 1963, and February 7, 1964, ARP 131–10B. Bennett Cerf to Elayne Kalberman, January 14, 1966, ARP 131–10C. Cerf described his relationship with Rand in *At Random: The Reminiscences of Bennett Cerf* (New York: Random House, 1977).

54. Ayn Rand, "The Objectivist Ethics," speech delivered to University of Wisconsin Symposium, "Ethics in Our Time," January 9, 1961, reprinted in *The Virtue Of Selfishness* (New York: Signet, 1964), 34.

55. Rand, *Virtue of Selfishness*, 114.

56. Rand, "For the New Intellectual," in *For the New Intellectual*, 55.

57. See, for example, Ayn Rand, *Capitalism: The Unknown Ideal* (New York: Penguin, 1967), 48, 216; Rand, *For the New Intellectual*, 43. "At the point of a gun" was a favorite libertarian catchphrase. Ludwig von Mises used it to describe collective bargaining. Mises quoted in Kimberly Phillips-Fein, *Invisible Hands: The Making of the Conservative Movement from the New Deal to Reagan* (New York: Norton, 2009), 105. It is unclear if Mises and Rand arrived at the phrase independently or if one learned it from the other.

58. Rand, *The Virtue of Selfishness*, 137, 131.

59. "Objectivist Calendar," *The Objectivist Newsletter*, April 1965, 18. Hessen, interview with author, December 11, 2007.

Chapter 8

1. Adriana Slifka, "Ayn Rand Pulls TV Mail," *Youngstown Vindicator,* December 19, 1967, ARP 006–4A; Edward Kuhn, New American Library, to AR, February 28, 1968, ARP 088–02A.

2. Turner Advertising Company erected the billboards in January 1967 in seven major southern cities: Atlanta (80 billboards), Covington, Kentucky (20), Charleston (24), Chattanooga (32), Richmond (40), and Roanoke (20). The cost was approximately eight thousand dollars, paid by Turner himself. "It's Message in Question on Rebirth of Man's Spirit," *Atlanta Journal Constitution,* February 5, 1967, 21; Ted Turner to Paul Gitlin, March 1, 1967, ARP 003–07x.

3. Although NBI does not appear to have kept exact numbers of students enrolled, based on the figures for these two years a conservative estimate would put the total number of students in the range of at least ten thousand (an average of two thousand students over at least five years; NBI existed from 1958 to 1968). The institute claimed a mailing list of forty thousand people.

4. Jerome Tuccille, *It Usually Begins with Ayn Rand* (New York: Stein and Day, 1971), 23; Karen Minto and David Oyerly, "Interview with Henry Mark Holzer," *Full Context,* July/August 2001, 5; Kay Nolte Smith quoted in Jeff Walker, *The Ayn Rand Cult* (La Salle, IL: Open Court Press, 1999), 175.

5. Nathaniel Branden, "A Report to Our Readers," *The Objectivist Newsletter,* December 1963, 47. In 1965 Nathan, accompanied by Rand, delivered the opening lecture for new NBI courses in Boston and Washington, D.C.

6. *Basic Principles of Objectivism,* NBI pamphlet, ARP 017–05B.

7 Ayn Rand, "Cashing In: The Student Rebellion," in *Capitalism: The Unknown Ideal* (New York: Penguin, 1967), 251.

8. AR to John Golden, July 10, 1966, ARP 042–02B.

9. Draft media release, 001–01A; AR to L. Kopacz, March 20, 1966, ARP 039–07A; Doris Gordon, "My Personal Contacts with Ayn Rand," *Full Context,* March/April 2001, 7.

10. Nathaniel Branden, "A Message to Our Readers," *The Objectivist Newsletter,* April 1965, 17.

11. Ibid.

12. Rothbard's activities during this time are covered in Brian Doherty, *Radicals for Capitalism: A Freewheeling History of the Modern Libertarian Movement* (New York: Public Affairs, 2007); Justin Raimondo, *An Enemy of the State: The Life of Murray N. Rothbard* (Amherst, NY: Prometheus Books, 2000). Rothbard's greatest coup was placing an article in *Ramparts,* the flagship magazine of the student left. Murray Rothbard, "Confessions of a Right-Wing Liberal," *Ramparts,* June 15, 1968, 48–52.

13. Richard Weaver, *Ideas Have Consequences* (Chicago: Regnery, 1948). Though Weaver disliked the title, which his publisher suggested, it captured an essential component of the conservative worldview. Barry Goldwater, *The Conscience of a Conservative* (New York: McFadden-Bartell, 1960), 10–11.

14. Rand, "Cashing In," 269, 268.

15. Robert Hinck, "New Group Arises to Battle SDS," *Columbia Owl*, March 29, 1967, 1.

16. Frank Bubb, "Demonstration or Coercion?," *Washington University Student Life*, December 13, 1968, 9.

17. Committee for Defense of Property Rights, *For a Civilized University*, pamphlet, 1967, ARP 005–18A.

18. Earl Wood to AR, January 6, 1966 and May 8, 1967, ARP 005–18A. The conference proceeded as planned and attracted nearly two hundred participants.

19. Ayn Rand, *The Objectivist*, April 1967, 256.

20. Jarret Wollstein, "Objectivism—A New Orthodoxy?," *The New Guard*. October 1967, 14–21.

21. Numerous eyewitness accounts bear this out. See Joy Parker, letter to the editor, *Playboy*, June 1964;"Born Eccentric," *Newsweek*, March 27, 1961, 104; John Kobler, "The Curious Cult of Ayn Rand," *Saturday Evening Post*, November, 11, 1961.

22. Don Ventura, Oral History, ARP; Ilona Royce Smithkin, Oral History, ARP. Anne Heller suggests that Frank may have suffered from Dupuytren's syndrome, which is often linked to alcohol abuse. Anne C. Heller, *Ayn Rand and the World She Made* (New York: Doubleday, 2009), 357.

23. Patrecia Scott to AR, April 6, 1967, ARP 003–13A.

24. Ayn Rand, *Atlas Shrugged*, 35th anniversary ed. (1957; New York: Penguin, 1992), 460.

25. Ayn Rand, *Philosophy: Who Needs It?* (New York: Signet, 1982), 17; Rand, *Atlas Shrugged*, 962.

26. Nathaniel Branden,"Intellectual Ammunition Department: Reason and Emotion," *The Objectivist Newsletter* 1, no. 1 (1962): 3.

27. Biographical Interview 17, April 19, 1961. Not surprisingly, Objectivist psychotherapy has spawned what Justin Raimondo calls "a whole literature of recovery," including Ellen Plasil, *Therapist* (New York: St. Martin's Press, 1985); Jeff Walker, *The Ayn Rand Cult* (Chicago: Open Court Press, 1999); Sidney Greenberg, *Ayn Rand and Alienation: The Platonic Idealism of the Objective Ethics and a Rational Alternative* (San Francisco: Sidney Greenberg, 1977). Branden himself described much of his later psychological work as an effort to undo the damage caused by Objectivist psychotherapy. See N. Branden, "Benefits and Hazards of the Philosophy of Ayn Rand," available at www.nathanielbranden.com/catalog/articles_essays/benefits_and_hazards. html [February 23, 2009].

28. The final stages of their relationship are traced in detail by Barbara Branden, *The Passion of Ayn Rand* (Garden City, NY: Doubleday, 1986); Nathaniel Branden, *Judgment Day: My Years with Ayn Rand* (Boston: Houghton Mifflin, 1989); James Valliant, *The Passion of Ayn Rand's Critics* (Dallas: Durban House, 2005).

29. Ayn Rand, "An Answer to Readers: About a Woman President," *The Objectivist*, December 1968, 561–63. For an exploration of Rand's ideas about gender, see Susan Love Brown, "Ayn Rand: The Woman Who Would Not Be President," in *Feminist Interpretations of Ayn Rand*, ed. Mimi Reisel Gladstein and Chris Matthew Sciabarra (University Park: Pennsylvania State University Press, 1999), 275–98.

30. B. Branden, *The Passion of Ayn Rand,* 338.

31. *The Objectivist,* June 1968, 480. As a point of comparison, *National Review* had eighteen thousand subscribers in 1957, the time of Whittaker Chambers's review of *Atlas Shrugged.* From there it grew rapidly, reaching a high of ninety thousand in 1964. John B. Judis, *William F. Buckley, Jr.: Patron Saint of the Conservatives* (New York: Simon and Schuster, 1988), 140, 221. Likewise *The New Republic* reached a circulation of around one hundred thousand during the 1960s. Richard H. Pells, *The Liberal Mind in a Conservative Era: American Intellectuals in the 1940s and 1950s* (Middletown, CT: Wesleyan University Press, 1989), 65. In contrast to these two, Rand's magazines did not accept advertising or charitable donations and had a far more modest budget. A better comparison might be with *Partisan Review,* which never exceeded fifteen thousand subscribers. Joseph Berger, "William Phillips, Co-Founder and Soul of Partisan Review, Dies at 94," *New York Times,* September 14, 2002.

32. "Atlas Shrugged," *Valley Morning News* (Harlingen, TX), August 1, 1966, ARP 006–04C; "Atlas Shrugged Coming True?," *Orange County Register,* February 10, 1963, C12; Muskegon Manufacturer's Association, circular letter W-80, June 15, 1962, 3, ARP 006–02D; "Unreasonable Quotas: Oil Import Curbs Are Damaging the National Interest," *Barron's,* November 27, 1961, 1. Other citations of Rand in *Barron's* include "Graven in Copper," January 10, 1966, 1; "Shape of Things to Come," September 9, 1965, 1. Rand's editorial "What Is Capitalism?" appeared January 3, 1966, 1. Although *Barron's* articles are unsigned, Rand's presence was likely due to *Barron's* longtime editor, Robert M. Bleiberg, an admirer of Rand and close friend of Alan Greenspan.

33. Honor Tracy, "Here We Go Gathering Nuts," *The New Republic,* December 10, 1966, 27–28.

34. Ayn Rand, "The Wreckage of the Consensus," in *Capitalism: The Unknown Ideal,* 223, 224.

35. Ibid., 226.

36. Ibid., 230, 232.

37. Rand, "Wreckage of the Consensus," 235.

38. Objectivist History Project DVD, vol. 2, "The Early Years."

39. Martin O. Hutchinson, letter to the editor, *National Review,* May 14, 1982, 520. Libertarian opposition to the draft is described in Doherty, *Radicals for Capitalism.*

40. William F. Buckley Jr. to M. Stanton Evans, February 28, 1967, Evans, M. Stanton, Box 43, William F. Buckley Papers, Sterling Memorial Library, Yale University. Evans was the author of *Revolt on Campus* (Chicago: H. Regnery, 1962) and a host of other conservative books, including the recent controversial defense of Senator Joe McCarthy, *Blacklisted by History: The Untold Story of Senator Joe McCarthy and His Fight against America's Enemies* (New York: Crown Forum, 2007). Stanton's early career is covered in John A. Andrew III, *The Other Side of the Sixties: Young Americans for Freedom and the Rise of Conservative Politics* (New Brunswick, NJ: Rutgers University Press, 1997), 65, 61–62.

41. M. Stanton Evans, "The Gospel According to Ayn Rand," *National Review,* October 3, 1967, 1067.

42. I discuss Evans's take on Rand more fully in Jennifer Burns, "Godless Capitalism: Ayn Rand and the Conservatives," *Modern Intellectual History* 1, no. 3 (2004): 1–27.

43. "Objectivist Calendar," *The Objectivist,* November 1967, 366.

44. Charles Frederick Schroeder, "Ayn Rand: Far Right Prophetess," *Christian Century,* December 13, 1961, 1494; "Born Eccentric," 104; Kobler, "The Curious Cult of Ayn Rand." Another representative characterization, which ends on the none too subtle note of an Objectivist praising Hitler, can be found in Nora Sayre, "The Cult of Ayn Rand," in *Sixties Going on Seventies* (Piscataway: Rutgers University Press, 2006), 173–77.

45. Dora Hamblin, "The Cult of Angry Ayn Rand," *Life,* April 7, 1967, 92–102; Tuccille, *It Usually Begins With Ayn Rand,* 23; Nathaniel Branden, "Intellectual Ammunition Department: What Is Psychological Maturity?," *The Objectivist Newsletter* 4, no 11 (1965): 53. It should be noted that the use of Rand as evidence was not confined to her publications. A writer for *The Freeman* cited her tale of a factory organized along collective lines as proof that Communistic principles would not work in business. See John C. Sparks, "Least of All—The Family," *The Freeman,* March 1963, 41.

46. Albert Ellis, *Is Objectivism a Religion?* (New York: Lyle Stuart, 1968); John Hospers to AR, May 25, 1960, ARP 146-H01.

47. *Letters,* 531, 532.

48. Ibid., 532, 535, 533.

49. Karen Reedstrom, "Interview with Laurence I. Gould," *Full Context,* November 1991, 3.

50. Jan Schulman, née Richman, September 26, 1997, Oral History, ARP; Martin Anderson, *The Federal Bulldozer: A Critical Analysis of Urban Renewal 1949–62* (Cambridge, MA: MIT Press, 1964); Martin Anderson, interview with author, January 11, 2008. Charles and Mary Ann Sures also emphasize the warmer side of Rand in *Facets of Ayn Rand* (Irvine, CA: Ayn Rand Institute, 2001).

51. Karen Reedstrom, "Interview with Roger Donway," *Full Context,* May 1992, 1; Karen Reedstrom and David Saum, "Interview with Ronald E. Merrill," *Full Context,* November 1995, 7.

52. NBI, Basic Principles of Objectivism flyer, 27–06-A; Reedstrom, "Interview with Laurence I. Gould," 1.

53. Plasil, *Therapist,* 45.

54. Sky Gilbert, *The Emotionalists* (Winnipeg: Blizzard, 2000), 10. Chris Sciabarra further explores this issue in *Ayn Rand, Homosexuality, and Human Liberation* (Cape Town, South Africa: Leap Publishing, 2003).

55. Kay Nolte Smith, quoted in Walker, *The Ayn Rand Cult,* 14. Details on the dresses and dining room table are from Iris Bell, Oral History ARP; Shelly Reuben, Oral History, ARP.

56. Roy A. Childs Jr., "Ayn Rand and the Libertarian Movement," in *Liberty against Power: Essays by Roy Childs, Jr.,* ed. Joan Kennedy Taylor (San Francisco: Fox and Wilkes, 1994), 278; Howard McConnel to AR, January 7, 1959, ARP 003–13B; Susan Reisel to AR, October 17, 1962, ARP 038–04C.

57. Author interview with Robert Hessen, December 7, 2007.

58. Karen Minto and David Oyerly, "Interview with Henry Mark Holzer," *Full Context,* July/Aug 2001, 5.

59. Edith Efron to AR, dated "Tuesday," ARP 020–01M. Efron later recovered from the shock of her expulsion and criticized the conformity of life in the Collective, while remaining appreciative of Rand's ideas. Leonard Bogart to author, private communication.

60. Karen Minto, "Interview with Barbara Branden," *Full Context,* September/October 1998, 9.

61. Valliant, *The Passion of Ayn Rand's Critics,* 241, 245.

62. Ayn Rand, *The Fountainhead,* 50th anniversary ed. (1943; New York: Signet, 1993), 496.

63. See B. Branden, *Passion of Ayn Rand,* 347; N. Branden, *Judgment Day,* 387–88.

64. Tod Foster, Oral History, ARP.

65. Karen Reedstrom, "Interview with George Walsh," *Full Context,* February 1991, 4. When Rand's attorney requested letters about Branden to support Rand's published claims against him, virtually all of Branden's close friends, including his sister, submitted lengthy statements about the faults and flaws in his character. The material was collected in response to Branden's threat of legal action. See finding aid, Ayn Rand Papers, Ayn Rand Institute.

66. Ayn Rand, "To Whom It May Concern," *The Objectivist,* May 1968, 449, 457. According to Rand's attorney and accountant, her veiled accusations of Branden's financial misdealing and theft were baseless. Reedstrom, "Interview with Henry Mark Holzer."

67. Nathaniel Branden, "In Answer to Ayn Rand," in Roy Childs Papers, Box 31, "Objectivism—Ayn Rand," Hoover Institute Archives, Stanford University.

68. Reedstrom, "Interview with George Walsh," 4.

69. *National Review,* December 17, 1968, 1257.

70. Sandra G. Wells to AR, April 7, 1969, ARP 155–04x.

Chapter 9

1. I use "Objectivist" to indicate persons who considered themselves significantly influenced by Rand, although not in complete agreement with her.

2. In "No War, No Welfare, and No Damn Taxation: The Student Libertarian Movement, 1968–1972," in *The Vietnam War on Campus: Other Voices, More Distant Drums,* ed. Mark Jason Gilbert (Westport, CT: Praeger, 2001), Jonathan Schoenwald frames the libertarian movement as "a minor third wave of 1960s student activism" and "the climax of a generation's efforts" (21, 22). Although Schoenwald is right to identify connections between the two activist movements, his analysis collapses left and right and overlooks the very different provenance, goals, and ideologies of each. He suggests that the Libertarian Party represented the "death blow" to the movement, but my own research suggests that the Libertarian Party grew out of a thriving subculture in which students and recent graduates played a key role. The Party ought to be considered the peak of that subculture rather than its end. See Jennifer Burns, "O Libertarian, Where Is Thy Sting?," *Journal of Policy History* 19, no. 4 (2007): 453–71. See also John L. Kelley, *Bringing the Market Back In: The Political Revitalization of Market Liberalism* (New York: New York University Press, 1997).

3. Rand was still friendly with the Hessens during this time, although they had relocated to Princeton, New Jersey, and met infrequently.

4. Nathaniel Branden, *The Psychology of Self Esteem* (Los Angeles: Nash, 1969). Branden described his later therapeutic practice as eclectic and experimental, drawing on gestalt therapy, Alexander Lowen's bioenergetic therapy, and his own sentence-completion methodology. Other approaches of interest to Branden were those of Wilhelm Reich, Arthur Janov, Abraham Maslow, and Thomas Szasz. "Break Free! An Interview with Nathaniel Branden," *Reason,* October 1971, 4–19. Branden's connections to and influence upon New Age psychology, which one commentator identifies as "the quest for the higher self," are well worth exploring. Richard Kyle, *The New Age Movement in American Culture* (Lanham, MD: University Press of America, 1995), 137. Although Branden had no connection to Esalen, Jeffrey Kripal's *Esalen: America and the Religion of No Religion* (Chicago: University of Chicago Press, 2007) suggests fruitful ways to understand the historical significance of pop psychology in the 1970s. Branden's books have sales figures to rival Rand's. According to his website, his twenty books have sold nearly six million copies. See www.nathanielbranden.com [March 5, 2009].

5. Ayn Rand, *The Fountainhead,* 50th anniversary ed. (1943; New York: Signet, 1993), vi.

6. Cynthia Peikoff, interview transcripts for "Sense of Life" documentary, December 2, 1994. ARP.

7. Leonard Peikoff, *The Ominous Parallels* (New York: Stein and Day, 1982). The Objectivist oral tradition is described in Allan Gotthelf, *On Ayn Rand* (Belmont, CA: Wadsworth, 2000), 26. Peikoff's *Objectivism: The Philosophy of Ayn Rand* (New York: Dutton, 1991) draws on this oral tradition. Rand's students in these last years included, among others, George Walsh, John Nelson, David Kelley, Michael Berliner, Harry Binswanger, Peter Schwartz, George Reisman, and John Ridpath. After her death Peikoff released two additional essay collections under her name, *Philosophy: Who Needs It?* (New York: Signet, 1982) and *The Voice of Reason,* ed. Leonard Peikoff (New York: New American Library, 1989).

8. Rand's loss of stature following the "Objecti-schism" is detailed in Sidney Greenberg, *Ayn Rand and Alienation: The Platonic Idealism of the Objective Ethics and a Rational Alternative* (San Francisco: Sidney Greenberg, 1977). Circulation figures are in *The Objectivist,* December 1969, 768. Karen Reedstrom, "Interview with Anne Wortham," *Full Context,* March 1994, 6; Anne Wortham, *The Other Side of Racism* (Columbus: Ohio State University Press, 1981). Wortham is currently a professor of sociology at Illinois State University and a Hoover Institution Fellow.

9. *The Rational Individualist* 1, no. 8 (1969): 1.

10. Roy Childs, "Open Letter to Ayn Rand," in *Liberty against Power: Essays by Roy A. Childs, Jr.,* ed. Joan Kennedy Taylor (San Francisco: Fox and Wilkes, 1994), 145, 155, italics in original. This letter was prefigured by another article by Childs: "The Contradiction in Objectivism," *Rampart Journal,* spring 1968.

11. *Western World Review Newsletter,* no. 2 (October 1969): 3, Box 18, David Walter Collection, Hoover Archives.

12. R. W. Bradford, "In the Beginning, There Were Anarchists," *Liberty,* June 1999, 40–42.

13. Ibid., 146.

14. Childs, "Open Letter to Ayn Rand"; Jerome Tuccille, *Radical Libertarianism* (New York: Bobbs Merrill, 1970), 4; Jerome Tuccille, *It Usually Begins with Ayn Rand* (New York: Stein and Day, 1971).

15. Ayn Rand, "A Statement of Policy," *The Objectivist,* June 1968, 472.

16. Ayn Rand, "The Nature of Government," in *The Virtue of Selfishness* (New York: Signet, 1964), 128–29.

17. Gary North, *Chalcedon Report,* no. 46 (June 1, 1969), Early Libertarian Movement, Box 26, Evers Papers, Hoover Institution, Stanford University.

18. "YAF: A Philosophical and Political Profile," *The New Guard,* January 1970, 21–22. Twelve percent of respondents identified as followers of Ludwig von Mises, a figure that likely indicates familiarity with the work of either Rand or Rothbard, the two most consistent promoters of the obscure economist. Taken together, the "poll" put Objectivist-libertarians at about 22 percent of YAF membership. "Keep a Good thing Going!," Ron Docksai for National Board, campaign leaflet, Miscellaneous, Box 2, Dowd Papers, Hoover Institution; Don Feder to Libertarian Caucus, undated, Letters Received, 1968–69, Box 1, Dowd Papers; Hubbard to Rodger C. Bell, July 14, 1969, Correspondence: Letters Received, 69–70, Box 1, Dowd Papers.

19. Events at the convention have been covered in multiple accounts, from which my rendition draws. I have also relied on documentary sources, as cited. See Tuccille, *Radical Libertarianism,* 96–109; Murray Rothbard, *For a New Liberty: The Libertarian Manifesto* (New York: MacMillan, 1973), 5–7; Gregory L. Schneider, *Cadres for Conservatism: Young Americans for Freedom and the Rise of the Contemporary Right* (New York: New York University Press, 1999), 134–37; Brian Doherty, *Radicals for Capitalism: A Freewheeling History of the Modern Libertarian Movement* (New York: Public Affairs, 2007), 355–59; Don Meinshausen, "Present at the Creation," *Liberty* 18, no. 6 (June 2004), available at www.libertyunbound.com/archive/2004_06/meinshausen-creation.html. [February 28, 2009].

20. Other goals included electing more libertarians to positions of power, establishing a permanent network of libertarian communications within the organization, and ensuring that all YAF members were educated about laissez-faire capitalism. "Libertarian Caucus: Credo," undated, YAF: 1969 Convention, Box 24, Evers Papers.

21. In 1970 the National Board passed a resolution including anarchy on a list of forbidden doctrines in YAF.

22. Tuccille, *Radical Libertarianism,* 106. YAF later identified the draft card burner as Lee Houffman, although Don Meinhausen identifies him as David Schumacher. Minutes of the Meeting of the Nat. Board of Directors, St. Louis, MO, August 31, 1969, National Board—printed matter and reports. Box 2, Dowd Papers.

23. Confidential Report to National YAF Leadership, January 16, 1970, 2, YAF National Convention, Box 24, Evers Papers.

24. Don Ernsberger to Murray Rothbard, August 25, 1969, Evers Papers, Box 24. Also see criticism of Rothbard in "TANSTAAFL! Report of the Libertarian Caucus," no. 2, YAF Convention Series, St. Louis, Mo., August 28–31, YAF: 1969 National Convention, Box 24,

Evers Papers. See, for example, *California Libertarian Report*, Post Convention Issue no. 1, YAF National Board, printed matter and reports, Box 2, Dowd Papers; Berle Hubbard to Patrick Dowd, October 31, 1969, Letters Received, 1969–1970, Box 1, Dowd Papers; Patrick Dowd to David Keene, December 6, 1969. I strongly disagree with Stephen Newman's contention, seconded by Jonathon Schoenwald, that Rothbard "deserves to be called the founder of the modern libertarian movement." Newman, *Liberalism at Wit's End: The Libertarian Revolt against the Modern State* (Ithaca, NY: Cornell University Press, 1984), 27. However much Rothbard wished to present himself as "Mr. Libertarian," the evidence simply does not support this claim. Rothbard certainly managed to hog the spotlight and convince outsiders that he was the major theorist of libertarianism, but his appeal was far more limited than Rand's. Furthermore Rothbard's extremism and poor strategic thinking did much to damage the movement and the Libertarian Party. Rothbard did, however, succeed in getting a book contract to write about libertarianism in *For a New Liberty: The Libertarian Manifesto* (New York: MacMillan, 1973).

25. See, for example, *California Libertarian Report*, Post Convention Issue no. 1, YAF National Board, printed matter and reports, Box 2, Dowd Papers; Berle Hubbard to Patrick Dowd, October 31, 1969, Letters Received, 1969–1970, Box 1, Dowd Papers.

26. Patrick Dowd to David Keene, December 6, 1969, Dowd Papers.

27. Society for Individual Liberty news release, November 21, 1969, SIL, Box 36, Evers Papers; "Worth Repeating," *Rational Individualist* 1, no. 13 (1969): 14, Box 15, David Walter Collection, Hoover Institution.

28. Libertarian Caucus/Society for Individual Liberty News, November 22, 1969, SIL, Box 36, Evers Papers; "The Year One in Retrospect," *SIL News* 1, no. 10 (1970): 5.

29. "Society for Individual Liberty Directory, 1972," SIL, Box 36, Evers Papers.

30. *A Is A Libertarian Directory*, January 1971, 1, Box 15, Walter Papers.

31. Ibid.

32. Ayn Rand, "Brief Summary," *The Objectivist*, September 1971, 1090.

33. *Chronicle*, Monthly Newsletter of the Libertarian International, 1, no. 9 (1982), Box 15, Walter Papers.

34. The disclaimer appeared in every issue. *New Libertarian Notes*, 1973, unlabeled folder, Box 18, Walter Papers.

35. Gilbert Nash, "The Beat + The Buck = The Bucknick," *Swank*, June 1967, 43–55.

36. Tuccille, *It Usually Begins with Ayn Rand*, 105–7.

37. Don Franzen, "Thoughts on the Post-revolutionary World," *SIL News* 1, no. 7 (1970), 1, Walter Collection, Box 3, Hoover Institution Archives, Stanford University. All further citations of *SIL News* are from this box and collection. Also printed in *Protos* 2, no. 4 (1970), Box 25, Evers Papers.

38. Ibid., 1. Tibor Machan defines libertarianism as a purely political ideology that "is a claim about the scope of permissible force or threat of force among human beings, including human beings who constitute the governing administration of a given human community; it is a political claim or theory and not some other, however much it may presuppose a variety of other, nonpolitical claims." Machan, "Libertarianism and Conservatives," *Modem Age* 24 (winter 1980): 21–33.

39. Franzen, "Forethoughts on the Post-Revolutionary World."

40. Bidinotto authored "Getting Away with Murder," a 1988 *Reader's Digest* article that brought Willie Horton to the attention of presidential candidates Al Gore and George Bush.

41. It was a libertarian truism that the Constitution was an authoritarian document, since it had been signed by only a few persons yet claimed jurisdiction over an entire nation. See *Hard Core News*, undated, postmarked November 1970, unlabeled folder, Box 24, Evers Papers; Kerry Thornley, letter to the editors, *Libertarian American* 1, no. 5 (1968), 2, Box 36, Evers Papers.

42. Ayn Rand, "Apollo 11," *The Objectivist*, September 1969, 709.

43. Jerome Tuccille, "Spotlighting the News," *Rational Individualist*, October 1969, 5, Mises Institute.

44. Ayn Rand, "The Anti-Industrial Revolution," *The Objectivist*, January 1971, 962, 978.

45. Ayn Rand, "The Anti-Industrial Revolution, Part II," *The Objectivist*, February 1971, 980.

46. This distinction is made by Andrew Kirk, *Counterculture Green: The* Whole Earth Catalog *and American Environmentalism* (Lawrence: University Press of Kansas, 2007). Whether this set of ideas transcends or represents yet another iteration of what Donald Worster called the dialectic of "arcadian" and "imperialist" ecology is an important question to explore. Worster, *Nature' s Economy: A History of Ecological Ideas* (Cambridge: Cambridge University Press, 1977/1994).

47. Stewart Brand, diary entries dated July 9, 1968 and August 16, 1968, Stewart Brand Papers, Stanford University Special Collections.

48. *The Last Whole Earth Catalog* (Menlo Park, CA: Portola Institute, 1971), 185. The catalogue included only books deemed either "useful as a tool" or "relevant to independent education," making mention tantamount to endorsement. It also recommended the *A Is A Directory* and Milton Friedman's *Capitalism and Freedom* (344). The *Atlas Shrugged* excerpt was from a speech by Rand villain Floyd Ferris, in which he tells Hank Rearden, "One declares so many things to be a crime that it becomes impossible for men to live without breaking laws." Rand may also have inspired Brand's later insistence that his hippy partners become comfortable with money and overcome their guilt about using it to reform the world. For libertarian and counterculture connections to cyberspace, see Fred Turner, *From Counterculture to Cyberculture: Stewart Brand, the Whole Earth Network, and the Rise of Digital Utopianism* (Chicago: University of Chicago Press, 2006); John Markoff, *What the Dormouse Said: How the Sixties Counterculture Shaped the Personal Computer Industry* (New York: Viking Penguin, 2005). Rand's intersection with the computer culture is noted in Christopher Hitchens, "Why So Many High-Tech Executives Have Declared Allegiance to Randian Objectivism," *Business 2.0*, August/September 2001, 129–32, and is surely worth further exploration.

49. Ayn Rand, "A Suggestion," *The Objectivist*, February 1969, 595–96; Ayn Rand, "Of Living Death," *The Objectivist*, October 1968, 534. Members of Frank O'Connor's extended family claimed that Rand herself had an abortion in the early 1930s, which they helped pay for. Heller, 128. Rand never mentioned this incident, but whatever

340 NOTES TO PAGES 263–267

her personal experience, her support of abortion rights was fully consonant with her emphasis on individualism and personal liberty.

50. Joan Didion made a nearly identical argument in "The Women's Movement," in *The White Album* (New York: Simon and Schuster, 1979), 110. Many feminists did indeed have Marxist roots. See Daniel Horowitz, *Betty Friedan and the Making of the Feminine Mystique: The American Left, the Cold War, and Modern Feminism* (Amherst: University of Massachusetts Press, 1998).

51. Ayn Rand, "The Age of Envy, Part II," *The Objectivist*, August 1971, 1076.

52. Susan Brownmiller, *Against Our Will: Men, Women, and Rape* (New York: Simon and Schuster, 1975), 315.

53. Barbara Grazzuti Harrison, "Psyching Out Ayn Rand," *Ms.*, September 1978, reprinted in Mimi Reisel Gladstein and Chris Sciabarra, eds., *Feminist Interpretations of Ayn Rand* (University Park: Pennsylvania State University Press, 1999), 70, 75, 72, 76.

54. Gladstein and Sciabarra, *Feminist Interpretations of Ayn Rand,* 49; "Sightings," *The Navigator: An Objectivist Review of Politics and Culture* 6, nos. 7–8 (August 2003), available at www.objectivistcenter.org/navigator/articles/nav+sightings-nav-6-78.asp [July 26, 2005]. Organizations dedicated to individualist feminism include Feminists for Free Expression, the Association of Libertarian Feminists, and the Independent Women's Forum. The last is analyzed in Ronnee Schreiber, *Righting Feminism: Conservative Women and American Politics* (New York: Oxford University Press, 2008). Joan Kennedy Taylor, the author of *Reclaiming the Mainstream: Individualist Feminism Rediscovered* (Amherst, NY: Prometheus Books, 1992) and a longtime friend of Rand, was an important figure in this movement. Wendy McElroy of www.ifeminist.com also identifies Rand as an influence.

55. Rand's remarks are printed in Ayn Rand, *Ayn Rand Answers: The Best of Her Q and A,* ed. Robert Mayhew (New York: New American Library, 2005), 91, 72.

56. *SIL News* 3, no. 12 (1972): 1.

57. This discussion of the Libertarian Party draws on my article, "O Libertarian, Where Is Thy Sting?" Other works that discuss the Party's history are Joseph Hazlett, *The Libertarian Party and Other Minor Political Parties* (Jefferson, NC: McFarland, 1992); Kelley, *Bringing the Market Back In.* The Libertarian Party pledge is found in *There Is No Middle Ground,* LP pamphlet, in "Campaign Literature 1972–1981," Box 1, Libertarian Party Papers (hereafter LPP), Albert and Shirley Small Special Collections Library, University of Virginia, Charlottesville.

58. Interview with David Nolan by Palmer, July 1, 1984, Interviews with Libertarian Party members, 1984, Box 11, LPP. A poll of activists found 36 percent identified as Objectivists and 75 percent were former Republicans. Doherty, *Radicals for Capitalism,* 391; *Colorado Libertarian,* February 1977, 2, Papers of the Colorado Libertarian Party, LPP. The second position belonged to a publication by Roger MacBride, the Party's 1975 presidential nominee. "You Are What You Read: Survey of CA Libertarian Party Members," *Colorado Liberty* 1, no 2 (1979); 1972 Libertarian Party pamphlet, *Tired of Being the Politicians' Puppet?,* Campaign Literature 1972–1981, LPP.

59. Don Ernsberger, "Politics and Social Change," *SIL News* 2, no. 11 (1971): 2–5.

60. Campaign figures are from Tom Palmer, interview with Edward Crane III, June 28, 1984, Interviews with Libertarian Party Members, 1984, Box 11, LPP; vote total from "Editorial Research Report: Libertarian's Alaskan Warm-up," *Congressional Quarterly*, August 17, 1982.

61. Before joining the Republican Party, Norton was active in Libertarian Party politics, particularly the 1980 presidential campaign. Laura Flanders, *Bushwomen: Tales of a Cynical Species* (New York: Verso, 2004).

62. Rand, *Ayn Rand Answers*, 72, 74, 73.

63. Edward H. Crane, "How Now, Ayn Rand?," *Option* 2, no. 2 (1974): 15, reprinted from *LP News*, December 1973, Box 3, Walter Papers.

64. Although two biographies of Greenspan credit his involvement with the campaign to Len Garment, both Greenspan and Anderson remember that Anderson was the person who introduced him to Nixon and involved him in the presidential campaign. Author interview with Martin Anderson, January 11, 2008; Alan Greenspan, personal communication to author, February 27, 2009; Justin Martin, *Greenspan: The Man behind the Money* (Cambridge, MA: Perseus, 2000), 45; Jerome Tuccille, *Alan Shrugged: Alan Greenspan, the World's Most Powerful Banker* (New York: Wiley, 2002). Anderson included an excerpt from Rand in Martin Anderson and Barbara Honegger, eds., *The Military Draft: Selected Readings on Conscription* (Stanford, CA: Hoover Institution Press, 1982). For more on the Gates Commission, see Bernard D. Rostker, *I Want You! The Evolution of the All-Volunteer Force* (Washington, DC: RAND Corporation, 2006).

65. The Austrians remained a tiny minority within the economics profession but established durable clusters at George Mason University, Auburn University, and the University of Nevada, Las Vegas. Karen Iversen Vaughn, *Austrian Economics in America: The Migration of a Tradition* (Cambridge: Cambridge University Press, 1994). The law and economics movement is described in Steven M. Teles, *The Rise of the Conservative Legal Movement* (Princeton, NJ: Princeton University Press, 2008), especially chapter 4. Although not libertarian per se, the work of rational choice theorists made thinkers in multiple academic disciplines more receptive to individualism. S. M. Amadae, *Rationalizing Capitalist Democracy: The Cold War Origins of Rational Choice Liberalism* (Chicago: University of Chicago Press, 2003).

66. Robert Nozick, *Anarchy, State, and Utopia* (New York: Basic Books, 1974), 115. Nozick addressed Objectivism directly in *Anarchy, State, and Utopia* (177–79) and in a separate essay, "On the Randian Argument," In *Socratic Puzzles* (Cambridge, MA: Harvard University Press, 1997), 249–64. Although he sharply criticized Rand's arguments, Nozick called her "an interesting thinker, worthy of attention." Nozick's encounter with libertarianism and Rothbard is described in *Socratic Puzzles*, 1, 7–8, and in Ralph Raico, "Robert Nozick: A Historical Note," available at www.lewrockwell.com/raico/raico15.html [November 27, 2008]. For a sympathetic treatment of Nozick that explains his relationship to other strains of libertarianism, see Edward Feder, *On Nozick* (Toronto: Wadsworth, 2004). Details of Nozick at the Libertarian Party convention are given in Ian Young, "Gay Rights and the Libertarians," *Libertarian Option*, January 1976, 9–30, Box 3, Walter Papers. Nozick argued that a gay candidate might attract urban and younger voters.

67. Paul Varnell, "Of Academic Interest," *A Is A* 2, no. 6 (1973): 3, and *A Is A* 2, no. 4 (1973): 4, Box 15, Walter Papers; "In Brief," *SIL News,* June–July 1971, 5.

68. "Break Free! An Interview with Nathaniel Branden."

69. Ayn Rand, "An Untitled Letter, Part II," *Ayn Rand Letter* 2, no. 10 (1973): 168. The review ran in two concurrent issues.

70. Ayn Rand, "A Last Survey," *Ayn Rand Letter* 4, no. 2 (1975): 382, 381.

71. Ibid., 382.

72. Details on the Koch brothers and Cato's founding can be found in Doherty, *Radicals for Capitalism,* 411–13. An alternative account crediting Murray Rothbard is given in Justin Raimondo's celebratory biography of Rothbard, *An Enemy of the State: The Life of Murray N. Rothbard* (Amherst, NY: Prometheus Books, 2000), chapter 5. Cato's strategy of direct policy intervention and advocacy represented a new direction for think tanks that was increasingly popular in the 1970s. Andrew Rich describes this transformation as one from expertise to advocacy in *Think Tanks, Public Policy, and the Politics of Expertise* (New York: Cambridge University Press, 2004). According to Rich's data, Cato was considered the fifth most influential think tank in 1993 and the third most influential in 1997 (81). Alice O'Connor identifies and critiques a similar shift in *Social Science for What? Philanthropy and the Social Question in a World Turned Rightside Up* (New York: Russell Sage Foundation, 2007). Conservative think tanks became increasingly important institutions in the 1970s, providing an institutional apparatus to support intellectuals and a direct conduit to policymakers. Kimberly Phillips-Fein, *Invisible Hands: The Making of the Conservative Movement from the New Deal to Ronald Reagan* (New York: Norton, 2009). Koch money also funded the Institute for Humane Studies, an organization that promotes libertarian ideas to students.

73. The Hessens moved to California in 1974 and started the Palo Alto Book Service after *The Ayn Rand Letter* closed, selling off Rand's inventory of newsletters. After their final break with Rand they continued a business relationship until her death and closed the service in 1986 after a dispute with Leonard Peikoff.

74. Edited by Leonard Peikoff and Harry Binswanger, *The Objectivist Forum* was published bimonthly from 1980 to 1987. *The Intellectual Activist,* started by Peter Schwartz in 1979, is still in existence after several editorial changes. Rand's stamp collecting is described in Charles and Mary Ann Sures, *Facets of Ayn Rand* (Irvine, CA: Ayn Rand Institute Press, 2001).

75. Barbara Branden, *The Passion of Ayn Rand* (New York: Random House, 1986), 396–400; Nathaniel Branden, *My Years with Ayn Rand* (San Francisco: Jossey Bass, 1999), 391–402.

76. Cynthia Peikoff interview for "Sense of Life," December 2, 1994, documentary outtakes, ARP.

Epilogue

1. William F. Buckley Jr., "Ayn Rand: RIP," *National Review,* April 2, 1982, 380; George Gilder, *Wealth and Poverty* (New York: Basic Books, 1981); Charles Murray, *Losing Ground: American Social Policy, 1950–1980* (New York: Basic Books, 1984); William Simon, *A Time*

for Truth (New York: McGrawReader's Digest Press, 1978); Maureen Dowd, "Where *Atlas Shrugged* Is Still Read—Forthrightly," *New York Times*, September 13, 1987.

2. Nicholas Dykes, letter to the editor, *Full Context*, February 1997, 10.

3. David Kelley, *The Evidence of the Senses: A Realist Theory of Perception* (Baton Rouge: Louisiana State University Press, 1986).

4. Peter Schwartz, "On Sanctioning the Sanctioners," *Intellectual Activist IV*, February 27, 1989; Leonard Peikoff, "Fact and Value," *Intellectual Activist V*, May 18, 1989; David Kelley, "Truth and Toleration" (1990), in *The Contested Legacy of Ayn Rand: Truth and Toleration in Objectivism*, 2nd ed. (New Brunswick, NJ: Transaction, 2000).

5. Peikoff, "Fact and Value"; Kelley, "Truth and Toleration."

6. "No Gods or Kings: Objectivism in Bioshock," available at www.kotaku.com/354717/no-gods-or-kings-objectivism-in-bioshock. [February 7, 2009].

7. The program was sponsored by the Telluride Association. Eitan Grossman, personal communication to author.

8. Tobias Wolff, *Old School* (New York: Knopf, 2003), 68.

9. Mary Gaitskill, *Two Girls Fat and Thin* (New York: Poseidon Press, 1991); Murray Rothbard, "Mozart Was a Red," available at www.lewrockwell.com/rothbard/mozart.html. [February 19, 2009]. Rand also appeared, thinly disguised, as the imperious baby-killer Vardis Wolfe in former Collective member Kay Nolte Smith's *Elegy for a Soprano* (New York: Villard Books, 1985).

10. Testimony of Dr. Alan Greenspan, Committee of Government Oversight and Reform, October 23, 2008, in Edmund L. Andrews, "Greenspan Concedes Error on Regulation," *New York Times*, October 23, 2008. Typical criticisms of Rand include David Corn, "Alan Shrugged: Greenspan, Ayn Rand, and Their God That Failed," *Mother Jones*, October 25, 2008, available at www.commondreams.org/view/2008/10/25–6 [February 5, 2009]; Jacob Weisburg, "The End of Libertarianism," *Slate*, October 18, 2008, available at www.slate.com/id/2202489 [February 6, 2009]. Weisberg's article drew a sharp retort from Richard Epstein, "Strident and Wrong," *Forbes.com*, available at www.forbes.com/2008/10/27/slate-libertarian-weisberg-oped-cx_re_1028epstein.html   [February 6, 2009]. Yaron Brook is quoted in Barrett Sheridan, "Who Is to Blame?," *Newsweek*, available at www.newsweek.com/id/173514 [February 6, 2009]. Sales of *Atlas Shrugged* are noted in "Atlas Felt a Sense of Déjà Vu," *The Economist*, February 26, 2009, available at www.economist.com/finance/displayStory.cfm?story_id=13185404&source=hpte xtfeature [March 4, 2009]. The trend of "going Galt" is described at the Liberty Papers blog, www.thelibertypapers.org/2009/03/06/will-atlas-shrug-an-compilation-of-blogo-sphere-commentary-about-going-galt/ [March 8, 2009]. Rush Limbaugh, "An Ayn Rand Sequel: Atlas Puked," available at www.rushlimbaugh.com/home/daily/site_121108/content/01125115.guest.html [March 2, 2009].

11. Katherine Mangu-Ward, "The Real Community Organizer," *Reason*, January 2009, available at www.reason.com/news/show/130353.html [February 7, 2009].

12. Clement C. Mason to AR, October 14, 1957, 22–05–03A, ARP.

13. *Journals*, 86.

14. Lee Clettenberg to AR, February 3, 1965, ellipses in original document, Box 43, folder 07–07E, ARP.

15. Ayn Rand, *The Fountainhead*, 50th anniversary ed. (1943; New York: Signet, 1993), ix.

Essay on Sources

1. Chris Sciabarra, "Bowdlerizing Ayn Rand," *Liberty*, September 1998.

2. Ayn Rand, *Letters of Ayn Rand*, ed. Michael S. Berliner (New York: Dutton, 1995), xvi–xvii.

3. To understand the differences between Rand's letters as written and as published, readers may wish to compare the edited version of Rand's August 1, 1946, letter to Leonard Read (*Letters*, 298–300) with a complete PDF of the original letter posted on the website of the Foundation for Economic Education (www.fee.org).

4. Ayn Rand, *Journals of Ayn Rand*, ed. David Harriman (New York: Dutton, 1997), 82. The original is in Second Hand Lives notebooks, Box 167, Ayn Rand Papers (henceforth ARP).

5. *Journals*, 162, and Box 167, folder 167–02D, 120, ARP.

6. For omission of Nock, see Sciabarra. Reference to Ingebretsen is deleted from *Journals*, 274, but can be found in Rand, Notes on the Moral Basis of Individualism, June 29, 1945, ARP 32–11A.

7. Reference to race is in notebook "Second-Hand Lives," December 4, 1935, 13, ARC 167–01B, and is deleted from *Journals*, 81. Reference to "nance" is in notebook "Second Hand Lives," March 28, 1937, 85, ARP 167–01D, and is deleted from *Journals*, 109.

BIBLIOGRAPHY

Archival Collections

Albert and Shirley Small Special Collections Library, University of Virginia
  Libertarian Party Papers
Ayn Rand Archives
  Ayn Rand Papers
Foundation for Economic Education, Irvington, New York
  Leonard Read Papers
Herbert Hoover Presidential Library, West Branch, Iowa
  Isabel Paterson Papers
  Rose Wilder Lane Papers
  William C. Mullendore Papers
Hoover Institution Archives, Stanford University
  Roy Childs Papers
  Sidney Hook Papers
  David Walter Papers
  Patrick Dowd Papers
  Williamson Evers Papers
John Hay Library, Brown University
  Gordon Hall and Grace Hoag Collection of Dissenting and Extremist Printed Propaganda
Library of Congress
  William Rusher Papers
  Ayn Rand Papers
Ludwig von Mises Institute, Auburn, Alabama
  Murray Rothbard Papers
  Ludwig von Mises Papers
Stanford University Special Collections
  Stewart Brand Papers
Yale University Library
  William F. Buckley Jr. Papers

Periodicals

The Ayn Rand Letter, 1971–1976
Full Context, 1988–2002
Journal of Ayn Rand Studies, 1999–2009
The Objectivist, 1966–1971
The Objectivist Forum, 1980–1987
The Objectivist Newsletter, 1962–1965

Published Works by Ayn Rand

Anthem. Expanded 50th anniversary ed. 1938; New York: Penguin, 1999.
The Art of Fiction: A Guide for Readers and Writers. Ed. Tore Boeckmann. New York: Plume, 2000.
Atlas Shrugged. 35th anniversary ed. 1957; New York: Penguin, 1992.
The Art of Non-Fiction: A Guide for Readers and Writers. Ed. Peter Schwartz. Plume, 2001.
Ayn Rand Answers: The Best of Her Q and A. Ed. Robert Mayhew. New York: New American Library, 2005.
The Ayn Rand Column. Ed. Peter Schwartz. Oceanside, CA: Second Renaissance Books, 1991.
Ayn Rand's Marginalia: Her Critical Comments on the Writings of Over 20 Authors. Ed. Robert Mayhew. Oceanside, CA: Second Renaissance Books, 1995.
Capitalism: The Unknown Ideal. New York: Penguin, 1967.
The Early Ayn Rand. Ed. Leonard Peikoff. New York: Penguin, 1986.
"A Faith for Modern Management." *Atlanta Economic Review* 8, no. 9 (1958).
For the New Intellectual. New York: New American Library, 1961.
The Fountainhead. 50th anniversary ed. 1943; New York: Signet, 1993.
Introduction to Objectivist Epistemology. New York: New American Library, 1979.
Journals of Ayn Rand. Ed. David Harriman. New York: Penguin, 1999.
Letters of Ayn Rand. Ed. Michael S. Berliner. New York: Penguin, 1995.
The New Left: The Anti-Industrial Revolution. New York: Penguin, 1971.
Night of January 16th. 1963; New York: New American Library, 1987.
Objectively Speaking: Ayn Rand Interviewed. Ed. Marlene Podritske and Peter Schwartz. New York: Lexington Books, 2009.
Philosophy: Who Needs It. New York: Signet, 1982.
The Romantic Manifesto. 1971; New York: Penguin, 1975.
Russian Writings on Hollywood. Ed. Michael S. Berliner. Irvine, CA: Ayn Rand Institute Press, 1999.
The Virtue of Selfishness. New York: Signet, 1964.
The Voice of Reason: Essays in Objectivist Thought. Ed. Leonard Peikoff and Peter Schwartz. New York: New American Library, 1989.
We the Living. 1936; New York: Signet, 1959.

Unpublished Interviews

Abarbanel, Sunny

Abrams, Larry

Anderson, Martin

Asher, Allison

Bell, Iris

Berliner, Judy

Berliner, Mike

Bokor, Sylvia

Bradford, Bruce

Branden, Barbara

Branden, Nathaniel

Brewer, Roy

Brown, Fern

Buechner, M. Northrup

Bungay, Jack

Childs, Roy

Cornuelle, Richard

Douglas, Robert

Drobysheva (née Rosenbaum), Nora

Eddy, Duane

Eikoff, Katherine

Elliott, Joan

Faragher, John Mack

Feingersh, Frederick

Forest, Gaina

Foster, Tod

Gillam, Jackie

Goldberg, Harvey

Gotthelf, Allan

Green, Daniel

Grossinger, Tania

Halpert, Wesley

Hassani, Lissette

Hendricksen, Bruce

Hessen, Robert

Higgins, John

Hill, Ruth Beebe

Holzer, Erica

Holzer, Henry Mark

Howard, John

Ingebretsen, James

Johnson, Bill

Knowlton, Perry

Kurisu, June

Lee, Dorothy

Lively, Anna

Lively, Della

Lively, Earl

Locke, Edwin

Ludel, Susan

Messenger, Doug

Miller, Gary

Nathan, Paul S.

Neal, Patricia

Newman, Arnold

Nickerson, Kathleen

Nickerson, Richard

O'Quinn, Kerry

Odzer, Howard

Petro, Sylvester

Phillips, Richard L.

Portnoy, Jack

Rabwin, Marcella

Ramus, Al

Reuben, Shelly

Ridpath, John

Rothbard, Murray

Salamon, Roger

Sandler, Ake

Sandler, Jane

Schulman, Jan

Schulman, Julius

Seltzer, Walter

Smith, Frances

Smithkin, Ilona Royce

Spillane, Mickey

Stack, Robert

Stanley, Scott

Sutton, Dan

Toffler, Alvin

Torigian, Rosemary

Ventura, Don

Wallace, Mike

Wilson, Rosalie

Winick, Eugene

Wolfe, Docky

Wright, Evan

Wright, Micky

Books and Articles

Adler, Les K., and Thomas G. Paterson. "Red Fascism: The Merger of Nazi Germany and Soviet Russia in the American Image of Totalitarianism, 1930s–1950s." *American Historical Review* 75, no. 4 (1970): 1046–64.

Allitt, Patrick. *Catholic Intellectuals and Conservative Politics in America, 1950–1985.* Ithaca, NY: Cornell University Press, 1993.

———. *The Conservatives: Ideas and Personalities throughout American History.* Cambridge, MA: Harvard University Press, 2009.

Alpers, Benjamin L. *Dictators, Democracy, and American Public Culture.* Chapel Hill: University of North Carolina Press, 2003.

Amadae, S. M. *Rationalizing Capitalist Democracy: The Cold War Origins of Rational Choice Liberalism*. Chicago: University of Chicago Press, 2003.

Anderson, Martin. *The Federal Bulldozer: A Critical Analysis of Urban Renewal 1949–62*. Cambridge, MA: MIT Press, 1964.

Anderson, Martin, and Barbara Honegger, eds. *The Military Draft: Selected Readings on Conscription*. Stanford, CA: Hoover Institution Press, 1982.

Andrew, John A., III. *The Other Side of the Sixties: Young Americans for Freedom and the Rise of Conservative Politics*. New Brunswick, NJ: Rutgers University Press, 1997.

Baker, James. *Ayn Rand*. Boston: Twayne, 1987.

Baker, Paula, "Liberty against Power: Defending Classical Liberalism in the 1930s." Unpublished paper.

Bannister, Robert C. *Social Darwinism: Science and Myth in Anglo-American Social Thought*. Philadelphia: Temple University Press, 1979.

Barnes, Hazel. *An Existentialist Ethics*. New York: Knopf, 1967.

Bass, Robert H. "Egoism versus Rights," *Journal of Ayn Rand Studies* 7, no. 2 (2006): 357–69.

Bell, Daniel. *The End of Ideology: On the Exhaustion of Political Ideas in the Fifties*. Glencoe, IL: Free Press, 1960.

———, ed. *The New American Right*. New York: Criterion Books, 1955.

———, ed. *The Radical Right*. 3rd ed. 1963; New Brunswick, NJ: Transaction, 2002.

Bellamy, Edward. *Looking Backward 2000–1887*. Ed. Alex McDonald. Petersborough, Ontario: Broadview Literary Texts, 2003.

Bellomy, Donald C. "'Social Darwinism' Revisited." *Perspectives in America History* 1 n.s. (1984): 1–129.

Bender, Thomas, and Carl E. Schorske. *American Academic Culture in Transformation: Fifty Years, Four Disciplines*. Princeton, NJ: Princeton University Press, 1997.

Bevir, Mark. "Fabianism, Permeation, and Independent Labor." *Historical Journal* 39, no. 1 (1996): 179–96.

———. *The Logic of the History of Ideas*. Cambridge, UK: Cambridge University Press, 1999.

Binswanger, Harry. *The Ayn Rand Lexicon*. New York: Penguin, 1986.

Blumenthal, Sidney. *The Rise of the Counter-Establishment: From Conservative Ideology to Political Power*. New York: Times Books, 1986.

Branden, Barbara. *The Passion of Ayn Rand*. Garden City, NY: Doubleday, 1986.

Branden, Nathaniel. "The Benefits and Hazards of the Philosophy of Ayn Rand." *Journal of Humanistic Psychology* 24, no. 4 (1984): 39–64.

———. *Judgment Day: My Years with Ayn Rand*. Boston: Houghton Mifflin, 1989.

———. *My Years with Ayn Rand*. San Francisco: Jossey-Bass, 1999.

———. *The Psychology of Self Esteem*. Los Angeles: Nash, 1969.

Branden, Nathaniel, and Barbara Branden. *Who Is Ayn Rand?* New York: Random House, 1962.

Braungart, Margaret M., and Richard Braungart. "The Life Course Development of Left and Right Wing Student Activist Leaders for the 1960s." *Political Psychology* 2 (1990): 243–82.

Brennan, Mary C. *Turning Right in the Sixties: The Conservative Capture of the GOP.* Chapel Hill: University of North Carolina Press, 1995.

Brick, Howard. *Transcending Capitalism: Visions of a New Society in Modern American Thought.* Ithaca, NY: Cornell University Press, 2006.

Brinkley, Alan. *The End of Reform: New Deal Liberalism in Recession and War.* New York: Knopf, 1995.

————. "The Problem of American Conservatism." *American Historical Review* 99, no. 2 (1994): 409–29.

————. *Voices of Protest: Huey Long, Father Coughlin, and the Great Depression.* New York: Knopf, 1982.

Britting, Jeff. *Ayn Rand.* New York: Overlook Press, 2004.

Brownmiller, Susan. *Against Our Will: Men, Women, and Rape.* New York: Simon and Schuster, 1975.

Buckley, William F. *Getting It Right: A Novel.* Washington, DC: Regnery, 2003.

————. *God and Man at Yale.* 1950; Washington, DC: Regnery, 1986.

————. *The Jeweler's Eye.* 1958; New York: G. P. Putnam's Sons, 1968.

Burgin, Angus. "Unintended Consequences: The Transformation of Atlantic Conservative Thought, 1920–1970." PhD diss., Harvard University, forthcoming.

Burns, Jennifer. "Godless Capitalism: Ayn Rand and the Conservatives." *Modern Intellectual History* 1, no. 3 (2004): 1–27. Reprinted in *American Capitalism: Social Thought and Political Economy in the Twentieth Century,* ed. Nelson Lichtenstein. Philadelphia: University of Pennsylvania Press, 2006.

————. "In Retrospect: George Nash's *The Conservative Intellectual Movement in America Since 1945.*" *Reviews in American History* 32 (2004): 447–62.

————. "Liberalism and the Conservative Imagination" In *Liberalism for a New Century,* ed. Neil Jumonville and Kevin Mattson. Berkeley: University of California Press, 2007.

————. "O Libertarian, Where Is Thy Sting?" *Journal of Policy History* 19, no. 4 (2007): 452–71.

Butler, Eamonn. *Ludwig Von Mises: Fountainhead of the Modern Microeconomics Revolution.* Aldershot, UK and Brookfield, VT: Gower, 1988.

Cain, Edward. *They'd Rather Be Right: Youth and the Conservative Movement.* New York: Macmillan, 1963.

Caldwell, Bruce. *Hayek's Challenge: An Intellectual Biography of F. A. Hayek.* Chicago: University of Chicago Press, 2003.

Campbell, Robert L. "Altruism in Auguste Comte and Ayn Rand." *Journal of Ayn Rand Studies* 7, no. 2 (2006): 357–69.

Carter, Dan T. *The Politics of Rage: George Wallace, the Origins of the New Conservatism, and the Transformation of American Politics.* Baton Rouge: Louisiana State University Press, 2000.

Cerf, Bennett. *At Random: The Reminiscences of Bennett Cerf.* New York: Random House, 1977.

Chamberlain, John. *A Life with the Printed Word.* Chicago: Regnery Gateway, 1982.

Chambers, Whittaker. *Odyssey of a Friend: Whittaker Chambers' Letters to William F. Buckley, Jr.* New York: G. P. Putnam's Sons, 1969.

————. *Witness*. New York: Random House, 1952.

Childs, Roy. *Liberty against Power: Essays by Roy Childs, Jr.* Ed. Joan Kennedy Taylor. San Francisco: Fox and Wilkes, 1994.

Clapper, Thomas H. "American Conservative Utopias." PhD diss., University of Oklahoma, 1983.

Colander, David C., and Harry Landreth. *The Coming of Keynesianism to America: Conversations with the Founders of Keynesian Economics.* Brookfield, VT: Edward Elgar, 1996.

Cole, Wayne S. *Roosevelt and the Isolationists, 1932–45.* Lincoln: University of Nebraska Press, 1983.

Cornuelle, Richard. *Reclaiming the American Dream: The Role of Private Individuals and Voluntary Associations.* New York: Random House, 1965.

Cookinham, Frederick. *The Age of Rand: Imagining an Objectivist Future World.* Lincoln, NE: iUniverse, 2005.

Cox, Stephen. "Ayn Rand: Theory versus Creative Life." *Journal of Libertarian Studies* 8 (1986): 19–29.

————. *The Woman and the Dynamo: Isabel Paterson and the Idea of America.* New Brunswick, NJ: Transaction, 2004.

Crespino, Joseph. *In Search of Another Country: Mississippi and the Conservative Counterrevolution.* Princeton, NJ: Princeton University Press, 2007.

Critchlow, Donald T. *The Conservative Ascendancy: How the GOP Right Made Political History.* Cambridge, MA: Harvard University Press, 2007.

————. *Phyllis Schlafly and Grassroots Conservatism: A Woman's Crusade.* Princeton, NJ: Princeton University Press, 2005.

————, and Nancy MacLean, *Debating the American Conservative Movement: 1945 to the Present.* New York: Rowman and Littlefield, 2009.

Crossman, Richard, Louis Fischer, Andre Gide, Arthur Koestler, Ignazio Silone, Stephen Spender, and Richard Wright. *The God That Failed: Six Studies in Communism.* London: Hamish Hamilton, 1950.

De Leon, David. *The American as Anarchist: Reflections on Indigenous Radicalism.* Baltimore: Johns Hopkins University Press, 1978.

Den Uyl, Douglas J. *The Fountainhead: An American Novel.* New York: Twayne, 1999.

Den Uyl, Douglas J., and Douglas B. Rasmussen. *The Philosophic Thought of Ayn Rand.* Urbana: University of Illinois Press, 1984.

Denning, Michael. *The Cultural Front: The Laboring of American Culture in the Twentieth Century.* Haymarket Series. New York: Verso, 1997.

Didion, Joan. *The White Album.* New York: Simon and Schuster, 1979.

Dionne, E. J. *Why Americans Hate Politics.* New York: Simon and Schuster, 1991.

Doenecke, Justus D. *Storm on the Horizon: The Challenge to American Intervention, 1939–1941.* Lanham, MD: Rowman and Littlefield, 2000.

Doenecke, Justus D., and Mark A. Stoler. *Debating Franklin D. Roosevelt's Foreign Policies, 1933–1945.* Lanham, MD: Rowman and Littlefield, 2005.

Doherty, Brian. *Radicals for Capitalism: A Freewheeling History of the Modern American Libertarian Movement.* New York: Public Affairs, 2007.

Drury, Shadia, B. *Leo Strauss and the American Right*. New York: St. Martin's Press, 1997.

Dunlap, Riley. "Radical and Conservative Student Activists: A Comparison of Family Background." *Pacific Sociological Review* 13 (summer 1970): 171–80.

Ebenstein, Alan. *Friedrich Hayek*. Chicago: University of Chicago Press, 2001.

Edsell, Thomas B., and Mary Edsell. *Chain Reaction: The Impact of Race, Rights, and Taxes on American Politics*. New York: Norton, 1991.

Efron, Edith. *The News Twisters*. Los Angeles: Nash, 1971.

Ellis, Albert. *Is Objectivism a Religion?* New York: Lyle Stuart, 1968.

Engerman, David C. *Modernization from the Other Shore: American Intellectuals and the Romance of Russian Development*. Cambridge, MA: Harvard University Press, 2003.

Eow, Greg. "Fighting a New Deal: Intellectual Origins of the Reagan Revolution, 1932–1952." PhD diss., Rice University, 2007.

Evans, M. Stanton. *Blacklisted by History: The Untold Story of Senator Joe McCarthy and His Fight against America's Enemies*. New York: Crown Forum, 2007.

———. *Revolt on Campus*. Chicago: H. Regnery, 1962.

Farber, David, and Jeff Roche. *The Conservative Sixties*. New York: Peter Lang, 2003.

Feder, Edward. *On Nozick*. Toronto: Wadsworth, 2004.

Finer, Herman. *The Road to Reaction*. Boston: Little, Brown, 1945.

Fitzgerald, F. Scott. *The Love of the Last Tycoon*. 1941; New York: Scribner, 1993.

Flamm, Michael. *Law and Order: Street Crime, Civil Unrest, and the Crisis of Liberalism in the 1960s*. New York: Columbia University Press, 2005.

Flammang, Janet, ed. *Political Women: Current Roles in State and Local Government*. Beverly Hills, CA: Sage, 1984.

Flanders, Laura. *Bushwomen: Tales of a Cynical Species*. New York: Verso, 2004.

Fones-Wolf, Elizabeth A. *Selling Free Enterprise: The Business Assault on Labor and Liberalism, 1945–60*. Urbana: University of Illinois Press, 1994.

Fox, Richard Wightman. *Reinhold Niebuhr: A Biography*. New York: Pantheon Books, 1985.

Fraser, Steve, and Gary Gerstle. *The Rise and Fall of the New Deal Order, 1930–1980*. Princeton, NJ: Princeton University Press, 1989.

Freeman, Joanne B. "The Culture of Politics: The Politics of Culture." *Journal of Policy History* 16, no. 2 (2004): 137.

Friedman, Milton, with Rose Friedman, *Capitalism and Freedom*. Chicago: University of Chicago Press, 1962.

———, and Rose D. Friedman. *Two Lucky People: Memoirs*. Chicago: University of Chicago Press, 1998.

Friedman, Milton, and George Stigler. *Roofs or Ceilings*, in *Verdict on Rent Control*. London: Institute of Economic Affairs, 1972.

Gabler, Neal. *An Empire of Their Own: How the Jews Invented Hollywood*. New York: Crown, 1988.

Gaitskill, Mary. *Two Girls, Fat and Thin: A Novel*. New York: Poseidon Press, 1991.

Gallup, Alec M. *The Gallup Poll Cumulative Index: Public Opinion, 1935–1997*. Wilmington, DE: Scholarly Resources, 1999.

Garrett, Garet, and Bruce Ramsey. *Salvos against the New Deal: Selections from the Saturday Evening Post, 1933–1940*. Caldwell, ID: Caxton Press, 2002.

Gilbert, Marc Jason. *The Vietnam War on Campus: Other Voices, More Distant Drums*. Westport, CT: Praeger, 2001.

Gilbert, Sky. *The Emotionalists*. Winnipeg: Blizzard, 2000.

Gilder, George F. *Wealth and Poverty*. New York: Basic Books, 1981.

Gillespie, J. David. *Politics at the Periphery: Third Parties in Two-Party America*. Columbia: University of South Carolina Press, 1993.

Gimpelevich, Zina. "'We' and 'I' in Zamyatin's *We* and Ayn Rand's *Anthem*," *Germano-Slavica* 10, no. 1 (1997): 13–23.

Gitelman, Zvi. *A Century of Ambivalence: The Jews of Russia and the Soviet Union, 1881 to the Present*. Bloomington: Indiana University Press, 2001.

Gladstein, Mimi Reisel. *Atlas Shrugged: Manifesto of the Mind*. New York: Twayne, 2000.

———. *The New Ayn Rand Companion*. Westport, CT: Greenwood Press, 1999.

Gladstein, Mimi Reisel, and Chris Matthew Sciabarra, eds. *Feminist Interpretations of Ayn Rand*. University Park: Pennsylvania State University Press, 1999.

Goldwater, Barry. *The Conscience of a Conservative*. New York: McFadden-Bartell, 1960.

Gottfried, Paul. *Conservatism in America: Making Sense of the American Right*. New York: Palgrave Macmillan, 2007.

Gotthelf, Allan. *On Ayn Rand*. Belmont, CA: Wadsworth/Thomson Learning, 2000.

Greenberg, Sidney. *Ayn Rand and Alienation: The Platonic Idealism of the Objective Ethics and a Rational Alternative*. San Francisco: Sidney Greenberg, 1977.

Greenspan, Alan. *The Age of Turbulence: Adventures in a New World*. New York, Penguin, 2007.

Hale, Grace. *Rebel, Rebel: Why We Love Outsiders and the Effects of This Romance on Postwar American Culture and Politics*. New York: Oxford University Press, 2009.

Handlin, Oscar. "Capitalism and Freedom." *Business History Review* 37, no. 3 (1963): 315–16.

Hargrove, Erwin C. *Prisoners of Myth: The Leadership of the Tennessee Valley Authority, 1933–1990*. Princeton, NJ: Princeton University Press, 1994.

Hayek, Friedrich A. von. *Verdict on Rent Control: Essays on the Economic Consequences of Political Action to Restrict Rents in Five Countries*. London: Institute of Economic Affairs, 1972.

Hayek, F. A. "Review of *Capitalism the Creator* by Carl Snyder." *Economica* 7, no. 28. (1940): 437–39.

———. *The Road to Serfdom*. Chicago: University of Chicago Press, 1944.

Haydn, Hiram. *Words and Faces*. New York: Harcourt College, 1974.

Hazlett, Joseph M. *The Libertarian Party and Other Minor Political Parties in the United States*. Jefferson, NC: McFarland, 1992.

Heinze, Andrew R. *Jews and the American Soul: Human Nature in the Twentieth Century*. Princeton, NJ: Princeton University Press, 2004.

Heller, Anne C. *Ayn Rand and the World She Made*. New York: Random House, 2009.

Hess, Karl. *Mostly on the Edge: An Autobiography*. Amherst, NY: Prometheus Books, 1999.

Himmelstein, Jerome L. *To the Right: The Transformation of American Conservatism.* Berkeley: University of California Press, 1990.

Hoberek, Andrew. *The Twilight of the Middle Class: Post–World War II American Fiction and White-Collar Work.* Princeton, NJ: Princeton University Press, 2005.

Hodgson, Godfrey. *The World Turned Right Side Up: A History of the Conservative Ascendancy in America.* Boston: Houghton Mifflin, 1996.

Hofstadter, Richard. *Social Darwinism in American Thought.* Revised ed. 1944; Boston: Beacon Press, 1955.

Holtz, William V. *The Ghost in the Little House: A Life of Rose Wilder Lane.* Columbia: University of Missouri Press, 1993.

Horowitz, Daniel. *Betty Friedan and the Making of the Feminine Mystique: The American Left, the Cold War, and Modern Feminism.* Amherst: University of Massachusetts Press, 1998.

Hospers, John. *An Introduction to Philosophical Analysis.* 2nd ed. Englewood Cliffs, NJ: Prentice-Hall, 1967.

Hudson, William. *The Libertarian Illusion: Ideology, Public Policy and the Assault on the Common Good.* Washington, DC: CQ Press, 2007.

Hulsmann, Jörg Guido. *Mises: The Last Knight of Liberalism.* Auburn, AL: Ludwig von Mises Institute, 2007.

Institute for Objectivist Studies. *The Fountainhead: A 50th Anniversary Celebration.* Poughkeepsie, NY: Institute for Objectivist Studies, 1993.

Isserman, Maurice. *Which Side Were You On? The American Communist Party During the Second World War.* Middletown, CT: Wesleyan University Press, 1982.

Isserman, Maurice, and Michael Kazin. *America Divided: The Civil War of the 1960s.* New York: Oxford University Press, 2000.

Jacoby, Susan. *Freethinkers: A History of American Secularism.* New York: Metropolitan Books, 2004.

Johnson, Donald Leslie. *The Fountainheads: Wright, Rand, the FBI and Hollywood.* Jefferson, NC: McFarland, 2005.

Jones, William M. *Stages of Composition: A College Reader.* Boston: D. C. Heath, 1964.

Judis, John B. *William F. Buckley, Jr.: Patron Saint of the Conservatives.* New York: Simon and Schuster, 1988.

Kamp, Joseph. *The Fifth Column in Washington!* New Haven, CT: Constitutional Education League, 1940.

Kauffman, Bill. *America First! Its History, Culture, and Politics.* Amherst, NY: Prometheus Books, 1995.

Kaufmann, Walter. *Nietzsche: Philosopher, Psychologist, Antichrist.* Princeton, NJ: Princeton University Press, 1974.

———, ed. *The Portable Nietzsche.* New York: Penguin, 1954.

Kazin, Michael. *The Populist Persuasion: An American History.* New York: Basic Books, 1995.

Kelley, David. *The Contested Legacy of Ayn Rand: Truth and Toleration in Objectivism.* 2nd ed. New Brunswick, NJ: Transaction, 2000.

————. *The Evidence of the Senses: A Realist Theory of Perception.* Baton Rouge: Louisiana State University Press, 1986.

————. *Truth and Toleration.* Verbank, NY: Institute for Objectivist Studies, 1990.

Kelley, John L. *Bringing the Market Back In: The Political Revitalization of Market Liberalism.* New York: New York University Press, 1997.

Kennedy, David. *Freedom from Fear: The American People in Depression and War, 1929–1945.* New York: Oxford University Press, 1999.

Keynes, John Maynard. *The General Theory of Employment, Interest, and Money.* Great Minds Series. Amherst, NY: Prometheus Books, 1997.

Kimmage, Michael. *The Conservative Turn: Lionel Trilling, Whittaker Chambers, and the Lessons of Anti-Communism.* Cambridge, MA: Harvard University Press, 2009.

King, Florence. *With Charity toward None: A Fond Look at Misanthropy.* New York: St. Martin's Press, 1992.

Kirk, Andrew G. *Counterculture Green: The* Whole Earth Catalog *and American Environmentalism.* Lawrence: University Press of Kansas, 2007.

Kirk, Russell. *Confessions of a Bohemian Tory.* New York: Fleet, 1963.

Kirzner, Israel M. *Ludwig Von Mises: The Man and His Economics.* Wilmington, DE: ISI Books, 2001.

Klatch, Rebecca E. *A Generation Divided: The New Left, the New Right, and the 1960s.* Berkeley: University of California Press, 1999.

————. *Women of the New Right.* Philadelphia: Temple University Press, 1987.

Klehr, Harvey. *The Heyday of American Communism: The Depression Decade.* New York: Basic Books, 1984.

Koerner, Steven. "The Conservative Youth Movement: A Study in Right Wing Political Culture in Activism, 1950–1980." PhD diss., University of Virginia, 2001.

Kresge, Stephen, and Leif Wenar, eds. *Hayek on Hayek: An Autobiographical Dialogue.* Chicago: University of Chicago Press, 1994.

Kripal, Jeffrey J. *Esalen: America and the Religion of No Religion.* Chicago: University of Chicago Press, 2007.

Kruse, Kevin. *White Flight: Atlanta and the Making of Modern Conservatism.* Princeton, NJ: Princeton University Press, 2007.

Kuklick, Bruce. *The Rise of American Philosophy: Cambridge, Massachusetts, 1860–1930.* New Haven, CT: Yale University Press, 1977.

Kyle, Richard. *The New Age Movement in American Culture.* Lanham, MD: University Press of America, 1995.

Lassiter, Matthew. *The Silent Majority: Suburban Politics in the Sunbelt South.* Princeton, NJ: Princeton University Press, 2006.

The Last Whole Earth Catalog. Menlo Park, CA: Portola Institute, 1971.

Lerner, Abba P. "Capitalism and Freedom." *American Economic Review* 53, no. 3 (1963): 458–60.

Lichtenstein, Nelson, ed. *American Capitalism: Social Thought and Political Economy in the Twentieth Century.* Philadelphia: University of Pennsylvania Press, 2006.

Loomis, Mildred J. *Alternative Americas.* New York: Universe Books, 1982.

Lowndes, Joseph. *From the New Deal to the New Right: Race and the Southern Origins of Modern Conservatism*. New Haven, CT: Yale University Press, 2008.

Machan, Tibor R. *Ayn Rand*. New York: Peter Lang, 1999.

———. *Human Rights and Human Liberties*. Chicago: Nelson Hall, 1975.

———. "Libertarianism and Conservatives." *Modern Age* 24 (winter 1980): 21–33.

———. *The Man without a Hobby: Adventures of a Gregarious Egoist*. Lanham, MD: Hamilton Books, 2004.

Maine, Henry. 1861; *Ancient Law*. New York: Henry Holt, 1864.

Markoff, John. *What the Dormouse Said: How the Sixties Counterculture Shaped the Personal Computer Industry*. New York: Viking Penguin, 2005.

Martin, James J. *Men against the State: The Expositors of Individualist Anarchism in America, 1827–1908*. 1953; Colorado Spring, CO: Ralph Myles, 1970.

Martin, Justin. *Greenspan: The Man behind Money*. Cambridge, MA: Perseus, 2000.

Mattson, Kevin. *Rebels All! A Short History of the Conservative Mind in Postwar America*. Piscataway, NJ: Rutgers University Press, 2008.

Mayhew, Robert J. *Ayn Rand and* Song of Russia: *Communism and Anti-Communism in 1940s Hollywood*. Lanham, MD: Scarecrow Press, 2005.

———, ed. *Essays on Ayn Rand's* Anthem. Lanham, MD: Lexington Books, 2005.

———, ed. *Essays on Ayn Rand's* Atlas Shrugged. Lanham, MD: Lexington Books, 2009.

———, ed. *Essays on Ayn Rand's* The Fountainhead. Lanham, MD: Lexington Books, 2007.

———, ed. *Essays on Ayn Rand's* We the Living. Lanham, MD: Lexington Books, 2004.

Mazmanian, Daniel A. *Third Parties in Presidential Elections*. Washington, DC: Brookings Institution, 1974.

McGirr, Lisa. *Suburban Warriors. The Origins of the New American Right*. Princeton, NJ: Princeton University Press, 2001.

McKeon, Richard, ed. *The Basic Works of Aristotle*. New York: Random House, 1941.

McNicholas, Joseph Colin. "Corporate Culture and the American Novel: Producers, Persuaders, and Communicators." PhD diss., University of Texas at Austin, 1999.

Mencken, H. L. *Letters of H. L. Mencken*. Ed. Guy Fogue. New York: Knopf, 1961.

Merrill, Ronald E. *The Ideas of Ayn Rand*. LaSalle, IL: Open Court Press, 1991.

Micklethwait, John, and Adrian Wooldridge. *The Right Nation: Conservative Power in America*. New York: Penguin Press, 2004.

Mises, Ludwig von. *Human Action*. 1949; 3rd revised ed. Chicago: Regnery, 196.

Morgan, Ted. *Reds: McCarthyism in Twentieth-century America*. New York: Random House, 2003.

Moser, John E. *Right Turn: John T. Flynn and the Transformation of American Liberalism*. New York: New York University Press, 2005.

Murray, Charles Augustus. *Losing Ground: American Social Policy, 1950–1980*. New York: Basic Books, 1984.

Namier, Lewis. "Human Nature in Politics." In *Personalities and Powers: Selected Essays*. New York: Harper and Row, 1965.

Nash, George H. "Forgotten Godfathers: Premature Jewish Conservatives and the Rise of *National Review*." *American Jewish History* 87, nos. 2–3 (1999): 123–57.

————. *The Conservative Intellectual Movement in America Since 1945*. New York: Basic Books, 1976.

Nathans, Benjamin. *Beyond the Pale: The Jewish Encounter with Late Imperial Russia*. Berkeley: University of California Press, 2002.

Neal, Steve. *Dark Horse: A Biography of Wendell Willkie*. Garden City, NY: Doubleday, 1984.

Newman, Stephen L. *Liberalism at Wit's End: The Libertarian Revolt against the Modern State*. Ithaca, NY: Cornell University Press, 1984.

Nickerson, Michelle. "'The Power of a Morally Indignant Woman': Republican Women and the Making of California Conservatism." *Journal of the West* 42 (summer 2003): 35–43.

Niebuhr, Reinhold. *The Children of Light and the Children of Darkness: A Vindication of Democracy and a Critique of Its Traditional Defense*. New York: Charles Scribner, 1944.

Nietzsche, Friedrich. *Beyond Good and Evil*. Trans. R. J. Hollingdale. New York: Penguin Books, 1973.

Nock, Albert Jay. *Memoirs of a Superfluous Man*. New York: Harper Brothers, 1943.

Nock, Albert Jay, and Frank W. Garrison, eds. *Letters from Albert Jay Nock, 1924–1945 to Edmund C. Evans, Mrs. Edmund C. Evans and Ellen Winsor*. Caldwell, ID: Caxton Printers, 1949.

Nock, Albert Jay, and Charles H. Hamilton. *The State of the Union: Essays in Social Criticism*. Indianapolis: Liberty Press, 1991.

Nozick, Robert. *Anarchy, State, and Utopia*. New York: Basic Books, 1974.

————. "On the Randian Argument." In *Socratic Puzzles*. Cambridge, MA: Harvard University Press, 1997.

O'Connor, Alice. *Social Science for What? Philanthropy and the Social Question in a World Turned Rightside Up*. New York: Russell Sage Foundation, 2007.

O'Neill, William F. *With Charity toward None: An Analysis of Ayn Rand's Philosophy*. New York: Philosophical Library, 1971.

Ortega y Gasset, José. *The Revolt of the Masses*. Notre Dame, IN: University of Notre Dame Press, 1985.

Parsons, Talcott. *The Structure of Social Action*. New York: McGraw Hill, 1937.

Paterson, Isabel. *God of the Machine*. 1943; New Brunswick, NJ: Transaction, 1993.

Patterson, James T. *Congressional Conservatism and the New Deal: The Growth of the Conservative Coalition in Congress, 1933–1939*. Lexington: University of Kentucky Press, 1967.

Peikoff, Leonard. *Objectivism: The Philosophy of Ayn Rand*. New York: Dutton, 1991.

————. *The Ominous Parallels: The End of Freedom in America*. New York: Stein and Day, 1982.

Pells, Richard H. *The Liberal Mind in a Conservative Era: American Intellectuals in the 1940s and 1950s*. Middletown, CT: Wesleyan University Press, 1989.

Perlstein, Rick. *Before the Storm: Barry Goldwater and the Unmaking of the American Consensus*. New York: Hill and Wang, 2001.

————. *Nixonland: The Rise of a President and the Fracturing of America*. New York: Scribner, 2008.

Peters, Charles. *Five Days in Philadelphia: The Amazing "We Want Willkie!" Convention of 1940 and How It Freed FDR to Save the Western World*. New York: Public Affairs, 2005.

Phillips, Kevin. *The Emerging Republican Majority*. New Rochelle, NY: Arlington House, 1969.

Phillips-Fein, Kimberly. *Invisible Hands: The Making of the Conservative Movement from the New Deal to Ronald Reagan*. New York: Norton, 2009.

Plasil, Ellen. *Therapist*. New York: St. Martin's Press, 1985.

Purcell, Edward A. *The Crisis of Democratic Theory: Scientific Naturalism and the Problem of Value*. Lexington: University Press of Kentucky, 1973.

Pye, Lucien, and Sidney Verba. *Political Culture and Political Development*. Princeton, NJ: Princeton University Press, 1965.

Radway, Janice A. *Reading the Romance: Women, Patriarchy, and Popular Literature*. Chapel Hill: University of North Carolina Press, 1991.

Raimondo, Justin. *An Enemy of the State: The Life of Murray N. Rothbard*. Amherst, NY: Prometheus Books, 2000.

———. *Reclaiming the American Right: The Lost Legacy of the Conservative Movement*. Wilmington, DE: Intercollegiate Studies Institute, 2008.

Ratner-Rosenhagen, Jennifer. "Neither Rock nor Refuge: American Encounters with Nietzsche and the Search for Foundations." PhD diss., Brandeis University, 2003.

Rawls, John. *A Theory of Justice*. Cambridge, MA: Belknap Press, 1971.

Redding, Arthur. "Closet, Coup, and Cold War: F. O. Matthiessen's *From the Heart of Europe*." *boundary 2* 33, no. 1 (2006): 171–201.

Reisman, David, with Denney, Reuel, and Glazer, Nathan. *The Lonely Crowd*. New Haven, CT: Yale University Press, 1950.

Ribuffo, Leo P. *The Old Christian Right: The Protestant Far Right from the Great Depression to the Cold War*. Philadelphia: Temple University Press, 1983.

Rich, Andrew. *Think Tanks, Public Policy, and the Politics of Expertise*. New York: Cambridge University Press, 2004.

Richman, Sheldon. "New Deal Nemesis: The 'Old Right' Jeffersonians." *Independent Review* 1, no. 2 (1996): 201–48.

Rogin, Michael Paul. *The Intellectuals and McCarthy: The Radical Specter*. Cambridge, MA: MIT Press, 1967.

Root, E. Merrill. *Brainwashing in the High Schools*. New York: Devon-Adair, 1958.

———. *Collectivism on Campus*. New York: Devon-Adair, 1955.

Rose, Jonathan. *The Intellectual Life of the British Working Classes*. New Haven, CT: Yale University Press, 2001.

Rosenstone, Steven J., Roy L. Behr, and Edward H. Lazarus. *Third Parties in America: Citizen Response to Major Party Failure*. Princeton, NJ: Princeton University Press, 1984.

Rostker, Bernard D. *I Want You! The Evolution of the All-Volunteer Force*. Washington, DC: RAND, 2006.

Rothbard, Murray Newton. *The Betrayal of the American Right*. Auburn, AL: Ludwig von Mises Institute, 2007.

———. *For a New Liberty: The Libertarian Manifesto*. New York: Macmillan, 1973.

————. "The Mantle of Science." In *Scientism and Values,* ed. Helmut Schoeck and James W. Wiggins. New York: D. Van Nostrand, 1960.

Rubin, Joan Shelley. *The Making of Middlebrow Culture.* Chapel Hill: University of North Carolina Press, 1992.

Ryant, Carl. *Profit's Prophet: Garet Garrett.* Selinsgrove, PA: Susquehanna University Press, 1989.

Sager, Ryan. *The Elephant in the Room: Evangelicals, Libertarians, and the Battle to Control the Republican Party.* Hoboken, NJ: Wiley, 2006.

Sayre, Nora. *Sixties Going on Seventies.* New York: Arbor House, 1973.

Schafer, Byron, and Richard Johnston. *The End of Southern Exceptionalism: Class, Race, and Partisan Change in the Postwar South.* Cambridge, MA: Harvard University Press, 2007.

Schaller, Michael. *Right Turn: American Life in the Reagan-Bush Era, 1980–1992.* New York: Oxford University Press, 2007.

Schlafly, Phyllis. *Feminist Fantasies.* Dallas: Spence, 2003.

Schleier, Merrill, "Ayn Rand and King Vidor's Film *The Fountainhead:* Architectural Modernism, the Gendered Body, and Political Ideology." *Journal of The Society of Architectural Historians* 61, no. 3 (2002): 310–31.

————. *Skyscraper Cinema: Architecture and Gender in American Film.* Minneapolis: University of Minnesota Press, 2009.

Schneider, Gregory L. *Cadres for Conservatism: Young Americans for Freedom and the Rise of the Contemporary Right.* New York: New York University Press, 1999.

————. *The Conservative Century: From Reaction to Revolution.* Critical Issues in American History Series. New York: Rowman and Littlefield, 2008.

Schoenwald, Jonathan M. *A Time for Choosing: The Rise of Modern American Conservatism.* New York: Oxford University Press, 2001.

————. "No War, No Welfare, and No Damn Taxation: The Student Libertarian Movement, 1968–1972." In *The Vietnam War on Campus: Other Voices, More Distant Drums,* ed. Mark Jason Gilbert. Westport, CT: Praeger, 2001.

Schreiber, Ronnee. *Righting Feminism: Conservative Women and American Politics.* New York: Oxford University Press, 2008.

Schulman, Bruce J., and Julian Zelizer. *Rightward Bound: Making America Conservative in the 1970s.* Cambridge, MA: Harvard University Press, 2008.

Schwartz, Richard B. *Cold War Culture: Media and the Arts, 1945–1990.* New York: Facts on File, 1998.

Sciabarra, Chris Matthew. *Ayn Rand, Homosexuality, and Human Liberation.* University Park: Pennsylvania State University Press, 2003.

————. *Ayn Rand: The Russian Radical.* University Park: Pennsylvania State University Press, 1995.

————. *Ayn Rand, Homosexuality, and Human Liberty.* Cape Town: Leap Publishing, 2003.

Sharp, Joanne P. *Condensing the Cold War: Reader's Digest and American Identity.* Minneapolis: University of Minnesota Press, 2000.

Shermer, Elizabeth Tandy. "Counter-Organizing the Sunbelt: Right-to-Work Campaigns and Anti-Union Conservatism, 1943–1958." *Pacific Historical Review* 78, no. 1 (2009): 81–118.

Simon, William E. *A Time for Truth*. New York: Reader's Digest Press, 1978.

Slezkine, Yuri. *The Jewish Century*. Princeton, NJ: Princeton University Press, 2004.

Slivinski, Stephen A. *Buck Wild: How Republicans Broke the Bank and Became the Party of Big Government*. Nashville, TN: Nelson Current, 2006.

Smart, Kevin J. *Principles and Heresies: Frank S. Meyer and the Shaping of the American Conservative Movement*. Wilmington, DE: ISI Books, 2002.

Smith, Adam. 1759; *Theory of Moral Sentiments*. New York: Cambridge University Press, 2005.

Smith, Kay Nolte. *Elegy for a Soprano*. New York: Villard Books, 1985.

Smith, Tara. *Ayn Rand's Normative Ethics: The Virtuous Egoist*. Cambridge: Cambridge University Press, 2006.

Snyder, Carl. *Capitalism the Creator: The Economic Foundations of Modern Industrial Society*. New York: Macmillan, 1940.

Sokol, Jason. *There Goes My Everything: White Southerners in the Age of Civil Rights, 1945–1957*. New York: Knopf, 2006.

Spadoni, Robert. "Guilty by Omission: Girding the 'Fountainhead' for the Cold War (Ayn Rand)." *Literature-Film Quarterly* 27, no. 3 (1999): 223–32.

Spencer, Herbert. *The Man versus the State*. Caldwell, ID: Caxton Printers, 1940.

Stigler, George Joseph. *Memoirs of an Unregulated Economist*. New York: Basic Books, 1988.

Sullivan, Andrew. *The Conservative Soul: How We Lost It, How to Get It Back*. New York: HarperCollins, 2006

Sumner, William Graham. 1883; *What Social Classes Owe to Each Other*. Caldwell, ID: Caxton Press, 2003.

Sures, Charles, and Mary Ann Sures. *Facets of Ayn Rand*. Irvine, CA: Ayn Rand Institute, 2001.

Sutton, F. X. "Capitalism and Freedom." *American Sociological Review* 28, no. 3 (1963): 491–92.

Szalay, Michael. *New Deal Modernism: American Literature and the Invention of the Welfare State*. Durham, NC: Duke University Press, 2000.

Tanenhaus, Sam. *Whittaker Chambers: A Biography*. New York: Random House, 1997.

Taylor, Joan Kennedy. *Reclaiming the Mainstream: Individualist Feminism Rediscovered*. Amherst, NY: Prometheus Books, 1992.

Teachout, Terry. *The Skeptic: The Life of H. L. Mencken*. New York: Harper Collins, 2002.

Teles, Steven Michael. *The Rise of the Conservative Legal Movement: The Battle for Control of the Law*. Princeton, NJ: Princeton University Press, 2008.

Torres, Louis, and Michelle Marder Kamhi. *What Art Is: The Aesthetic Theory of Ayn Rand*. Chicago: Open Court Press, 2000.

Toy, Eckard V., Jr., "The Right Side of the 1960s: The Origins of the John Birch Society in the Pacific Northwest," *Oregon Historical Quarterly* 105, no. 2 (2004): 260–283.

Tuccille, Jerome. *Alan Shrugged: Alan Greenspan, the World's Most Powerful Banker*. New York: Wiley, 2002.

―――. *It Usually Begins with Ayn Rand*. New York: Stein and Day, 1971.

―――. *Radical Libertarianism*. New York: Bobbs Merrill, 1970.

Turner, Fred. *From Counterculture to Cyberculture: Stewart Brand, the Whole Earth Network, and the Rise of Digital Utopianism*. Chicago: University of Chicago Press, 2006.

Valliant, James S. *The Passion of Ayn Rand's Critics*. Dallas: Durban House, 2005.

Vaughn, Karen Iversen. *Austrian Economics in America: The Migration of a Tradition*. Cambridge: Cambridge University Press, 1994.

Vidal, Gore. *Rocking the Boat*. New York: Little, Brown, 1962.

Walker, Jeff. *The Ayn Rand Cult*. LaSalle, IL: Open Court Press, 1999.

Weaver, Richard. *Ideas Have Consequences*. Chicago: Regnery, 1948.

West, Nathanael. *Miss Lonelyhearts and The Day of the Locust*. New York: New Directions, 1962.

Westby, David, and Richard Braungart. "Class and Politics in the Family Backgrounds of Student Political Activists." *American Sociological Review* 31 (1996): 690–92.

White, Morton. *Social Thought in America: The Revolt against Formalism*. New York: Viking, 1949.

Wills, Garry. Introduction to Lillian Hellman, *Scoundrel Time*. Boston: Little Brown, 1976.

Wills, Garry. *Nixon Agonistes: The Crisis of the Self-made Man*. New York: New American Library, 1979.

Wolff, Tobias. *Old School: A Novel*. New York: Knopf, 2003.

Wolfskill, George. *Revolt of the Conservatives: A History of the Liberty League, 1934–1940*. Boston: Houghton Mifflin, 1962.

Wolfskill, George, and John A. Hudson. *All but the People: Franklin D. Roosevelt and His Critics*. London: Macmillan, 1969.

Worster, Donald. *Nature's Economy: The Roots of Ecology*. 1977; Cambridge: Cambridge University Press, 1994.

Wortham, Anne. *The Other Side of Racism: A Philosophical Study of Black Race Consciousness*. Columbus: Ohio State University Press, 1981.

Wright, Frank Lloyd. *Autobiography of Frank Lloyd Wright*. New York: Longmans, Green, 1932.

Younkins, Edward Wayne. *Ayn Rand's Atlas Shrugged: A Philosophical and Literary Companion*. Aldershot, UK: Ashgate, 2007.

―――. *Philosophers of Capitalism: Menger, Mises, Rand, and Beyond*. Lanham, MD: Lexington Books, 2005.

Zamyatin, Yevgeny. *We*. Trans. Mirra Ginsburg. New York: Viking Press, 1972.

INDEX

DATE DUE